PERSPECTIVES ON LISTENING

THE COMMUNICATION AND INFORMATION SCIENCE SERIES
Series Editor: BRENDA DERVIN, The Ohio State University

Subseries:
Progress in Communication Sciences: Brant R. Burleson
Interpersonal Communication: Donald J. Cegala
Organizational Communication: George Barnett
Mass Communication/Telecommunication Systems: Lee B. Becker
User-Based Communication/Information System Design: Michael S. Nilan
Cross-Cultural/Cross-National Communication and Social Change: Josep Rota
International Communication, Peace and Development: Majid Tehranian
Critical Cultural Studies in Communication: Leslie T. Good
Feminist Scholarship in Communication: Lana Rakow
Rhetorical Theory and Criticism: Stephen H. Browne
Communication Pedagogy and Practice: Gerald M. Phillips
Communication: The Human Context: Lee Thayer

PERSPECTIVES ON LISTENING

edited by

Andrew D. Wolvin
and
Carolyn Gwynn Coakley

University of Maryland-College Park

ABLEX PUBLISHING CORPORATION
NORWOOD, NEW JERSEY

Printed in the United States of America

Library of Congress Cataloging-in-Publication Data

Perspectives on listening / [edited by] Andrew D. Wolvin, Carolyn Gwynn Coakley.
    p.   cm.
    Includes bibliographical references and index.
    ISBN 0-89391-879-2 (hard).—ISBN 0-89391-925-X (pbk.)
    1. Listening. 2. Oral communication. I. Wolvin, Andrew D. II. Coakley, Carolyn Gwynn.
P95.46.P47 1993
302.2′242—dc20

92-42454
CIP

Ablex Publishing Corporation
355 Chestnut Street
Norwood, New Jersey 07648

FTW
AGE 5603

Contents

About the Authors

Andrew D. Wolvin (Ph.D., Purdue University) is Professor and Chair of the Department of Speech Communication at the University of Maryland-College Park. He and Carolyn Coakley have co-authored *Listening* (Wm. C. Brown), *Listening Instruction* (ERIC), and *Experiential Listening* (Spectra), and many papers and journal articles on listening behavior. He is a past president and an inductee of the Hall of Fame of the International Listening Association.

Carolyn Gwynn Coakley (M.A., University of Maryland) is a listening and communication consultant. A former secondary school teacher of Speech Communication, she was awarded one of the first Christa McCauliffe fellowships and received the Washington *Post* outstanding educator award and the Speech Communication Association outstanding teacher award. With Andrew Wolvin, she has co-authored *Listening, Instruction,* and *Experiential Listening,* as well as a number of papers and journal articles. She also has authored *Teaching Listening.* She is a past president and an inductee of the Hall of Fame of the International Listening Association.

Alice Ridge is on the faculty of the Department of Communication and Theatre Arts at the University of Wisconsin-Eau Claire. A recent inductee into the International Listening Association Hall of Fame, she has taught listening for 14 years at Eau Claire and in England and Malaysia. She has authored a K-12 listening curriculum for the state of Wisconsin and has presented over 200 workshops, seminars, and speeches on listening to business, civic, and education groups.

Belle Ruth Witkin (Ph.D., University of Washington) is a Visiting Scholar at the University of Washington. She is a specialist in Speech and Hearing Pathology and has done extensive research in the area of audiological perception.

Renee Edwards (Ph.D., Florida State University) is Associate Professor of Speech Communication at Louisiana State University. Her interest in cognitive theory has led to the study of listening, especially the role that prior knowledge plays in the listening process. Her other research areas

Renee Edwards (Ph.D., Florida State University) is Associate Professor of Speech Communication at Louisiana State University. Her interest in cognitive theory has led to the study of listening, especially the role that prior knowledge plays in the listening process. Her other research areas include metaphorical invention, communication and the self, and imagined interaction.

Janet L. McDonald (Ph.D., Carnegie-Mellon University) is Assistant Professor of Psychology at Louisiana State University. Her research in psycholinguistics includes first and second language comprehension and the integration of semantic and syntactic information.

Sheila C. Bentley (Ph.D., Arizona State University) is a communication consultant based in Memphis. She has taught numerous training seminars on listening and memory to a variety of corporations, organizations, and school systems. Her clients include Honeywell, Motorola, Holiday Corporation, International Paper, the City of Memphis, Scottsdale Public Schools, and the American Institute of Banking. She also has taught at Arizona State University and Memphis State University. She has held various offices in the International Listening Association.

Sara W. Lundsteen (Ph.D.) is a reading specialist who has published extensively in the field of reading and elementary language arts education. Her work, *Listening: Its Impact on Reading and the Other Language Arts,* is a seminal book on listening pedagogy.

Billie Thompson (Ph.D., Arizona State University) is Director of the Sound Listening and Learning Center in Phoenix. After working as a teacher and administrator in several Arizona public school districts, she started the Center to bring together a unique set of educational and human development programs and materials to provide both corrective and enrichment techniques. She is co-editor of *About the Tomatis Method.*

Jack Johnson (Ph.D., University of Denver) joined the faculty of the University of Wisconsin-Milwaukee in 1978, where he has been responsible for teaching and conducting research related to applied communication and communication interventions in organizational settings. His long-term interest in listening and inner speech rests on his conviction that inner speech is central to both the production and the reception of spoken language and that applications of communication should be based on theoretical understandings of the communicative process.

Tom Bruneau (Ph.D., Pennsylvania State University) has been teaching listening behavior for 18 years. He is a contributing member of the International Listening Association and serves on the editorial board of the *Journal of the International Listening Association.* His publications concern empathic listening, communicative silences, intrapersonal communication, and nonverbal aspects of temporality (chronemics).

Paul Friedman (Ph.D., Pennsylvania State University) is an Associate Professor in the Department of Communication Studies at the University of Kansas. His teaching and research for over 25 years has been concerned in one way or another with listening. He is the author of *Listening Processes: Attention, Understanding, Evaluation*, published by the National Education Association. Chapters in several of his other books also deal with listening, and he has presented numerous convention papers on the topic. In 1990, he was named to the International Listening Associates Hall of Fame.

Steven Rhodes (Ph.D., Pennsylvania State University) is a Professor of Speech Communication and Director of the Center for Communication Research at Western Michigan University. He teaches a graduate seminar in listening theory and research and serves as a listening consultant for business and education. He has presented numerous papers and written articles and book chapters about listening. Three of his papers have received the Ralph G. Nichols Award presented by the Institute for Study of Intrapersonal Processes in recognition of outstanding scholarship in listening research.

Judi Brownell is an Associate Professor of Managerial Communication at the School of Hotel Administration at Cornell University. She teaches both graduate and undergraduate courses as well as a variety of executive education programs on listening and related topics. She is author of *Building Active Listening Skills* (Prentice-Hall, 1986) and co-author of *Organizational Communication and Behavior* (Holt, Rinehart and Winston, 1989). She has written numerous articles on listening which have appeared in communication, management, and hospitality journals. She has received the International Listening Association's research award and has held a number of ILA offices, including the Vice Presidency/Presidency.

Donald Rubin (Ph.D., University of Minnesota) is Professor in the Departments of Speech Communication and Language Education at the University of Georgia. He conducts research in areas of applied linguistics such as gender and writing style, students' responses to nonnative English speaking instructors, and sociolinguistic bias in personnel testing. Rubin has also published in the area of orality/literacy. He was Director of Project Synapse, supported by the U.S. Fund for Improvement of Postsecondary Education, which developed oral communication exercises to improve the academic writing of underprepared students, University of Cincinnati.

Introduction

Andrew D. Wolvin
Carolyn Gwynn Coakley

Department of Speech Communication
University of Maryland at College Park

The study of listening behavior came into its own in the last decade. As scholars became increasingly interested in exploring the intricacies of this most complex of human functions, it was clear that there is much that we have yet to discover about listening as communication. Indeed, the Research Committee of the International Listening Association identified 27 separate topics to be addressed by listening scholars. One of the key topics was "conceptualizations of listening and synthesis of existing conceptualizations" (Emmert, 1988).

As a result of the research, theory building, and curriculum development on listening during the 1980s, we have come to recognize that listening is an important communication activity. Corporate America has been especially active in communicating the message that listening is critical to organizational effectiveness and human productivity. Corporate listening themes, training activity, and advertising campaigns have all contributed to a greater American awareness of the significant role that listening does play in professional and in personal lives.

We also know that listening is a complex human behavior. Listening involves the cognitive and affective processing of verbal and nonverbal messages through an intricate internal system which we are just beginning to understand. We can recognize the role of short-term and long-term memory and the significance of cognitive schema in receiving, attending to, and interpreting messages.

Likewise, listening is recognized as a variable communication activity. A listener will function differently depending upon his or her purpose for listening. And listening further depends upon any of a number of factors which can facilitate or detract from the process at any given time—factors such as the speaker, the message, the channel used, the environment, and the listener's psychological and/or physical state.

We also know that listening is a skill that can be improved. Education in and about listening behavior has provided thousands of students in academic and corporate classrooms with knowledge about the complexities of the process, changing attitudes about the role of listening in human interaction, and new skills to enhance listening ability. Training in listening has been found to have a positive effect on those who receive it, suggesting that listening pedagogy ought to be central to communication education at all levels.

Conceptualizations of listening, then, center on an understanding of the process nature of this communication phenomenon. Reviewing many of the definitions of listening, the authors (Wolvin & Coakley, 1988) have concluded that listening is a process of "receiving, attending to and assigning meaning to aural stimuli" (p. 91).

How the process is approached, however, remains a base for interesting theoretical interpretation. While much of the work on listening, to date, stems from a skills perspective, and while much of the study of listening is still in its "infancy," it is significant to note the development of other views of this complex communication act. As a result, we have assembled this volume of original essays by listening scholars to address various current perspectives which inform our understanding of the listening process.

A theoretical basis for understanding listening comes at an important juncture in the development of this field of study. Fisher (1978) has argued that theoretical perspectives significantly influence how we conceptualize and understand the communication process. Goss (1982) has extended Fisher's argument to stress that listening research requires a theoretical grounding that will allow for the "integration of a number of essential components of listening. Such a point of view should focus on the listening act itself and not just its products" (p. 304).

A solid theoretical foundation for understanding the listening act is important for providing the basis for research about listening as a communication behavior. Such a foundation also provides the means for facilitating the application of this research to the actual act of listening. Much of current listening pedagogy is based more on intuitive "prescriptions" for listening effectiveness than on well-substantiated listening paradigms.

The purpose of this book, then, is to provide readers with an analysis of listening behaviors from current perspectives developed by scholars in various disciplines (communication, psychology, reading, learning skills) concerned with the way humans process oral messages. It is hoped that this collection of chapters, written especially for this volume, will offer a useful base for applying what we know about this complex human behavior to improving listening skills in personal relationships in academic, work, and social settings at all levels of learning.

Since the skills perspective is historically so pervasive in listening research and pedagogy, we begin this volume with a review of that approach to understanding listening. Ridge reviews Nichols's and others' early work, which has shaped the study of listening to the present day.

Our chapter on our listening taxonomy is intended to expand the view of listening as a communication skill, especially as the taxonomy is used as the framework for a great deal of listening pedagogy today. We have come to understand listening as guided by the listener's purpose(s) and how one's listening behaviors will be modified according to the objective.

The involved process of listening may best be understood today as a function of human information processing. That approach is reviewed by Witkin as it stems from information theory. She focuses on auditory processing and attention, both central to the cognitive processing which listeners undertake.

Expanding on the model of listening as information processing, Edwards and McDonald offer a summary of current understanding of schema theory from cognitive psychology. Schema theory provides an important framework for understanding how listeners retrieve information and then use that information to interpret messages.

The retrieval of information is critical to the listening process. Bentley offers a thorough summary of theory and research in memory and how memory influences listening behavior at every stage of the process. She makes a case for utilizing different memory strategies to handle information according to the listener's purpose.

The human information processing model can be seen to incorporate other aspects of the listening act. Johnson explores one of those aspects—inner speech. He details the process of subvocalized speech used to generate or to make associations between or among concepts by listeners. This decoding process is integral to comprehending the speaker's intended meaning.

Central to the utilization of one's understanding of the listening process is *metacognition*—one's awareness of personal cognitive performance, and the use of that awareness to alter that performance. Lundsteen details our current understanding of metacognition and how developmental research has enhanced the study of the related receptive behavior of reading. She offers an important link to her theory of metacognitive listening.

Applications of metacognitive listening are especially relevant in considering the disabled listener. Thompson reviews the literature that impacts on listening disabilities and describes the Tomatis Method as one current approach for enabling disabled listeners to cope with their listening problems.

Just as listening has been understood from the standpoint of skills development, listening is identified with Rogers's (1961) concept of "active listening," which hinges on the principle of empathy. Bruneau provides us with a review of the concept of empathy and how it relates to listening. He argues that empathy is central to effective communication.

An important basis for building empathy is to listen to an individual's stories. Friedman explores the nature of listening to narratives. He observes that stories serve a major communication function in everyday discourse, so listeners should be more discerning in the way that they process narrative discourse.

Rhodes then places listening into a relational context. He describes the transactional process of communication as a measure of predictability in the communication patterns. He makes a case for expanding the notion of listening as receiving, attending, and interpreting messages to also include responding in dyadic relationships.

Listening in relationships is shaped by, and also serves to shape, the communication environment. In her analysis of the listening environment, Brownell builds a case for developing effective listening attitudes and behaviors to enhance the quality of the environment, both in the workplace (the focus of much of the current research in this area) and in personal settings of all kinds.

Understanding the intricacies of listening both intrapersonally and interpersonally offers a theoretical base for also understanding what makes a message listenable. Rubin explores the concept of listenability, describing elements of oral-based style and "considerateness," the ease of processing of a message.

These perspectives on listening, both intrapersonal and interpersonal, provide us with an expanded base for understanding the process of listening. Such a base should serve listening researchers and teachers to further our theoretical framework for testing, predicting, and teaching about effective listening behaviors.

REFERENCES

Emmert, P. (1988). Future directions for listening research. In J. Brownell (Ed.), *Cornell conference on listening*. Ithaca, NY: Cornell University.

Fisher, A. (1978). *Perspectives on human communication*. New York: Macmillan.

Goss, B. (1982). Listening as information processing. *Communication Quarterly, 30*, 304–307.

Rogers, C. (1961). *On becoming a person*. Boston: Houghton Mifflin.

Wolvin, A.D., & Coakley, C.G. (1988). *Listening*. Dubuque, IA: William C. Brown.

Chapter 1

A Perspective of Listening Skills

Alice Ridge

Department of Communication and Theater Arts
University of Wisconsin-Eau Claire

This chapter explores, first, the subject of listening skills; second, the concept of a listening strategy; and last, competence as a product of strategy and skills. A *strategy* is a plan derived from a context that determines which skills to apply. Listening competence turns on the ability of the listener to choose a strategy, then select among skills appropriate to that context and employ those skills. Explored are a discussion of the scope of the skills approach, the composition of competence, the need for strategy, and evaluation of listening competence. The implications for teachers are that strategies, not just isolated skills, need to be taught. The listener may achieve a greater degree of homophily with the message and sender as strategies direct the appropriate choice of skills.

INTRODUCTION AND PURPOSE

The federal Education Act of 1978 amended the Education Act of 1965 to include oral communication in its definition of basic skills for K–12 students. Until then, generally, few outside of the speech communication profession had thought of oral communication as a basic skill, and fewer still had thought of listening as a skill that was separately teachable and measurable. State departments of education, school districts, writers of basic communication texts, and elementary and secondary school teachers with little experience or understanding about listening competency or skills were faced with implementing this mandate. In an effort to comply with the mandate, some states such as Wisconsin, New York, and others funded various attempts to design listening curricula (Ridge, 1981; Wisconsin Department of Public Instruction, 1977, 1986; State University of New York, 1979). Universities and school districts hosted workshops in the teaching of basic communication skills, and, in many of those workshops, listening was included as a separate discipline for the first time.

In a parallel development, the International Listening Association was founded in 1979 and it began to encourage the exploration of a myriad of aspects of listening, including definition and assessment considerations. Publications and yearly conventions featured skill-building activities.

One outcome of the curriculum effort and the work of the International Listening Association is that many now believe that we listen more than we read or write or speak in both the classroom and the workplace, and, more importantly, that listening skills can be taught.

But the question arises: What skills should be taught? Historically, the study of listening has focused on skills, but does possession of a collection of listening skills constitute competence?

This chapter explores, first, the subject of listening skills; and, second, the concept of a listening strategy. Finally, it will be suggested that listening competence is the product of the effective welding of an appropriate strategy with effective skills and practice.

LISTENING SKILLS

Listening Skills as Genre

A sampling of the history of thinking about listening in terms of its "elements" or specific skills may be seen in the following few, brief citations.

Perhaps the origin might be seen as stemming from the field's seminal work by Paul Rankin, who listed in his 1926 doctoral dissertation 32 prominent and subskills as necessary for an individual to be rated "high in his ability to obtain meaning from spoken language" (Duker, 1966, p. 25–26). Listening scholar and popularizer Ralph G. Nichols (1948) set a trend when he isolated, through the interview process, several factors which influenced listening comprehension. Over the years, those skills became reworded and presented as 10 bad listening habits in a variety of media including "Six Bad Habits" in *Are You Listening?* by Nichols and Stevens (1957). Today one need only pick up a current business magazine to see reprinted yet again a version of Nichols's 10 (cf. Watkin, 1984). *Nation's Business* reprinted in 1987 an article it ran 30 years ago by Ralph Nichols entitled "Listening is a 10 Part Skill" (Nichols, 1987). The magazine noted that this article had drawn the greatest number of requests for reprints of the hundreds of articles they published on successful management techniques. It has been this author's experience to know business people whose only contact with the subject of listening has been through their own professional journals, which carried the same 10 bad habits, and who immediately recall Nichols's name in that context.

Lundsteen identified skills she considered necessary to critical listening and worked them into lesson plans for fifth and sixth graders (1963) and furthered the codification of such skills in later years (1979). In 1977 the Speech Communication Association fostered a skills approach when it created a task force to establish speaking and listening competencies and attendant skills for high school graduates (Bassett, Whittington, & Staton-Spicer, 1979). The Speech Communication Association (1978) followed this with competency models for prospective communication and theatre arts teachers, including the teaching of several listening skills.

Wolff, Marsnik, Tacey, and Nichols (1983), Floyd (1985), and Wolvin and Coakley (1988) all offer suggestions to help the reader improve upon listening skills needed for varying purposes of listening. In a more recent text, Roach and Wyatt (1988) speak of skills in a unique way, not listing selected ones but linking skills to rhetorical acts such as "choosing listening goals, analyzing the situation, and choosing an appropriate strategy."

In the field of second-language teaching, a skills approach is revealed by Richards (1983), who offers 33 "microskills for conversational listening" and 18 "microskills for listening to lectures." Although these skills are presented as aids to nonnative English speakers, they appear to be applicable to anyone attempting to listen to a foreign tongue. Ferrer and Whalley (1985) utilize skill-building predominantly in their workbook for nonnative speakers. Emphasized are skills such as listening for analogies, for main points, for chronological order, for arguments for and against, for digressions from a message, and for humor.

What Are Listening Skills?

A way of looking at listening skills may be through a definition of *listening*. The final chapter on a definition has not yet been written, and disagreement upon its breadth exists. For instance, the inclusion or exclusion of "response" by a listener as a necessary component of a definition of listening seems to be a point of disagreement among listening scholars. Rhodes, in a thorough examination of listening and the systems theory principle of entropy, concludes that "one function of the feedback process (the response dimension of listening) is to arrest the amount of entropy in the system" (1986, p. 20). Response, regarded here as a tool for assisting the speaker in creating a message, differs from Wolvin and Coakley's (1988) concept of overt response as beginning a new stimulus, thus leaving the realm of listening.

The inclusion or exclusion of *memory* in a definition of listening has also been a point of disagreement, the argument centering around memory as being indigenous to the process of listening or only an adjunct to it. Varying perceptions of what constitutes this behavioral act prevent a single definition from emerging. However, Ethel Glenn (1989) discovered, through content analysis of 50 definitions of listening, some similarity in key terms. *Interpreting* or assigning meaning appeared in 36 of the 50; *perceiving* or receiving signals appeared in 32; *attention* was in 22; *memory* appeared in 13. *Response* of listener as a necessary component was mentioned in 16 definitions, but no distinction was made between overt and covert response. If definitions shape theories and suggest methodologies, perhaps the commonality of some descriptive or delimiting terminology in the various definitions of listening point to a similarity of perception of components, or *skills,* related to listening.

How then shall *skill* be defined? What building blocks about listening theory does the term *skill* provide? In this perspective a listening skill is a behavior, which, if carried out as part of a strategy, will most probably result in the listener perceiving with fair approximation of accuracy an aural message. Competence as an overall capability is often spoken of in terms of component skills. The strategy of selecting among skills, and the use of the selected skills, are not the same. A skillful listener is one who comprehends the context of the listening instance, produces from his or her repertoire a plan or strategy for selection of the appropriate skills, and executes those chosen skills.

Identifying those skills which a listener needs to choose among to be judged competent may imply that listening is made up of an endless list of skills. Indeed, Anderson's (1988) view is that considering listening as a composite of subskills is folly and unnatural. To him, listening is "creative experiencing" (p. 12). Kelly (1967) questioned whether listening skills could be tested at all; denying a unitary skill, he stated that it was a "complex of activities" (p. 465). His argument was with the listening tests extant; his plea was to test less, skill by skill, and teach more about listening. Also, Rhodes, Watson and Barker (1989, p. 20) warn of a certain arbitrariness accompanying extant lists of skills. Rhodes (1986) also concludes that "such a focus [on identification and assessment of specific listening skills] has done little to contribute to the continuing process of theory development" (p. 24). Roberts (1988) reminds us that no research is extant that proves that possessing particular skills facilitates listening.

Those lists alone do not constitute good listening. However, if skills are looked at as topoi or places for ideas that suggest appropriate listening behaviors, and if skills are made part of a strategy, a discussion of specific skills has something to offer as building blocks for competence. Pedagogically speaking, the identification of strategies and skills allows instructional procedures and curricula to be devised for the development of those skills. Teaching strategies and behaviors that represent practical helps to the listener in a variety of contexts is more efficient, more participatory, concrete, and image-producing than encouraging, say, "creative experiencing." The concept of teaching skills as a result of a strategy would seem to make practical sense.

Commonly Enumerated Skills

A review of the listening skills selected by various authors of listening curricula and texts reveals a wide variety of skills, with a large core of them commonly cited.

The following selection of skills is offered as suggested skills only and is not purported to be complete. The selected skills may be grouped for convenience according to function. The *Wisconsin Alternative Curriculum Design* (Wisconsin Department of Public Instruction, 1977), as well as *An Activity Guide for Speaking and Listening* (Wisconsin Department of Public Instruction, 1990), for instance, have used the five functions espoused by the Speech Communication Association (Allen & Brown, 1976): informing, controlling, imagining, feeling, and ritualizing. The below-listed skills could be arranged according to those five functions as well. However, the schema outlined below is based on Lyman Steil's S.I.E.R. model (Steil, Barker, & Watson, 1983), which reflects the process of listening rather than function. Many definitions of listening are process oriented, their descriptors and delimiters providing key building blocks to a perception of necessary skills. In the Steil model (S.I.E.R.), S stands for sensing the message, I represents interpreting or understanding the message, E refers to evaluating the message, and R represents responding to the message. This model was selected because of the wide latitude it affords for the inclusion of skills, thus precluding a narrow contextual field. The skills listed below are not necessarily those of Steil, but represent typical skills most relevant to each part of the model.

Some listening skills of a sensing nature (S):

- attending purposefully
- discerning between intended message and noise

- concentrating on one stimulus instead of many
- getting "set" to listen
- attending to metaverbals such as quality of sound
- discriminating among phonemes such as p–b, k–g, f–v, and morpheme endings
- perceiving direction of source of sound
- discriminating among environmental sound patterns vs. speech sound patterns
- noting differences in accents and dialects
- noting "turn taking" in conversation and role responsibilities of speaker and listener
- discriminating between words as spoken and words as meant
- noting differences in tone of voice

Some listening skills of an interpreting or understanding nature *(I)*:

- recognizing main points vs. supporting points
- discerning between literal and symbolic meaning
- recognizing fact from fiction
- gaining meaning of words through contextual clues
- following a sequence of instructions
- recognizing relationships among sources of messages
- conceptualizing
- recognizing language as coming from other cultures and statuses
- recognizing different purposes of the source
- recognizing differences between words as spoken and words as meant by recognizing figures of speech
- noting the meaning of silence
- noting organization
- drawing justifiable inferences

Some listening skills of an evaluative nature *(E)*:

- noting purposes for listening
- noting strategies of the source
- noting reasoning, arguments
- recognizing differences between assumption and fact, opinion, inference
- recognizing the language of persuasion vs. information
- assessing the credibility of the message
- assessing the credibility of the speaker
- recognizing the emotional self and other barriers to listening

Some listening skills of responding *(R)*:

- asking questions
- giving appropriate feedback commensurate with purpose of speaker
- responding in consonance with speaker/situation/mood
- withholding preparation of response until speaker has finished
- paraphrasing or checking back for understanding

The Steil model used above includes *response* as a part of listening. As mentioned earlier, the inclusion or exclusion of *response* as a part of the listening process is argued. Some (cf. Wolvin & Coakley, 1988) say that an overt response is legitimately part of a new communication cycle, with the response constituting an initiative of the sender. Others, such as Rhodes (1986), in the above discussion, argue that communication is incomplete without a receiver acknowledging that a message did exist; thus, there is a need for confirmation of that message by the receiver. Experience alone has shown that lack of feedback to a speaker is oftentimes interpreted as *ignoring* the speaker, disagreeing with the speaker, or, in the extreme, decimating the speaker. Thus, skills involved with responding would seem to be no less important than others when one discusses the total listening setting.

To demonstrate how common the skills approach is, the following examples are offered. The Maryland State Board of Education (1988) has arrayed skills under the functional headings of "Goals and Subgoals." A goal of "listening for a variety of purposes" is supported by subgoals or skills of listening to comprehend content and intent of speaker, listening empathically, listening critically, listening for pleasure or aesthetic enjoyment. A goal of "developing a positive attitude toward listening" is supported by subgoals or skills of developing a willingness to listen actively, developing a curiosity, and valuing the significant role of listening.

The legislature of the state of Florida mandated that minimal communication skills be established for second-year college students. The listening skills selected by educators were grouped, again functionally, under purposes of literal and critical comprehensive listening, emphasizing listening for main points, details, evidence, and structure of the message (Quianthy, 1984). A similar, function-based selection of skills was made by Clayton State College in Georgia, with specific skills supporting listening purposes of "literal, inferential, and critical comprehension" (Coakley & Wolvin, 1990, p. 42).

Brownell (1986) has arranged skills in an order of process. Selected skills are supportive of a perceived six-part process of listening: hearing, understanding, remembering, interpreting, evaluating, and responding.

LISTENING STRATEGY

In this perspective, a strategy is a plan derived from a context that determines which skills to apply at that moment of listening. It would seem, then, that listening competence would turn on the ability of the listener to apply a strategy and then (a) select among skills available, and (b) employ those selected skills to perceive with fair approximation the content, context, and intent of a given communication.

The purposes for which we listen differ. We may perceive that judgments are required of us as we listen to persuasive messages. We perceive that some messages have as their purpose entertainment and may call for less than critical responses. We may perceive that someone is asking for our help with a matter of personal decision making; thus, we realize that "listening from the other person's shoes" is necessary. The process of attending and cognitive structuring may well be the same in the temporal lobe of the brain. But we weigh various aspects of each message differently. Creating a strategy or a plan that would assist in selecting the skills needed for comprehension at that moment seems sensible. The competent listener recognizes the unique context of the message that calls for a strategy to help determine the skills most useful in identifying accurately the purposes of the message sender, his or her coding system, and the cloak of meaning surrounding all. For instance, if a listener comprehends an incoming message as demanding empathy, the recognition of that context would identify the strategy that calls for skills of patience, withholding of judgment, and a perception of the uniqueness of the sender. The more sensitive to context the listener is, (a) the more accurate the strategy or plan which would call forth the appropriate skills, and (b) the more potential for competence he or she may be said to possess.

Allen and Brown (1976) define *communication competence* in terms of four characteristics possessed by the competent communicator: (a) an available repertoire of experiences, (b) an ability to select appropriate strategies from the repertoire, (c) the willingness to implement the strategies, and (d) the ability to evaluate the performance of communicative behaviors (p. 248).

Although their reference goes beyond listening to include all of communication, listening seems closely allied with the Allen and Brown perception of competence, because acquiring appropriate experiences (skills) and selecting and implementing strategies are suggested as separate aspects of competence. Since listening is carried on in varying contexts, a strategy must be created by the listener to select among available skills those which best address the current communication context.

Knowing the role of listening in the communicative process helps the effective listener to perform that role. A strategy specifies, for instance, when to remain silent and when to be empathic. A strategy could render a listener competent if he or she performs skills consistent with the strategy. A competent listener should have a repertoire of skills including those of attending, decoding, and evaluating messages; divining the speaker's purpose; and creating a strategy to help choose among those skills.

LISTENING COMPETENCE

It is the position of this perspective that skills are related to *competence,* despite that term's enervescence and ambiguity. Gerald Phillips (1984) has said, "Defining 'competence' is like trying to climb a greased pole. Every time you think you have it, it slips" (p. 25). To him, competence is not a 'thing' but rather an evaluation, a judgment call. Furthermore, the term may have one meaning to a theorist and another to a teacher (Phillips, 1984). However subjective the term may be, exploration of its relationship to skills seems warranted, for a skills perspective influences how we conceptualize listening and how we determine the constituents of competence. Defining competence, Spitzberg and Cupach (1984) speak of *fundamental competence,* which reflects "two interrelated concerns: (a) the cognitive capabilities leading to consistent personal effectiveness and (b) the developmental processes that facilitate or inhibit the acquisition of general adaptability" (p. 36). Spitzberg and Cupach also speak of competence as "appropriateness" which, along with "adaptability," implies a contextual factor. Listening, they suggest, is a behavioral act dependent upon context, and effective listening is the product of the listener's adaptability to that context (p. 64).

Moore (1981) states that competence is "product bound" (p. 7). This seems particularly fitting to describe listening. The "product" of listening rests in the listener's mind. It is the conclusion drawn or the fact retained or the mood of the speaker perceived or the music appreciated. A measure of competence is assigned to the degree that the listener responds appropriately, overtly or covertly, to the intent of the source of a communication within a communicative context.

McCroskey (1982, 1984) draws a distinction between knowing about a behavior and performing it. He has argued that it is not sufficient to be able to describe proper communication behavior in order to be adjudged competent; the communication also must be performed adequately. The above views of competence appear to reflect agreement that there is a difference between "knowing about" and being able "to do or perform" appropriately, and that competence seems to demand both. Phillips (1984), however, would argue that this view would suggest a basis for criticism rather than scientific knowledge.

It is the position of this chapter that competence is demonstrated by the creation of an appropriate strategy for selecting skills and the performance of those selected skills. Knowing about the listening process and its attendant processes of reception, attention, concentration, and memory systems is important to carrying out effective listening, which demands hearing, selective attention, concentration strategies, and memory. Knowing that people have different purposes for commanding the listener's attention helps the listener to respond appropriately to the intent of the message. Knowing the role of the listener in the communicative process helps the effective listener to perform that role.

Evaluating Listening Competence

Current evaluation is based primarily on evaluating the application of skills, not strategy. Research exists to verify the theory that a separate, testable listening dimension does exist in the comprehension of information that is received aurally. Fitch Hauser and Hughes (1987) cite various researchers including Brown, Wilson, Spearitt, and Lundsteen, who studied listening as a discreet, unique skill. Brown, an early researcher, found in 1954 that something called "auding" was a unique ability in the communication process. Wilson administered the Sequential Test in Educational Progress (STEP) 4A-language listening test and several tests of music listening. A correlation between the two types of listening was positive but low, implying some commonality among types of listening but much uniqueness in the two skills. Spearritt presented a battery of 34 tests to Australian school children. The tests included tests of listening comprehension, attention, memory, vocabulary, and reading comprehension. His factor analysis revealed a separate factor he called "comprehension of verbal material presented in spoken form." Testing fifth and sixth graders, Lundsteen correlated the pre- and posttest scores with various other measures and supported the existence of something she called "critical listening," suggesting that listening could be broken down into various subskills.

Listening classes often employ self-reporting tools, such as surveys, that ask students to generalize about their skills in a context of everyday life. With no scale by which to measure competence, those self-reporting surveys serve little purpose except, perhaps, that of alerting the student to the subject of listening in general. However, the tests of listening skills in some classes frequently are instance-specific, based, for example, upon a few minutes of a taped message. Upon these instances, judgments are then made about competence. If listening is context dependent, it would seem that competence in listening would demand a correlated context such as intent of speaker/source, frame of reference of the source, and so on, clues which oftentimes are not available in short samples.

If self-reporting surveys do not produce an accurate picture of listening competence, and short tests are unrealistic, how is one to assess listening skills? Lists of skills would suggest options for behavior but do not speak to a relative success in employing these options because of the lack of context. Strategies which reflect the context of messages need to be learned, but skill-building drills tend to emphasize knowledge of individual skills. The short exercises teach skills but do not represent the whole listening context.

It is upon this premise of the existence of subskills that all of the present listening tests are built. The Brown-Carlsen Listening Comprehension Test (Brown & Carlsen, 1955), the Watson-Barker Listening Test (Watson & Barker, 1987), and the Kentucky Comprehensive Listening Test (Bostrom & Waldhart, 1981), for instance, test subskills of short-term memory, long-term memory, main idea detection, following directions, and lecture comprehension. The Kentucky Comprehensive Listening Test has an added feature of testing empathic listening. Two Canadian tests, the Listening Comprehension Test and the Alberta Listening Test, test for elements related to comprehensive listening such as prediction, relationships, and understanding of content in addition to sentence recognition, literal comprehension, interpretive comprehension, and critical comprehension (Plattor, 1988).

Of the tests on the market today, it seems that the Watson-Barker and Kentucky Comprehensive Test have more acceptable reliability over older tests (Rhodes et al., p. 27) partly because developers and critics have produced more rigorous validation requirements and partly because the tests have some "context" built in by means of "conversations" carried on between people in "real" settings as seen on videotape or as heard on audio tape. Subskills contained in "assigning meaning," or in "attention" or in "sound discrimination" or in "memory," the skills most mentioned in the 50 definitions of listening studied by Glenn (1989), are separately tested but within a "real" context.

Consideration of evaluating listening competence through both strategies and individual skills should be sought.

IMPLICATIONS

Implications for further study of strategies as an aid to skill selection are apparent. Testing and measurement of skills seem to occupy some listening scholars, but the concept of using strategies sensitive to context to select skills needs to be explored. Methods for teaching sensitivity to context and related strategies need to be devised, along with teaching the skills themselves.

Listeners who learn to consider context and strategies as necessary conditions for skill selection may become more efficient listeners than those taught skills alone. Also, a greater degree of homophily may develop as comprehension of context and strategies directs the choice of skills. Consider an analogy: The person who sets out to memorize poetry without knowing something about rhyme scheme will probably have a less satisfying product; it is context and strategy consideration that may lead to a more satisfying skill selection.

The teacher who disappears behind a screen and rattles keys and then asks the kindergarten children to identify the noisy item may be teaching the skill of attending, but without prior experience with keys, the child cannot be expected to name the item. Teaching children to describe the sound, and teaching them ways of classifying like sounds, is to teach them strategies which may be more useful to them in the long run than learning that they misnamed an item.

A perspective of listening skills that includes strategies developed with sensitivities to context to aid in choosing skills, plus the practice of those choices, may help in our understanding of this ubiquitous behavioral act we call listening.

REFERENCES

Allen, R.R., & Brown, K.L. (Eds.) (1976). *Developing communication competence in children: A report of the speech communication association's national project on speech communication competencies.* Skokie, IL: National Textbook Company.

Anderson, R. (1988, April). *Listening is not a skill: The technique ethic and an experientialist alternative.* Paper presented at the Central States Speech Association Convention, Schaumburg, IL.

Bassett, R.E., Whittington, N., & Staton-Spicer, A. (1979). The basics in speaking and listening for high school graduates: What should be assessed? *Communication Education 27,* 298–302.

Bostrom, R., & Waldhart, E. (1981). *Kentucky comprehensive listening skills test.* Lexington, KY: University of Kentucky.

Brown, J., & Carlsen, G.R. (1955). *Brown-Carlsen listening comprehension test.* New York: Harcourt, Brace and World. (This test is now available through CDI, St. Paul, MN.)

Brownell, J. (1986). *Building active listening skills.* Englewood Cliffs, NJ: Prentice-Hall.

Coakley, C., & Wolvin, A. (1990). Listening pedagogy and androgeny: The state of the art. *Journal of the International Listening Association, 4,* 33–61.

Duker, S. (1966). *Listening: Readings*. New York: The Scarecrow Press.

Ferrer, J., & Whalley, E. (1985). *Mosaic: A listening/speaking skills book*. New York: Random House.

Fitch Hauser, M., & Hughes, A. (1987). A factor analytic study of four listening tests. *Journal of the International Listening Association, 1*, 129–147.

Floyd, J.J. (1985). *Listening: A practical approach*. Glenview, IL: Scott, Foresman and Co.

Glenn, E. (1989). A content analysis of 50 definitions of listening. *Journal of the International Listening Association, 2*, 21–31.

Kelly, C.M. (1967). Listening: Complex of activities—and a unitary skill? *Speech Monographs, 34*, 455–465.

Lundsteen, S.R. (1963). *Teaching abilities in critical listening in the fifth and sixth grades*. Unpublished doctoral dissertation, University of California at Berkeley.

Lundsteen, S. (1979). *Listening: Its impact at all levels on reading and the other language arts*. Urbana, IL: ERIC Clearinghouse.

Maryland State Board of Education. (1988). *English language arts: A Maryland curricular framework*. Annapolis, MD.

McCroskey, J.C. (1982). Communication competence and performance. *Communication Education, 31*, 1–8.

McCroskey, J.C. (1984). Communication competence: The elusive construct. In R.N. Bostrom (Ed.), *Competence in communication: A multidisciplinary approach* (pp. 259–268). Beverly Hills, CA: Sage Publications.

Moore, M. (1981, December). *A dynamic vs. a static perspective of communication competence*. Paper presented at the meeting of the speech communication association, Anaheim, CA.

Nichols, R.G. (1948). *Factors accounting for differences in comprehension of materials presented orally in the classroom*. Unpublished doctoral dissertation, State University of Iowa, Ames.

Nichols, R.G. (1987). Listening is a 10 part skill. *Nation's Business, 75*(9), 40.

Nichols, R.G., & Stevens, L.A. (1957). *Are you listening?* New York: McGraw-Hill Book Company.

Phillips, G.M. (1984). A competent view of "competence." *Communication Education, 33*(1), 25–36.

Plattor, E. (1988). Assessing listening in elementary and junior high schools: An examination of four listening tests. *Journal of the Instructional Listening Association, 2*, 41–44.

Quianthy, R. (1984, March). *The Florida speaking and listening test: What's it all about, Alfie?* Paper presented at the International Listening Association Conference, Scottsdale, AZ.

Rhodes, S. (1986, March). *An approach to listening research using the systems theory principle of entropy*. Paper presented at the International Listening Association conference, San Diego, CA.

Rhodes, S., Watson, K., & Barker, L. (1989, March). *Issues and methods in listening assessment: 1989*. Paper presented at the Interdisciplinary Conference on Theory, Issues, and Methodology of the International Listening Association, Atlanta, GA.

Richards, J.C. (1983). Listening comprehension: Approach, design, procedure. *TESOL Quarterly, 17*(2), 219–240.

Ridge, A. (1981). *K–12 listening skills curriculum.* University of Wisconsin Extension Division, unpublished manuscript.

Roach, C.A., & Wyatt, N.J. (1988). *Successful listening.* New York: Harper and Row.

Roberts, C.V. (1988). The validation of listening tests: Cutting the gordian knot. *Journal of the International Listening Association, 2,* 1–19.

Speech Communication Association. (1978). *Preparation of elementary and secondary teachers in speech communication and theatre.* Falls Church, VA: American Theatre Association and the Speech Communication Association.

Spitzberg, B.H., & Cupach, W.R. (1984). *Interpersonal communication competence.* Beverly Hills, CA: Sage.

Steil, L., Barker, L., & Watson, K. (1983). *Effective listening: Key to Your success.* Reading, MA: Addison-Wesley Publishing Company.

State University of New York/The State Education Department. (1979). *English language arts.* Albany, NY: Author.

Watkin, E. (1984). The business of listening. *Today's Office, 18*(9), 46.

Watson, K., & Barker, L. (1987). *Watson-Barker listening test.* Auburn, AL: Spectra, Inc.

Wisconsin Department of Public Instruction. (1977). *The Wisconsin alternative curriculum design in basic English/communication skills.* Madison, WI: Author.

Wisconsin Department of Public Instruction. (1986). *A guide to curriculum planning in English language arts.* Madison, WI: Author.

Wisconsin Department of Public Instruction. (1990). *An activity guide for speaking and listening.* Madison, WI: Author.

Wolff, F., Marsnik, N., Tacey, W., & Nichols, R. (1983). *Perceptive listening.* New York: Holt, Rinehart, Winston.

Wolvin, A.D., & Coakley, C.G. (1988). *Listening* (3rd ed.). Dubuque, IA: Wm. C. Brown.

Chapter 2

A Listening Taxonomy

Andrew D. Wolvin
Carolyn Gwynn Coakley
Department of Speech Communication
University of Maryland at College Park

This chapter addresses the need for a classification system of listening purposes. The authors review the various listening taxonomies developed in the field and detail their own taxonomy of listeners' objectives and how those objectives affect listening behaviors. The taxonomy has been found to be a useful framework for listening education.

A classification system is central to natural sciences (Cole, 1984). Likewise, the classification of human behaviors is basic to the behavioral sciences. Classification can assist in the description of behaviors as well as in the establishment of theories by which particular behaviors can be explained and predicted (Hempel, 1965). A classification taxonomy, then, can serve as a useful model for understanding a behavior and how it functions (Fabrega, 1976). Indeed, today, taxonomy (the science of classification) is "pervasive in practically every field of study" (Mezzich & Solomon, 1980, p. 2).

Chafetz (1986), recognizing the crucial role of building a taxonomy in the field of psychology, stresses that a taxonomy is "a model helpful in subsequent theory building because it provides lawful representation of the elements that comprise a theory" (p. 121). Just as in the study of psychology, a taxonomic model of listening behaviors may be useful in expanding our understanding of this complex human behavior.

King (1988), who has proposed a taxonomy for classifying language studies in intercultural communication, stresses that a taxonomy can be helpful for understanding what is currently known and for identifying those areas most in need of additional research. He believes that a taxonomy is "one way to impose coherence on what is now incoherent and to provide direction for research efforts that are currently uncoordinated" (p. 220). Such an objective is descriptive, not only of intercultural communication, but also of listening studies.

One perspective on listening behaviors that lends itself to a classification scheme is that of listening purposes. Research in reading behavior suggests that the reader who understands the purpose he/she has for reading a particular passage can be assisted, then, in the comprehension of that passage because the purpose can help the reader to focus on the specific aspects of a selection (Harris & Smith, 1980, pp. 248–253). It is possible, therefore, that the listener also can be assisted in listening by identifying and recognizing just what purpose he or she has for a specific listening experience. Further, these purposes may function in a hierarchical order, building from basic listening goals or objectives to more particular kinds of responses.

Listeners function in the complex process of listening with a variety of purposes. These purposes of listening have been identified variously in the literature. Lundsteen (1971/1979), one of the first to analyze listening skills as a hierarchy, offered an instructional taxonomy of listening skills in general and of critical listening skills in particular. Lundsteen was concerned with building a listening curriculum, so she stressed the value of looking at levels of listening skills: Level A, the lowest level, is acuity or sound perception; Level B represents basic discrimination among sounds; and Level C is the comprehension of sounds. Skills at these levels may form a hierarchy, stresses Lundsteen (1979), "because persons who fail to discriminate sound differences with finesse probably also fail to symbolize much verbal meaning from those sounds" (p. 54).

Another early examination of listening as a hierarchy was proposed by Weaver and Rutherford (1974). Like Lundsteen, these authors were concerned with assisting teachers in building listening skills in children. They stressed auditory discrimination from the prenatal stage to the sixth grade. They distinguished between environmental skills (distinguishing between/among sounds other than verbal) and discrimination skills (distinguishing between/among verbal sounds). Two other categories have been proposed by Barker and by Mills. Barker (1971) defined listening contexts as social and serious. These categories were explicated further by Steil, Barker, and Watson (1983) as social listening, which includes appreciative, conversational, courteous listening, and listening to indicate love or respect, while serious listening was classified as either selective or concentrated. Mills (1974) described listening *targets* as *responsive listening* (agreeing with the speaker), *implicative listening* (identifying what is not being said), *critical listening* (evaluating the message), and *nondirective listening* (providing a sounding board for the speaker).

In a 1976 publication, Allen and Brown (1976) presented a matrix of listening skills based on communication functions. These functions were identified as becoming informed, being controlled, imaging (to visualize), feeling, and ritualizing (to facilitate and maintain relationships).

Yet another categorization of listening types was proposed by Devine (1982). This reading specialist suggested that instruction in listening could be built around *accurate listening* (paying attention), *purposeful listening* (following spoken discourse), and *critical listening.*

Foreign language educators also have developed taxonomies of listening comprehension as a foundation for enabling students to process the acquisition of the new language. One of the leading proponents of teaching listening comprehension in foreign language education is Richards (1983, 1985), who has developed an extensive taxonomy of "microskills" required for conversational listening and for academic listening. *Conversational listening* involves such skills as the ability to retain chunks of language of different lengths for short periods, discriminate among the distinctive sounds of the language, recognize the stress patterns of words, detect sentence constituents, process speech at different rates, and adjust listening strategies to different kinds of listener purposes or goals. *Academic listening* includes such skills as the ability to identify purpose and scope of lecture, identify relationships among units within discourse, deduce meanings of words from context, and recognize markers of cohesion.

Another foreign language specialist, Ur (1984), categorizes listening as *listening for perception* and *listening for comprehension.* Using the taxonomy to prepare students for language acquisition, she identifies listening for perception as listening to perceive correctly the "different sounds, sound-combinations and stress and intonation patterns of foreign language" (p. 33). Listening for comprehension, then, is described as ranging from a very "passive" act where the learner "simply listens, making little or no response" to "active" listening as preliminary to or the basis for other language skills "and imaginative or logical thought" (p. 33). As with all other taxonomies, Ur stresses that the classification is not intended to represent a strict chronology for application to learning a foreign language; rather, it is a suggested range of possible listening choices.

More recently, additional categorical systems have been posited. Wolff, Marsnik, Tacey, and Nichols (1983) focus on listening comprehension, appreciative listening, and empathic listening. Glatthorn and Adams (1983) identify three types of listening for managers: hearing, analyzing, and empathizing. In her work for managers, Brownell (1986) emphasizes the need to build active listening skills based on a classification utilizing the acronym HURIER: hearing, understanding, remembering, interpreting, evaluating, and responding.

Further extending the previous work on the hierarchical nature of listening skills, we (Wolvin & Coakley, 1979, 1988) have developed a taxonomy of listening functions that correlate with five general purposes of listeners (aligned with general purposes of speakers): discriminative, comprehensive, therapeutic, critical, and appreciative. Just as there are specific listening skills unique to each of these listening purposes, we believe that the skills developed and used operate in a hierarchical sequence—depending upon what each listener's intended objective or objectives for listening might be at any particular time. Too, we believe that, regardless of the listening purpose, listening always involves a basic process of receiving, attending to, and assigning meaning to messages. These elements of the listening process make up the listener's behaviors while functioning in any of the listening categories. Furthermore, we recognize that the listening purposes are not always discrete categories. There are times when an individual may listen for multiple purposes. A review of listening behaviors for the different purposes in the Wolvin-Coakley Listening Hierarchy can illustrate the listening process.

Discriminative listening is distinguishing the auditory and/or visual stimuli. Discriminative listening involves developing careful concentration on, and sensitivity to, the various stimuli to differentiate between/among them accurately. Effective discriminative listening requires sensitivity to the verbal and nonverbal cues offered by the communicator source and a concerted effort to identify the auditory and the visual messages.

The importance of listening to discriminate is readily apparent. Parents quickly learn discriminative listening skills when listening to the cries of their newborn infant. Auditory discrimination serves as the base for reading readiness programs for young children. Panhandlers are experts at visually discriminating as "easy mark" on the street. Professionally, auto mechanics rely on sound discrimination to understand the malfunctioning of a car. Musicians must discriminate sounds in order to perform at a professional level. Speech and hearing specialists work to distinguish speech sounds in order to assist clients in overcoming speech disorders.

Discriminative listening serves as the *base* for all other purposes of listening behavior. The receptive stage in the process requires the listener to identify and interpret carefully the auditory and visual cues in order to deal effectively with the information being received.

Listening for comprehension extends from the discrimination of the stimulus to an understanding of the message. Comprehensive listeners listen to lectures, briefings, reports, conferences, television and film documentaries, telephone messages, traffic alerts, and so on, to comprehend the information presented. Clearly, much of the educational process is based on comprehensive listening. Students are asked to listen carefully to lectures and class discussions in order to understand and retain vast amounts of information.

The effective comprehensive listener actively strives to understand and to retain the information in the message. To assign the meaning intended by the speaker instead of assigning his or her own meaning, the listener avoids critical judgment of the message, the speaker, the channel, or the language used. In addition to not being evaluative, the listener requires proficiency at listening for comprehension by having a well-developed vocabulary, skill at making accuracy checks through questioning, and even notemaking strategies. Understanding and retaining the information presented requires the listener to develop memory skills— skills that enable the listener to initially hold the incoming information in the short-term memory, rehearse the information to ensure that it is placed in the long-term memory store, and to draw on the long-term memory store to assign meaning. All of these memory skills depend on intense concentration, an essential key to effective listening comprehension.

Careful concentration, however, is made more difficult by the fact that listeners can process information (or listen and think) as much as four times faster than the normal conversation rate (125 to 180 words per minute) of the speaker. Research by Nichols (1957) on this differential between the speech speed and the thought speed reveals that the listener, consequently, is tuning in and tuning out throughout any presentation. An effective comprehensive listener must work to refocus and maintain focus on the speaker's message by utilizing internal summaries and other identifiers to assist in the concentration process.

Therapeutic (also referred to as *empathic)* listening requires that the listener serve as a "sounding board" to provide the speaker with the opportunity to talk through a problem to the speaker's own solution of it. Effective therapeutic listening builds from discrimination and comprehension of the message in order for the listener to provide the necessary supportive behaviors and responses that enable the speaker to talk through the problem. While serious psychological problems must be handled by qualified therapists, an empathetic ear can be all the assistance needed for many people to deal with daily concerns. An effective therapeutic listener must be careful not to evaluate or judge what is said. The therapeutic listener operates from the principle of empathy—putting one's self in another's position in order to understand the feelings and thoughts communicated. By applying principles of nondirective listening, the listener offers just the necessary responses to keep the speaker communicating without directing the speaker to any one particular solution (Rogers, 1961).

Successful therapeutic listening demands a supportive communication climate in which the speaker feels free to express his or her feelings and thoughts without judgment (Gibb, 1961). Likewise, the therapeutic listener must work to remain an empathetic listener without offering a great deal of advice. It is a difficult task because so many individuals will say, "What do you think I should do?" and we have a very natural tendency to want to respond with "If I were you, I would..."

Critical listening, unlike therapeutic, requires that a listener evaluate what is being said (Wolvin & Coakley, 1988, chap. 8). Once the critical listener has discriminated and comprehended the message, it is necessary then to form judgments about the message in order to accept or reject the persuasive appeals.

Listeners respond to persuasive messages at various levels. The credibility (trustworthiness, dynamism, and believability) of the speaker is influential. Further, listeners respond to the structure and support of the speaker's arguments. Since effective persuasive communicators will utilize a variety of psychological appeals to get listeners to respond at appropriate need levels, the conscientious critical listener must know what speakers are doing to develop persuasive messages and, consequently, why and how he or she is responding to them.

Critical listeners do well to train themselves in recognizing argument fallacies, particularly hasty generalizations drawn from too little or no evidence. And emotional language can distract listeners if they are not careful to recognize the "red flags" that lead to strong emotional responses. Further, critical listeners should be able to assess the impact that a speaker may be having on their responses to the persuasive message. Effective critical listening clearly involves sound judgment and awareness of the persuasive strategies being used.

Appreciative listening, the fifth purpose, is listening to enjoy or to gain a sensory impression from the material (Wolvin & Coakley, 1988, chap. 9). Listening to music, to environmental sounds, or to a television presentation all represent forms of appreciative listening.

Although listening for appreciation also builds from discrimination and comprehension of appreciative experiences, it results from a very individual response. Tastes and standards for appreciation vary widely. Some specialists argue that awareness of the background and the style of the material may provide a more meaningful base for appreciating that material. Thus, music appreciation courses, for example, frequently stress music history, form, and composition. Other specialists, however, encourage listeners to "go with the experience" and not be terribly concerned about analyzing the elements.

The effective listener, then, will make some determination as to what purpose for listening is appropriate in any given communication situation and adapt his or her listening responses accordingly. While not discrete categories (a person may both appreciate and evaluate some material, for instance), the taxonomy of listening purposes has proven to be helpful to listeners in understanding their own listening behavior and in developing strategies for functioning more effectively with the different purposes.

While the taxonomy serves as a useful instructional frame, Arnold (1990) argues against this classification system by suggesting that "these distinctions do not hold up in practice and they provide little in sight into the processes of listening" (p. 3). As a result, he proposes to look at listening as a continuum from listening to information on the left side to listening with empathy on the right side of the continuum.

It is apparent that listening, whether viewed as a continuum or as a taxonomy, is a complex communication behavior, involving a process of receiving, attending to, and assigning meaning to verbal and/or nonverbal stimuli. Throughout the process, listeners are influenced by variables that can facilitate and/or distract from the process. The listener functions at different purposes depending upon his or her objective as well as the speaker's goal in the communication. As a result, research and pedagogy in the listening process must be based on a clear understanding of these intricacies and their effects on the individual listeners. Indeed, a classification taxonomy of listening purposes can assist listeners in developing a clear understanding of the essential behavioral science of listening.

REFERENCES

Allen, R.R., & Brown, K. (Eds.). (1976). *Developing communication competence.* Skokie, IL: National Textbook.

Arnold, W.E. (1990, March). *Listening: A conceptualization.* Paper presented to the International Listening Association, Indianapolis.

Barker, L.L. (1971).*Listening behavior.* Englewood Cliffs, NJ: Prentice-Hall.

Brownell, J. (1986). *Building active listening skills.* Englewood Cliffs, NJ: Prentice-Hall.

Chafetz, M.D. (1986). Taxonomy in psychology: Looking for subatomic units. *The Journal of Psychology, 120,* 121–135.

Cole, C.J. (1984). Taxonomy: What's in a name? *Natural History, 93,* 30–34.

Devine, T.G. (1982). *Listening skills schoolwide: Activities and programs.* Urbana, IL: ERIC Clearinghouse on Reading and Study Skills.

Fabrega, H., Jr. (1976). The biological significance of taxonomies of disease. *Journal of Theoretical Biology, 63,* 191–216.

Gibb, J.R. (1961). Defensive communication. *Journal of Communication, 11,* 142.

Glatthorn, A.A., & Adams, H.R. (1983). *Listening your way to management success.* Glenview, IL: Scott Foresman.

Harris, L.A., & Smith, C.B. (1980). *Reading instruction.* New York: Holt, Rinehart & Winston.

Hempel, C. (1965). *Aspects of scientific explanation.* New York: The Free Press.

King, S.W. (1988). A taxonomy for the classification of language studies in intercultural communication. In L.A. Samovar & R.E. Porter (Eds.), *Intercultural communication: A reader.* Belmont, CA: Wadsworth.

Lundsteen, S.W. (1979). *Listening its impact at all levels on reading and the other language arts.* (2nd ed.). Urbana, IL: ERIC Clearinghouse on Reading and the Other Language Arts. (original work published 1971)

Mezzich, J.E., & Solomon, H. (1980). *Taxonomy and behavioral science.* New York: Academic Press.

Mills, E.P. (1974). *Listening: Key to communication.* New York: Petrocelli Books.

Nichols, R.G. (1957). Listening is a 10-part skill. *Nation's Business, 45,* 4.

Richards, J.C. (1983). Listening comprehension: Approach, design, procedure. *TESOL Quarterly, 17,* 219–240.

Richards, J.C. (1985). *The context of language teaching.* Cambridge, UK: Cambridge University Press.

Rogers, C.R. (1961). *On becoming a person.* Boston: Houghton Mifflin.

Steil, L., Barker, L.L., & Watson, K.W. (1983). *Effective listening key to your success.* Reading, MA: Addison-Wesley.

Ur, P. (1984). *Teaching listening comprehension.* Cambridge, UK: Cambridge University Press.

Weaver, S.W., & Rutherford, W.L. (1974). A hierarchy of listening skills. *Elementary English, 51,* 1148–1149.

Wolff, F.I., Marsnik, N.E., Tacey, W.W., & Nichols, R.G. (1983). *Perceptive listening.* New York: Holt, Rinehart & Winston.

Wolvin, A.D., & Coakley, C.G. (1979). *Listening instruction.* Urbana, IL: ERIC Clearinghouse on Reading and Other Communication Skills.

Wolvin, A.D., & Coakley, C.G. (1988). *Listening.* Dubuque, IA: William C. Brown.

Chapter 3

Human Information Processing

Belle Ruth Witkin

Department of Speech Communication
University of Washington

Human information processing is discussed from two perspectives: information theory, and the stages of acoustic events as they occur and interact over time. The focus of the chapter is on listening as an active cognitive process and on the listener's activity at the stages of pattern processing, particularly perception and attention. Several models are discussed, as well as research methods in attention and perception with adults, children, and infants. Implications from the research for the listener are information processing under adverse environmental conditions, listening in the classroom, listening assessment, everyday listening, and the listening of older people.

It is scarcely possible to understand listening without a knowledge of how the listener processes the information heard—that is, perceives, understands, and remembers it. Goss (1982) argues that an information-processing approach to listening would alleviate a good deal of conceptual confusion. The focus of research, then, would be on the listening *act* itself—on how humans process information, rather than just on the products of listening.

CONCEPTUALIZATIONS OF
INFORMATION PROCESSING

The idea of the human being as an information processor is a metaphor (Tulving, 1979). The meaning of that metaphor changes with the theoretical and research interests of the investigator. In a sense, the concepts of every chapter in this book could be subsumed under the rubric of human information processing. So vast is the field that Craig (1979) noted at least 39 relevant topics—among them psychophysics, perception, attention, pattern recognition, concept formation, reasoning, decision making, memory, language comprehension, cognitive complexity, message and channel variables, overload, and cybernetic systems.

According to Craig (1979), the basis underlying the information-processing perspective is systems theory, which is of great interest to communicology. He finds, however, that, except for persuasion and information seeking, most of the important literature on specific aspects of individual information processing lies, not in communicology, but in the field of cognitive science, in which a central concern is the cognitive processing and representation in memory of information from discourse. Cognitive science is an interdisciplinary field that draws from psychology, linguistics, and artificial intelligence, with psychology being the richest source of knowledge.

As might be expected, conceptualizations of information processing vary with the focal concerns of the investigator. Massaro (1975) uses an information-processing model for the theoretical analysis of speech perception, reading, and psycholinguistics. He views language processing as the abstraction of meaning from an acoustic signal or from printed text, "a sequence of processing stages or operations that occur between stimulus and meaning" (p. 5). The flow of information can be tracked through the processes of feature detection, recognition, and recoding. For the listener, "deriving meaning from the speech signals involves a sequence of successive transformations that give the system larger and larger chunks of information" (p. 16).

Other researchers find support for conceiving the human information-processing system as one "which acts to minimize negative or noxious psycho-emotional states produced by either understimulation or over-stimulation" (Donohew, Palmgreen, & Duncan, 1980, p. 305).

The field is complex, with research coming from at least two different perspectives. In one perspective, information-processing theories of intelligence have taken their place along with trait theories and general theories of thinking (Lohman, 1989), and an information-processing hierarchy is used to explain various components of intelligence. Similarly, models of information processing are used to study specific cognitive processes such as attention and memory. In the other perspective, research on such processes as attention and memory is undertaken to elucidate the nature of information processing per se.

The focus in the present chapter is on the light that theories and research on human information processing (HIP) can throw on listening— that is, on auditory rather than visual processing and particularly on the processes occurring *at the moment of listening*. The major sections address these topics: (a) What is meant by information processing. (b) How humans process information, with special focus on perception and attention. (c) Selected methods of research. (d) Implications of the research on information processing for the understanding of listening. The topics and their treatment must of necessity be representative, rather than exhaustive. The underlying physiological and neurological factors of information processing are beyond the scope of this chapter.

WHAT IS MEANT BY INFORMATION PROCESSING?

There are many approaches to the study of human information processing, principally from the field of psychology. Some of them are primarily concerned with the nature of thought, or with visual processing and memory for events. This chapter draws mainly on two disciplines— cognitive science and speech (or acoustic) science—which in my view clarify the role of listening processes within the larger field of human communication. Within these perspectives the concept of information processing can be further studied from two different but related theoretical bases: *information theory* and a continuum of *information flow*.

Information Theory

Some of the earliest research on information theory was that of Shannon (1948), who viewed information as essentially a selection among alternatives, a numerical quantity that measures the uncertainty in the outcome of an utterance. Information theory defines the processing of information as the *reduction of uncertainty*. The underlying philosophy of information theory as applied to listening is that the listener's recognition of patterns in a spoken utterance is significantly affected by one's concept of the total set of patterns that might be encountered. As Sanders (1977) explains, "the amount of information which can be extracted from a complex stimulus is proportional to the degree of uncertainty it represents. That is to say, if a person is aware of all the possible combinations and, most importantly, of the probabilities of occurrence of each combination, he will quickly recognize patterns" (p. 82); and that principle explains the rapid speech perception of individuals who are acquainted with a particular set of language rules.

Another way of putting it is that information theory deals *statistically* with information, with the probability that a particular pattern of speech sounds or features will appear in a given context, and with the measurement of its content in terms of its distinguishing essential characteristics or by the number of alternatives from which it makes a choice possible.

In the context of information theory, then, *information* does not carry the everyday denotations of "knowledge," "facts," or "meaning." It is

> the occurrence of one out of a set of alternative discriminative stimuli.... The *content of the information* concerns the particular discriminative stimulus that does occur. The *amount of the information* concerns the range of possible alternatives that could occur.... Our definition does not say that the listener must be able to decode the message. The amount of information is the measure of a talker's freedom of choice when he selects a message. It is a measure, not of a particular message, but of a total situation. (G. A. Miller, 1951, p. 41)

For example, in the English language there is a high probability that any utterance beginning with the marker *the* will be followed by a noun form or a phrase containing a noun and modifiers. The language permits the construction *the dog* or *the large dog* but not *dog the*. The utterance might even be *the skorter* or *the grufous skorter,* which the listener would not be able to decode but which would be recognized as a particular grammatical form in English and which might be decodable from the context of a larger utterance.

Information exists whenever a given system is in one possible state rather than another. By definition, then, information is transmitted when the state of one system is somehow contingent on the state of another. When the nervous system of a listener acquires structure from sound waves, we say that the system has *processed* the information. According to Neisser (1976), however, that statement may be misleading. The information itself is not changed, since it was already in the sound waves or light waves. Furthermore, as cognitive scientists argue, *meanings* reside not in messages but in people (Roberts & Maccoby, 1985). Therefore the messages sent by a speaker are never exactly the same as those received by the listener.

Mathematically, the amount of information is defined as the logarithm of the number of alternatives. Information theorists use this definition to investigate the amount of information carried by sound waves as well as the amount conveyed by the verbal elements. The relative frequencies of phonemes, syllables, and words in a language, and the effects of communication contexts on the standard curves of those frequency distributions, are the concerns of information theorists. Anyone who does crossword puzzles or acrostics uses principles of information theory to complete words or sentences in the puzzle. Thus, the letter that belongs in a space standing alone is more likely to be *a* or *I* than any other; and the letter belonging in a word that ends in -*ng* is most likely to be *i*. Similarly, the listener unconsciously rules out any sequence of acoustic events in a spoken message that is unlikely to occur in the language.

Fortunately, it is not necessary to hear and understand every phoneme and lexical unit in ongoing speech to derive meaning from it. G.A. Miller (1951) notes, "The secret of the resilience of the spoken word is that it contains far more information than the listener actually needs" (p. 69). All languages are characterized by redundancy—that is, some sequences of verbal units are favored more than others—and this redundancy effectively reduces the amount of information that must be encoded per unit. In English, for example, we distinguish 41 phonemes. But when the average value of the logarithms of their probabilities is calculated, the result is only $\log_{28}$ units of information per phoneme, not $\log_{41}$ units. Miller explains, "In other words, we could convey just as much information per sound with a language that has only 28 sounds but uses them all equally often as we can with our present language of 41 sounds that are not used equally often" (1951, p. 103). A completely phonetic language such as Hawaiian functions quite well with only 13 phonemes—5 vowels and 8 consonants.

Not only phonemes but also lexical units are redundant. Typically, in a sentence of 11 words only about 5 carry the freight of meaning—mainly nouns and verbs. The rest are markers, modifiers, and connectives. Thus, we can readily understand the utterance, "I go beach early August," when the complete sentence might be "I plan to go to a sandy beach early in August," or even "I go to the beach in early August each year." The exact interpretation would depend on the context.

Information Flow

The second perspective on information processing in listening is concerned not so much with the statistical properties of information as the reduction of uncertainty, but rather with how the listener processes acoustic events as they occur in a flow over time, and with relationships between sources of information, messages, channels, and receivers. In a continuum of input–processing–output–feedback there are more or less well-defined stages. Rumelhart (1977) suggests:

> The points at which fluctuations in patterns of energy in the environment are translated into fluctuations of neural activity are of special importance to the information processing theorist. It is through these points that the

information flow begins. The theoretical problem is to characterize the form of the information as it enters the system and then to observe the changes which occur with time after its entrance. (p. 4)

Rumelhart posits five general stages in the continuum of information flow: *sensing* disturbances in the environment that affect the sense organs; *recognizing patterns* through attention and perception, coding complex sensory inputs, and matching them with stored memory patterns; *understanding language* by discovering the meaning of the linguistic inputs; *remembering,* including information decay and loss with time, as well as the organization of long-term memory structures; and *reasoning,* the processes operating on structured memories that allow us to make inferences (Rumelhart, 1977).

Other communication theorists propose somewhat different models. The listening model of Goss (1982), for example, is composed of three interlocking parts: signal processing, literal processing, and reflective processing. In the Goss model, signal processing is roughly analogous to Rumelhart's stages of sensing and pattern recognition, literal processing to understanding language, and reflective processing to reasoning.

How is the concept of a continuum of information flow related to information theory? According to Sanders (1977), the *patterns* and transformations of energy at the sense receptors are what generate *information.* The ability to identify or impose patterns upon a changing sensory environment lies at the basis of all perception.

The five stages in Rumelhart's model and the three in Goss's are not independent but interact in a complex manner so that their separation for descriptive purposes is somewhat artificial. This chapter focuses on the stage of pattern recognition (or signal processing), and especially on theories and research on perception and attention—the phenomena that occur in the listener *at the moment of listening.* The stage of memory is dealt with in detail by Bentley in Chapter 5 in the present volume.

Eco (1984) takes issue with what information theorists have proposed as the standard communication model, in which there is a sender, a message, and an addressee (receiver), and "in which the message is decoded on the basis of a Code [sic] shared by both the virtual poles of the chain" (p. 5). Instead of a simple continuum of flow of information, Eco postulates a complex model in which the "message" is really a *text,* a network of different messages depending on different codes and working at different levels of signification. There is a reciprocal interaction between the *message-expression* as a source of information, including private codes and ideological biases of the sender, ambiguities of expression and content, and various subcodes that represent knowledge that the addressee supposedly shares with the sender; and the *message-content* as interpreted text, which includes private codes and ideological biases of the addressee, aleatory[1] connotations, interpretive failures, and subcodes that represent the "real patrimony of [the] addressee's knowledge" (Eco, 1984, p. 6).

Perception and attention in listening are intimately related to listening *comprehension*. According to Ortony (1978), much of what we consider listening comprehension is based on the implicit assumption that whatever is *perceived* is converted into an underlying *representation* of its *meaning*, which is then stored in *memory* and added to the listener's knowledge.

Ortony argues, however, that it is necessary to distinguish between *comprehension* and *memory*, since not everything that is understood is remembered and not everything that is remembered is understood. He points out that people are not tape recorders and that there can be considerable distortion in *recall* of material that was processed and understood. We acknowledge that "comprehension involves the utilization of knowledge. Memory, on the other hand, involves the retrieval, recognition, and in some cases even the regeneration of *representations* of knowledge.... [It] becomes clear that comprehension is a process *prior* to and *distinct* from the creation of a memory representation" (Ortony, 1978, p. 57; emphasis added).

Types of Information

In relating types of information to the larger concept of how listeners select and process information it is useful to consider two broad categories distinguished by G. R. Miller (1969): *Information 1*, consisting of all external stimuli to which an individual is exposed at a given moment, each representing a unit of information potential; and *Information 2*, the individual's internal storehouse of knowledge and prior learning experiences. This available response repertory "helps fix the possible response alternatives [and] also the probability of each of these alternatives occurring under particular environmental circumstances" (p. 53).

According to Miller, those who have stressed the importance of Information 1 have been learning theorists. Those who have stressed the primacy of Information 2 have been perceptual theorists. In Miller's view, "most scientifically useful generalizations concerning human information processing will have to take account" of both types of information— environmental stimuli and the individual's background of experience (1969, p. 53).

A related distinction particularly applicable to listening comprehension

---

[1] Aleatory: depending on an uncertain event or contingency; relating to luck, especially bad luck.

is what Samuels (1987) terms *inside-the-head* and *outside-the-head* factors. The *outside* factors, corresponding to Information 1, are the discussion topic, speaker awareness of audience need, clarity and speaker effectiveness, and context. The *inside* factors, corresponding roughly to Information 2, are intelligence, language facility, background knowledge and schemas, speech registers and awareness of contextual influences, metacognitive strategies, kinesics, and motivation (Samuels, 1987, pp. 298–299).

A problem of major importance in the research on HIP by psychologists is that almost all attention is paid to manipulating Information 1, while researchers rarely inquire into the storehouse of Information 2 that subjects bring to the experiment—that is, their attitudes and previous experiences with the variables under study ("pre-experimental assessments of subjects' phenomenal states," G.R. Miller, 1969, p. 55). Miller cites the constructs of dissonance, anxiety, attitude, and credibility as being inextricably bound to human information processing. A similar concern from the perspectives of psychotherapy and interpersonal communication is that, regardless of context, any message between persons not only conveys content, or bits of information, but also reflects the relationships of the participants.

In recent years, considerable light on Information 2 has come from *schema theory* (discussed by Edwards and McDonald in Chapter 4 of this volume), a construct that forms a bridge between attention to complex auditory signals, and interpretation and memory. Norman (1976, 1979) postulates that experience and knowledge are organized into structural frames or schemas that can be used to characterize any experience. He assumes that the processing system consists of an autonomous collection of schemas, each acting as an independent processing structure.

According to Norman, processing should be viewed not as "analysis by sequential stages" but as "analysis by a pool of memory schemas." Thus stages of processing disappear. He further notes, "Schemas play an active role in guiding the flow of information-processing activities, and the flow cannot be characterized as traveling in any particular direction" (Norman, 1979, p. 138).

HOW DO HUMANS PROCESS INFORMATION?

Contrary to what earlier researchers thought, information processing is not passive. Craig (1979) notes, "The human as an information processor...*seeks* information from the environment and recodes and stores that information for later retrieval and use" (Craig, 1979, p. 101; emphasis added). In this view, coding efficiency, memory phenomena, and capacity of the channel are central. Theorists also distinguish between *structural features* of the system, such as memory stores, and *control processes,* such as attention, rehearsal, and retrieval (Atkinson & Shiffrin, 1968; cited in Craig, 1979, p. 101). A frequent analogy is to the electronic computer—the brain is likened to the hardware and the mind to a set of programs or software for recoding and transmitting information. Although advances in computer capabilities have made it possible to link artificial intelligence (AI) with psychology and linguistics to investigate information processing, there are many objections to making too close an analogy between AI and HIP. Lohman (1989) points out that, recently, there has been a tempering of enthusiasm for the use of AI in investigating intelligence and information processing. Among other considerations, although computers are programmed to consider all factors in a problem before deciding on a course of action, "humans tend not to consider all aspects of a problem... before deciding upon a course of action.... [T]he computer begins to drown in computation as problems increase in complexity" (Lohman, 1989, p. 364).

A full treatment of how humans process information would include physiological, neurological, sensory, cognitive, linguistic, and many other factors, as well as an explication of all the stages in Rumelhart's model of information flow. This chapter, however, limits the discussion to the pattern recognition stage, especially the processes of perception and attention.

Perception

The auditory perception of language, or speech perception, is "a process of interpreting the instructions imprinted on the acoustic wave by the speaker over a time span" (Sanders, 1977, p. 98). Some researchers make a distinction between *language processing* and *auditory processing,* since deaf individuals do acquire and process language but do not do it auditorially. Speech perception, however, is heavily dependent upon the listener's familiarity with the rules of language processing (Pierce, 1969). A factor that makes computer recognition of speech so difficult is that "the human listener depends very little upon the information in the acoustic signal and very heavily upon his knowledge of the linguistic rules constraining the speaker" (Sanders, 1977, p. 141).

There are two sets of phenomena in auditory processing: (a) the acoustic, linguistic, and statistical characteristics of the *message* (speech signal, inputs); and (b) the psycholinguistic and perceptual processes occurring in the *listener.* Although this chapter deals mainly with processes in the listener, it includes some research on the effects of variables and distractors in the speech signal on listener processing and comprehension.

Certain early experimental studies in auditory processing had as their purpose the development of models of perception (e.g., Hanley, 1956; Witkin, 1962). Fairbanks (1966) enlarged the scope of inquiry with research on delayed auditory feedback, time compression/expansion of speech, the specification of the vowel, and signal detection and intelligibility. Other early studies investigated auditory discrimination, auditory memory and synthesis, and the relationship of speech perception to speech production.

Like so many other aspects of listening, there is no one generally accepted model of auditory information processing, although there has been a great deal of interest in model building. The question is, How can information be structured internally to yield perceptual value? Sanders (1977) asserts that the *recognition of patterns* by the perceptual system is critical to an understanding of speech perception. The parameters of intensity and frequency interact over time to generate various patterns of complex speech sounds, each of which can be identified by its distinctive features. However, "different individuals may require significantly different amounts of information to identify the same stimulus" (Sanders, 1977, p. 82). Once the pattern is identified, the speech stimulus may be analyzed in a step-by-step process (serial processing) or by simultaneous examination of its features (parallel processing).

There have been four general theories of pattern recognition:

1. *Template theories* view the task as one of correlating, or matching input pattern information to an internal standard pattern. These theories do not appear to be adequate in explaining speech perception (Sanders, 1977).
2. *Filtering theories* envisage information as passing through banks of filters that permit the sorting of data into identifiable categories (Fant, 1967).
3. A radical modification of filter theory is *feature detection theory,* which posits the concept of active neural units that select rather than filter. In this model, of which there are many variations, the system is comprised of discrete detectors, each sensitized to a certain potential pattern component or feature. Sanders (1977) cautions, "It is important to note that the input data will be perceived, not in terms of the external stimulus, but *in terms of how the system has processed them.* The processing is subject to both internal and external influences" (p. 87; emphasis added).
4. The *analysis-by-synthesis* model involves the identification of patterns predicted on the basis of the constraints operating at a given

time (Stevens & Halle, 1967). At the synthesis stage, the pattern is an expectancy, or computed probability. Analysis is performed by comparing the *predicted* signal with the received input of the *actual* signal.

Researchers are interested in how our perceptual mechanisms can possibly cope with speech signals that are as fast and complex as the production process has made them (Pierce, 1969). In this regard Sanders (1977, pp. 100–101) supplies a useful abstract of active and passive theories of speech perception. *Passive* models are nonmediated, with direct decoding; both neurological and acoustic models have been proposed. These models also use the concept of distinctive features. *Active* models are mediated, with indirect decoding. Active models assume that a listener is one "who actively participates in producing speech as well as listening to it in order that he may compare his internal utterances with the incoming one" (Cooper, 1972, p. 42). Two major schools of thought have been that of motor theory, investigated by the group at Haskins Laboratories (Liberman, Cooper, Shankweiler, & Studdert-Kennedy, 1967); and the analysis-by-synthesis model based upon hypothesis testing (Stevens & Halle, 1967).

There has been a great deal of controversy in the field of speech science about these two types of models. The proponents of each have modified their views to some extent; other researchers have concluded that neither theory alone can entirely explain the perception of speech (Sanders, 1977) and that normally we may use several different methods simultaneously (Denes, 1967).

As noted in the discussion of Information 1 and Information 2, auditory perception in the mature listener always involves an interaction of sensory input and past knowledge. There may also be separate but interrelated systems for processing speech elements, such as segmental and suprasegmental (intonation) phonemes. Doehring (1983) notes that fully interactive models are limited; for example, information about temporal order might be lost. He proposes a model that does not make a direct connection between brief sensory storage and higher-level perceptual systems. In such a model these two aspects would be treated separately.

Attention

Psychologists from the time of James have alternately noticed or ignored the whole question of attention; or, as Solley and Murphy (1960) put it, "In short, the problem of attention is a pesky creature that keeps circling us like a Socratic gadfly" (p. 177). They viewed the attentional act as very complex, "embracing the *moment before and during* reception of a potential perceptual stimulus" (p. 178; emphasis in original).

In postbehavioristic psychology the term *attention* has been used to "provide a label for some of the internal mechanisms that determine the significance of stimuli" (Kahneman, 1973, p. 2). There are several distinct subcultures among students of attention; those interested in audition and in visual perception are only two. Each has developed its own language and biases.

Attention is the factor responsible for determining whether or not the visual or auditory signal is processed and proceeds into short-term memory (STM). It refers to "the allotment of processing resources to one or another processing activity. We are said to attend to something when we allot our resources to the processing of that thing" (Rumelhart, 1977, p. 277).

Auditory attention is the ability to direct and sustain attention to sounds, to select a relevant stimulus from a background of irrelevant stimuli, and to continue to attend selectively to this stimulus. Of particular interest to listening research are the concepts of focusing on a figure in relation to ground, attention span, and tracking a spoken message accurately. According to Sticht, Beck, Hauke, Kleiman, and James (1974), in tracking a spoken message a listener uses three levels of analysis: *acoustic* (frequency, speech quality, rate), *linguistic* (phonetic constituents, phonemic sequences, grammatical structures), and *semantic* (meaning).

The ability to pay attention is a developmental one. Highly distractible children who have difficulty learning language are not able to attend to relevant information in the face of a multitude of unweighted sensory stimuli. As Sanders (1977) points out, "In order for a person to perceive a given message, he must be able to follow its developing pattern over time against a background of ongoing activity in the same medium" (p. 202).

Failures in listening comprehension and effectiveness often begin with failures of attention. Because of the redundancy of spoken language, however, attention to meaningful connected speech need not always be continuous. Normally a listener is able to decode a message without attending to every syllable, particularly if the message is rich in context. It should be noted that tests of recall of strings of unrelated words or digits, which are often used to study memory span in listening, are as much a test of attention as they are of memory.

An important difference between auditory and visual attention is that "auditory perception requires spatiotemporal grouping while the visual analysis of unmoving objects involves only spatial grouping. Auditory attention to one message in a medley is analogous to [the vastly more complex case of] visual attention to one dancer in an ensemble" (Kahneman, 1973, p. 135).

Selective Attention. Psychologists identify two basic aspects of attention: *selective* and *intensive*. In *selective* attention the listener appears to control the choice of stimuli that will be allowed, in turn, to control behavior; that is, the organism *selectively attends* to some stimuli in preference to others. Selective processing is of prime importance to the listener, since otherwise we would be totally overwhelmed by the amounts of auditory stimuli that reach the sensory nerve endings (Sanders, 1977).

Selective attention is related to the experience of figural emphasis in visual figure–ground experiments, such as the well-known picture in which the viewer alternately sees a vase or two faces in profile. In attending to a radio announcement while people in the same room are talking loudly, the listener may select the announcer's voice as figure and the other sounds as background. Selective attention tasks are easier if the inputs to be attended to form a distinct unit, or contrast with the simultaneous background message. It is easier if the two messages are in quite different voices, or separate inputs to the two ears, or meaningful speech contrasted with noise, or (in the case of similar voices) if the voice to be attended to is at least 5 decibels (db) louder or softer than the voice to be ignored (that is, a signal-to-distraction ratio of +5 or −5db). But selective attention is very difficult with two similar voices, or binaural input, or two simultaneous meaningful messages, or when the signal-to-distraction ratio of meaningful stimuli is 0 db (Witkin, Butler, Hedrick, & Manning, 1973; Witkin, Butler, & Whalen, 1977).

According to Sanders (1977), "*control* of the figure-ground relationship, the preattentive processes, and the development of perceptual expectancies are all aspects of the same perceptual process" (p. 93; emphasis added). This auditory control contrasts with visual perception, where selective focusing on figure vs. ground is an innate ability rather than a matter of control.

There has been considerable investigation of selective attention in relation to age of listeners, types of messages attended to, and attention in various environmental contexts. Tasks that are used to investigate attention will be described in the section on research methods below.

In some of the earliest research on selective listening with children, Maccoby and Konrad (1966) found that ability to attend to a given voice and ignore the other improved with age, that performance improved with practice, and that scores were better for all ages if the different voices were presented to different ears. An increase in accuracy with age was also found by Hedrick (1967; Hedrick & Kunze, 1974), who studied the development of selective listening ability in children from kindergarten to fifth grade. The relative *intensity* of the competing messages most affected children in grades K–2, but the message *content* most affected those in grade 3.

Augustine (1973) studied relationships in 6-year-olds between an observational measure of attention, an overt behavioral measure (a vigilance task), and a physiological measure (auditory evoked response, AER). He found positive significant correlations between vigilance and AER, both in the level of attention and in change of attention, but not between observation and vigilance or AER. In their research on fig-ure–ground discrimination in children, Witkin et al. (1973) found that teacher observations of listening attention correlated more highly with students' reading scores than with their listening scores.

The ability to attend to continuous auditory messages has been studied with both shadowing and monitoring tasks. The *shadowing* task requires continuous overt responses—the subject must repeat what has been heard as quickly as possible; in the *monitoring* task the listener must respond only to occasional target items. In a variety of experiments, some using fast rates of presentation, Kahneman (1973) and his colleagues found that selective attention was less effective in the recognition experiments than in studies of shadowing.

Another research question has centered on the nature of selective attention to nonattended stimuli (Gillespie, 1969). Subjects were trained to shadow lists of 1,000 words presented at .75 seconds to the right ear. A second (distractor) list, paired word for word, was presented simulta-neously to the left ear. The second list contained a small proportion of words belonging to a particular experimental class to which subjects might be expected to respond (due to previous training conditions). Results indicated that the presence of a nonattended sensitized word in the distractor list was associated with a slight delay in the shadowing of the paired attended word and an increase in shadowing errors to the following attended word. Gillespie's findings contradicted Broadbent's (1958) model, which provided for filtering out of nonattended stimuli at a low processing level; but they were consistent with Treisman's (1970) model, which allowed for a lower threshold for word recognition units under certain conditions.

Intensive Attention. The second major aspect of attention is *intensive*. It has to do with effort and may be present with either involuntary or voluntary attention. Some types of information-processing activities can be triggered solely by an input of information. Others require an additional input of attention or effort. As Kahneman (1973) observes, "Because the total quantity of effort which can be exerted at any one time is limited, concurrent activities which require attention tend to interfere with one another" (p. 12).

Two models of attention have been proposed: (a) a structural model, in which cognitive activity is limited by a bottleneck, or station, at which parallel processing is impossible; and (b) a capacity model, in which the limited capacity determines which activities can be carried out together. In Kahneman's view, neither model is adequate alone.

These models are incompatible and contradictory. But it is possible to reconcile them by recognizing that two different but related phenomena are subsumed under the construct *attention*. One is our ability to focus on certain aspects of the world in order to increase the detail with which it is perceived. The other is our apparent inability to process simultaneously and deeply all aspects of the stimuli impinging on our sense organs. Attention thus is a tradeoff between *depth of processing* and *breadth of processing* (Rumelhart, 1977). This fact has led to different kinds of questions and different kinds of models about the mechanism of attention. Rumelhart's pattern recognition model attempts to reconcile the differences between single- and multiple-channel models.

Attention and Localization of Sound. Much of the pioneering work in attention was done by Broadbent (1958), who studied the role of auditory localization in attention and memory span, listening between and during practiced auditory distraction, and the effects of noise on behavior. Among other findings he discovered that sounds tend to be grouped if they originate from the same location or if they share certain physical characteristics.

The ability to localize a sound source is a crucial aspect of attention. Because of an "acoustic shadow" cast by the head, there is a decrease in intensity of sounds arriving at the ear opposite the source of the sound. The localization permitted by this phenomenon improves the detectability of sounds to be attended to in the presence of other competing sounds. Sounds occurring simultaneously, but emanating from different locations in space, activate different groups of cells in the auditory pathway of the brain stem.

Persons with monaural hearing losses or with substantial differences in hearing ability between the two ears are unable to use this mechanism of localization in attention. They therefore have significant problems of discriminating sounds in a noisy environment. Thus, although attention is a perceptual rather than a purely sensory phenomenon, it is affected by hearing thresholds. What a classroom teacher regards as inattention or auditory distractibility may in fact be due to some degree of hearing loss.

Attention, Distraction, and Preattentive Processes.

Students frequently claim that they can study very well while the radio or television is on. Armstrong and Greenberg (1990), however, report that, when television is used as a secondary activity, it interferes with performance on otherwise intellectually demanding tasks. In addition, "there is evidence that people are not very good at knowing when they are being distracted" (Reisberg & McLean, 1985; cited in Armstrong & Greenberg, 1990, p. 378). It is true that it is easier to attend to a visual task in the presence of auditory distraction than to an auditory task with auditory distraction. Visual and auditory processing use different nerve pathways, and therefore interference from one mode is not as distracting as if two messages were present in the same mode. Furthermore, in humans "a visual stimulus is clearly dominant over a concurrent auditory stimulus, and it captures both awareness and response" (Kahneman, 1973, p. 141). On the other hand, Mowbray (1954) found that subjects could not listen to one story while reading another. Altogether, there is substantial research evidence that attentional distractions can seriously interfere with auditory processing, especially of complex cognitive tasks.

Among the variables that affect attention, an increasingly important one is environmental noise. The effects of noise on attention and other aspects of auditory processing have only begun to be examined. But the data are mounting to indicate, not only that ambient noise affects attention to an immediate task, but that continued exposure to high levels of noise causes reduced hearing acuity and associated perceptual problems that seriously affect auditory processing.

Perceptual readiness to recognize and attend to a stimulus is strongly related to our interests and familiarity with the event. A friend whose professional career was focused on the prevention and reduction of racial and religious discrimination recounted an incident in which he caught a glimpse of a billboard advertising a product. He thought he saw the words racial issues, when in fact the message was about facial tissues. Such misperceptions have been studied in the context of mindfulness and mindlessness (Langer, 1989), automatic human information processing (Schneider & Schiffrin, 1977), and hidden preattentive processes (Broadbent, 1977). Broadbent cites research to show that preattentive processes act like pigeonholes to constrain our choices of those aspects of auditory and visual stimuli that we will attend to. Research on the semantic effects of context, word frequency, and emotionality argue for the existence of preattentive processes, although the research is contradictory as to whether the processes are active or passive. In a larger context, Langer's research over a 15-year period shows the harmful effects of chronic mindlessness and automatic information processing to the individual and to society.

Attention in Infants. Attention has been studied in infants as well. Researchers have observed that infants of 6 weeks will pay attention to speech and nonspeech stimuli that are pulsed (with a silent interval between stimuli). They will also attend to nonpulsed speech stimuli, but not to nonpulsed nonspeech stimuli (sine waves). Kuhl (1983) found that an infant's response to speech and sound is dictated not only by its linguistic but also by its social significance.

Conflicting Models of Attention. The research and development of theories on attention have been confused and often contradictory. We have previously noted that attention appears to be a tradeoff between *depth of processing* and *breadth of processing,* and that different models have been developed to account for those differences. Other perspectives on attention as studied in the experimental laboratory have led to other conflicting views of models of auditory processing. As Norman (1976) summarizes the problem: "Some processing proceeds from the input signals, a bottom-up, data driven sequence of processing. Other processing proceeds from internally generated hypotheses or conceptualizations, a top-down, conceptually driven sequence of processing. Above all, there is some limit on how much processing can be performed at any one time" (p. 80).

Butler (1984) proposes a reconciliation of *multistore* and *levels of processing* models by suggesting that the key to language processing is really "halfway up the down staircase." She points out that, in listening to language, there is a reciprocal and integrative relationship between and among perception, attention, and memory, all functions that are under the control of higher order mental processes. The ability of children to redirect attention is part of expanding competence related to maturation of the nervous system, as well as to their understanding of language. Individuals may ignore information selectively, focusing and shifting their attention to various aspects of a stimulus or situation. The concept of attention shift and attention span is important in understanding any auditory learning, particularly in the case of children diagnosed as having learning disabilities, who are often described as having a short attention span. Yet Maxwell and Wallach (1984) caution, "We might ask, 'Short for what?' As we all know, many learning-disabled children, as well as normally acquiring children, attend for very long periods of time—to things that interest them" (p. 30).

The subject of attention is of major importance. The effectiveness with which humans process and remember auditory information is directly related to those aspects of the message to which they attend, as well as to aspects that compete for the listener's attention (Cohen, 1989).

SELECTED METHODS OF RESEARCH ON PATTERN PROCESSING

A large body of listening research is designed to measure individual differences in ability to understand and recall information from spoken messages. Short-term memory (STM) tasks are typically studied by responses of various kinds to strings of digits or numbers, under varying conditions of delay, interference, or contexts (Bostrom, 1990). Long-term memory (LTM) is often studied using a lecture or other passages of from a minute to perhaps 15 minutes in length, after which listeners respond to questions on content, vocabulary connotations, transitions, emotional content, or directions of varying complexity. Answers are usually on multiple-choice forms.

The tape-recorded message/multiple-choice response design yields data as to *what* or *how much* listeners remember or variations in response to different kinds of messages, but not much about *how* listeners process information. For that we must look to methods used to investigate auditory attention and perception—the pattern-processing stages in the information flow of the Rumelhart model.

Research Methods in Speech Perception

Research on how humans perceive and process speech is concerned, ramong other things, with comparing the *acoustic parameters* of a spoken message with the listener's *perception* of the message. A principal tool is the sound spectrograph, which analyzes the acoustic information encoded in the speech signal, making visible the bands of acoustic energy in spoken language.

Spectrograms are produced in speech (acoustic) science laboratories by means of high-speed digital computers. The stimulus usually consists of short segments of speech. These inputs are tape-recorded, the signal is digitized and "massaged" in various ways, and resultant acoustic analyses are printed out in either two-dimensional or three-dimensional displays. Sound spectrograms show the amount and patterns of energy in the different formant regions of the speech signal. Energy patterns of vowels and consonants and their changes over time can be analyzed in many ways.

The acoustic scientist is interested, not only in the characteristics of the speech signal, but in the listener's perception of the spoken message. How do listeners contend with the extreme acoustic variations that occur in speech? Variations in the phonetic percept arise from the talker who produces the utterance, the context in which it occurs, and the rate of utterance (Minifie & Kuhl, 1991). How can theories of speech perception explain how the perceptual system equates physically different acoustic events?

Researchers have found that there is no one-to-one relationship between the information in the speech signal and what the listener reports hearing—that is, acoustic processing per se cannot account for speech perception (Cooper, 1972). For example, listeners can perceive the fundamental pitch of an utterance even when there is more energy in the second or third formant regions than in Formant$_1$, the fundamental. Using the sound spectrograph and speech synthesizers and varying the nature of the speech signal by controlling the formant regions of vowels, researchers have made extensive changes in the signal without altering the perceptual experience of the listener.

Another line of research using computers and spectrographic analyses is being pursued by Minifie and his colleagues, who are conducting studies on how perceptions of consonants shift with changes in rate of speech. Stimuli sentences are produced by an adult male talker, stored in a tape recorder, then digitized on a computer at a sampling rate of 15 KHz. The rate of utterance for each sentence is systematically increased by deleting every third segment in all sections of the sentence, and spectrograms are used for analysis of formant transitions (Minifie & Kuhl, 1991).

In this research, the perceptual shift of interest is from the phoneme /w/ to /b/ in various sentence contexts, for example, "Wetter days are ahead" and "Is Bob wetter now?" At some point as the utterance becomes faster there is a perceived consonant shift, and the listener perceives, "Better days are ahead" and "Is Bob better now?"

These studies are being used to test hypotheses about a relational theory of speech perception, in which the shift in perceptual boundary is related to the contextual environment, including rate of speech. Other procedures manipulate, not only rate, but also stress patterns. According to Minifie, there is some indication that the *internal* clock of the listener is more relevant than the *clock time* (or absolute time) measures used as research variables.[2]

---

[2] Personal communication from Fred Minifie, Professor of Speech and Hearing Science, University of Washington, December 18, 1990.

Perception and Discrimination in Children

Researchers in language development and speech/language pathologists are interested in children's ability to perceive and recognize a word when the signal has been changed to segment the word into individual phonemes. A words such as *cat* is spoken with the phonemes /k/ae/t/ presented at intervals of 1/2, 1, 2, or 3 seconds. The stimulus may be presented by a trained speaker with live voice, tape recording, or tapes of synthetic speech, in which digital computers produce speech sounds conforming to spectrographic analyses of live voice.

The longer the delay between phonemes, the more difficult it is for the listener to synthesize them in STM and to recognize the word. Studies of mentally retarded children show that, if the inputs are too slow, the listener has difficulty keeping the information in STM; if the inputs are too fast, the listener cannot attend adequately and does not have enough time to decode. The optimum band of rate of phonemic synthesis is probably narrower for such children than for listeners of average or above average intelligence.

Research Methods on Infant Perception of Speech

The study of the perception of speech by infants is only a decade old. Several behavioral techniques have been developed. One procedure uses heart rate as an index of attention to a novel event. The response decreases in magnitude as a novel stimulus becomes "familiar" and increases if a second novel stimulus is presented. A second procedure is operant conditioning, in which the index of discrimination is the infant's changes in sucking on a pacifier in response to a familiar versus a novel stimulus. The high-amplitude sucking (HAS) technique produced valuable findings but had severe limitations.

A more promising technique is that of the operant head-turn (HT), which in recent years was adapted by a team of clinical audiologists at the University of Washington to study speech-sound discrimination in infants in the 5 to 12-month age range. A speech sound is presented constantly as a "background" stimulus. The infant is trained to produce a head-turn response toward a loudspeaker when an auditory signal is presented. The infant sits on the parent's lap in the experimental room, a trained observer watches behind a one-way mirror, and correct HT responses are reinforced with the presentation of a visual stimulus of interest to infants, such as an animated toy. The following description is extracted from Kuhl (1985):

> Four types of reinforcement were examined: (a) no reinforcement; (b) social
> reinforcement (a smile, verbal praise, and/or a pat on the shoulder); (c) simple

visual reinforcement (a blinking light); and (d) complex visual reinforcement (an animated toy).

The stimulus was a complex noise presented at a level well above threshold. Each infant...was given 40 trials; each trial consisted of a 4-second observation interval during which head-turn responses were judged by both an assistant and an experimenter. (p. 226)

Research using the HT response is yielding data that infants respond discriminatively to speech sounds at a much younger age than had been thought previously.

Research Methods on Attention

Attention relies on selecting features from the acoustic stimuli to which energy is allocated. Following are brief descriptions of laboratory methods for studying *selective attention* and *figure-ground relationships*.

Selective Attention. Auditory perception involves the checking out of perceptual expectancies. Thus it is usually not necessary for a listener to pay attention to individual components in an utterance unless the context is unfamiliar or unexpected, or when there is very little redundancy in the message signal (as in letter or word strings), or when a speech pattern differs markedly from one's own, as in listening to a foreign language or foreign dialect (Sanders, 1977).

Attention tasks may require subjects to select inputs (stimuli) from a particular source, or targets of a particular type, or a particular attribute of objects, or outputs (responses) in a particular category. The ability to select out of the acoustic stimulus certain features may be researched using a variety of methods. In a previous section there was a brief description of two types of tasks: *shadowing* of continuous speech, in which the subject repeats the message aloud as quickly as possible; and *monitoring* of continuous speech, in which the listener must attend to the entire message but respond only to occasional target items randomly presented.

Selective attention is also studied by presenting auditory information of two different kinds or from two different sources, either live and free-field or through earphones. The Maccoby and Konrad (1966) research referred to earlier studied age trends in selective listening in children in primary grades. They used male and female voices, with messages spoken in a free-field environment, and children were instructed to pay attention to one voice and to disregard the other.

Hedrick (1967; Hedrick & Kunze, 1974) refined the method by using tape-recorded messages presented to both ears. The speech stimuli competed with background noise or speech. Systematic variations were produced in intensity of the signal, content of the message, and ratios of the signal to the distracting background. Manning (1964) adapted the method for research with adult listeners.

There are four experimental procedures for presenting auditory information from two sources to the two ears through earphones: (a) *monaural* presentation, in which both sounds (A and B) are presented to one ear only; (b) *binaural,* in which the two sounds are mixed together and presented to both ears so that the two ears hear the same material; (c) *dichotic,* in which the messages from the two channels are fed into separate ears so that the left ear hears only A and the right ear only B; and (d) *stereophonic,* in which both A and B are fed through loudspeakers placed at different positions from the listener (Norman, 1976, p. 21).

Figure—Ground Relationships. A related aspect of selective attention is the ability of the listener to separate out an acoustic stimulus of interest against a background of speech or noise of varying degrees of similarity to the signal. This is sometimes called a competing message (CM) task.

Variations of the CM task have been used in diagnostic test batteries to identify auditory processing deficits in children or to use in training children and adults in auditory attention. Hedrick and Manning (Witkin et al., 1973) refined the procedure as part of a 3-year research and development project on listening in elementary school children. They constructed tape recordings using inputs from two channels, in which the competing messages were varied by phonemic content, voice quality, and intensity. Relative intensities of the signal and distraction were systematically varied electronically, from +15db to −15db; the two signals were mixed and presented binaurally through earphones or loudspeaker.

The CM tasks used three types of voices (adult male, adult female, young boy) as the signal against various types and intensities of distraction (noise, music, single words, a running narrative of high interest, different voices, similar voices). The competing messages also varied in similarity or difference in linguistic and phonemic content (e.g., door/floor, or door/deer). Children were instructed to attend only to one (identified) voice, and to ignore the "noisy friend" or other noise. This particular CM research revealed that the amount of intensity *separation* of the two messages was crucial—that is, it is easier to attend to a "wanted" message that is 5 or 10 db *softer* than the background, than when the signal and distraction are the same—at 0 db. The CM tasks were also found to be a factor different from other processing tasks such as phonemic and suprasegmental phoneme discrimination, speech sound analysis, auditory closure, and synthesis (Witkin et al., 1977).

Synthesis of Auditory Units. The ability to segregate one auditory unit from another has also been studied using CM. When pairs of computer-synchronized auditory units (e.g., the nonsense syllables TAV and SEM) are presented either binaurally or dichotically, the listener tends to mix the phonemes from the two stimuli and respond with TEV. But the confusion is reduced when a nonsense syllable is presented to one ear and a digit to the other (Treisman, 1970).

Vigilance Tasks. A variation of CM to study selective attention requires the listener to respond to intermittent signals of a specified type in an ongoing stream of auditory stimuli. This type of attention is particularly important in situations such as air-traffic control.

Methods of Studying Rates of Speech Processing

Although we suspect that listeners can process information four or five times faster than the average person speaks (Nichols, 1948), what are the limits of rate of auditory processing? To what extent can oral message rates depart from the norm and still be understood?

The invention of the speech compressor (see Fairbanks, 1966) made it possible to study rates and limits of auditory processing and to correlate the ability to process speech at faster rates with other characteristics of listeners. The compressor electronically compresses or expands the time factor in speech without changing the fundamental pitch—thus eliminating the "Donald Duck" effect that occurs when an ordinary tape recording is speeded up. The compression is accomplished by mathematically removing very small segments from the speech flow. The message can be heard immediately at the new speed or recorded for later use. The rate can also be reduced by systematically doubling sound segments. In the slowed speech mode, however, there may be some lowering of pitch or a tremolo in the signal, so that the message does not sound as "normal" as does the rate altered by compression.

The average speaking rate is about 125 to 175 words per minute (wpm). Rate-controlled speech technology has been used to investigate the ability of listeners to process speech at input rates of from 75 to 450 wpm (Carver, Johnson, & Friedman, 1970; Sticht, 1971). Most college students can learn to listen at rates up to 350 wpm after becoming familiar with the reader's voice. A study of blinded veterans found that 86% could comprehend material compressed to almost 475 wpm.

Research has also been conducted on the trainability of listening comprehension to speeded discourse; the effects of practice, of difficulty of material, and of different verbal and visual presentation patterns on comprehension (Olson, 1985); the effects on comprehension of rate-controlled speech of varying linguistic complexity (Thompson, 1973); applicability of slowed speech to foreign language education (Flaherty, 1979); and the relationship of comprehension of speeded speech to gender, academic grades, and field-dependence (De L'Aune, Lewis, Needham, & Nelson, 1977). Duker (1974) published three volumes of an anthology, and an exhaustive bibliography of research.

Effects of Speech Compression on Processing. Research with compressed speech has revealed a threshold in speech rate beyond which listener comprehension drops rapidly. This is because

> it takes a fixed amount of time to relate the stimulus, or input words, to the long-term stored information, and a certain minimum number of these chunks of information must remain in short-term storage in order for the chunks to get processed. When this minimum time requirement is exceeded...there is no information processed. (Carver, 1973, pp. 124–125)

Other studies, using compressed speech with adjunct pictures (Tantiblarphol & Hughes, 1984), found that fourth- and fifth-grade students increased their recall at higher rates when pause time was added between sentences, and when pictures were added to the story. Olson and Berry (1982) discovered a different band of optimum rate of input for children and adults, both for individual phonemes and for connected speech. Others have learned, not only that 30% compression did not interfere with performance of children with auditory processing problems, but that the higher rate appeared to neutralize the decay of stimuli from STM (Manning, Johnston, & Beasley, 1977; cited in Olson & Berry, 1982).

Does training in listening to faster speech result in more effective listening in real time? Sullivan (1982) cites research to support the fact that training in progressively compressed speech may result in better overall listening skills. There is anecdotal evidence, however, to suggest that, once listeners are trained to process speech at faster rates, they can become bored when listening to slower speakers, and must work harder to keep on track with the speaker and prevent attention lapses. Also, because of the time factor in storing in STM, if the inputs are too slow, less material gets stored at one time, and there is more likely to be greater loss between STM and LTM.

Online Monitoring. Compressed speech has been used to investigate relationships between listening and reading-processing abilities (Sticht, 1971; Sticht & Beck, 1976), with a research variation called *online monitoring*. The listener silently reads a script and simultaneously listens to the script read aloud, at four increasingly rapid rates of speed. The spoken messages contain mismatches with the written script, inserted in random fashion, the substituted words having the same grammatical construction and relevance to the context as the written words. The listener circles each word that does not match what is heard.

The method is based on a model of oracy and literacy that postulates a certain relationship in the developmental curves of listening and reading comprehension (Sticht et al., 1974). The online monitoring task, which has been normed for young adults, assesses automaticity of decoding. Studies by Sticht and his colleagues have shown that listening comprehension should exceed reading comprehension for individuals who have not acquired automatic reading-decoding skills.

Problems in Methodology

There are many methodological problems in studying aspects of HIP. One is that, for a long time, the preponderance of research was on visual perception and attention, not on auditory. Solley and Murphy's (1960) important work, for example, devoted one paragraph in an entire chapter on figure–ground to auditory figure–ground. In later works, such as Kahneman's (1973) on attention and effort, descriptions of research on auditory theories are often buried in discussions of attention in general. A similar situation prevails in research on memory and language processing.

Auditory processing is not exactly analogous to visual processing, because of the different spatiotemporal nature of auditory and visual inputs as well as different neural pathways. In listening, we never have the total pattern of an utterance before us, no matter how small the unit may be; even a single phoneme or syllable takes time. Thus, the internal representation of an acoustic event must be held in storage until it is progressively synthesized (Sanders, 1977). Further, since speech is a continuous phenomenon, "the auditory system must wait until sufficient information has entered to permit the processing of the smallest sized unit [before it can] perform analysis with any degree of sophistication" (Sanders, 1977, p. 150).

Another problem has been in extrapolating data from experiments on perception of noise, tone, or square wave patterns to inferences on perception of speech. Significant research has been done on temporal sequencing of sounds and on holistic pattern recognition of acoustic components (Warren, 1982), but the methodology is much less exact and conclusive for speech perception.

The research of the 1960s and 1970s from acoustics, psycholinguistics, experimental phonetics, and auditory perception has begun to be reexamined; and findings from disparate disciplines are being brought together to provide a better understanding of the complex nature of auditory processing and to furnish a basis for hypotheses to direct future research. A new synthesis of a vast body of information was undertaken by

Warren (1982). Of particular interest is his work on perception of acoustic sequences—rate of occurrence of components, identification of components and their order in varying types and lengths of sequences, holistic pattern recognition, and perceptual restoration of missing sounds.

Results of experiments in auditory perception can be profoundly affected by whether the subjects are trained or untrained. Warren (1982) cautions, "[Subjects trained to recognize temporal order and holistic acoustic patterns] can give much more sensitive responses and make distinctions not possible for untrained subjects. On the other hand...subjects can inadvertently be trained to provide correct rote naming of temporal order of sounds lasting only a few milliseconds, even when this information is not provided directly" (p. 132).

Still another problem lies with the role of the phoneme in speech perception. The phoneme has been an important and perhaps indispensable construct in studies of speech production and for linguistic analysis, and much data on listener processing comes from spectrographic studies of the phoneme, such as the work in progress by Minifie cited earlier. As Warren notes, however, "perceptual models based on the recovery of phonemes from speech have run into difficulties, often attributable to the 'acoustic-phonetic non-invariance problem'" (1982, p. 172).

Research on perception requires a certain level of literacy in subjects. Studies with both children and adults have shown that there is a close relationship between literacy in alphabetic writing and the ability to detect phonemes. Illiterate adults, as well as those learning a second language, often have difficulty segmenting continuous speech phonetically, or into separate words, and in children the ability to do so is closely related to their reading ability. This relationship between literacy and phonemic detection is also related to juncture, which in running speech is not the same as in writing. Thus, *an apple* may be heard as *a napple*. (But languages change over time. *Nuncle* for *uncle* is found in Shakespeare.) There is also experimental evidence that "listeners do not perceive phonemes in running speech directly, but that their presence is inferred following identification of larger units" in syllables and words (Warren, 1982, p. 175).[3]

An important constraint on research in auditory attention is that it cannot be accurately observed by another person. In research on reading, an observer can record eye movements and other overt signs of attention

---

[3] This phenomenon is illustrated by an incident when I had difficulty decoding two words in an indistinct message left on my telephone answering machine. The speaker assured me that she would "cut spaces" with me. From the context I finally gathered that she would "touch bases" with me; I had accurately perceived the phonemic content of the vowels, but not that of the stop-plosive consonants.

to the printed page. But overt signs of listening attention or inattention can be misleading, as any lecturer knows. In our research on auditory perception of primary school children (Witkin et al., 1977), we found that a seemingly attentive child could be very inaccurate in processing, while another whose attention appeared to wander (as shown by body position, head movements, etc.) processed the material quite accurately. Because of the design of the audiotaped inputs—no nonverbal signals, no redundancy or contextual clues—strict auditory attention was necessary to ensure correct processing.

In some respects, research methods on perception and attention yield less ambiguous results than research on broader constructs such as "listening" or the global concept of information processing. This is partly because tasks of *memory* or auditory *language* processing inevitably involve *perception* of and *attention* to the auditory signal. Failure on a memory task, therefore, might be attributable to failure of perception or attention. The greater precision in results of many pattern-processing research tasks may be offset by the fact that such tasks often bear little resemblance to real-life listening situations, and generalizations to information processing as a whole could be problematical. Exceptions would be vigilance tasks such as might be used by air-traffic controllers. At one level, then, we can say that research has given us a good deal of information about how the listener perceives and makes patterns of the stream of incoming auditory information at the moment of listening. But at another level, we still have a great deal to learn about how the listener processes information in complex real-life situations (Cohen, 1989).

IMPLICATIONS FOR LISTENING

Not all human information processing is listening—but in a sense, all listening (to speech) is information processing. Among teachers and researchers of listening, there has been a pronounced interest in what the listener understands and remembers—in the *products* of listening. A recognition of the importance of listening *processes* provides a healthy counterbalance, as well as the possibility of fruitful new avenues of observation and research. In this final section we consider some implications for the communication environment, listening in the classroom, listening assessment, everyday listening, and listening of older people.

The Communication Environment

Information processing is adversely affected by even moderate levels of noise or other distraction in the environment or by conditions that affect the intelligibility of the signal. Armstrong and Greenberg (1990) and Hoffner, Cantor, and Thorson (1989) stress the nature of background TV as an inhibitor. Although many listeners apparently adapt well to constant ambient noise, attention to the spoken word suffers. On both the conscious and unconscious levels, the listener learns to "tune out" much of the information in the environment, and then often fails to "tune in" when it is important to do so. In addition, there is evidence that repeated exposures to high noise levels exact an emotional as well as cognitive toll on the human organism.

Listening in the Classroom

Provision of a communication environment that is conducive to good information processing is particularly important in the classroom, and all teachers should be aware of perceptual and attention factors that are critical to listening and learning. Speech pathologists and others involved in special education are usually alert to possible auditory processing problems in children who have learning or speech disabilities. One school of thought holds that these problems are due to central processing disorders that have a neurological basis, but the view is by no means universally accepted. Another controversial area is that of so-called attention deficits in learning-disabled or hyperactive children. Whether or not such problems are neurologically based, the classroom teacher should recognize that inattention may be more closely related to information-processing difficulties than simply to inappropriate behavior.

Environmental noise is also an important factor. The vogue in some quarters for "open classrooms" in elementary schools puts a premium on flexibility of the learning environment at the expense of attentional factors. Sanders (1977) cites a body of research confirming that ambient noise levels in normal classrooms are surprisingly high, particularly in early grades. He also notes that competing environmental stimuli often cause problems for children with learning disabilities because of their difficulty in holding figure-ground relationships for any length of time. Behavioral symptoms of children with learning disabilities "may include apparent unawareness by the child that he has been spoken to, or failure to persevere with a listening task...for more than a few minutes...[and] unusual levels of distractibility" (Sanders, 1977, p. 204).

Knowledge of constructs in perception and attention is also important in the foreign language classroom, as well as for the teacher of listening skills at any grade level. Wolvin and Coakley (1988) point out that *listening* is often incorrectly equated with *attention*—that is, the teacher may assume that effective listening is simply a matter of "paying attention," whereas attention is only one factor in the listening process. Listening training would benefit from incorporation of strategies to assist all students in understanding their own processing habits and to help them develop better attentional and other processing skills.

Listening Assessment

The construction of listening assessment instruments and procedures would likewise benefit from awareness of the roles that perception and attention pay in listening. As mentioned earlier, we tend to measure a listener's effectiveness by *outputs*—by evidence that a message has been understood and remembered. Yet we have few methods for analyzing precisely where in the flow of information the breakdowns in listening occur. In fact, results on listening comprehension tests are often confounded by insufficient consideration or control of the perceptual factors in information processing.

Some instruments to assess auditory processing have been developed for children, but there is almost nothing available for teenagers or adult listeners. Researchers might consider developing diagnostic procedures in perception and attention, which could be used as adjuncts to listening comprehension tests in cases where other known factors appear not to account for low scores.

When group tests are administered, the teacher should be aware of the role of noise or distraction in the environment. In a three-year research project that used competing messages and other perceptual tasks (Witkin et al., 1973), sound pressure levels were taken at various times in the participating classrooms. At all the project schools, sound levels were found to be unacceptably high, even though teachers had made an effort to minimize distractions. Failures of attention on some of the listening tasks were traced to sudden bursts of noise outside or to high levels of continuous ambient noise. These findings were supported by the research reported above by Sanders (1977).

Everyday Listening

A short list of information-processing factors affecting how well we listen in everyday situations includes deliberate or inadvertent distortion of the information, relevant and irrelevant communication distractors (Buller, 1986), communication underload or overload (Housel & Waldhart, 1981), and vague messages that lead to a distortion of memory cues (Williams, 1980). The listener must consider the role of context in information seeking (Rubin, 1977, 1979), be able to process paralanguage (Clark,

1989), use second guessing to gather selected bits of information from messages (Doelger, Hewes, & Graham, 1986), and use imagery in the organization of information (Paivio, 1975).

Still other factors that have been found to affect auditory information processing are sleep deprivation, anxiety and other psychological stress, perceptual or central-processing disabilities, and attitudes of the listener. Two decades ago G.R. Miller argued that attitude research should be "placed in its proper perspective as only one of many important dimensions of human information processing" (1969, p. 63). He also emphasized the role that information processing could play in fostering conflict resolution and engendering personal growth.

Certain occupations require excellent auditory processing skills: pilots, air-traffic controllers, shorthand writers, persons on police or crisis "hot lines," and medical personnel come to mind. Therapists and counselors must pay close attention to message nuances that go beyond the denotation of the language used. Listening in such occupations puts a premium on preventing mind wandering, on tracking rapid speech accurately, on processing in the presence of auditory or visual distractions, on recognizing the importance of paralanguage, and on inferring meaning from nonverbal, incomplete, or distorted cues in the message.

The average citizen may also face special situations where close attention and accurate processing are essential. Two of them are receiving information from a doctor or nurse, and serving on a jury. A large body of legal and communication research has accumulated to indicate that jurors in long and complex trials are prone to information overload, memory lapses, and serious misunderstanding of judge's instructions (*Jury Comprehension in Complex Trials*, 1989; Witkin, 1991).

Listening of Older People

Two listening factors that appear to concern older people the most are decrements in hearing acuity and inability to remember what has been said. Anxiety about both of these could be alleviated by attention to improving processing skills.

For example, people with mild or moderate hearing losses can receive aural rehabilitation that gives training in inferring meaning from minimal or distorted cues and that teaches strategies for avoiding or compensating for distracting environments. Yet many hearing-impaired individuals receive no help beyond being fitted with a hearing aid.

As for memory loss, "we cannot deny *that an object once attended to will remain in memory,* whilst one inattentively allowed to pass will leave no traces behind" (Norman, 1976, p. 11). At whatever age, therefore, anyone wishing to improve memory in listening situations can do so to a large extent by applying techniques for paying closer *attention* to the message at the moment of listening and by learning to shut out distractions.

Research evidence shows that it is relatively harder for older people to concentrate on a task in the presence of distraction or when dividing attention between two different tasks (West, 1985). Misinformation due to faulty perception or to inattentiveness also interacts with memory, so that, for example, names that are not clearly heard and understood are later recalled with errors of pronunciation, or addition or deletion of phonemes and syllables.

IMPLICATIONS FOR LISTENING RESEARCH

Communication scholars who pursue research in listening in the broad sense deal with different theoretical constructs and research hypotheses than do researchers in the speech and hearing sciences who focus on such factors as perception and attention. They pose different questions and use different research methods. There is a great need for better syntheses of the research from these diverse areas.

Laboratory experiments such as are necessary for investigating many aspects of pattern processing put listening in a highly artificial context. Much more research is needed on how the listener processes information in everyday situations. Because listening is a highly interactive situation, many factors in the message, the source, the context, and characteristics of the listener can affect experimental results (Cohen, 1989).

Most of the time we are not aware of how we process information, especially in the context of continuous, rapid speech. But often failures in perception or attention remind us how complex the process is and what demands the process places on the listener. We are amused when a child says *pisghetti* for *spaghetti;* we are less amused when we hear our name pronounced variously Wilkins, Wickens, Watkins, or Whitcomb, even when we have carefully pronounced and spelled it out for the listener; and we become acutely aware of processing demands when a shorthand writer, courtroom reporter, or note taker has difficulty in tracking running speech. As for attention, we have all had the experience of mind-wandering while someone else is talking. This is an area in which qualitative research, such as trained observations, self-reports, and certain methods of failure analysis might add to our understanding of *how* individuals listen, not just *how well* they listen.

As we have seen, much of the research in cognitive science either does not address listening directly or does not indicate whether the experiments used visual or auditory inputs. Yet we cannot assume that information processing is the same regardless of the modality. Jaynes (1976) emphasizes the uniqueness of the aural modality:

> Sound is a very special modality. We cannot handle it. We cannot push it away. We cannot turn our backs to it. We can close our eyes, hold our noses, withdraw from touch, refuse to taste. We cannot close our ears though we can partly muffle them. Sound is the least controllable of all sense modalities, and it is this that is the medium of that most intricate of all evolutionary achievements, language. We are therefore looking at a problem of considerable depth and complexity.
>
> Consider what it is to listen and understand someone speaking to us. In a certain sense we have to become the other person; or rather, we let him become part of us for a brief second. We suspend our own identities, after which we come back to ourselves and accept or reject what he has said. But that brief second of dawdling identity is the nature of understanding language. (p. 96)

Despite the fact that we cannot necessarily draw conclusions about auditory information processing from models based on research with visual processing, there is certainly an intimate connection between the two modalities. Many readers find it necessary to use inner speech to convert the visual image into an auditory one in order to get it into short-term memory.

The reader can test this proposition by translating from the Slurvian the following excerpts from that classic of deathless prose, LADLE RAT ROTTEN HUT. (For elucidation of the origins and research possibilities of Slurvian, see Tiffany, 1963.)

"Wants pawn term dare worsted ladle gull, hoe lift widow mutter honor itch offer lodge dock florist." And the sad tale concludes, "MURAL! Yonder nor sorghum stenches suture ladle gull torque wet strainers!"

If your visual processing has not been adequate, try reading it aloud—or better yet, have someone else read it to you. The exercise will confirm the role that auditory information processing plays even in the processing of the printed word.

REFERENCES

Armstrong, G.B., & Greenberg, B.S. (1990). Background television as an inhibitor of cognitive processing. *Human Communication Research, 16,* 355–386.

Atkinson, R.C., & Shiffrin, R.M. (1968). Human memory: A proposed system and its control processes. In K.W. Spence & J.T. Spence (Eds.), *The psychology of learning and motivation: Advances on research and theory* (Vol. 2, pp. 89–196). New York: Academic Press.

Augustine, L.E. (1973). *A correlational study of three measures of auditory attending behavior in children.* Unpublished doctoral dissertation, University of Washington, Seattle.

Bostrom, R.N. (1990). *Listening behavior: Measurement and application.* New York: Guilford Press.

Broadbent, D.E. (1958). *Perception and communication.* London: Pergamon Press.

Broadbent, D.E. (1977). The hidden preattentive processes. *American Psychologist, 32,* 109–118.

Buller, D.B. (1986). Distraction during persuasive communication: A meta-analytic review. *Communication Monographs, 53,* 91–114.

Butler, K.G. (1984). Language processing: Halfway up the down staircase. In G.P. Wallach & K.G. Butler (Eds.)., *Language learning and disabilities in school-age children* (pp. 60–81). Baltimore: Williams & Wilkins.

Carver, R.P. (1973). Effect of increasing the rate of speech presentation upon comprehension. *Journal of Educational Psychology, 65*(1), 118–126.

Carver, R.P., Johnson, R.L., & Friedman, H.L. (1970). *Factor analysis of the ability to comprehend time-compressed speech* (Final report for National Institute of Health). Washington, DC: American Institutes for Research.

Clark, A.J. (1989). Communication confidence and listening competence: An investigation of the relationships of willingness to communicate, communication apprehension, and receiver apprehension in comprehension of content and emotional meaning in spoken messages. *Communication Education, 38,* 237–248.

Cohen, G. (1989). *Memory in the real world.* Hove and London (UK); Hillsdale, NJ: Erlbaum.

Cooper, F.S. (1972). How is language conveyed by speech? In J.F. Kavanagh & I.G. Mattingly (Eds.), *Language by ear and by eye: The relationships between speech and reading* (pp. 25–45). Cambridge, MA: The MIT Press.

Craig, R.T. (1979). Information systems theory and research: An overview of individual information processing. *Communication Yearbook 3,* 99–121.

Denes, P.B. (1967). On the motor theory of speech perception. In W. Wathen-Dunn (Ed.), *Models for the perception of speech and visual form* (pp. 309–314). (Proceedings of a symposium sponsored by the Data Sciences Laboratory, Air Force Cambridge Research Laboratories, Boston, November 1964.) Cambridge, MA: The MIT Press.

De L'Aune, W., Lewis, C., Needham, W., & Nelson, J. (1977). Speech compression: Personality correlates of successful use. *Journal of Visual Impairment and Blindness, 71,* 66–70.

Doehring, D.G. (1983). Theoretical aspects of auditory perceptual development. In S.E. Gerber & G.T. Mencher (Eds.), *The development of auditory behavior* (pp. 269–286). New York: Grune & Stratton.

Doelger, J.A., Hewes, D.E., & Graham, M.L. (1986). Knowing when to "second-guess": The mindful analysis of messages. *Human Communication Research, 12*(3), 301–338.

Donohew, L., Palmgreen, P., & Duncan, J. (1980). An activation model of information exposure. *Communication Monographs, 47,* 295–303.

Duker, S. (1974). *Time-compressed speech: An anthology and bibliography* (3 vols.). Metuchen, NY: Scarecrow Press.

Eco, U. (1984). *The role of the reader. Explorations in the semiotics of texts.* Bloomington: Indiana Press.

Fairbanks, G. (1966). *Experimental phonetics: Selected articles.* Urbana: University of Illinois Press.

Fant, G. (1967). Auditory patterns of speech. In W. Wathen-Dunn (Ed.), *Models for the perception of speech and visual form* (pp. 111–125). (Proceedings of a symposium sponsored by the Data Sciences Laboratory, Air Force Cambridge Research Laboratories, Boston, November 1964.) Cambridge, MA: The MIT Press.

Flaherty, E. (1979). *Rate-controlled speech in foreign language education* (CAL-ERIC/CLL Series on Language and Linguistics, No. 61). Washington, DC: National Institute of Education. ERIC Document Reporduction Service No. ED 102 991.

Gillespie, A.R. (1969). *Selective listening: The processing of simultaneous auditory stimuli.* Unpublished doctoral dissertation, University of Washington, Seattle.

Goss, B. (1982). Listening as information processing. *Communication Quarterly, 30,* 304–307.

Hanley, C.N. (1956). Factorial analysis of speech perception. *Journal of Speech and Hearing Disorders, 21,* 76–87.

Hedrick, D.L. (1967). A developmental investigation of children's abilities to respond to competing massages varied in intensity and content (Doctoral dissertation, University of Washington, Seattle). *Dissertation Abstracts International, 28,* 1926A-27A.

Hedrick, D.L., & Kunze, L.H. (1974). Diotic listening in young children. *Perceptual and Motor Skills, 38,* 591–598.

Hoffner, C., Cantor, J., & Thorson, E. (1989). Children's responses to conflicting auditory and visual features of a televised narrative. *Human Communication Research, 16,* 256–278.

Housel, T.J., & Waldhart, E. (1981). The effects of communication load and mode on perceived decision quality and satisfaction. *Southern Speech Communication Journal, 46,* 361–376.

Jaynes, J. (1976). *The origin of consciousness in the breakdown of the bicameral mind.* Boston: Houghton Mifflin.

Jury Comprehension in Complex Cases. (1989). Report of the Special Committee on Jury Comprehension of the Section on Litigation of the American Bar Association. Chicago: American Bar Association.

Kahneman, D. (1973). *Attention and effort.* Englewood Cliffs, NJ: Prentice-Hall.

Kuhl, P.K. (1983). The perception of speech in early infancy: Four phenomena. In S.E. Gerber & G.T. Mencher (Eds.), *The development of auditory behavior* (pp. 187–218). New York: Grune & Stratton.

Kuhl, P.K. (1985). Methods in the study of infant speech perception. In G. Gottlieb & N. Krasnegor (Eds.), *Measurement of audition and vision in the first year of postnatal life.* Norwood, NJ: Ablex Publishing Corp.

Langer, E.J. (1989). *Mindfulness.* Reading, MA: Addison-Wesley.

Liberman, A.M., Cooper, F.S., Shankweiler, D.P., & Studdert-Kennedy, M.G. (1967). Perception of the speech code. *Psychological Review, 74,* 431-461.

Lohman, D.F. (1989). Human intelligence: An introduction to advances in theory and research. *Review of Educational Research, 59,* 333–373.

Maccoby, E.E., & Konrad, K.W. (1966). Age trends in selective listening. *Journal of Experimental Child Psychology, 3,* 113–122.

Manning, C.C. (1964). *A study of the intelligibility of competing messages as a function of relative intensity and message similarity.* Unpublished doctoral dissertation, University of Washington, Seattle.

Manning, W.H., Johnston, L.L., & Beasley, D.S. (1977). The performance of children with auditory perceptual disorders on a time-compressed speech discrimination measure. *Journal of Speech and Hearing Disorders, 42,* 77–84.

Massaro, D.W. (Ed.). (1975). *Understanding language. An information-processing analysis of speech perception, reading, and psycholinguistics.* New York: Academic Press.

Maxwell, S.E., & Wallach, G.P. (1984). The language-learning disabilities connection: Symptoms of early language disability change over time. In G.P. Wallach & K.G. Butler (Eds.), *Language learning disabilities in school-age children* (pp. 15–34). Baltimore: Williams & Wilkins.

Miller, G.A. (1951). *Language and communication.* New York: McGraw-Hill.

Miller, G.R. (1969). Human information processing: Some research guidelines. In R.J. Kibler & L.L. Barker (Eds.), *Conceptual frontiers in speech communication* (pp. 51–68). (Report of the New Orleans Conference on Research and Instructional Development.) New York: Speech Association of America.

Minifie, F.D., & Kuhl, P.K. (1991). Perception of /b/ and /w/ during changes in rate of speech. Working paper.

Mowbray, G.H. (1954). The perception of short phrases presented simultaneously for visual and auditory reception. *Quarterly Journal of Experimental Psychology, 6,* 86–92.

Neisser, U. (1976). *Cognition and reality.* San Francisco: W. H. Freeman.

Nichols, R.G. (1948). Factors in listening comprehension. *Speech Monographs, 5,* 154–163.

Norman, D.A. (1976). *Memory and attention: An introduction to human information processing.* New York: John Wiley.

Norman, D.A. (1979). Perception, memory, and mental processes. In L.-G. Nilsson (Ed.), *Perspectives on memory research: Essays in honor of Uppsala University's 500th anniversary* (pp. 121–144). Hillside, NJ: Erlbaum.

Olson, J.S. (1985, January). *A study of the relative effectiveness of verbal and visual augmentation of rate-modified speech in the presentation of technical materials.* Paper presented at meeting of the Association for Educational Communications and Technology, Anaheim, CA. ERIC Document Reproduction Service No. ED 256 329.

Olson, J.S., & Berry, L.H. (1982, May). *The state of the art in rate-modified speech: A review of contemporary research.* Paper presented at the meeting of the Association for Educational Communications and Technology, Dallas, TX. (ERIC Document Reproduction Service No. ED 223 229).

Ortony, A. (1978). Remembering, understanding, and representation. *Cognitive Science, 2,* 53–69.

Paivio, A. (1975). Imagery and long-term memory. In A. Kennedy & A. Wilkes (Eds.), *Studies in long term memory* (pp. 57–85). London: John Wiley.

Pierce, J.R. (1969). Whither speech recognition. *Journal of the Acoustical Society of America, 49,* 1049–51.

Reisberg, D., & McLean, J. (1985). Meta-attention: Do we know when we are being distracted? *Journal of General Psychology, 112,* 291–306.

Roberts, D.F., & Maccoby, N. (1985). Effects of mass communication. In G. Lindzey & E. Aronson (Eds.), *Handbook of social psychology* (Vol. 2, pp. 209–223). New York: Random House.

Rubin, R.B. (1977). The role of context in information seeking and impression formation. *Communication Monographs, 44,* 81–90.

Rubin, R.B. (1979). The effect of context on information seeking across the span of initial interactions. *Communication Quarterly, 27*(3), 13–20.

Rumelhart, D.E. (1977). *Introduction to human information processing.* New York: John Wiley.

Samuels, S.J. (1987). Factors that influence listening and reading comprehension. In R. Horowitz & S.J. Samuels (Eds.), *Comprehending oral and written language.* San Diego: Academic Press.

Sanders, D.A. (1977). *Auditory perception of speech: An introduction to principles and problems.* Englewood Cliffs, NJ: Prentice-Hall.

Schneider, W., & Shiffrin, R.M. (1977). Controlled and automatic human information processing: I. Detection, search, and attention. *Psychological Review, 84,* 1–66.

Shannon, C.E. (1948). A mathematical theory of communication. *Bell System Technical Journal, 27,* 379–423, 623–656.

Solley, C.M., & Murphy, G. (1960). *Development of the perceptual world.* New York: Basic Books.

Stevens, K.N., & Halle, M. (1967). Remarks on analysis by synthesis and distinctive features. In W. Wathen-Dunn (Ed.), *Models for the perception of speech and visual form* (pp. 88–102). (Proceedings of a symposium sponsored by the Data Sciences Laboratory, Air Force Cambridge Research Laboratories, Boston, November 1964.) Cambridge, MA: The MIT Press.

Sticht, T.G. (1971). *Learning by listening in relation to aptitude, reading, and rate-controlled speech: Additional studies* (Tech. Rep. No. 71–5). Alexandria, VA: Human Resources Research Organization.

Sticht, T.G., & Beck, L.J. (1976). *Development of an experimental literacy assessment battery.* Alexandria, VA: Human Resources Research Organization.

Sticht, T.G., Beck, L.J., Hauke, R.N., Kleiman, G.M., & James, J.H. (1974). *Auding and reading: A developmental model.* Alexandria, VA: Human Resources Research Organization.

Sullivan, L.L. (1982). *Compressed speech technology: Implications for learning and instruction.* (ERIC Document Reproduction Service No. ED 228 998).

Tantiblarphol, S., & Hughes, L.H. (1984, January). *Processing time and question type in the comprehension of compressed speech with adjunct pictures.* Paper presented at the meeting of the Association for Educational Communications and Technology, Dallas, TX. (ERIC Document Reproduction Service No. ED 243 437).

Thompson, N.W. (1973, November). *Comprehension of rate-controlled speech of varying linguistic complexity by normal children.* Paper presented at the meeting of the American Speech and Hearing Association, Detroit.

Tiffany, W.R. (1963). Slurvian translation as a speech research tool. *Speech Monographs, 30,* 23–30.

Treisman, A.M. (1970). Perception and recall of simultaneous speech stimuli. *Acta Psychologica, 33,* 132–148.

Tulving, E. (1979). Memory research: What kind of progress? In L.-G. Nilsson (Ed.), *Perspectives on memory research: Essays in honor of Uppsala University's 500th Anniversary* (pp. 19–34). Hillsdale, NJ: Erlbaum.

Warren, R.M. (1982). *Auditory perception: A new synthesis.* New York: Pergamon Press.

West, R. (1985). *Memory fitness over 40.* Gainesville, FL: Triad Publishing Co.

Williams, M.L. (1980). The effect of deliberate vagueness on receiver recall and agreement. *Central States Speech Journal, 31,* 30–41.

Witkin, B.R. (1962). *An analysis of some dimensions of phonetic ability.* Unpublished doctoral dissertation, University of Washington, Seattle.

Witkin, B.R. (1991, March). *Listening in the public interest: The juror as information processor.* Paper presented at annual meeting of International Listening Association, Jacksonville, FL.

Witkin, B.R., Butler, K.G., Hedrick, D.L., & Manning, C.C. (1973). *Auditory Perceptual Training.* Hayward, CA: Alameda County Office of Education.

Witkin, B.R., Butler, K.G., & Whalen, T.E. (1977). Auditory processing in children: Two studies of component factors. *Language, Speech, and Hearing Services in Schools, 8,* 140–154.

Wolvin, A., & Coakley, C.G. (1988). *Listening* (3rd ed.). Dubuque, IA: Wm. C. Brown.

Chapter 4

Schema Theory and Listening

Renee Edwards
Deptartment of Speech Communication
Louisiana State University

Janet L. McDonald
Department of Psychology
Louisiana State University

Schema theory details how people store and use knowledge about a domain. The theory predicts what information people will select for memory storage, that the information will be abstract, and that the information will be interpreted in light of existing knowledge and integrated into the existing network. Evidence from listening tasks offers support for the predictions of schema theory, with people having better recall for information consistent with their schemas. Schemas also appear to help process information by reducing processing load. We extend the predictions of schema theory to listening in two ways. First, the richness of a schema should affect listening positively for messages that add new information to an existing schema (activating and supplemental messages) but in an inverted u-shaped pattern for messages that repeat or contradict existing knowledge (repetitive and inconsistent messages). Second, schemas should be particularly helpful for listening during conversation and when a message is complex because they aid in reducing processing load.

For nearly 25 years, much scientific examination of memory has been guided by the notion that knowledge is stored in *schemas*, which direct the selection, interpretation, and retrieval of information. The first social scientific exploration of schemas was reported by Bartlett in 1932. This text was the inspiration for most modern schema theories, although it was largely ignored for 40 years. Modern schema theory was introduced in the mid-1970s with the publication of several papers (for example, Minsky, 1975; Schank & Abelson, 1977). These pieces have stimulated an extensive body of theoretical and empirical research; this body of literature will be loosely referred to as *schema theory* in this chapter.

Schema theory is important for listening theory and research for several reasons. First, selection, interpretation, and retrieval of information are components of listening. When listeners are presented with a message, they are thought to engage in selective processes that permit them to attend to some parts of a message more than others. They then interpret the message subjectively and may remember a distorted or incomplete version. Schema theory provides one explanation for these effects.

Second, a database involving orally administered tasks already exists in schema theory research (e.g., Kintsch & Greene, 1978, Mandler, 1978; Voss, Vesonder, & Spilich, 1980). Subjects in experiments have listened to messages and then have responded to them using both oral and written formats. Communication theorists can examine these results for insights into the listening process as well as for conclusions about the role of schemas.

The purpose of this chapter is to review schema theory and discuss its implications for listening. The first section of the chapter will examine definitions, propositions, and limitations of schema theory. The next section will describe a sample of schema research that has used orally administered tasks, while the third section will discuss cognitive processing implications. Finally, the chapter will examine implications of schema theory for listening and make recommendations for future research.

SCHEMA THEORY

Researchers and theorists have not achieved consensus in defining *schema* (Taylor & Crocker, 1981), although a simple definition is that it is "the general knowledge a person possesses about a particular domain" (Alba &

Hasher, 1983).[1] Brewer and Nakamura (1984) suggest that "schemas[2] are the unconscious cognitive structures that underlie human knowledge and skill" (p. 136), while Taylor and Crocker (1981) provide a more detailed definition:

> A schema is a cognitive structure that consists in part of the representation of some defined stimulus domain. The schema contains general knowledge about that domain, including a specification of the relationships among its attributes, as well as specific examples or instances of the stimulus domain. (p. 91)

Thorndyke and Yekovich (1980) discussed several specified properties of schemas: *concept abstraction, hierarchical organization, instantiation, prediction,* and *induction.* According to these characteristics, a schema is an abstraction containing slots in which the relevant properties of a prototypical instance are denoted. These slots are arranged hierarchically, so that some constituents of a schema include lower-level constituents. Instantiation occurs in the schema when information about a particular instance is matched to a slot; prediction occurs when no information about a slot is provided and a default value is used to predict the most likely filler. The default value is the property that is assumed when there is no information to the contrary. Schemas are thought to develop after repeated exposures to instances of a concept through an inductive process.

For example, the statement "We went to the mall" would activate one's schema for "mall." Mall is an *abstract concept* that has several characteristics: it is a very large, enclosed structure containing stores, movie theaters, and restaurants; it has a large parking lot, etc. Each of these properties has a particular *slot* in the mental schema for "malls." These are arranged *hierarchically,* so that the slot for "stores" is subdivided into department stores, specialty shops, clothing stores, and so on. Each time an individual goes to a mall, *instantiation* occurs through the matching of experience with schema. In the example, the sources did not identify which mall they went to, but the listener knows which one they usually go to. That particular mall is the default value. In making the assumption that they went to the same mall, the listener engages in *prediction.* Finally, a

---

[1] Some researchers advance the concepts of nodes and links as components of schemas. *Nodes* are basic ideas or concepts, while *links* are the associations among them. For other researchers, nodes are clusters of information (e.g., person nodes), comparable to schemas.

[2] The terms *schemas* and *schemata* have both been used as the plural form of *schema.* We use the former except when referring to a source text that uses *schemata.*

person's schema for "malls" comes from personal experiences of shopping in them through a process of *induction*. A person who has been to many malls or who shops at them frequently will have a more developed schema than someone who has only been once or twice.

Central Processes

Although many different researchers make use of the schema construct, there is no single, overriding theory concerning schemas. Alba and Hasher (1983), however, identified four central processes assumed by schema research: *selection, abstraction, interpretation,* and *integration.* The following discussion explores these processes.

The notion of *selection* posits that information from a message or event will be stored in memory when three conditions hold: when the information is related to an existing schema, when the existing schema is activated, and when the information is important to the schema. A variety of research has provided empirical support for these effects. For example, Chase and Simon (1973) found that skilled chess players can remember the location of pieces on a chessboard from an actual game better than novices because of the existence of a "chess" schema for the experts. Bransford and Johnson (1972) found that providing a title for a short passage of text led to better memory for it than did presenting the text without a title; the title activated the relevant schema.

The process of *abstraction* (Alba & Hasher, 1983) suggests that, when persons are presented with a message, their schema leads them to focus on the meanings rather than on other details of presentation. This is based on the notion that schemas are organized around particular meanings, so that meaning is more important than specific word choice and syntactic structure. Empirical support for this process has shown that persons recall or misrecognize synonyms of presented words (Anderson & Bower, 1980).

Schemas also lead to distortions in memory by biasing the information that is presented through a process of *interpretation* (Alba & Hasher, 1983). Schema theory suggests that persons interpret and store incoming stimuli in a way that is consistent with existing knowledge. The distortions that occur may be pragmatic implications of statements—notions that may be true but are not necessarily so. For example, Brewer (1977) presented subjects with the statement "The flimsy shelf weakened under the weight of the books." When given the cue of "the flimsy shelf," subjects were more likely to recall that it "bent," "gave way," "swayed," "broke," "collapsed," or "fell" than that it "weakened" or "lost strength." The schema for a "flimsy shelf" leads people to make an inference about the statement and encode a distortion of it. Interpretation also occurs when persons make inferences that fill in missing details, simplify complex information, or make vague information more concrete. Johnson, Bransford, and Solomon (1973) found that subjects presented with a passage describing a person pounding a nail will assume that a hammer was used, and include that in their memory for the event. These kinds of inferences represent interpretations or distortions because they supplement or alter the presented information.

The last defining feature of schemas that Alba and Hasher (1983) identify is *integration*. According to this notion, information that is selected or inferred from a stimulus message is incorporated into a complex semantic network. When a schema already exists for the topic, the "new" information becomes indistinguishable from the "old" information in the schema. In support of integration, Fischhoff (1975) and others have found empirical support for the "knew-it-all along" phenomenon. This effect occurs when a person is presented with new information that is contrary to an earlier estimate or prediction he or she has made. After learning the new information, the person is asked to recreate the original estimate or judgment. Research reveals that subjects overestimate their original correctness. They cannot accurately recall their initial judgments and bias them in the direction of the new information. The notion of integration suggests that the old and new information have become inseparable, so that accurate retrieval of previously held knowledge becomes practically impossible.

Limitations of Schema Theory

Brewer and Nakamura (1984) offered the conclusion that "schema theory is one of the most intellectually exciting areas of current cognitive psychology" (p. 120). Other less enthusiastic theorists note a number of problems with current conceptualizations (e.g., Alba & Hasher, 1983; Sypher & Applegate, 1984). Most criticisms of schema theory revolve around three issues: definitional problems, theoretical inadequacies, and empirical evidence that contradicts the basic processes.

The problem of definition is that there is no fixed understanding for schema. Hastie (1981) responded to this absence by identifying three distinct types of schemas (central tendency, template, and procedural); however, Sypher and Applegate (1984) observed that "the bulk of research...does not utilize these more articulated definitions" (p. 314). Consequently, systematic examination of the construct has been limited by the use of many different definitions and operationalizations.

A second problem is that schema theory at times makes contradictory claims and predictions, often based on post hoc explanations. Thorndyke and Yekovich (1980) criticize schema theory for its lack of explicit processing assumptions. They note that, while the theory is plausible and does an excellent job in giving a unified framework for describing or accounting for results after the fact, its processing mechanisms are not well enough specified to allow for clear predictions or tests of the theory. They note that schema theory is "relatively impervious to disconfirming data while remaining capable of explaining post hoc most empirical results" (p. 41).

Finally, schema theory is limited by empirical evidence that contradicts some of the central processes. For example, Yekovich and Thorndyke (1981) conducted an empirical test of some of the assumptions of schema theory, including the prediction that the importance of a proposition will influence whether it is encoded in memory. Schema theory assumes that important information will be stored in memory, while less important information will be lost (see the earlier discussion of "selection").

Two methods for testing memory are recall and recognition tests. Recall tests (also called *free recall*) involve providing a subject with an open-ended instruction to recall as much of the stimulus material as can be remembered. Recognition tests employ more extensive materials in which a subject is provided with a set of items and asked if each were included in the original stimulus.[3]

Using both kinds of tests, Yekovich and Thorndyke (1981) found support for the schema theory prediction using the recall test *but not using the recognition test*. Both important and unimportant information were apparently encoded into memory, but only recognition testing led to the retrieval of unimportant information. Consequently and in contradiction to schema theory, the schema effect of selection does not operate at the time of encoding information into memory but rather takes effect at the point of retrieval. Schemas may operate to facilitate retrieval of information but do not necessarily restrict the quantity or quality of information that is stored in memory.

Summary

No single definition or theory exists for schema or schema-related processes, although there are several specific schema theories (e.g., frame theory by Minsky, 1975, and script theory from Schank & Abelson, 1977). In general, schema theory predicts that schemas are abstract cognitive representations of concepts or activities. They are thought to guide

---

[3] An intermediate approach is sometimes called *cued recall*—subjects are provided with a portion of the original stimulus and asked to recall the remainder.

information processing by influencing selection of stimuli from the environment, by coding meanings rather than the lexical or syntactic features of a message, by supplying inferences and missing details, and by integrating new information into existing knowledge.

Limitations of schema theory include the absence of a unifying definition or theory, theoretical limitations, and empirical evidence that contradicts some of the predictions of schema theory.

SCHEMA RESEARCH USING ORALLY ADMINISTERED TASKS

While the goal of schema research has been to explore mental structures, several studies have employed oral tasks to test their hypotheses. Because of the central role of listening, this section will discuss three of these studies in detail.

In his original work on schemas, Bartlett (1932) found that subjects who were presented a story included many inaccuracies and distortions when retelling it. Kintsch and Greene (1978) attempted to replicate Bartlett's findings of distortions using an oral task. These researchers began with two types of stories: one conformed to Western cultural story schema (schema consistent) while the other did not (schema inconsistent). One set of subjects listened to one of the stories and then retold it on tape. Additional subjects listened to the tape-recorded retelling and then retold their version of the story on tape. This continued for a series of five subjects. Kintsch and Greene compared the final retellings of the schema-consistent stories and the schema-inconsistent stories to the original versions of the stories. Unlike Bartlett, these researchers found that subjects had fairly accurate recall for both types of stories—about 84% of what they recalled was correct. However, consistent with the claims of schema theory, significantly more of the gist of the schema-consistent story was recalled than of the schema-inconsistent story. Thus, Kintsch and Greene (1978) found that, in an oral story-retelling task, people recall accurate information but recall more when the story is consistent with the cultural schema.

A second study using an oral task compared children and adults listening to a story with two episodes in it (Mandler, 1978). In the first condition, subjects listened to one episode followed by the other. In the second condition, the episodes were intermixed: the first sentence from episode one was followed by the first sentence from episode two, and so on. A day after hearing the studies, subjects recalled them orally. Mandler found that subjects who heard the jumbled or intermixed episodes displayed two types of errors in their retellings, compared to the subjects who heard the straightforward version. First, they introduced more distorted pieces of information such as confusing characters or events or inserting details that were not present in the original story. The second error they displayed was to reorder the story into two separate episodes rather than retell it in the original alternating fashion. This was especially true for the children but also occurred for adults. Thus, the use of a story schema as a retrieval strategy causes at least two types of distortions. It may make retrieval of some schema nonconforming information difficult resulting in the substitution of plausible information, and it may distort the order of input to conform more to the order present in the schema.

A final example of schema research using an orally administered task comes from a series of studies using baseball as the stimulus domain. Voss, Vesonder, and Spilich (1980) identified subjects with high and low knowledge of baseball who when listened to six different descriptions of a half inning of a baseball game. Three of these descriptions were generated by high baseball knowledge people; the other three by low baseball knowledge people. In general, the descriptions generated by the high-knowledge people were more complex and presented more information than those generated by low-knowledge people. After hearing each half inning, subjects were asked to recall it. Results revealed that high-knowledge subjects had better recall, both for content and sequence of events, than did the low-knowledge subjects, but this superiority for the high-knowledge subjects generally only held true for the passages generated by high-knowledge people. Recall by the high- and low-knowledge subjects tended to be similar for the less complex accounts generated by low-knowledge people. This research suggests that, although high-knowledge subjects did show an advantage on a few measures, it is mainly on more complex texts that the advantage of knowledge (or schemas) is shown.

Summary

Studies involving oral tasks in which subjects must recall consistent versus schema-inconsistent information generally find an advantage for schema-consistent information. This advantage may show up in more complete recall or recall with fewer distortions. The advantage of schema-consistent materials may be exaggerated as the materials increase in complexity.

SCHEMA THEORY AND PROCESSING LOAD

While most studies on schema theory have examined structural relationships concerning knowledge and memory, another approach is to consider how schemas help or hinder the cognitive system in general. This approach appears to be of special value for understanding the role that schemata play in listening.

A simple model of the human information processing system identifies three stages of information processing architecture. The first stage is a *sensory store,* a very short-lived memory trace in which direct sensory input is maintained in its entirety but is lost after a half to two seconds if it is not renewed by additional sensory input. From the sensory store, information is taken into *short-term memory,* a somewhat longer-lived memory (around 30 seconds) that can be maintained or renewed through rehearsal. An important feature of short-term memory, also called *working memory* (Baddeley, 1986), is its limited capacity. Rather than representing all incoming information, short-term memory can only process approximately seven units or chunks of information at a time. In processing information, humans are limited by the bottleneck of short-term memory capacity. The third state is *long-term memory,* the system in which semantic and real-world knowledge, including schemas, is stored. This memory system has no apparent capacity limit, and its duration is thought to be permanent. Short-term or working memory is often viewed as the active portion of long-term memory (Craik & Lockhart, 1972).

How, then, does this information-processing architecture relate to schema theory? Consider a woman listening to a story about an event for which she has a schema in a long-term memory. As she listens, she takes the incoming sensory information into her visual and audio sensory store; from there it is shunted off to short-term memory. Within short-term memory, the meanings of the words she is hearing must be accessed from long-term memory, and then the relationships among the words must be integrated together to make sense of the sentences she is hearing. Sentences must be integrated together to make sense of the discourse. If the story-appropriate schema is activated in long-term memory as she hears the story, it may aid her in accessing words relevant to that schema and in integrating actions together into schema-relevant larger units.

Using a reading task in an experimental situation, Sharkey (1986) found direct support for the effect of a script on information processing. A *script* is schema for an event in which various actions that take place in prototypical instance are represented (Schank & Abelson, 1977). For example, the script for "going to a movie" would include actions such as waiting in line at the ticket box, buying a ticket, giving it to the attendant at the door who tears it in half, taking back half of the torn ticket, and so on. The subjects in Sharkey's experiment read a story that included words that were relevant and irrelevant to the script. He found that subjects read script-related words faster than words not related to the script, and this effect was more pronounced at the end of a sentence than at the beginning.

From this data he concluded that the activation of a script serves both to activate related lexical items and to help in integrating a sentence with what came previously. Thus, the use of a schema may help reduce the processing load in short-term memory in two ways. Lower-level processes such as lexical retrieval may be facilitated by prior activation from the schema, and higher-level comprehension and integration may be aided by the structure inherent in the schema.

Other research, including the baseball-related studies mentioned earlier, has examined the role of knowledge (or schemas) on information processing capacity. In one experiment, people with different levels of prior knowledge about baseball were asked to read sentences dealing with baseball or with neutral topics (Fincher-Kiefer, Post, Greene, & Voss, 1988). The twist in the experiment, though, was that, after reading a set of sentences, they were asked to recall the last word they had read. This is known as a *reading span task* (Daneman & Carpenter, 1980) and is a way of measuring working memory capacity during reading.

Under this formulation, working memory consists of two parts: one part is devoted to processing, and the remaining capacity may be used for storage. These two factors trade off, so that devoting large amounts of memory to one function decreases the amount available for the other function. Thus, if a great deal of capacity is needed for reading, there will be less space left in which to store the final words of the sentences. However, if less capacity is needed for reading, more working memory space will be left to store the words. Therefore a reading span test can detect factors that decrease capacity needed for the reading process. If prior knowledge about baseball lessens the reading load on baseball sentences, we would expect high baseball knowledge subjects to have higher reading spans on baseball materials than low baseball knowledge subject. Reading spans for the two groups should be similar for non-baseball-related material.

In the first experiment, Fincher-Kiefer et al. (1988) asked subjects simply to read the baseball-related sentence groups and to recall the last words. They found *no* differences between the high- and low-knowledge subjects in their recall of the final words. In the second experiment, the researchers developed a more complex task. In addition to recalling the final word of the sentence, subjects were asked to recall the contents of the various sentences. Using this task, clear differences emerged between the high- and low-knowledge subjects. High baseball knowledge subjects had significantly higher spans on the baseball materials than did the low-knowledge subjects, while the groups did not have different spans when tested using neutral material.

These researchers interpret the results to mean that prior knowledge about a topic does not lessen processing load on the microlevel of simply reading individual sentences (Fincher-Kiefer et al., 1988). However, when subjects must also set up a retrieval pathway for the *contents* of the sentences, differences in span do occur. Therefore, prior knowledge appears to have its effect when the task is more complex and requires development of additional retrieval structures.

Additional evidence for the role of knowledge in building retrieval structures is provided by Voss and his colleagues. Chiesi, Spilich, and Voss (1979, Experiment 5) asked high and low baseball knowledge subjects to recall a target sentence. This sentence was initially presented either by itself or with one or two relevant sentences to provide context. High-knowledge subjects were aided by the presentation of a one or two sentence context, while low-knowledge subjects were hurt by this context. Thus, when retrieval structures must be built in order for sentence content to be recalled, high-knowledge subjects are able to utilize prior knowledge (i.e., existing schemas) with context to build better structures, while low-knowledge subjects are hurt, probably because they are not able to use the contextual information to aid in building a retrieval pathway.

Summary

The presence of a schema in long-term memory can affect the processing load that occurs during reading. It may aid the access of related words and help in higher level integration (Sharkey, 1986). In addition, it may help alleviate load when retrieval structures must be built, because the schema itself can help to form these structures. We claim similar effects should occur with listening tasks, especially when listeners must build retrieval structures, because they expect they will have to recall the information later.

SCHEMA THEORY AND LISTENING

Listening theory and schema theory share a common problem: lack of unifying definition of the central construct. The leading listening theorists take very different perspectives in defining and modeling listening (Wolvin, 1989). Steil, Barker, and Watson (1983) conceptualize listening as a series of four steps including sensing, interpreting, evaluating, and responding. Bostrom and Waldhart (1980, 1988) exclude hearing (the sensing stage of Steil et al., 1983) and interpreting as components of listening; they argue that listening research can add little to the already extensive body of literature on selective attention and perception (Bostrom & Waldhart, 1988). Goss (1982; Goss & O'Hair, 1988), on the other hand, provides for signal processing, literal processing, and reflecting processing. Similarly, Wolvin and Coakley (1988) include receiving, attending to, and interpreting stimuli but do not include a "responding" component. In contrast, Rhodes (1989) argues that responding is an essential component of listening, so that communicators are able to "monitor progress toward understanding and to modify subsequent communicative choices" (p. 554). Not unexpectedly, conceptual disagreement and confusion have hindered systematic research in listening.

Another factor that has limited research is the pedagogical nature of interest in listening. There seems to be a consensus that people need to be taught to "listen better," a notion that is furthered by various state legislatures mandating training in listening (Backlund, Brown, Gurry, & Jandt, 1982) as well as federal legislation that targets listening as a basic skill (Rubin, Daly, McCroskey, & Mead, 1982). In response to this call, various research efforts have been devoted more to developing tests of individual listening skills than to developing theory (e.g., Watson & Barker, 1983; Rubin & Roberts, 1987).

One especially noteworthy program of research has explored theoretical relationships while developing a listening test. Bostrom and his colleagues Waldhart and Bryant (Bostrom & Waldhart, 1980, 1988; Bostrom & Bryant, 1980) have examined types of listening that correspond to the cognitive architecture of short-term, rehearsal-supplemented short-term, and long-term memory systems. Their research reveals these to be distinct forms of listening, offering needed definition and empirical evidence to the study of listening. This research also evidences the value of using established cognitive theory to promote listening theory and research.

So what contributions can schema theory make to the study of listening? We argue that schema theory identifies a number of theoretically significant issues for listening theory and provides a research agenda that can complement the work being done by Bostrom and his colleagues.

The first and perhaps most significant contribution of schema theory is to identify the central role that existing knowledge plays in processing stimuli. While cognitive theorists treat knowledge structures as a central force in information processing, few researchers have examined the relationship between knowledge and listening. In a study that examined the relationship between listening ability and academic achievement, McClarty (1958) found that listening ability was significantly related to general knowledge and an understanding of the basic concepts of a message. More recently, Beatty and Payne (1984) found that cognitive complexity is associated with listening. Cognitively complex individuals, who are theorized to have more differentiated constructs for perceiving others (i.e., more schemas for persons), were found to have greater listening recall than less complex individuals.

Other listening theorists have treated knowledge as an "intervening variable" in test development. Watson and Barker (1984) caution that cognitive factors may account for problems of validity and reliability in testing listening. They note that listening tests must control for content familiarity because individuals who are more familiar with a topic will perform better on listening tests that incorporate it. While this is tacit recognition that listening is affected by existing knowledge, there has been little "listening" research pursuing this important relationship.

The relationship between schemas or knowledge and listening is theoretically interesting and significant. Schema theory suggests that knowledge level is a much more important predictor of listening than are other variables. One can easily argue that persons with greater knowledge of a topic will recall more of a message than will persons with no knowledge of the topic. Greater schematic development allows individuals to comprehend related information. But although schematic development may facilitate listening, extensive schemas may also interfere with listening. Because schemas influence the perception of information in top-down processing, one possibility is that they will lead to inaccurate perception of information, particularly when it is schema inconsistent.

We anticipate that the effect of a schema on listening will be influenced by whether the incoming message functions primarily to activate, to repeat, or to supplement information stored in the schema. Take, for example, a message concerning baseball. We identify an *activating message* as one that utilizes existing knowledge but presents new information, perhaps concerning a particular game: "The scorer called it a single rather than an error." Existing knowledge concerning scorekeeping, singles, and errors is activated (at least for high-knowledge persons); the new information concerns the official designation of this particular play. On the other hand, a *repetitive message* is one that duplicates information already present in the schema. For a high-knowledge person, the following is a repetitive message: "a single is scored when the batter hits the ball into fair territory, runs to first base and is safe there, and no one has committed an error in allowing the batter to get to first base." This information is already available in the schema and essentially repeats what the person knows. A *novel message* is unrelated to any schema, while a *supplemental message* is one that adds to the information a person possesses. The definition of a single would be novel for a European with no experience with baseball, and supplemental for someone who may have some knowledge of baseball but perhaps not a technical understanding of scoring. Finally, an *inconsistent message* contradicts information in the schema. The definition of a single would be inconsistent for a high-knowledge person if it said that a single is scored whenever a batter gets to first base. Thus, the degree to which a message is repetitive, novel, supplemental, or inconsistent is a function of the amount of information that an individual possesses, that is, the extensiveness of the schema. Similarly, the degree of activation is also a function of the amount of knowledge a person has.

Based on schema theory, we speculate that different types of messages will have different effects on listeners as a function of knowledge levels. For activating messages, we posit a strong, positive effect for knowledge, so that high-knowledge persons will listen more efficiently and have better recall than moderate knowledge persons, who in turn will perform better than low-knowledge persons. For example, after listening to a baseball game, high-knowledge listeners should have the best recall and recognition of game events, while low-knowledge persons should have the worst. This is consistent with the results of Voss et al. (1980). We further anticipate that these effects will hold for short-term, short-term with rehearsal, and long-term listening.

However, a more complex pattern of relationships might emerge for other kinds of messages concerning baseball. Imagine a situation in which a speaker is giving a 10-minute talk on the basic rules of baseball. The audience consists of baseball experts (high-knowledge), baseball novices (low-knowledge), and a group with a moderate amount of knowledge. After the speech, audience members recall the particular rules they heard and take a recognition test. For this situation, a curvilinear pattern may emerge. Experts may listen less well and misrecall or misrecognize rules that were not actually presented in the speech because the information is repetitive. Novices should also perform poorly (worse than the experts), but persons with moderate knowledge may perform better because the rules will be more distinctive for them—the information is supplemental. This pattern may be exaggerated with a test of long-term listening. One week later, experts may perform as poorly as novices, with moderate knowledge persons performing the best.

This research idea reveals both the best and the worst of schema theory. Because schema theory is concerned with existing knowledge frameworks, it raises interesting questions about how knowledge affects the processing of incoming stimuli. Unfortunately, schema theory does not specify precise processing mechanisms and does not make specific predictions.

Another fruitful area of research may be the role of schemas on processing load while listening. We expect that the relationship between processing load and schemas to be even more important for listening than for reading, because the processing load carried by a listener should be generally greater than for a reader. Given equivalent stimuli, a higher processing load should occur for listeners, because they have limited control over the input rate whereas readers can vary their reading rate as a function of text difficulty. Second, a higher load is imposed because listeners are not able to go back and "rehear" information that they failed to understand on the first pass; readers can go back and reread material that causes problems. Therefore, while schemas may mediate processing load in both listening and reading, we would expect the effect to be more pronounced in listening. Research testing this notion might use the listening span task developed by Daneman and Carpenter (1980), similar to the reading span task for assessing cognitive load described earlier. This kind of task might also be used for development of various tests of short-term listening. For example, a test of how "listenable" a passage is could employ a listening span task as well as a test over content.

Finally, we speculate that schemas should be more important for interactive, conversational listening than for "lecture" listening. Based on the findings of Fincher-Kiefer et al. (1988) and Chiesi et al. (1979), it appears that processing load is greatest when people are required to process stimuli and to develop retrieval structures for recalling the information simultaneously. When a person is engaged in a conversation, he or she must build a message that is responsive to the current message *at the same time* that he or she is listening to the current message; this dual task places an additional burden on processing load. In listening to a lecture or a narrative, people can concentrate all their energy on the incoming message. Consequently, they may have sufficient processing capacity to build a schema while listening to a lecture but may need to rely on existing schemas for engaging in conversation. This process may explain in part the inchoate, rambling "oral" nature of conversation described by Rubin (1989). Consequently, we anticipate that schemas facilitate memory for conversation even more than they facilitate memory for a message to which the listener is not expected to make a response.

Because of the lack of research examining the relationship between schemas and listening, the practical implications of this approach are limited. If our analysis is correct, however, listening can generally be improved by increasing the knowledge of the targets of messages. This principle should hold for four situations in particular: (a) when the target is engaged in conversation, (b) when the target begins with little or no knowledge of the topic, (c) when the message is complex, and (d) when the message is activating. Listening to repetitive messages may be facilitated by adding supplemental information to them or by including activating components such as narratives.

CONCLUSION

Schema theory is concerned with the organization of information in memory and how existing knowledge influences the encoding of new information and its retrieval from memory. While stimulating a great deal of theorizing and empirical research, schema theory has yet to offer a clear explanation of its central terms and processing mechanisms.

The role of schemas in communication has been explored by researchers in the areas of persuasion (e.g., Smith, 1982), relationships (Planalp, 1985), and marriage (Fitzpatrick, 1989). This chapter has examined implications of schema theory for listening theory and offered three avenues for research. We recommend that research evaluate activating, repeating, and supplemental messages for their effects on short-term, short-term with rehearsal, and long-term listening. Second, research should compare the effects of schemas on cognitive load for listening and reading; we hypothesize that they will exhibit a stronger effect for listening. Finally, the heavier cognitive load for conversation leads to the prediction that schemas should have more of an effect when participating in a conversation than when listening to a lecture. We are currently exploring some of these relationships and encourage other researchers to do the same.

REFERENCES

Alba, J.W., & Hasher, L. (1983). Is memory schematic? *Psychological Bulletin, 93,* 203–231.

Anderson, J.R., & Bower, G.H. (1980). *Human associative memory: A brief edition.* Hillsdale, NJ: Erlbaum.

Backlund, P.M., Brown, K.L., Gurry, J., & Jandt, F. (1982). Recommendations for assessing speaking and listening skills. *Communication Education, 31,* 9–17.

Baddeley, A. (1986). *Working memory.* Oxford: Clarendon.

Bartlett, F.C. (1932). *Remembering: A study in experimental and social psychology.* London: Cambridge University Press.

Beatty, M.J., & Payne, S.K. (1984). Listening comprehension as a function of cognitive complexity: A research note. *Communication Monographs, 51,* 85–89.

Bostrom, R.N., & Bryant, C. (1980). Factors in the retention of information presented orally: The role of short-term listening. *Western Journal of Speech Communication, 44,* 137–145.

Bostrom, R.N., & Waldhart, E.S. (1980). Components in listening behavior: The role of short-term memory. *Human Communication Research, 6,* 221–227.

Bostrom, R.N., & Waldhart, E.S. (1988). Memory models and the measurement of listening. *Communication Education, 37,* 1–13.

Bransford, J.D., & Johnson, M.K. (1972). Contextual prerequisites for understanding: Some investigations of comprehension and recall. *Journal of Verbal Learning and Verbal Behavior, 11,* 717–726.

Brewer, W.F. (1977). Memory for the pragmatic implications of sentences. *Memory and cognition, 5,* 673–678.

Brewer, W.F., & Nakamura, G.V. (1984). The nature and functions of schemas. In

R.S. Wyer, Jr. & T.K. Srull (Eds.), *Handbook of social cognition* (Vol. 1, pp. 119-160). Hillsdale, NJ: Erlbaum.

Chase, W.G., & Simon, H.A. (1973). Perception in chess. *Cognitive Psychology, 4,* 55–81.

Chiesi, H.L., Spilich, G.J., & Voss, J.F. (1979). Acquisition of domain-related information in relation to high and low domain knowledge. *Journal of Verbal Learning and Verbal Behavior, 18,* 257–273.

Craik, F., & Lockhart, R. (1972). Levels of processing: A framework for memory research. *Journal of Verbal Learning and Verbal Behavior, 11,* 671–684.

Daneman, M., & Carpenter, P. (1980). Individual differences in working memory and reading. *Journal of Verbal Learning and Verbal Behavior, 19,* 450–466.

Fincher-Kiefer, R., Post, T.A., Greene, T.R., & Voss, J.F. (1988). On the role of prior knowledge and task demands in the processing of text. *Journal of Verbal Learning and Verbal Behavior, 27,* 416–428.

Fischhoff, B. (1975). Hindsight ne foresight: The effect of outcome knowledge on judgment under uncertainty. *Journal of Experimental Psychology: Human Perception and Performance, 1,* 288–299.

Fitzpatrick, M.A. (1989, November). *Towards a theory of family interaction.* Paper presented at the meeting of the Speech Communication Association, San Francisco.

Goss, B. (1982). Listening as information processing. *Communication Quarterly, 30,* 304–307.

Goss, B., & O'Hair, D. (1988). *Communicating in interpersonal relationships.* New York: Macmillan.

Hastie, R. (1981). Schematic principles in human memory. In E.T. Higgins, C.P. Herman, & M.P. Zanna (Eds.), *Social cognition: The Ontario Symposium* (Vol. 1, pp. 39-88). Hillsdale, NJ: Erlbaum.

Johnson, M.K., Bransford, J.D., & Solomon, S.K. (1973). Memory for tacit implications of sentences. *Journal of Experimental Psychology, 98,* 203–205.

Kintsch, W., & Greene, E. (1978). The role of culture-specific schemata in the comprehension and recall of stories. *Discourse Processing, 1,* 1–13.

Mandler, J.M. (1978). A code in the node: The use of story schema in retrieval. *Discourse Processing, 1,* 14–35.

McClarty, E.L. (1958). Auding ability related to achievement in two telecourses. *Dissertation Abstracts, 18,* 531–532.

Minsky, M. (1975). A framework for representing knowledge. In P.H. Winston (Ed.), *The psychology of computer vision.* New York: McGraw-Hill.

Planalp, P. (1985). Relational schemata: A test of alternative forms of relational knowledge as guides to communication. *Human Communication Research, 12,* 3–29.

Rhodes, S.C. (1989). Listening and intrapersonal communication. In C.V. Roberts & K.W. Watson (Eds.), *Intrapersonal communication processes: Original essays* (pp. 547–569). New Orleans: Spectra.

Rubin, D.L. (1989, February). *Orality, considerate text, and the social construction of listening.* Paper presented at the Research Preconference of the International Listening Association, Atlanta.

Rubin, D.L., Daly, J., McCroskey, J.C., & Mead, N.A. (1982). A review and critique of procedures for assessing speaking and listening skills among preschool through grade twelve students. *Communication Education, 31,* 285–303.

Rubin, R.B., & Roberts, C.V. (1987). A comparative examination and analysis of three listening tests. *Communication Education, 36,* 142–153.

Schank, R.C., & Abelson, R. (1977). *Scripts, plans, goals, and understanding.* Hillsdale, NJ: Erlbaum.

Sharkey, N.E. (1986). A model of knowledge-based expectations in text comprehension. In J. Galambos, R. Abelson, & J. Black (Eds.), *Knowledge structures.* Hillsdale, NJ: Erlbaum.

Smith, M.J. (1982). Cognitive schema theory and the perseverance and attenuation of unwarranted empirical beliefs. *Communication Monographs, 49,* 115–126.

Steil, L.K., Barker, L.L., & Watson, K.W. (1983). *Effective listening: Key to your success.* Reading, MA: Addison-Wesley.

Sypher, H.E., & Applegate, J.L. (1984). Organizing communication behavior: The role of schemas and constructs. In R. N. Bostrom (Ed.), *Communication yearbook 8* (pp. 310–329). Beverly Hills, CA: Sage.

Taylor, S.E., & Crocker, J. (1981). Schematic bases of social information processing. In E.T. Higgins, C.P. Herman, & M.P. Zanna (Eds.), *Social cognition: The Ontario Symposium* Vol. 1, pp. 89–134). Hillsdale, NJ: Erlbaum.

Thorndyke, P.W., & Yekovich, F.R. (1980). A critique of schema-based theories of human story memory. *Poetics, 9,* 23–49.

Voss, J.F., Vesonder, G.T., & Spilich, G.J. (1980). Text generation and recall by high-knowledge and low-knowledge individuals. *Journal of Verbal Learning and Verbal Behavior, 19,* 651–667.

Watson, K.W., & Barker, L.L. (1983). *Watson-Barker listening test.* Auburn, AL: Spectra.

Watson, K.W., & Barker, L.L. (1984). Listening behavior: Definition and measurement. In R.N. Bostrom (Ed.), *Communication yearbook 8* (pp. 178–197). Beverly Hills, CA: Sage.

Wolvin, A.D. (1989). Models of the listening process. In C.V. Roberts & K.W. Watson (Eds.), *Intrapersonal communication processes: Original essays* (pp. 508–527). New Orleans: Spectra.

Wolvin, A.D., & Coakley, C.G. (1988).*Listening.* Dubuque, IA: William C. Brown.

Yekovich, F.R., & Thorndyke, P.W. (1981). An evaluation of alternative functional models of narrative schemata. *Journal of Verbal Learning and Verbal Behavior, 20,* 454–469.

Chapter 5

Listening and Memory

Sheila C. Bentley

Department of Curriculum and Instruction
Memphis State University

This chapter explores the relationship between the listening and memory processes. The focus is on memory, its structure and the processes involved, and the possible effects that memory limitations and abilities could have on listening skill and ability. Both structure and processing models of memory are reviewed, as well as a variety of other perspectives from which memory is being viewed, such as the type of information stored, the instructions given at encoding, and the type of test task and recall conditions. Techniques for improving recall are examined for possible application in common listening situations.

Although there is not yet a universally accepted theory or model of listening, most listening models include some reference to memory as an aspect, phase, or process of listening (Brownell, 1986; Wolff, Marsnik, Tacey, & Nichols, 1983; Weaver, 1972; and Barker, 1971). Also, there is currently no universally accepted theory or model of memory, which only makes it more difficult to develop theories or models of listening, for we cannot fully understand the listening process if we do not understand one of its components.

One difficulty in resolving this dilemma is that the research on the relationships between listening and memory has been sparse. A second difficulty lies in separating the two processes so that we know which one we are viewing with any given observation.

This chapter reviews theories of memory with the intent of enhancing our understanding of the relationships between listening and memory. The chapter explores issues such as how many types of memory there are and what is the structure and function of each, which types are involved in listening, and how our listening ability is influenced by the limitations or structure of our memory.

WHAT *IS* MEMORY?

Endel Tulving (1983)—remarked on the difficulty of this basic question of what is memory: "Few problems that inquiring minds have attempted to resolve by the methods of science have resisted understanding as stubbornly as have problems of memory" (p. 1). Although philosophers, physiologists, brain scientists, and psychologists have studied memory for over 2,000 years, until recently our general understanding of memory was not greatly different from what it was 100 years ago. Only within the last 20 years have we made "genuine progress" (Tulving, 1983, p. 2).

In the simple view of memory, we look at what items have been put into the memory system (such as a list of words read to the subject), and then we compare what can be retrieved at some later time. The output is subsequently perceived to be "in memory." However, looking at the output does not tell us what happens to the information, why we remember certain words and not others, or why we are more likely to remember the words if they are at the first and last of a list. Consequently, in order to understand better what memory is, we also look at complicating factors which affect what the learner remembers. Such factors include:

1. *What the learner knew before we orally presented the list of words to him or her* (prior knowledge). What the learner already knows about the words will have an impact on whether he or she retains the words Bobrow & Norman, 1976; Hirst, 1988).
2. *What other information the learner was being exposed to at the time of presentation.* We cannot assume that, just because we are presenting a list of words to the subject, the subject is listening only to the list. There may be considerable other input from the five senses as well as the individual's own self-talk.
3. *What the words themselves are that are being input.* Different types of words are recalled more easily than others. For instance, concrete nouns are more easily recalled than abstract nouns. Thus, recall of information is somewhat dependent on the information itself.

4. *What the relative position of specific words in the list is.* The first words and the last ones are more likely to be remembered (Ebbinghaus, 1885/1964).
5. *What the learner does as he or she is listening to the information.* The type and level of processing given to the information can determine what is remembered (Craik & Lockhart, 1972; Pressley, Levin, & Delaney, 1982; Dickel & Slak, 1983).
6. *What occurs between the time of input and the recall test.* Some factors (such as proactive and retroactive interference) may affect what we have input (Underwood, 1957).
7. *What cues are available at recall.* What a person can reproduce at the time of recall under one set of circumstances (cued recall vs. free recall and encoding specificity) may not be the same as under other circumstances (Tulving, 1983; Ratcliff & McKoon, 1989).

Therefore, when we study memory for a piece of information, we cannot look only at a point on a line—what is produced at recall—but must look at the whole continuum. What a person remembers from a particular incident where information is input is affected by what came before the information was presented, what was occurring at the time of presentation, the information itself, how the information was input and encoded, what occurred after the information was input, and finally what the circumstances were during recall.

Ratcliff and McKoon (1989) emphatically support the importance of retrieval conditions at recall: "Memory cannot be assessed independently of retrieval, and a theoretical description of memory cannot be formulated without specification of the retrieval environment" (p. 73). (See Ratcliff & McKoon, 1989, for a review of memory models with varying degrees of commitment to cue-dependent retrieval.)

A review of memory literature makes it readily apparent that there is not a predominant concept of what memory is. In fact, much of the recent literature deals with the many perspectives from which memory can be examined.

STRUCTURE VERSUS PROCESSING VIEWS OF MEMORY

For the past 30 years, memory research has taken a *structure* vs. *process* approach. The question has been: Is memory performance due to the physiology of human memory and its inherent strengths and physical limitations, or does remembering depend on applying appropriate processes at encoding and retrieval? (There are also cross-over theories in which remembering depends on both physical limitations and the processes applied at encoding and retrieval.)

Structure Theories of Memory

Structure theories of memory suggest that what we are able to remember is determined by the physiology and biochemistry of the brain. Structure theorists are concerned with how many physically or biochemically different types of memory there are and with what the structural capabilities and limitations of each is. Influential structure theorists have included James (1890), Hebb (1949), Broadbent (1958), and Atkinson and Shiffrin (1968).

A primary issue is whether there exist separate memory systems (a multistore system) with different processing capabilities and limitations, or whether there is only a unitary store that encodes and retrieves different types of information in different ways. In the single-memory theory, different types of information—such as item information, associative information, or propositional information—are stored in a common memory or set of connections (Murdock, 1989). In contrast, in the multiple memory theory, different types of information are stored in separate memories. Thus, experimental differences in memory performance could be due to separate memory systems, or they could be due to the action of different limitations within a single memory system.

Tulving (1983) assumes there is no such structure as "the memory"; rather that we must distinguish between different forms of memory. This may somewhat beg the question, but a popular approach is to define memory by subdividing it into different types or different functions. However, there is considerable disagreement on what the types of memory are.

The multiple stores theory is often supported by research techniques that produce differences in performance, such as processing time differences in word identification versus recognition. These differences, referred to as *dissociations,* support the multistore theory with the premise that the difference in processing time is a result of two different memory systems being accessed. However, these findings could also reflect only different retrieval processes for different types of information or with different cues for retrieval from a single-store system (see Richardson-Klavehn & Bjork, 1988, for discussion).

The idea that memory might not be a single system dates back at least to William James (1890), with his introduction of the terms *primary* and *secondary memory.* Hebb (1949) suggested a distinction between long-

and short-term memory and that there might be two neurophysiologically separate storage systems within the brain, one electrically based and one representing a permanent change based on a growth of links between nerve cells, forming what Hebb called *cell assemblies.*

Some research in the biochemistry of memory now focuses on molecular transformations within neurons. According to Black, Adler, Dreyfus, Friedman, LaGamma, and Roach (1988), "Critical molecular processes appear to be in constant flux, influenced by environmental stimuli and conditions" (p. 4). Molecular changes caused by the environment may be one way that external information is translated into neural language. Molecules in the peripheral and central nervous systems encode and store information over time, indicating that the potential for storing information is not limited to certain cell populations in the brain but rather is widespread. Apparently, even the single neuron can exhibit mnemonic mechanisms. Cell processes that sense environmental change, transsynaptic communication, and membrane depolarization cause a series of cellular and nuclear mechanisms that store information. Long-term information storage may occur as impulse activity activates and represses different families of genes. Black et al. (1988) conclude, "The particular physiological, behavioral, or cognitive manifestations of information storage may simply reflect the specific neural populations involved" (pp. 17–18).

A number of past studies have shown that small amounts of material (well within the memory span) are rapidly forgotten if rehearsal is prevented. For example, Broadbent (1957) conducted a sequence of studies in which subjects listened to two different series of spoken digits— presented simultaneously in each ear. Subjects were then told which ear to recall first. Subjects performed well on recall of the digits to the first ear but showed marked forgetting on the digits to the second ear. These results supported the assumption that the delay in recall allowed the memory trace to decay, and thus, forgetting was due to decay of the memory trace, a physiological or structural cause.

In reviewing evidence of *short-term memory* (STM), Broadbent (1958) concluded that short-term forgetting appeared to be caused by trace decay, and long-term forgetting was caused by interference; thus, the two must be based on separate systems. Broadbent's information processing model of short-term memory (1958) is still influential today, even though his conclusions about the causes of forgetting have been challenged.

George Miller's (1956) classic paper, "The Magical Number Seven," added credibility to Broadbent's theory in that Miller found that subjects can handle only about seven bits or chunks of information at a time. This finding suggested a possible general limitation on human information processing for at least one type of memory (short-term memory).

However, in 1963 Arthur Melton argued for a unitary theory of memory based on two main points. First, he demonstrated that across a range of short-term memory (STM) tasks, the tasks are influenced by variables known to influence *long-term memory* (LTM). Second, he argued that all of the phenomena of STM can be accounted for by using the same interference theory concepts that are applied to LTM. Thus, it is more parsimonious to assume a single system. Melton cited studies demonstrating how proactive interference could produce forgetting in STM. However, the results are not entirely consistent, as interference is less after a longer delay between STM tasks than with a short delay, and the classic interference theory would not predict this phenomenon. This occurrence would be evidence more in support of a trace theory.

Waugh and Norman's study (1965) supported interference over decay as the source of forgetting, but the researchers suggested that forgetting in this paradigm results from displacement of items from a limited capacity short-term store. And in his review of short-term or *working memory,* Baddeley (1986) concluded that trace decay as an explanation for forgetting in STM is at best a gross oversimplification.

One of the most influential models of the 1970s was Atkinson and Shiffrin's 1968 "modal" model. The modal model was one of the first cross-over theories, because, while it focused on the structure of types of memory, it introduced the concept that the processes applied to the incoming information and during retrieval affect what is remembered.

The Atkinson-Shiffrin (1968) model has three major components: the *sensory stores,* the *short-term store* (STS), and the *long-term store* (LTS). The sensory stores each hold information from one sense. These stores feed information into STS, which acts as a working memory that plays a crucial role in a wide range of other tasks. STS is assumed to be a necessary intermediate stage in processing information into LTS. Long-term learning occurs as a result of maintaining information in STS; the longer the material is maintained, the greater the probability of transfer.

STS is also assumed to play an important role in selecting processing strategies and in maintaining and operating strategies for retrieval from long-term memory. STS is capable of using a range of control processes and strategies, and Atkinson and Shiffrin investigated the strategy of rote verbal rehearsal most extensively.

During the 1970s several problems with the modal model emerged although other theorists still supported a three-store system. For example, a number of studies called into question: (a) the assumption that long-term learning depended on the amount of time an item was held in STS (Craik & Watkins, 1973; Baddeley, 1986; Tulving, 1966; Beherian and Baddeley, in Baddeley, 1986); (b) the assumption that both the recency effect in free recall and memory span are manifestations of the same limited capacity STS (Baddeley, 1986); (c) the type of coding done in the two memory stores. The modal model suggests that STS operates entirely on phonological codes and LTS on semantic codes. However, it would seem obvious that LTM involves a wide range of coding dimensions, including phonological speech coding, since without such long-term coding, how could a person learn to speak or understand a spoken language?

The modal model was subsequently left to decay, as most of its supporters moved on to other topics.

One Memory System or Two?

While there are theorists who support a unitary-store memory system (and these will be discussed later), there is considerable evidence supporting at least the two systems, short-term and long-term memory. For example, in free recall tasks, the recency effect (recalling the last few items more successfully than the middle items) leads to a high level of performance on the last few items when tested immediately but is dissipated by a short delay. Performance on the rest of the list, however, is relatively resistant to delay.

Furthermore, the recency effect is influenced by very different variables from the rest of the free recall curve. Performance on the more durable items at the beginning and middle of the list can be influenced by factors such as speed of presentation and imageability, which are known to affect long-term learning. But these factors do not influence the size of the recency effect.

Also, LTM has an enormous capacity for storage coupled with relatively slow input and retrieval, while STM has a limited capacity store with rapid input and retrieval. In addition, STM relies principally on phonological coding, while LTM relies on semantic coding. There is considerable evidence for these differences. Further, Jacoby and Dallas (1981) interpreted various dissociations obtained in their studies to support a multistore model of memory.

Much work on amnesics and brain-damaged individuals also supports a dual stores system. (It should be noted here that many researchers use the terms *short-term store,* or STS, and *long-term store,* or LTS, in place of *short-term memory* and *long-term memory.*) For example, there is clear evidence that patients can have normal STS coupled with a grossly defective LTS, or with the opposite pattern of defects (Baddeley, 1986).

But if long-term learning depends on STS, as was proposed by Atkinson and Shiffrin (1971), then a patient with defective STS should also show impaired learning—in fact, a general impairment in intellectual capacity.

However, there are patients who do not show this long-term impairment in spite of defective STS.

As a result of some of the problems with the modal model and with structure theories in general, memory researchers began to explore other avenues of memory that could possibly account for differences in performance, as well as provide a general explanation for memory performance.

Processing Models of Memory

A precipitating factor in the decay of the modal model, as well as a movement away from structure models of memory, was the development of the *levels of processing* framework of memory, which is a processing model. Although this model does recognize different types of memory, such as short-term and long-term memory, the emphasis is on the cognitive processes applied at the time of input of the information and at recall, rather than the structure of memory, that determine what is remembered.

Craik and Lockhart's (1972) model stressed processing and suggested that trace durability, and therefore memory, were a direct consequence of the process of encoding, with deeper and more elaborate encoding leading to more durable memory traces.

Craik and Lockhart (1972) argued that learning involves processing information through a succession of ever deeper states, starting with the peripheral sensory stimulus and ending with an elaborate semantic integration of the material into the subject's existing knowledge with the deeper the processing, the better the learning or retention. Each stage of processing was assumed to leave a memory trace, with the memory trace becoming more durable with increasing depth. Rehearsal was assumed to be of two kinds, *maintenance rehearsal,* where an item is recirculated without changing the level of processing, and *elaborative rehearsal,* where each successive processing increases the depth of encoding. Learning was achieved exclusively through elaborative processing, whereas maintenance rehearsal, although ensuring an item could be recalled and tested immediately, had no influence on long-term memory. Craik and Lockhart assumed that the relevant processing was carried out by a primary memory system, but others felt the need for a dual memory system was made unnecessary by levels of processing.

As with the structure models of memory, the levels of processing framework began to run into difficulties in the 1970s as exceptions to the generalization were found. Four of these exceptions are discussed below.

Evidence exists that long-term retention can be influenced by maintenance rehearsal, particularly on recognition tests. However, the amount of learning resulting from repetition is typically small and dependent on the type of material. What repetition does not seem to accomplish is to build up complex associations between items, which is an important pre-requisite of recall under many standard verbal learning paradigms. Consequently, the levels of processing distinction between maintenance and elaborative rehearsal is incomplete in suggesting that maintenance rehearsal has no effect on LTM.

Second, the levels of processing framework suggests that an item encoded in terms of superficial features produces a memory trace that dissipates rapidly. More recent studies, though, advocate the concept of *transfer appropriate processing,* rather than the depth of processing, as the critical variable. This suggests that visual processing would be optimal when visual distinctions must be made, and semantic processing would be best when retrieval of meaning is crucial (see Tulving, 1983, for elabora-tion of this principle). However, semantic cues tend to be more effective over long delays than phonological or visual cues.

A third argument suggests that processing a word does not necessarily follow a linear sequence—that is, from a grapheme to a phoneme to a semantic representation. Instead, processing has been found to occur both in a bottom-up and a top-down manner, and several researchers are advocating parallel distributed processing models.

A fourth argument involves the problem of measuring processing depth. Craik and Tulving (1975) found that the deeper levels of processing took more time and questioned whether time could be used as an independent measure of processing depth. However, they found that it could not. They devised shallow processing tasks which took considerable processing time but did not produce good recall. For example, if C means consonant and V means vowel, does the word *rabbit* conform to the pattern CVCCVC? Craik and Tulving also found that a question evoking a "yes" response was retained better and took less processing time than did one evoking a "no" response. In addition, they noted that the more elaborately an item was processed, the better it was recalled. Thus, the sentence, "The wizened old man hobbled across the castle courtyard and dropped the gold watch down the well" would lead to better recall than "The man dropped the watch" (Baddeley, 1986, p. 27). But this is not a depth of processing—consequently it shows that levels of processing does not entirely account for human memory.

Finally, the levels of processing framework does not apply to amnesics; even though they can process information at deeper levels, they cannot retain the information. Thus, their memory deficit does not stem from a coding deficit.

As with the modal model, because the levels of processing framework does not explain the full range of differences in memory performance and provide an explanation for general memory performance, researchers are again seeking new avenues from which to approach the problem.

Structure vs. Process Memory Models and Listening

In the structure vs. process debate, there are several points which should be of considerable interest to listening theorists. For example, the theory of trace decay as a cause of forgetting should be of particular interest, because it would indicate that *time* is a critical factor in preserving what has been listened to and that appropriate processing must take place within a given time period in order to retain the information.

In addition, the concept of a limited capacity short-term memory (Miller, 1956) should be extremely important to listening researchers, since it would predict that if the individual is hearing more than seven bits of information at a time, he or she would not be able to hold them in short-term memory. Consequently, the *amount* of information being listened to would be a critical factor in determining what will be remembered.

The role of long-term memory in short-term memory tasks should be of interest as well. For example, a subject given the words January, February, March, April, May, and so on, in their usual order would be much more successful at recalling them than if given these words in a scrambled order. This suggests that much of what we are able to remember from a spoken message is dependent on what we already know about the topic. Furthermore, the structure of memory is a significant question for listening theorists to consider, because listening ability and skill are intimately involved with the storage and retrieval of information, and a key factor in listening ability could lie in which type of memory is being accessed and how the structure of it affects performance.

Interference and trace decay as the causes of forgetting present another significant matter for listening research, since typically in a spoken message, the listener cannot control the flow of information. If interference is the cause of forgetting, later information may replace earlier information before the listener has a chance to process the information into the long-term store. On the other hand, if trace decay is the cause of forgetting, then time for processing is the critical factor.

Bostrom and Waldhart (1988) propose yet another significant view of the relationship between memory and listening. They suggest a distinction between short-term memory and short-term with rehearsal. Bostrom and Waldhart propose that a distinction between short-term memory for verbal and nonverbal items is necessary and that "short-term listening" is an appropriate label for this aspect of memory (p. 5).

Consequently, additional research is needed in the structure versus process debate to enable more definitive answers about how memory affects listening abilities and skill and especially to provide guidance for how best to improve listening skill.

OTHER PERSPECTIVES ON MEMORY

Recently, memory researchers have begun looking at memory from other perspectives, such as the type of information stored, the instructions given at the time of presentation, and the type of test task. These other perspectives have produced different categories of memory, including:

Direct memory measures vs. Indirect memory measures
Explicit memory measures vs. Implicit memory measures
Incidental learning vs. Intentional learning
Semantic memory vs. Episodic memory
Procedural memory vs. Declarative (Propositional) memory
Data-driven processing vs. Conceptually driven processing
Memory system vs. Habit system.

Richardson-Klavehn and Bjork (1988) summarize this trend as "general agreement that some type of classificatory distinction between forms of memory is necessary" (p. 485), such as between memory with and without awareness, between implicit and explicit forms of memory, and between memory for personal experiences and other forms of memory, such as habits, skills, and general knowledge.

Many researchers have based the distinction between at least two types of memory on whether success in the memory test is determined by the subject's knowledge of events that occurred when he or she was personally present in a particular spatiotemporal context or not. Task instructions that refer to an episode in the subject's personal history have been referred to as autobiographical, direct, episodic, explicit, and intentional. Those tasks which involve no reference to an event in the subject's personal history, but are still influenced by such events, are classified as implicit, indirect, incidental, and semantic (Richardson-Klavehn & Bjork, 1988).

A brief explanation of each of the more popular classifications of memory follows.

Direct vs. Indirect Memory Measures

Direct memory measures test memory of an event in the personal history of the subject such as by mentioning the time of day, date, or environment in which the event occurred (Richardson-Klavehn & Bjork, 1988). Presenting a list of words, pictures, or sentences and then asking the subject to discriminate between words presented during the target event and new words would be examples.

Indirect measures do not refer to a previous experience. The subject is engaged in some cognitive or motor activity, and the instructions refer only to the task at hand without reference to prior events. The test measures any improvement in task performance by comparing performance with relevant prior experience to performance without such experience. Indirect measures include tests of factual, conceptual, lexical, and perceptual knowledge; tests of procedural knowledge, such as skilled performance and problem solving; measures of evaluative response; and other measures of behavioral change.

Explicit vs. Implicit Memory Measures

Explicit and implicit memory measures are similar to direct and indirect memory measures. Explicit measures test subjects directly on recent experience. In performing the tasks, subjects are asked to remember events and presumably are aware that they are recalling recent experiences. In implicit memory measures, subjects are not told to remember events but simply to perform some task. Retention is then measured by transfer from prior experience, and conscious recollection is not necessarily involved (Roediger, Weldon, & Challis, 1989).

Most memory studies involve explicit memory tasks. They include free recall, cued recall, recognition, and various judgments such as frequency, modality, and feeling-of-knowing. Explicit memory tests require conscious recollection of previous experiences and conscious awareness of the learning episode for successful performance. However, involuntary explicit memory refers to a subject's becoming aware of a prior event without having consciously intended to do so (Ebbinghaus, 1885/1964).

Implicit tasks are transfer tasks; the critical task is influenced by prior experience without the prior experience necessarily being reflected on explicit measures. That is, the subject may not be able to recall an item, but the item may affect performance on another related task, such as reading inverted text, naming fragmented words or pictures, or naming words or pictures from brief displays.

Roediger et al. (1989) reviewed studies which showed a dissociation between implicit and explicit memory measures and found that the most popular explanation of these dissociations is to propose separate memory systems, with the leading candidates being Tulving's episodic and semantic systems and Squire's procedural and declarative systems.

An important question regarding implicit and explicit memory, however, is whether these are forms of memory, possibly involving different memory systems, or are simply methods of testing memory. Richardson-Klavehn and Bjork (1988) conclude, "The hypothesis that different testing methods reveal different forms of memory can be entertained only when *dissociations* between those methods of measurement are observed" (p. 483).

Incidental vs. Intentional Learning

Intentional learning occurs when we have been directed to recall information and have consciously made an attempt to store the information. Incidental learning occurs when we have not been directed to recall something, but we do anyway without taking any conscious steps to do so (such as recalling what happened in a movie without making a conscious effort).

While the direct/indirect and explicit/implicit categories apply to the type of test instructions given at recall, the intentional incidental categories apply to the directions given or steps taken at encoding.

Episodic vs. Semantic Memory

Endel Tulving (1972) changed the course of the structure versus process debate significantly with his proposal of the classifications of *episodic* and *semantic memories*. These terms describe the *type of information* stored, and Tulving proposed separate memory systems for storing the two types of information.

Tulving (1972) defines episodic memory as memory which "receives and stores information about temporally dated episodes or events, and temporal-spatial relations among these events" (p. 385). Episodic memory is probably very susceptible to transformation and loss of information and would be of the form: "I did something in a certain place and at a certain time." Typical episodic memory experiments include such tasks as list learning. Accuracy of performance is then measured as input versus output, correct or incorrect. Tulving explains semantic memory as follows:

> Semantic memory is the memory necessary for the use of language. It is a mental thesaurus, organized knowledge a person possesses about words and other verbal symbols, their meaning and referents, about relations among them, and about rules, formulas, and algorithms for the manipulation of these symbols, concepts, and relations. (p. 386)

Forgetting appears to occur more in the episodic than semantic system. And although we don't know a lot about how information is lost from semantic memory, we do know a great deal about loss from episodic. Retrieval into episodic memory may lead to changes in the contents and the retrievability of these contents. Thus, forgetting probably takes place as a result of a transformation of the information as a consequence of interference with the temporal coding of stored events. Since information is always temporally coded in episodic memory, and since it can only be retrieved if its temporal date is specified by the retrieval cue, interference with the temporal coding might make access to the to-be-retrieved material difficult or impossible.

Retrieval in semantic memory leaves the contents unchanged and is probably much less susceptible to involuntary transformation and loss of information. In addition, information can be recorded piecemeal into semantic memory, and events that do not occur at the same time can become closely related in semantic memory. Information in semantic memory is usually encoded as part of a "rich, multidimensional structure of concepts and their relations" (Tulving, 1972, p. 391). This embeddedness protects the stored information from interference by other inputs.

Semantic variables also play a significant role in the retrievability of material in episodic memory; however, the processes involved in semantic encoding of perceptual events aren't well understood at all. For example, why is it easier to remember that word B was seen at the same time as A in a pair of words if the concepts of the words are closely related, such as night–day?

The two systems also differ in capabilities. Episodic memory does not include the capabilities of inferential reasoning or generalizations, whereas semantic memory includes reasoning, generalizing, application of rules and formulas, and use of algorithms. It is possible for a person to know something that he or she didn't learn by relying on semantic memory.

The two systems can function independently. Sensory impressions can probably be remembered without the intervention of the semantic system, and the semantic system can probably function independently of episodic memory. But little is known about the role the perceptual system and episodic memory play in the storage of information into semantic memory. In his 1972 article, Tulving concluded that episodic and semantic memory are two parallel and partially overlapping information-processing systems, but he later modified this position.

As a result of much debate on the distinction between the two memory systems, Tulving (1983) updated his original theory, adding the suggestion that there is a larger framework in which there are two more memory systems—lexical memory and procedural memory. This new work also received considerable attention in the field. In 1984 Tulving responded with the revised theory that episodic memory is a distinct but interactive subsystem embedded within semantic memory, rather than being a separate system. Between 1972 and 1984, Tulving's original article received more than 500 citations in the *Social Science Citation Index* (McKoon, Ratcliff, & Dell, 1986).

In reviewing Tulving's theories, McKoon et al. (1986) summarized that "Tulving (1983) proposed that semantic information is highly interconnected and organized, relatively permanent, and context dependent, whereas episodic information was less well organized, highly susceptible to forgetting, and context dependent" (p. 295). This distinction could be applied to interpreting experimental results that concerned context effects, forgetting, and retrieval, and it could be used to interpret neuropsychological data concerning amnesia and brain damage. For example, when the subject's ability to form new autobiographical memories is lost, yet old memories are retained, it could be concluded that the episodic system is damaged but the semantic system is intact.

However, McKoon et al. (1986) conclude that the distinction is of great heuristic and pragmatic use, but that the case for the distinction is weak. Their article, in fact, systematically takes the findings Tulving used to support his theory and shows how the support can be contradicted or that the conclusions Tulving draws are weak.

First, they assert that intuition would suggest that overlearned personal events should be part of permanent semantic knowledge, but by definition are part only of episodic knowledge. Next, they raise these questions:

> Are events in episodic memory not related to existing knowledge? Do the events not contain information about the referents of the objects involved in the events? The events of episodic memory are said to be propositional, but that term usually involves abstract properties; what would such properties be in episodic memory? How is the beginning and the end of an event known, if not by reference to the event's meaning? (McKoon et al., 1986, p. 296)

These authors conclude that we must understand what semantic information is allowed into episodic memory in order to distinguish between episodic and semantic memory. In an earlier work Schank (1975) also illustrates the difficulty in making the distinction, especially where language processing is involved. The process of analyzing the meaning of a message is "inextricably tied up with the problem of finding out what the individual words mean and cannot be separated from the knowledge of the world contained in those words. Moreover, memory for past events sometimes determines the meaning of an input sentence" (Schank, 1975, p. 165).

The third argument involves Tulving's assertions that organization in the episodic system is temporal, that episodic memory has little inferential capability, and that access for episodic information is deliberate and conscious, whereas for semantic memory, it is automatic.

However, earlier studies of McKoon et al. (1986) showed that information in episodic memory can reflect an organization based on meaning rather than the temporal order of the words in the sentence. These same kinds of priming experiments also showed that access to newly acquired information can be automatic. In addition, access to information in semantic memory can be slow and strategic, as would be shown by the time required to think of a "fruit beginning with the letter k."

Furthermore, McKoon et al. (1986) questioned Tulving's conclusions about differences in retrieval mechanisms within the two systems. They cite a number of studies that show that context plays a role in retrieval in both episodic and semantic memory. Thus, the effect of context on retrieval does not provide a distinction between episodic and semantic memory. In fact, they conclude that "the similarities between semantic and episodic retrieval far outweigh the differences and that there is little evidence for separation of the two systems on the basis of retrieval" (p. 297).

Finally, Tulving distinguished between episodic and semantic memories in their vulnerability to forgetting. Tulving says that episodic memory is more susceptible to forgetting than semantic memory. But McKoon et al. (1986) ask how these two can be equated in dimensions such as degree of learning, difficulty of material, and so on so that accurate measures of forgetting can take place. Besides, some studies with amnesics have shown that forgetting appears to occur at the same rate for episodic and semantic information.

McKoon et al. (1986) concluded that the experiments cited by Tulving as support for the episodic–semantic distinction follow the logic of dissociation. However, dissociations as support for separate systems have been criticized on several grounds. For example, a dissociation might reflect different processes rather than different systems, and it is difficult to know for which of the many dissociations that could be found experimentally there should be new memory systems proposed. Tulving has used a wide range of evidence from amnesia studies to support the episodic–semantic distinction. But McKoon et al. (1986) propose that, in amnesics, what is spared is procedural memory. They cite research by Baddeley, Cohen, Graf, Squire and Mandler, and Moscovitch as support. Amnesia studies show various results which may or may not support a distinction. For example, some amnesics cannot recall preamnesia events but can add new events to episodic memory, while others can recall childhood incidents (i.e., preamnesic) but cannot add new events to episodic memory. A popular view now is that amnesia supports a procedural/declarative distinction.

Procedural vs. Declarative (or Propositional)

Declarative memory is knowing *that* (stating knowledge propositionally), while *procedural* memory is knowing *how* (skills or operating on the environment in ways that may be difficult to verbalize, such as riding a bike).

To clarify these views of memory, Squire (1987, p. 170 proposed the following model of the relationships between various types of memory:

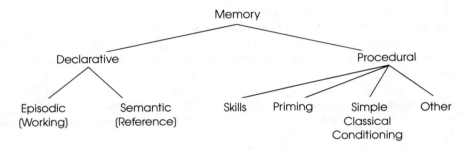

(From *Memory and Brain* by Larry R. Squire. Copyright © 1987 by Oxford University Press, Inc. Reprinted by Permission.)

As can be seen in this model, Squire perceives both episodic and semantic memories to be subsystems of declarative memory.

Data-driven vs. Conceptually Driven Processing

Yet another perspective on memory looks at the type of processing given to the incoming information. In differentiating between *data-driven* and *conceptually driven* processing in memory, the critical factor is between the *No Context* and the *Generate* conditions within a generation experiment (Roediger et al., 1989). Reading a word without an appropriate semantic context (No Context condition) involves data-driven processing, while generating a word (Generate condition) from a synonym or associated word involves conceptually driven processing. Thus, when a subject says 'cold' following a stimulus of XXX-COLD, the processing is mainly bottom-up or data driven. On the other hand, when the subject responds with 'cold' following the stimulus of 'hot-????', the processes are top-down, or conceptually driven because no 'data' for *cold* were displayed (Roediger et al., 1989). Reading a word in context (hot-COLD), would presumably involve both data-driven and conceptually driven processing. Priming in perceptual identification is a strongly data-driven task, while typical recognition, free recall, and semantic cued recall tests are conceptually driven (although recognition tests may have a small data-driven component).

According to Roediger et al. (1989), data-driven tests are affected by manipulations of surface information between study and test but relatively immune to manipulations involving conceptual elaboration. Conversely, conceptually driven tests are relatively unaffected by manipulations of surface information but strongly affected by conceptual elaboration.

These authors examined manipulation of surface variables such as modality (visual vs. auditory), symbolic form (word vs. picture), and language (same language vs. foreign language), and found that these variables have no effect on conceptually driven tests such as free recall. However, data-driven tests are sensitive to manipulations of surface features. There are many studies that support the view that conceptually driven processing tasks at encoding lead to improved performance on conceptually driven tests (free recall and recognition), such as levels of processing (Craik & Lockhart, 1972), imagery (Paivio, 1986), and organization (Tulving, 1968).

Roediger et al. (1989) also feel that test instructions play a role in determining processing mode. For example, explicit test instructions seem to encourage conceptually driven processing. This is probably because normally we are concerned with retrieving the meaning of events. The authors do note difficulty in applying their transfer-appropriate processing theory to amnesics. It fits only up to a certain point.

These authors surmise that it is likely that more than one memory system exists in the human brain for comparative and phylogenetic reasons: "The human brain is larger and more complex than any other brain, and it seems likely that more complicated mechanisms exist than in many creatures with less complex neural structures and relatively simple abilities to learn" (Roediger et al., 1989, p. 36).

Retrieval—Encoding Specificity

In addition to categories of memory, another important perspective receiving research attention is the retrieval aspect of memory. Roediger et al. (1989) reviewed studies that showed that category names could function as excellent retrieval cues in aiding recall of words belonging to semantic categories, especially when compared to performance under free recall conditions. In fact, the advantage of cued recall vs. free recall exceeded 200 percent in some of their conditions. This points out the importance of "distinguishing between the information available in memory (what is stored) and the information accessible on a test (what can be retrieved under a particular set of conditions)" (Roediger et al., 1989, p. 5). Consequently, memory tests tell only what a person remembers under a particular set of retrieval conditions, and therefore, memory theories must always specify the set of conditions operating during retrieval.

The term *encoding specificity* provides a label for this concept. Tulving (1983) explains the encoding specificity principle as follows: "recollection of an event, or a certain aspect of it, occurs if and only if properties of the trace of the event are sufficiently similar to the properties of the retrieval information" (p. 223). To illustrate this principle, Tulving proposed the following encoding retrieval paradigm (Tulving, 1983, p. 220):

Encoding/Retrieval Paradigm

		Retrieval Condition	
		A'	B'
Encoding Condition	A	AA'	AB'
	B	BA'	BB'

From *Elements of Episodic Memory,* by Endel Tulving. Copyright © 1983 by Oxford University Press. Reprinted by Permission.

According to this paradigm, retrieval should be better in conditions A-A' and B-B' than in A-B' and B-A', in which the encoding and retrieval conditions aren't as well matched. This is probably why we can better remember people's names that we have just learned as long as they stay seated in the same place. But if they move or we see them somewhere else, we don't remember the names as well because the retrieval conditions don't match the encoding conditions.

Studies have shown that levels of processing effects can disappear or even be reversed under the appropriate test conditions (Roediger et al., 1989). Some researchers (notably Tulving) even suggested that the levels of processing theory might be superfluous and that results could be better explained by the encoding specificity principle. On the other hand, other researchers explained the phenomena with a "transfer-appropriate processing" hypothesis: "study conditions foster good performance on later tests to the extent that the test permits appropriate transfer of the knowledge gained during study" (Roediger et al., 1989, p. 7).

ONE-SYSTEM ARGUMENTS

Although much of this chapter has described various multistore models or separate systems of memory, not all theorists subscribe to the separate systems theories. For example, Roediger et al. (1989) propose four assumptions that could explain the dissociations between implicit and explicit measures of retention:

1. They assume that memory tests benefit to the extent that the tasks required by the test match or overlap the encoding tasks.
2. Explicit and implicit memory tests require different retrieval operations (or access different forms of information) and consequently will benefit from different types of processing during learning.
3. Explicit memory tests rely on the encoded meaning of concepts, or on semantic processing, elaborative encoding, mental imagery, and the like; hence, explicit tests require conceptually driven processing.
4. Most standard implicit tests rely heavily on the match between perceptual processing during the learning and test episodes—they tap the perceptual record of past experience and therefore are data driven.

Roediger et al. (1989) do not consider the distinction between data-driven and conceptually driven processing as a dichotomy into which all memory tasks must be divided, but rather as endpoints on a continuum. The authors explain the dissociations between implicit and explicit tests of several studies involving recall of words as follows: Recognition and recall tests, which are explicit tests, are assumed to be mainly conceptually driven, and so should be affected by variations in levels of processing. On the other hand, the data or words presented during the study are assumed to be processed through the visual system in order to achieve lexical access no matter what further processing is required. This processing of data, which would be data-driven, would transfer equally to the data-driven implicit memory tests.

However, the authors do note that dissociations can be equally well explained in terms of separate memory systems, that recognition and recall could be manifestations of operations in the declarative or episodic memory system(s), and priming on implicit tests could result from changes registered in the semantic or procedural systems.

Roediger et al. (1989) argue that if dissociations can be produced *within* the memory systems (i.e., *within* the episodic system or *within* the semantic system), this might then mean that additional subsystems of memory would then need to be postulated to explain these dissociations (and in fact, such dissociations have already been observed). They therefore feel that the distinction between conceptually driven vs. data-driven tasks (transfer-appropriate processing) is a more parsimonious explanation of these dissociations.

After examining Blaxton's 1985 studies, which produced dissociations within (rather than between) the episodic and semantic memory systems, Roediger et al. (1989) concluded that the distinctions between modes of processing provides a better explanation of dissociations than does postulation of different memory systems.

TYPES OF MEMORY AND LISTENING MODELS

Let us next examine how these memory theories might relate to listening models. In relating direct or indirect or explicit and implicit memory measures to listening, it would seem reasonable to assume that all of these types of memory could be involved in a typical listening situation. For instance, many daily listening situations involve consciously remembering what someone told us yesterday, and the situation may even have involved explicit directions to remember what was being said. For example, our boss might instruct us, "Please remember to file all correspondence from Frank Jones in the Abraham Construction file." Implicit memory would be involved when we filed the Jones correspondence correctly without consciously recalling the instructions. Also, explicit memory would be involved if our boss asked, "What file did I ask you to file Frank Jones's letters in yesterday?"

It is also possible for listening situations to involve only implicit memory. For instance, radio or television advertisements may influence us to buy a product even though we may not consciously remember hearing the advertisement or even be able to explain why we have picked a particular brand when we need a product.

The relationship of both direct and indirect memory and explicit and implicit memory measures would be important ones for listening researchers to explore. When we listen, do we retain information better when we have been explicitly told to remember something, or is unconscious application of the information a more efficient or accurate type of memory?

While we might assume that in a typical listening situation we are more effective at recalling information when we have taken intentional steps to store the information, this topic deserves research attention—especially to explore what steps people can consciously take as they are listening to improve recall of what they are hearing. There have been some steps in this direction, such as Bostrom and Bryant (1980), and other studies that have dealt with improving listening skill in specific listening situations, such as Mendelsohn's (1984) suggestions for second-language listeners, but there certainly is a need for more of this type of research.

Regardless of the relationship between episodic and semantic memory, most listening tasks would seem to involve both types of memory. As listeners, we are generally called upon to use the mental thesaurus of semantic memory in order to understand what is being said and assign meaning to it, but at the same time, all of the spatiotemporal and contextual aspects of what is being said must be received and processed so that if required, we will know who told us something, when, and under what circumstances. Furthermore, the episodic aspects of the listening situation help us to determine which specific meaning to assign to the message (Schank, 1975). In listening, not only must we understand and remember what the message is, but who said it, and under what circumstances. This may be a limiting factor with listening. It may be that we cannot record information into the two systems simultaneously, so we must do constant switching. Or it may be that we can only receive or process a portion of the incoming information in each system. Consequently, much information of both types is missed. At any rate, this would be an area for further listening/memory research.

Additionally, the concept of data-driven vs. conceptually driven processing is important to the field of listening. This principle would mean that such features as male voice vs. female voice, pitch, loudness, and listened-to vs. read should have minimal effect on free recall (which is the typical, everyday listening task), whereas the level of processing (deeper, semantic processing) and the application of memory techniques would affect free recall in these situations. This would be because the information would be being encoded using conceptually driven processing and would be being retrieved using conceptually driven processing (since the data-driven cues would more than likely be absent in the typical free recall task of listened-to material). For instance, the question, "What did so and so say to me yesterday?" does not provide cues for data-driven processing.

APPLICATION

In practical terms, perhaps the proposal by Roediger et al. (1989) is of most use. These authors emphasize that the mental operations performed during learning experiences and during test episodes, and the interrelation of the two, are of most importance. Performance will improve to the extent that test procedures recapture the procedures used during prior learning, and an important dimension lies in whether procedures are directed more at surface features of items during study and test (data-driven processing) or at the deeper meaning of the stimuli (conceptually driven processing).

The Roediger et al. (1989) approach could account for why the deeper levels of processing (semantic as opposed to phonemic) lead to better recall in a typical listening situation because usually we are expected to remember the meaning of what was said rather than the exact words that were said.

Roediger et al. (1989) conclude that a memory theory encompassing memory systems and something like processing modes or procedures would probably be the correct one:

> A theory specifying both structural bases and processing assumptions is needed...but those presently on the scene emphasize either structure to the relative neglect of processing assumptions (the systems approach) or process-ing assumptions to the relative neglect of structure (our own approach). (p. 36).

They defend their bias as more practical because it focuses attention on the procedural aspects of memory performance and focuses attention away from identifying possible hidden memory systems and wondering what complex arrangements they might have. Certainly, this theory would provide a basis for ways of improving recall for certain types of informa-tion. If we want to recall the meaning of the message, then conceptually driven processing is more appropriate.

Hirst (1988) provides other suggestions for remembering more of what we hear. He notes the distinction that Tulving makes between episodic and semantic memory and says that when people complain about their memory, they are often talking about their episodic memories. They can't remember what someone said to them yesterday or when they are supposed to go to a meeting, or what someone's name is. Most jobs, however, require semantic memory. In performing a job, it doesn't matter where or when you learned how to do something, you just have to know how to do it. Thus, a study of memory techniques for a job should concentrate on mnemonics for semantic memories (i.e., using conceptually driven processing), but the memory technique must be tailored to the situation. We should first consider the task—"Memory for what?"—before designing a method for improving memory. We would use different techniques for learning the lines for a play than for how to operate equipment.

Hirst emphasizes the importance of what a listener does while listening over innate abilities:

> Memory performance depends on what one does while memorizing or remembering or, to use the jargon, encoding and retrieving. Difficulties arise because of the way information is encoded, the way one tries to retrieve the information, or both. Thus, differences in memory performance are often a consequence of what people do when memorizing and remembering, not what their capacity is. (p. 221)

In addition, superior memory can often be traced to what we do with the material as a consequence of our superior knowledge. For example, a French cook will typically remember a recipe for French food better than one for Chinese food (Hirst, 1980, in Hirst, 1988). He also observes that experiences aren't automatically memorized; they often must be transformed into a form more easily memorized: "Memorizing can be thought of as an activity in which people transform and manipulate experience in order to make it more memorable" (p. 222).

Most memories are involuntarily memorized—we remember something even though at the time our conscious intention was not to commit that something to memory. However, there are ways to make remembering more efficient when we *do* intend to remember the information. Substantial research, for instance, has established that the more connections we form between to-be-remembered information, the better we can remember the information (Pressley et al., 1982). In addition, these findings support the conclusion that conceptually driven processing enhances memory in free recall tasks.

One such technique is to relate the to-be-remembered material to what is already known. According to Hirst (1988), researchers often use the concept of *schema* (internal representation of an organized body of knowledge) in discussing elaboration. Schemata are best represented as scripts (procedural knowledge that is tied together by a small set of contingency relations) and generally contain information for how to act in different contexts, such as placing an order in a restaurant.

The concepts of script and schema specify more exactly the belief that knowledge is a set of associated concepts and that new information is learned by building associations to the existing network of associated concepts. Consequently, if the material is difficult to understand, it will also be difficult to memorize. If we can make the material more comprehensible, it will be easier to memorize (Hirst, 1988).

The importance of imagery in facilitating memory has been known since the early Greeks (Yates, 1966), and it has become a topic of significant recent research (Paivio, 1971, 1986). This facilitation effect is probably a result of our being forced to make connections and fit the new material into existing schemas in order to form the images. Kosslyn's (1984) work is laying important theoretical groundwork for how mental representations are formed so that we can better understand how to capitalize on the positive memory effects. And Sheikh's (1983) book provides a comprehensive look at theory, research, and application of imagery.

Possibly one of the more frustrating aspects of day-to-day memory tasks is the experience of knowing that we know something but not being able to recall or access the piece of information when we want it. Thus, memories can be available but not accessible (Tulving & Pearlstone, 1966). The trace can be somewhere in memory but cannot be successfully retrieved. It isn't enough to memorize something so that it is stored away. It must be memorized so that one can successfully retrieve it. Hirst (1988) advises that to make memories more accessible, we must study them with the recall demands in mind, and certainly Tulving's (1983) encoding specificity theory would support this. When we don't know what the retrieval cues will be, or we don't know what the exact circumstances will be when we are asked to recall the to-be-remembered information, the best approach is to encode the material along as many dimensions as possible. Here, mnemonic devices would help as would levels of processing information.

Motivation, it appears, is also an important factor in successful voluntary memorization, but only indirectly. When people are more motivated, they tend to use more of the strategies that will improve recall.

Actions are also more important than intentions. The deeper the level of processing, the more likely is recall, regardless of whether the learner had the intention of memorizing. Thus, orienting tasks that require a deeper level of processing produce better recall (Craik & Tulving, 1975).

In addition, the "generation effect" shows that elaboration of a word list is a more effective mnemonic if the elaboration is subject generated rather than experimenter provided (Dickel & Slak, 1983; Slamecka & Graf, 1978). Consequently, recall can be improved by requiring or encouraging the listener to generate the elaborations, rather than having the experimenter (or speaker) provide the elaborations.

Hirst (1988) concludes that "memory is an active process and that good, effective, and efficient memorizing and remembering involves the careful use of strategies" (p. 240). To help learners memorize, both the curricula and the design of the to-be-remembered material should be concerned with mnemonic principles. Certainly, it would be advantageous for students to be directly taught memory strategies and how to apply them so that they can more efficiently acquire the vast amounts of knowledge that are given to them in lectures in school.

Perhaps this is a most valuable message for us as listeners and as listening researchers. As listeners, we should become familiar with and learn to apply the memory strategies that are best suited to the type of information we are listening to, to the conditions under which recall will occur, and to the type of encoding and retrieval processes that will provide the best match between these processes and conditions.

To make this advice more practical, further research is required to specify which factors at encoding while listening are likely to produce the best performance under which conditions at recall. While listening, we must learn to anticipate what the recall conditions will be so that we can modify our encoding strategies to match those recall conditions. As has been mentioned by several of the memory researchers, we can improve our recall by applying certain strategies. However, which strategies we use depends on the specific circumstance. Further research will help us determine to what extent we need to be aware of distinctions between memory systems, types of information, types of processing, and types of test tasks so that we can apply strategies appropriate to those circumstances.

REFERENCES

Atkinson, R.C., & Shiffrin, R.M. (1968). Human memory: A proposed system and its control processes. In K.W. Spence & J.T. Spence (Eds.), *The psychology of learning and motivation: Vol. 2. Advances on research and theory* (pp. 89–196). New York: Academic Press.

Atkinson, R.C., & Shiffrin, R.M. (1971). The control of short-term memory. *Scientific American, 225,* 82–90.

Baddeley, A. (1986). *Working memory.* Oxford: Clarendon Press.

Barker, L.L. (1971). *Listening behavior.* Englewood Cliffs, NJ: Prentice-Hall.

Black, I.B., Adler, J.E., Dreyfus, C.F., Friedman, W.F., LaGamma, E.F., & Roach, A.H. (1988). Experience and the biochemistry of information storage in the nervous system. In M.S. Gazzaniga (Ed.), *Perspectives in memory research* (pp. 3–22). Cambridge, MA: The MIT Press.

Bobrow, D.A., & Norman, D.G. (1976). On the role of active memory processes in perception and cognition. In C.F. Cofer (Ed.), *The structure of human memory* (pp. 114–132). San Francisco: W.H. Freeman.

Bostrom, R.N., & Bryant, C.L. (1980). Factors in the retention of information presented orally: The role of short-term listening. *The Western Journal of Speech Communication, 44,* 137–145.

Bostrom, R.N. & Waldhart, E.S. (1988). Memory models and the measurement of listening. *Communication Education, 37,* 1–13.

Broadbent, D.E. (1957). A mechanical model for human attention and immediate memory. *Psychological Review, 64,* 205–215.

Broadbent, D.E. (1958). *Perception and communication.* London: Pergamon Press.

Brownell, J. (1986). *Building active listening skills*. Englewood Cliffs, NJ: Prentice-Hall.

Craik, F.I.M., & Lockhart, R.S. (1972). Levels of processing: A framework for memory research. *Journal of Verbal Learning and Verbal Behavior, 11,* 671–684.

Craik, F.I.M., & Tulving, E. (1975). Depth of processing and the retention of words in episodic memory. *Journal of Experimental Psychology: General, 104*(3), 268–294.

Craik, F.I.M., & Watkins, M.J. (1973). The role of rehearsal in short-term memory. *Journal of Verbal Learning and Verbal Behavior, 12,* 599–607.

Dickel, M.J., & Slak, S. (1983). Imagery vividness and memory for verbal material. *Journal of Mental Imagery, 7*(1), 121–126.

Ebbinghaus, H. (1964). *Memory* (H.A. Ruger & C.E. Bussenius, Trans.). New York: Dover. (Original work published in 1885).

Hebb, D.O. (1949). *The organization of behavior.* New York: Wiley.

Hirst, W. (1988). Improving memory. In M.S. Gazzaniga (Ed.), *Perspectives in memory research* (pp. 219–244). Cambridge, MA: MIT Press.

Jacoby, L.L., & Dallas, M. (1981). On the relationship between autobiographical memory and perceptual learning. *Journal of Experimental Psychology: General, 110*(3), 306–340.

James, W. (1890). *The principles of psychology.* New York: Holt, Rinehart and Winston.

Kosslyn, S.M. (1984). Mental representation. In J.R. Anderson & S.M. Kosslyn (Eds.), *Tutorials in learning and memory* (pp. 91–117). San Francisco: W.H. Freeman and Co.

McKoon, G., Ratcliff, R., & Dell, G.S. (1986). A critical evaluation of the semantic-episodic distinction. *Journal of Experimental Psychology: Learning, Memory, and Cognition, 12*(2), 295–306.

Melton, A.W. (1963). Implications of short-term memory for a general theory of memory. *Journal of Verbal Learning and Behavior, 2,* 1–21.

Mendelsohn, D.J. (1984). *There ARE strategies for listening.* Vancouver, B.C.: Teachers of English as an Additional Language. (ERIC Document Reproduction Service No. ED 246 648)

Miller, G.A. (1956). The magical number seven, plus or minus two: Some limits on our capacity for processing information. *Psychological Review, 63,* 81–97.

Murdock, B.B., Jr. (1989). The past, the present, and the future: Comments on Section 1. In H.L. Roediger, III & F.I.M. Craik (Eds.), *Varieties of memory and consciousness: Essays in honour of Endel Tulving* (pp. 93–98). Hillsdale, NJ: Erlbaum.

Paivio, A. (1971). *Imagery and verbal processes.* New York: Holt, Rinehart and Winston.

Paivio, A. (1986). *Mental representations: A dual coding approach* New York: Oxford University Press.

Pressley, M., Levin, J.R., & Delaney, H.D. (1982). The mnemonic keyword method. *Review of Educational Research, 52*(1), 61–91.

Ratcliff, R., & McKoon, G. (1989). Memory models, text processing, and cue-dependent retrieval. In H.L. Roediger, III & F.I.M. Craik (Eds.), *Varieties of memory and consciousness: Essays in honour of Endel Tulving* (pp. 73–92). Hillsdale, NJ: Erlbaum.

Richardson-Klavehn, A., & Bjork, R.A. (1988). Measures of memory. *Annual Review of Psychology, 39,* 475–543.

Roediger, J.L., III, Weldon, M.S., & Challis, B.H. (1989). Explaining dissociations between implicit and explicit measures of retention: A processing account. In H.L. Roediger, III & F.I.M. Craik (Eds.), *Varieties of memory and consciousness: Essays in honour of Endel Tulving* (pp. 3–41). Hillsdale, NJ: Erlbaum.

Schank, R.C. (1975). The role of memory in language processing. In C.N. Cofer (Ed.), *The structure of human memory* (pp. 162–189). San Francisco: W.H. Freeman.

Sheikh, A.A. (1983). *Imagery: Current theory, research, and application.* New York: John Wiley & Sons.

Slamecka, N.J., & Graf, P. (1978). The generation effect: Delineation of a phenomenon. *Journal of Experimental Psychology: Human Learning and Memory, 4,* 592–604.

Squire, L.R. (1987). *Memory and brain.* New York: Oxford University Press.

Tulving, E. (1966). Subjective organization and effects of repetition in multi-trial free-recall learning. *Journal of Verbal Learning and Verbal Behavior, 5,* 193–197.

Tulving, E. (1968). Theoretical issues in free recall. In T.R. Dixon & D.L. Horton (Eds.), *Verbal behavior and general behavior theory* (pp. 2–36). Englewood Cliffs, NJ: Prentice-Hall.

Tulving, E. (1972). Episodic and semantic memory. In E. Tulving & W. Donaldson (Eds.), *Organization of memory* (pp. 382–403). New York: Academic Press.

Tulving, E. (1983). *Elements of episodic memory.* Oxford: Clarendon Press.

Tulving, E. (1984). Precis of *Elements of Episodic Memory. The Behavioral and Brain Sciences, 7,* 223–268.

Tulving, E., & Pearlstone, Z. (1966). Availability versus accessibility of information in memory for words. *Journal of Verbal Learning and Verbal Behavior, 5,* 381–391.

Underwood, B.J. (1957). Interference and forgetting. *Psychological Review, 64*(1), 49–60.

Waugh, N.C., & Norman, D.A. (1965). Primary memory. *Psychological Review, 72,* 89–104.

Weaver, C.H. (1972). *Human listening.* Indianapolis: Bobbs-Merrill Educational Publishing.

Wolff, F.I., Marsnik, N.C., Tacey, W.S., & Nichols, R.G. (1983). *Perceptive listening.* New York: Holt, Rinehart and Winston.

Yates, F.A. (1966). *The art of memory.* Chicago: The University of Chicago Press.

Chapter 6

Metacognitive Listening

Sara W. Lundsteen

College of Education
University of North Texas

The aims of this chapter are twofold: to give an explanation of a perspective for investigating metacognitive listening, while reviewing relevant literature and research. Moreover, this chapter offers implications for the study of listening that are both theoretical and practical as they relate to metacognition, or monitoring one's thinking while listening.

EXPLANATION OF THE PERSPECTIVE AND REVIEW OF RELEVANT LITERATURE AND RESEARCH

Metacognition is a specific focus of cognitive psychology that can further increase our understanding of the complexities of a listening process—the higher mental aspects. Metacognition refers to an individual's awareness of personal cognitive performance and the use of that awareness to alter that performance. To use an analogy, this process is something like laying one overhead transparency over another as one thinks about one's thinking and that of others in a communication endeavor. That is, such a model of cognitive processing demands self-monitoring in order to be aware of one's own cognitive activity; then one can control that activity as one differentiates one's perspective from that of others (Brown, 1978).

Research by Brown (1980) and by Flavell (1979) on metacognition has implications for enhancing our understanding of the listening process as a model for listening to oneself.

So just what is metacognition? Metacognition refers to the examination of factors influencing an individual's control of strategies while learning. It includes: (a) an awareness of one's own cognitive activity; and (b) a monitoring of one's own cognitive processes while attempting a learning task (Brown & Palincsar, 1982; Flavell, 1981; Flavell, Speer, Green, & August, 1981; Singer & Flavell, 1981). Seen here is a knowledge of one's own cognitive limitations and a knowledge of varying processing require- ments of different learning tasks. Thus, in order to use cognitive monitor- ing one requires: (a) a selection of appropriate learning strategies; (b) a monitoring of the effectiveness of these strategies; and (c) a revision of ineffective strategies. For example, a child might think: "Those directions on how to get there aren't clear; something's missing; I'll get him to use 'turning right and left' instead of 'north and south'." In essence, during this metacognitive process one has something of a split mental focus that can correct and enhance meaning.

To repeat for emphasis, metacognition refers to an awareness of, and a capitalization on, one's own knowledge and thought process as they apply to a specific task (Flavell, 1976). With reference to listening, metacogni- tion is that general knowledge that guides listeners in monitoring their comprehension processes, selecting and implementing specific strategies in pursuit of a goal. Moreover, metacognition can be divided into two differing clusters (Baker & Brown, 1984). The first cluster concerns (a) learners' awareness of any mismatch between available knowledge and the task complexity; the second cluster (not necessarily independent), con- cerns (b) the active self-monitoring of cognitive processes while listening. Use of productive strategies relates directly to metacognitive awareness of drawbacks and appropriate monitoring.

Additionally, research by Snyder (1974) relates thinking about thinking to facial and vocal behaviors. That is, individuals differ in the extent of monitoring, through self-observation and control, in the areas of both expressive behavior and self-presentation—implying again strategies for listening to oneself while communicating with others. In essence, applica- tion of the inquiry on metacognition can be helpful to understanding one's own listening behavior, and one's use of specific strategies. Then one monitors strategies to enhance listening. Such productive activity can be a prime target for teaching behaviors. It is wise, however, not to overload the learner, but to focus on one or a few metacognitive strategies at a time, as we shall see. Otherwise all of this thinking about thinking could become so cumbersome that it actually interferes with communication and problem solving (Brown, 1978).

A Related Page from Reading Research

There have been detailed comparisons of constructs for the process and similarities and differences between reading and listening (e.g., Lundsteen, 1979, 1989). This section gleans ideas from that complimentary language art. Research, for example by Kurtz and Borkowski (1987), demonstrates superior performance by children in reading summarization after metacognitive training. With respect to comprehension of print, researchers have examined children's metacognitive knowledge about reading (and writing) using interviewing and questioning (e.g., Myers & Paris, 1978; Armbruster, Echols, & Brown, 1983). The results of these studies indicate developmental trends in children's acquisition of metacognitive awareness about the reading process. Apparently young children tend to associate reading with rather peripheral overt behaviors rather than with meaning-seeking processes.

Moreover, Sparks (1990), in a report of two comparative reading investigations of metacognitive self-regulation, found that this variable fluctuates in relation to primary task, topic interest, content familiarity, and perceived task difficulty. Her results with intellectually gifted seventh graders who were skilled or less skilled readers suggested that metacognitive functioning is not a unitary process, even within a single individual.

One example of metacognitive strategies in the field of reading is a *prereading plan* (PReP)—a usually rather teacher-directed strategy for helping a reader anticipate what prior knowledge will be needed to understand new information. Activities within this strategy are:

1. *Initial association with the concept in question*: "Tell anything that comes to mind when you hear the word 'Congress.'
2. *Reflections on initial associations*: "What made you think of...[whatever the student responded]?"
3. *Reformulation of knowledge*: "Now have you developed any new ideas about...?" (Alvermann, 1987; Langer, 1982, p. 154).

Another reading strategy, *reciprocal teaching of comprehension monitoring*, makes use of four separate cognitive activities: summarizing, clarifying, questioning, and predicting (Palincsar & Brown, 1985). Each activity is used in an authentic reading situation (real, genuine); for example, children use summarizing to tell themselves, the teacher, or a group what they understood. Children clarify *only* when communication is unclear. Children, not just the teachers, generate questions. The activity of predicting treats students to an active engagement in comprehending the next portion. As a final strategy example from the area of reading, note taking apparently can increase student's ability to remember what they read (Anderson & Armbruster, 1984).

While such studies have provided glimpses of children's metacognitive knowledge of the language art of reading (and one may be tempted to draw implications and ideas for the auditory mode), relatively few studies have examined children's metacognitive knowledge about listening.

A Page from Developmental Psychologists

Those few studies that have examined children's metacognitive knowledge about listening have been conducted largely by developmental psychologists. Research indicated that young children of kindergarten age have not yet developed the ability to analyze a message in order to see how adequate it is in conveying information (Robinson, 1981; Flavell et al., 1981). When asked to do a task, for example, choosing an object, young children were likely to make their choices on the assumption that the message is totally adequate. Proficient listeners realize that much material that comes their way contains insufficient information, and they ask for more. A mature act of comprehension monitoring (metacognitive processing) involves the following: (a) a listener's ability to know without explicit feedback that a communication is inadequate; (b) why it is inadequate; and (c) whose fault it is. Inadequacies may contain; uninterpretable segments, ambiguous references, contradictions, incomplete directions, or directions that could not be carried out.

As children get older, they do improve; by about age 8 functional operation is well in place, though no ceiling of competency is achieved. Memory is apparently not a significant factor in the ineptitude of the young children (Flavell et al., 1981).

Two experiments tested the hypothesis that development of children's comprehension monitoring skills in referential communication is based in part, however, on ability to differentiate the literal sentence meaning from the meaning that a speaker wished to convey (Bonitatibus, 1988). Another study investigated whether or not 7- and 10-year-olds, and adults, are sensitive to their own and another listener's failure to understand literal and nonliteral (sarcastic) uses of utterances (Ackerman, 1986).

Ackerman found that children aged 7 and 10, and 18-year-old college students, all had correct understanding of a speaker's sarcastic intent, and were sensitive to their own incomprehension. Vocal intonation cues were a help to 7-year-olds. Seven-year-olds, however, did not evaluate *another* listener's understanding effectively. A problem here (besides memory overload) may have been that 7-year-olds did not use their own interpretation of speaker intent as a monitoring/evaluative standard. Ability to assess another person's understanding appears to develop with age, and appears later than self-assessment. A sample story and questions from Ackerman's work follows:

Sarcastic Context

Billy struck out five times and was terrible in the baseball game. His sister Cheryl [the listener] watched the game. Later Billy's coach said to Cheryl, "Billy had a really great game, didn't he?" Cheryl said, "The coach said you played very badly."

Questions

1. Did the coach mean that he was pleased with how Billy played? (Speaker Intent)
2. Did you understand the coach? (Self-understanding)
3. Did Cheryl understand the coach? (Listener Understanding)

The successful self-monitoring results from Ackerman were at variance with results found by Markman (1977, 1979, 1981), who suggested that young children are relatively insensitive to their own comprehension failures. They fail to detect inconsistencies and their own incomprehension; they are generally deficient in comprehension monitoring. One reason for the variance may be that most other investigators besides Ackerman have not distinguished clearly between the "evaluation" and the "regulation" of comprehension and their sources. Evaluation concerns the detection of inconsistency, while regulation concerns repair processes used to resolve the problem. That is, children may (a) not detect inconsistency (—lack evaluative process), (b) detect but ignore inconsistency, or (c) detect and resolve inconsistency in a way unanticipated by the experimenter—(undetected regulative processes).

Promising thrusts for intervention in the field of listening have come from the work of developmental psychologists such as Robinson and Robinson (1982) and Flavell et al. (1981). E. J. and W. P. Robinson started their research at the University of Bristol in England, where they examined whether, when, and how children used metacognitive listening. This research was followed by experimental treatments intended to enhance the process in kindergarten children. The Robinson and Flavell studies indicated that preschool and kindergarten children apparently were not able to do metacognitive listening, in the researcher's context.

One explanation is that of developmental constraints, similar to those suggested by Piaget. That is, very young children simply do not think about thinking. Such abstract activity needs concrete operational thought, including the holding of many absent variables in the mind at the same time (e.g., the message sent, one's responsive behavior, the result, and a revisitation of the initially sent message). Metacognitive behavior is complex and abstract for an egocentric, authority-impressed child. The young child thinks, "If I didn't build that block pattern right, it must be that I didn't listen good." The explanation would not occur to the child that the sender sent a faulty, unclear, ambiguous message in the first place. In the research by Flavell et al. (1981), the message was masked by pretend sneezes and equally viable alternatives that could lead to vastly different results.

Flavell (1981) did think that an alternative hypothesis for young children's failure to do metacognitive listening might be simply the use of mature experimenters who are unwittingly a constraining authority figure for a young child. In remedy, he invented a child confederate (taped) who gave the ambiguous instructions. Moreover, Flavell used a puppet who was considered as immature and inept as the sender. Still the young children in his research did not bring themselves to ask for clarification. They apparently thought that the instructions listened to were perfect, and if their constructed block pattern didn't match the hidden model, then they themselves were solely at fault as listeners.

The Robinsons (Robinson & Robinson, 1982) have suggested the explanation that young children *lack models* for being a demanding, metacognitive listener. That is, when a young child sends an ambiguous, unintelligible message, adults do not say, "Hey, that's not clear to me; try again." Instead (and appropriately and supportively so) adults try probes, ask veiled questions, try to formulate testable hypotheses, and use roundabout means to get a clear message from the child. It is not until children go to school that the environment shows them models of demanding meaning when listening. Armed with this thought, Robinson (1981) mounted experiments with varied treatments, including modeling and feedback seeking, with some success. Teachers modeled seeking feedback and children took the message-sending role. The Flavell group has tried to take the listening tasks out of the more artificial laboratory game context and make the material more oriented to typical school activities.

Strategies. At the University of Oklahoma research was planned with respect to varied strategies in metacognitive listening (Tompkins, Friend, & Smith, 1984). The research was ultimately designed to examine many strategies that an effective older child listener might use or might try to teach a younger child to use. The assumption is that older students' instructions will reveal the strategies felt to be most successful in the particular learning task. Examples of listening strategies follow later. The methodology included individual differences (good and poor listeners) with respect to varied strategies of metacognitive listening. The thrust tried to look at process and strategy in listening by not only asking the child, "What did you do?" but also more indirectly by having the children act as tutors for a younger peer. That is, the tutors tried to explain to the younger peer strategies that they themselves would recommend. Users of this peer method (e.g., Brown, 1980) assume that the older student's instructions will reveal the strategies felt to be most successful in the particular learning task. The next section examines in detail ideas concerning strategies as applied to metacognitive listening and the classroom.

SELF-MONITORING TECHNIQUES AND CLASSROOM IMPLICATIONS

What, more precisely, are some of these metacognitive strategies with respect to classroom implementation? First consider the real-life context of state adopted goals for listening instruction. In the curriculum for the state of Maryland one will find a subgoal (paraphrased): Use self-monitoring techniques to assess own listening effectiveness. This subgoal is found under a large goal: Be aware of and use stages of a listening process (Wolvin, Fogler, Brownell, Cochran, Denniston, McDonough, Moffitt, & Slaughter, 1985). As indicated earlier, this metacognitive part of a listener process has been researched to some extent. But also, long ago, such related productive (and less productive) listener patterns have been at least pointed out (e.g., by Nichols in Nichols & Stevens, 1957). The instructional point with regard to strategies is to help children become aware of patterns and guard against those unproductive ones when the occasion warrants. Essential skills in monitoring communication are: (a) realizing that problems can occur; (b) recognizing when they do; and (c) knowing how to remedy them (Revelle, Wellman, & Karabenick, 1985). Next, examine listener patterns that relate to some teachable ideas adapted from Nichols.

First of all, patterns may take place in what we might call "leftover thinking space." Usually only a fraction of thinking time is spent in physically hearing most messages. Thought is faster than most people's delivery of a message. How one uses any leftover thinking space makes a considerable difference in success in understanding and using messages. The amount of leftover thinking space varies, but generally people can count on a usable amount, even as much as 90%, depending on the material (see Figure 6.1). Figure 6.1 shows a pie diagram and possible mental activities, concepts, and processes, besides that of physical hearing and auditory intake, almost simultaneously occurring within a time frame that is closely the same. With what else does one fill this leftover space?

Figure 6.1.   Thinking Space.

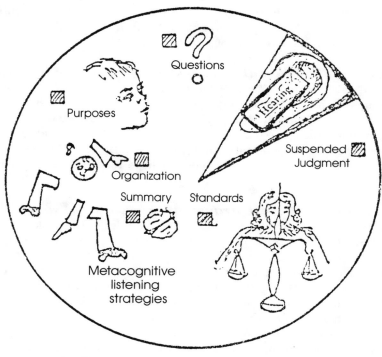

You normally use only about 10% of your thinking space for hearing.
There is time and space to monitor listening metacognitively.

Four listener patterns are typical during use of leftover thinking space. These patterns show alternative ways of interacting with material. One of the patterns is effective for literal listening, and the other three are not. (One might say some are skills and some are "antiskills.") To illustrate, consider a message in the context of a drama about a rattlesnake that children have improvised in a classroom (Lundsteen, 1989). Josephine chose the character of a lady with a small child to be the one to find the snake, and volunteers filled the other roles. Then the teacher said to Karina, who had volunteered, "What does the child say?" Now, with this message and context in hand, consider the first pattern often occupying leftover thinking space.

Pattern #1. Small departures from the communication line. Suppose Karina had taken small productive departures with her leftover thinking space. Say she imagined a small child, similar to her baby brother, and then imagined what he might dialogue in response to seeing a snake for the first time. If she did this she would have made effective use of her leftover thinking space. Such mental activity is apparently evidenced in her dialogue, "Mommie, look at the short rubber hose; it's moving!" (A representation of pattern #1, small productive departures, is in the first part of Figure 6.2.)

Pattern #2. Tangent. But let's suppose, instead, that the moment someone said "*snake*," Karina's leftover-thinking space became totally preoccupied with the terrible slithery creature. Suppose she went off on a tangent with her mind dwelling on her terror of snakes, never to return to the communication line (until lunch time). Her pattern would probably look like the second representation in Figure 6.2. She would probably not have even listened further and would not have realized that she missed anything.

Pattern #3. Private argument. Or suppose that when a "lady with a small child" was decided upon as the finder of the snake, Karina had chosen to fill her thinking space with private arguments. Let's say she really wanted a unicorn to be the chosen character for the improvised drama. "That could be much more fun," she could be arguing to herself, "Who wants to play the part of a lady with a small child! I've got enough of them at home!" She could argue privately for the rest of the activity session, missing the fun, the class assignment, and the homework task.

Sometimes this pattern is related to a distortion called *self-preoccupation*. An example is being introduced to people and then not remembering their names perhaps because of other thoughts. Sometimes people get wrapped up in their own parallel argument and never realize how close their position might be to that of their supposed antagonist. (This pattern, private argument, is the third in Figure 6.2).

Sometimes the metacognitive "fix-up" strategy of thinking that the "very next words may completely change my life," helps even the most prone to wander. Up to a certain point, instructors can help young individuals to learn to quiet themselves, discipline their attention, and do metacognitive listening. Individuals can visualize on target so as to enhance the message with an appropriate amount of relevant, image-enriching experience during leftover-thinking space. Figure 6.2 represents all four listener patterns adapted from Nichol's early work.

As for instructional implications and interventions, younger children might dramatize the first three patterns in Figure 6.2 with puppets, after modeled examples. Older children might role-play all five contrasting patterns. The next section details some further self-monitoring techniques and strategies (and a few more teaching implications).

Figure 6.2.   Listener Patterns.

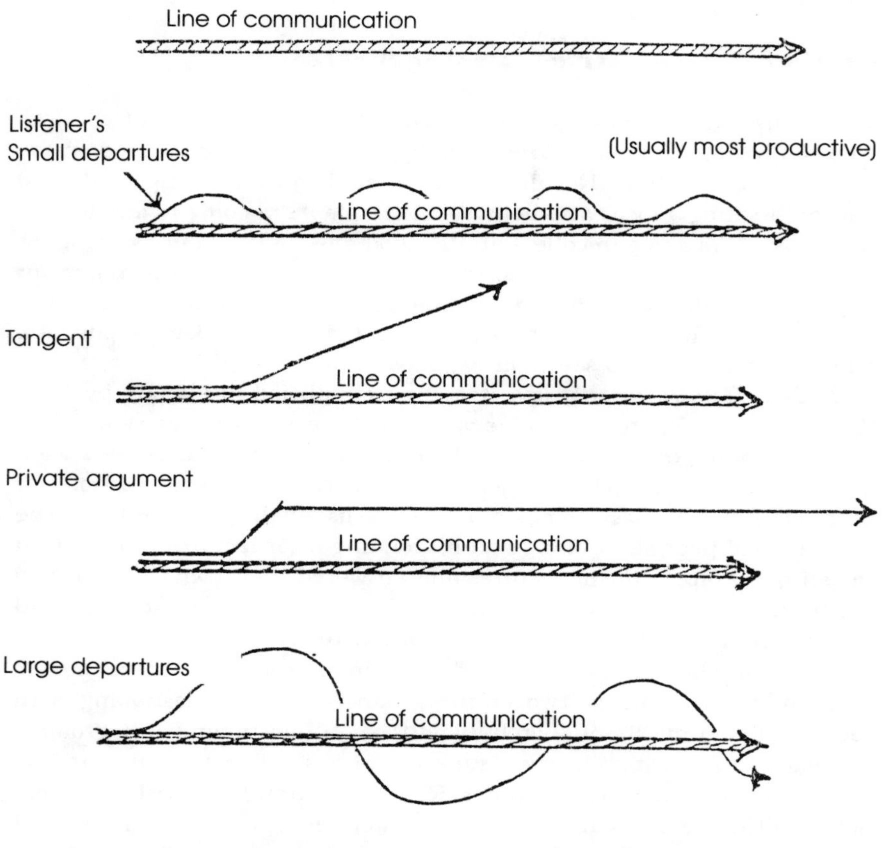

Line of communication

Listener's
Small departures

(Usually most productive)

Line of communication

Tangent

Line of communication

Private argument

Line of communication

Large departures

Line of communication

A skilled listener can monitor and to some extent control such patterns
metacognitively.

Pattern #4. Large departures. To illustrate the final pattern,
"Large Departures," suppose Karina had directed her attention fairly well
to the line of communication, but had let her mind play extensively with
images and wander too much (fourth pattern in Figure 6.2). For example,
she might have grasped some of the choices in response to selection of
locale for the drama; but left the communication line after "the department store" was mentioned. Then she might either be at a loss as to how to
improvise because of the big gaps, or give an inappropriate response. Too
large a departure from a line of communication has plagued listeners with

worries or enticing daydreams, even when they were motivated, really wanted to listen, and had some grasp of self-monitoring and the listening process.

Further Metacognitive Listening Strategies

1. **Attention directing** may receive a boost, in the case of children who can write, with note taking, mainly to keep attention focused on the line of communication. (Recall the reading study on notetaking mentioned earlier.) Picking a focus also helps, for example, "I'm going to aim for the big ideas"; "I'm going to collect all the good anecdotes"; "I'm listening for anything that shows the character was really brave"; "I'm listening for anything I could use in the classroom tomorrow." In essence children tell themselves, "Get ready, get set, tune out all else, select a purpose, LISTEN (and watch to see what happens to the process)."

2. **Self-Questioning** is a strategy exemplified in a study by King (1989). In an effort to determine whether the metacognitive strategy of self-questioning enhances lecture comprehension, 56 ninth graders were assigned to four conditions. Subjects: (a) were trained to pose questions for themselves during classroom lectures and to use their questions to engage in reciprocal peer-questioning and responding after lectures; (b) engaged in self-questioning during lectures and answered their own questions; (c) discussed lecture material in small cooperative groups; and (d) reviewed the lecture material independently, as a control condition.

On both postpractice and 10-day maintenance tests these honors program participants in two of the groups—the self-questioning with reciprocal peer-questioning group, and the self-questioning only group—showed lecture comprehension superior to that of participants in the discussion and in the control groups. Results apparently suggested that not only can the use of a self-questioning strategy improve comprehension of lectures, but that students can maintain this strategy when external prompts are removed. That is, such a metacognitive strategy can be taught to high school students and incorporated into their classroom learning environment.

3. **Memory enhancing** is a strategy or action that children can take when the problem seems to be memory overload. Basics that help are imposing organization on the seemingly unorganized message, categorizing, labeling, and rehearsing. Applying the organization of different speaker discourse patterns may help, (e.g., cause-effect, temporal, topical, revelation). *Word signals* may help. Younger children can watch for word cues such as "first," "second," "third"; older children for "in contrast," and "as another example." The use of an *advance organizer* (outline, web, study guide) helps a child with labels and categories. It is good to have

fewer concepts in such a guide for the young child, more detail for the older ones.

Most of us *chunk* phone numbers to enhance memory, saying, "dial 361 thirty-four, twenty-four" (instead of 3,4,2,4). Many children un-consciously use the strategy of *rehearsal*, repeating under their breaths over and over, for example, "Go to the office; ask Mrs. Lawrence for a pad of pink slips, a pair of scissors, and some tape. Go to the office..." and so on. Thus they assure (hopefully) with this strategy that a message listened to will not be forgotten.

Young children may use the strategy of *mouthing*, of forming words soundlessly with their lips as the message is received in order to hang on to the words. "Ridiculous, rilicudous, ridiculous. That's reliicudous," *almost* triumphed a 4-year-old listener, in pursuit of acquiring and using a lovely, long, new word.

What is the nature of research on this topic of metamemory? In one research project, two variables—the relationship between knowing that organization during study will facilitate performance (metamemory) and grouping pictures by semantic category—were examined in a free-recall task for 60 first-grade and 48 fourth-grade children. Results suggest that how and when such reflective metacognitive activity occurs may be crucial for learning and study effectiveness (Andreassen & Waters, 1989). Two studies looked at the knowledge of 320 college students about the use of memory strategies for different tasks and the relationships of this knowledge to use of strategy and performance. Results, apparently supporting current models of metamemory, indicated that the adult students did know the relative effectiveness of different memory strat-egies (Justice & Weaver-McDougall, 1989).

4. **Enhancing the communication** is a strategy pertaining to requests for clarity, active feedback, paraphrasing, and parasupports. Examples of parasupports are head nodding, phrases such as "Did you really!"; "Well!"; "Un-huh." Enabling words of active feedback might be, "Would this be an example of what you mean?" Words related to paraphrasing might be, "What I've learned so far is..."; "Is this what you're saying, that..." Deliberate, active, metacognitive use of feedback and summarizing can help memory, attention, and meaning during listening.

5. **Enhancing the meaning** is a strategy mentioned positively in connection with the first listener pattern with small productive depar-tures in the first part of Figure 6.2. Teachers can help children to elaborate the message with appropriate mental images, pictures in the mind, referral to previous experience, and self-questioning. Examples: "'*Metacognitive*'...ah, like an overhead projector with one transparency laid over another, thought overlaying thought to improve the communica-

tion—I see" (elaborating with imagery). "He said, 'I *know* about you.' I wonder what he meant? (self-questioning).

In sum, a number of strategies exist for enhancing listening. Most children and adults could profit from becoming students of their metacognitive listening processes and applying appropriate strategies. Unfortunately, few if any strategies are typically at a sufficient level of awareness and conscious use by young children (Tompkins, Friend, & Smith, 1987). On the other hand even some young children aged 3 and 4 can realize ambiguities and puzzlements in communication and will rather directly seek to clear them up after monitoring a situation highly *meaningful* to them (Revelle et al., 1985). Sonnenschein (1986) described two experiments comparing how children evaluate three types of uninformative messages (ambiguous, incomplete, inconsistent) and whether and why the speaker's age apparently is related to the evaluation of each.

Perhaps the main implication for educators is to know the learners and then help them with the following: (a) selection of appropriate *strategies*; (b) *monitoring* of the effectiveness of a selected listening strategy; and (c) *revision* of an ineffective listening strategy. That is, the implication is to help children attend and give self-alerts when the activity is not proceeding properly.

Researchers (e.g., Brown, 1978; Reeve & Brown, 1984) suggest that teachers need to find appropriate places for instruction regarding strategies and not use isolated practice of this split mental focus. That is, avoid seeking to clarify or summarize when nothing needs it. Instruction is not a matter of 15 minutes here and there with your metacognitive listening cap on; it is not a matter of a "quick fix." Instruction involves a sense of communication responsibility that teachers as models can seek to transfer to children's own use when it comes up naturally in the course of each day.

SUGGESTED RESEARCH

Part of any upcoming research thrust in this area needs to be creation and validation of an array of assessment means to form a base of "thinking young" about metacognitive listening. In addition, there are several hypotheses about the relation of style (Rosenberg, 1968) and metacognitive listening that future research might address. For instance, since individuals with a *rigid, inhibited style* have a dearth of information (relatively little internal and external), and relatively low level of abstractness in thought—one hypothesis is that such individuals would show up as the poorest metacognitive listeners. The individual with the *undisciplined style* might listen most skillfully to self (but not to others); the *acceptance anxious style* individual might listen most skillfully to "significant others" with some blocking in the higher and more creative levels, because of too much anxiety about pleasing the sender. Finally, a hypothesis about the *creative style* might be that these individuals would be the most adept metacognitive listeners. Why? Because those with this style use both listening material from without and call up material from within. They are willing to risk trying various metacognitive strategies and they receive the reinforcement of much pleasant feeling tone from simply enjoying the whole metacognitive process.

Apparently, researchers in metacognitive listening will need to continue investigation during the early years, kindergarten in particular. Studies by Donaldson (1979) show some of the Piagetian tasks can be handled by many young children when the social and emotional context is highly relevant. Donaldson has modified some of the Piagetian perspective tasks by switching from dolls, mountains, and pictures to a police-officer doll and child doll separated by partitions (more relevant to young children). Donaldson also uses the Piagetian conservation of number task where "naughty Teddy Bear" comes out of a drawer to mess up, to spread apart the second row of matched pennies. In this more real-life context, previously nonconserving children did conserve. It may be that socially oriented and highly meaningful, problematical thought has a different schedule of development than more purely cognitive thought (such as entailed in traditional Piagetian tasks for young children). In a 1985 study some young children aged 3 and 4 realized ambiguities and puzzlements in communication and sought rather directly to clear them up after monitoring a situation highly *meaningful* to them (Revelle et al., 1985). Further research could be informative.

More studies are needed which use the technique of socially personalizing the metacognitive listening situation for young children, and which use creative problem solving in activities that genuinely engage children's minds with long-term projects. Investigations need to take into account the variable of the linguistic material sent that may affect a young listener's comprehension. The approaches of the longitudinal study and the ethnographer might help with some of the following questions:

1. What are metacognitive strategies (if any) that young children use and grow to use while listening? What are some strategies they could use beyond simple demand for clarity?
2. Does a socially personalized and highly motivated context of listening, hinged to creative problem solving, produce a different schedule of metacognitive listening development?
3. Are good and poor metacognitive listeners matched with certain learning and solving styles (e.g., rigid inhibited, undisciplined acceptance anxious, and creative)?

4.   Are individuals locked into these styles and accompanying listening patterns, or do these change over time and across context?
5.   Do subtle aspects of language material act to affect a child's effective use of metacognitive listening?
6.   If a child exhibits an apparent improved metacognitive listening behavior, does an improved clarity in message sending or speaking occur, too?

Finally, there are some provocative ideas growing out of Gardner's theory of multiple intelligences (Gardner & Hatch, 1989) that could be of interest to those in the field of listening. This work on seven intelligences is generally an important thrust to rethink and retool the assessment of intelligence and construct related school curriculum. Gardner's sixth and seventh intelligences are called *interpersonal* and *intrapersonal*. The person with a high-profile element in interpersonal intelligence may end up with the job of therapist or salesperson with capacities to discern and respond appropriately to the moods, temperaments, motivations, and desires of other people. The person with a high-profile element in intrapersonal intelligence is likely to end up being a person with detailed, accurate self-knowledge. This person can well assess his own feelings, discriminate among them, and draw upon them to guide behavior. This person has knowledge of his own strengths, weaknesses, desires, and intelligences. One might hypothesize that these two intelligences, plus the linguistic intelligence of being sensitive to meanings and different functions of language, are crucial for effective metacognitive listening. Accordingly, one might research such ideas with respect to the field of listening.

SUMMARY

In summary, metacognition in listening refers to an awareness of one's own knowledge and thought processes in terms of a specific listening task. Metacognition is what listeners know about their sensitivities, abilities, and capacities, about the message sender and message they are to listen to, about the requirements of the task to be completed while providing evidence of learning, and about whether or not they have appropriate strategies to help complete the task.

Metacognitive strategies for listening include listening for meaning (comprehension) and listening for studying and remembering—hopefully also with comprehension. Listening for meaning includes comprehension monitoring strategies for listening given in this chapter. Individual appreciation of problems amenable to "fix-up strategies" vary across age and probably across ability level, though such limits may not be as constraining as was believed. Younger and less able listeners tend not to apply productive metacognitive strategies (such as self-questioning). Well-informed guidance, however, can help both younger and older listeners with an important goal: Use self-monitoring techniques to assess own listening effectiveness—as part of being aware of stages in a listening process.

REFERENCES

Ackerman, B.P. (1986). Children's sensitivity to comprehension failure in interpreting a nonliteral use of an utterance. *Child Development, 57,* 485–497.

Alvermann, D.E. (1987). Metacognition. In D.E. Alvermann, D. Mann, D.W. Moore, & M.W. Conley (Eds.), *Research within reach: Secondary school writing* (pp. 153–168). Newark, DE: International Reading Association.

Anderson, T.H., & Armbruster, B.B. (1984). Studying. In P.D. Pearson (Ed.), *Handbook of reading research* (pp. 657–679). New York: Longman.

Andreassen, C., & Waters, H.S. (1989). Organization during study: Relationships between metamemory, strategy use, and performance. *Journal of Educational Psychology, 81,* 190–195.

Armbruster, B.B., Echols, C.H., & Brown, A.L. (1983). *The role of metacognition in reading to learn: A developmental perspective* (Reading Education Report # 40). Champaign, IL: Center for Studies of Reading. University of Illinois.

Baker, L., & Brown, A.L., (1984). Cognitive monitoring in reading. In J. Flood (Ed.), *Understanding reading comprehension* (pp. 21–44). Newark, DE: International Reading Association.

Bonitatibus, G. (1988). Comprehension monitoring and the apprehension of literal meaning. *Child Development, 59,* 60–70.

Brown, A.L. (1978). Knowing when, where, and how to remember: A problem of metacognition. In R. Glaser (Ed.), *Advances in instructional psychology.* Hillsdale, NJ: Erlbaum.

Brown, A.L. (1980). Metacognitive development and reading. In R.J. Spiro, B.C. Bruce, & W.F. Brewer (Eds.), *Theoretical issues in reading comprehension.* Hillsdale, NJ: Erlbaum.

Brown, A.L., & Palincsar, A.S. (1982). *Inducing strategic learning from texts by means of informed, self-control training.* Cambridge, MA: Bolt, Beranek, & Newman; Urbana, IL: Center for the Study of Reading.

Donaldson, M. (1979). *Children's minds.* New York: Norton.

Flavell, J.H. (1976). Metacognitive aspects of problem solving. In L.B. Resnick (Ed.), *The nature of intelligence.* Hillsdale, NJ: Erlbaum.

Flavell, J.H. (1979). Metacognition and cognitive monitoring: A new area of cognitive-developmental inquiry. *American Psychologist, 34,* 906–911.

Flavell, J.H. (1981). Cognitive monitoring. In W.P. Dickson (Ed.), *Children's oral communication skills* (pp. 35–58). New York: Academic Press.

Flavell, J.H., Speer, J.R., Green, F.L., & August, D.L. (1981). The development of comprehension monitoring and knowledge about communication. *Monographs of the Society for Research in Child Development* (Serial No. 192), *46* (5).

Gardner, H., & Hatch, T. (1989). Multiple intelligences go to school: Educational implication of the theory of multiple intelligences. *Educational Researcher, 18* (8), 4–10.

Justice, E.M., & Weaver-McDougall, R.G. (1989). Adults' knowledge about memory: Awareness and use of memory strategies. *Journal of Educational Psychology, 81*, 214–219.

King, A. (1989, March). *Effects of a metacognitive strategy on high school students' comprehension of lectures.* Paper presented at the Annual Meeting of the American Educational Research Association, San Francisco.

Kurtz, B.E., & Borkowski, J.G. (1987). Development of strategic skills in impulsive and reflective children: A longitudinal study of metacognition. *Journal of Experimental Child Psychology, 43*, 128–148.

Langer, J.A. (1982). From theory to practice: A prereading plan. *Journal of Reading, 24*, 152–156.

Lundsteen, S.W. (1979). *Listening: Its impact on reading and the other language arts.* Urbana, IL: ERIC Clearinghouse for Reading and Communication Skills.

Lundsteen, S.W. (1989). *Language arts: A problem solving approach.* New York: McGraw-Hill.

Markman, E.M. (1977). Realizing that you don't understand: A preliminary investigation. *Child Development, 48*, 986–992.

Markman, E.M. (1979). Realizing that you don't understand: Elementary school children's awareness of inconsistencies. *Child Development, 50*, 643–655.

Markman, E.M. (1981). Comprehension monitoring. In W.P. Dickson (Ed.), *Children's oral communication skills* (pp. 61–84). New York: Academic Press.

Myers, M., & Paris, S.G. (1978). Children's metacognitive knowledge about reading. *Journal of Educational Psychology, 70*, 680–690.

Nichols, R., & Stevens, L.A. (1957). *Are you listening?* New York: McGraw-Hill.

Palincsar, A.S., & Brown, A. (1985). Reciprocal teaching: Activities to promote "reading with your mind." In T.L. Harris & E.J. Cooper (Eds.), *Reading, thinking, and concept development: Strategies for the classroom* (pp. 147–160). New York: The College Board.

Reeve, R.A., & Brown, A.L. (1984). *Metacognition reconsidered: Implications for intervention research* (Technical Rep. No. 328). Champaign, IL: Center for the Study of Reading. University of Illinois at Urbana-Champaign.

Revelle, G.L., Wellman, H.M., & Karabenick, J.D. (1985). Comprehension monitoring in preschool children. *Child Development, 56* (3), 654–663.

Robinson, E.J. (1981, August). *The advancement of children's verbal referential communication skills: The role of metacognitive guidance.* Paper given at the Sixth Biennial Meeting of the International Society for the Study of Behavioral Development, Toronto.

Robinson, E.J., & Robinson, W.P. (1982). Knowing when you don't know enough: Children's judgments about ambiguous information. *Cognition, 12,* 267–280.

Rosenberg, M.B. (1968). *Diagnostic teaching.* Seattle, WA: Special Child Publications.

Singer, J.B., & Flavell, J.H. (1981). Development of knowledge about communication: Children's evaluations of explicitly ambiguous messages. *Child Development, 52,* 1211–1215.

Snyder, M. (1974). Self-monitoring of expressive behavior. *Journal of Personality and Social Psychology, 30,* 526–637.

Sonnenschein, S. (1986). Development of referential communication: Deciding that a message is uninformative. *Developmental Psychology, 22,* 164–168.

Sparks, B. (1990, May). *Metacognitive self-regulation of reading by gifted children.* Paper presented at the thirty-fourth Annual Convention of the International Reading Association, Atlanta, GA.

Tompkins, G.E., Friend, M., & Smith, P.L. (1984, April). *Children's metacognitive knowledge of listening.* Paper presented at the 1984 American Educational Research Association, New Orleans.

Tompkins, G.E., Friend, M., & Smith, P.L. (1987). Strategies for more effective listening. In C.R. Personke & D.D. Johnson (Eds.), *Language arts and beginning teaching* (pp. 30–41). Englewood Cliffs, NJ: Prentice-Hall.

Wolvin, A.D., Fogler, C.L., Brownell, L., Cochran, C., Denniston, C., McDonough, J., Moffitt, F., & Slaughter, P. (1985, March). *Illustrative objectives for listening.* Paper presented at the annual meeting of the International Listening Association, Scottsdale, AZ.

Chapter 7

Listening Disabilities: The Plight of Many

Billie M. Thompson

Sound Listening and Learning Center
Phoenix, AZ

Listening is the most important and most basic of human communication and learning skills. Before we speak, read, or write, we learn to listen. In fact, listening provides the foundation for learning itself. The way the ear functions and integrates information from within the body (vestibular) and outside the body (sound) represents the context of this chapter for understanding how listening impacts our development and learning as humans and how listening disabilities must be understood from a functional and motivational context. A review of recent and significant educational, medical, and paramedical research and literature about learning disabilities, reading problems, attention deficit, speech/language problems, motor control, music, and foreign language problems points toward poor listening as a source of many of these problems, but only when one understands the perspective of the ear's functions and the distinction between listening and hearing. Some of the most interesting questions and insights into how to improve listening come from the work of noted French ear, nose, throat specialist Dr. Alfred Tomatis. If it is true that listening provides the foundation for all speech, language, social communication, music, learning, and literacy skills, the implications for most areas of our lives are huge. The question to answer is whether we will focus on listening disabilities, the plight of many, or listening abilities, the right of all.

LISTENING DISABILITIES: THE PLIGHT OF MANY

The more I go into it, the more I'm convinced that those who know how to listen are the exceptions. Most people hear, they're equipped with ears, and think that they have reached the summit. No. That's a passive phenomenon—you let yourself be bathed in sound, but you don't integrate any of it. But listening is integrating, and the will is an essential part of it, so that we go from a passive phenomenon to an active one. (Alfred Tomatis, in Michaud, 1989, p. 203).

If the 1990s and the early 2000s are to be, as some suggest, the Age of Integration, then it is indeed time to take a vigorous look at listening and listening disabilities. Understanding the ear and its myriad responsibilities will open new avenues to us in our fight against learning disabilities and other listening-related problems. Seeing the ear as integrator for the body and listening as integrator for all communication and learning endeavors is the key.

Dr. Alfred Tomatis (1979), French physician, psychologist, and educator, defines the major role of the ear as integrator. He says the ear is "a structuring organization which, neurologically speaking, coordinates the various levels of the nervous system" (p. 10). During a lifetime spent investigating the ear and its profound impact upon our connections to self, others, and the world, he has observed the relatedness of the following:

- the ear to the voice
- the ear to the entire body
- the ear to levels of personal energy
- audiovocal control to listening problems
- one's developmental history to one's desire to communicate
- listening to language acquisition and development
- posture, music, chant, and word repetition to listening improvement
- auditory processing patterns to listening and learning difficulties
- the mother's voice to communication motivation
- the prenatal development of the ear of the fetus to the phylogenetic development of the ear of the species

All these relationships undeniably connect listening to receptive and expressive language, learning, motor control, motivation, and one's developmental history. It is no wonder, then, that listening disabilities can cause such pervasive problems, both to individuals and to society.

Listening disabilities are significant and not uncommon. Sadly the plight of many, they often go unrecognized and untreated. Personally, educationally, and professionally, such disabilities can have disastrous effects that we are only now beginning to understand and address. Specialists in areas such as education, psychology, performing arts, foreign language, and health care areas (such as medicine, speech pathology, audiology, occupational therapy, osteopathy, physical therapy, homeopathy) all must deal with the problems of listening disabilities. In fact, so must everyone who comes in contact with those who have them.

It is imperative that we begin to appreciate the ear and its relationships to our bodies and our abilities if we are to somehow understand and correct listening disabilities. Identifying the important questions and reviewing what has already been discovered will help us do so. What exactly is listening, and how does it develop? What are listening disabilities and their symptoms? How can we test for them? Who has them and what is their impact? Can they be eliminated, or must we learn to live with them?

WHAT IS LISTENING AND HOW DOES IT DEVELOP?

We have a host of definitions for listening, as Wolvin and Coakley (1991) demonstrate, and others for auditory perception (Myklebust, 1954) and hearing (Tomatis, 1963, 1974a,b, 1989a; Hudspeth, 1989). As Roberts (1988) concludes in a recent *International Listening Association Journal* article about listening tests, we have had difficulty evaluating listening because we have not yet decided what it is. We need before all else to define listening and listening disabilities so we might find ways to test listening, improve listening, and prevent listening disabilities whenever possible.

It is critical to use the context of the nature of matter to establish these definitions and to understand the role of the ear in human development and functioning. To begin, physicists in the past two decades have shown us that our solid world is not so solid. Remarkable photographs and videos by Jenny (1974) introduce us to cymatics and give us visible proof that movement, rhythm, and sound create the form of all matter. From this context, that humans are creatures of movement, rhythm, and sound, the ear becomes a key player as the organ for integrating, organizing, and analyzing these elements.

Tomatis understands the ear from this context. He developed a method to improve listening, and an insightful (some would say revolutionary) theory of hearing which can account for many phenomena traditional theories of hearing cannot explain, including that of listening. He defines listening as the desire to communicate as well as the ability to focus the ear on the specific sounds to be analyzed. Having both a motivational and functional component to his definition is not unlike other definitions of listening proposed by leading researchers and theorists in the field (see Wolvin & Coakley, 1991). However, what is different is defining the ability to listen in specific neurophysiological terms. Tomatis proposes that the distinction between hearing and listening is one that begins at the periphery, the middle ear to be specific.

Tomatis offers valuable insight into the problems connected with poor listening. He stresses that we listen with our whole body, that one of the primary functions of the ear is to create cortical charge for the brain, and that we can only learn to think well if we can listen well. This approach differs from the cognitive listening training programs, which propose that one can listen better if one can think better.

Tomatis observes that we begin to listen prenatally and that the mother's voice plays a major role in inviting the fetus to communicate, develop language, and learn. He has discovered that the voice can produce only what the ear can hear, and he suggests that good listening is critical to our well-being, both to individuals and to society.

By reviewing some of the ear's anatomy and functions, we can better understand listening and the causes of listening disabilities. Without this review, we may continue to overlook the role of the ear in the entire learning process and the role of listening to tuning in to ourselves, others, and the cosmos.

Two Views of the Ear: Orthodox and Tomatis

Orthodox View. Pickles (1988) provides a comprehensive description of the orthodox view of the physiology and functioning of the ear. Weeks (1989, 1991) presents a summary of the orthodox view of the ear and the view of Tomatis as originally described in *Vers l'écoute humaine* (1974ab). Assisted by the U.S. National Fund for Medical Education, Weeks reviewed and summarized much about the ear's functions in light of Tomatis's research.

In general, the orthodox view of the ear is that it is composed of three parts: the outer, middle, and inner ears. Bone vibrations of the skull create sound waves in the outer ear to excite the tympanic membrane. Sound is transmitted via the ossicles from the tympanic membrane to the oval window. From there the endolmyph fluid takes the kinetic energy to the cells of Corti. The tectorial membrane anchors the Corti cells to facilitate the shearing force needed to set up an active potential, which will propagate along the 8th cranial nerve to the brain where the information is decoded and given meaning. The cochlea contains fluid and its kinetic force so as to preserve sound fidelity. The round window dampens kinetic energy.

Listening, when it is considered to be distinct from hearing, is usually defined conceptually as a cognitive process mediated by the brain; little is noted about neurological, neurophysiological, or neuropsychological aspects of listening. Listening can be improved through better or more efficient cognitive skills and is highly dependent on one's motivation or desire. Many listening training approaches achieve success, but not without addressing and mobilizing the individual's motivation. Tomatis says that while motivation is important, the functional ability to listen is equally important, beginning with the middle ear.

Tomatis's View. Tomatis (1974a,b, 1989a) proposed a different view of the ear than Von Békésy (1960), who was awarded a Nobel prize for his theory, because as his method of improving voice and listening evolved, the orthodox view did not explain his results. He has from time to time changed his theory as he gained new insights and as he learned from the research of others. He is the first to say that, if someone can provide a theory which better explains why his method works, he will be the first to listen.

Here are Tomatis' findings. First, he proposes for the ossicles a role other than the conduction of sound. Too much distance separating the incus and stapes and the presence of collagen there prevent the occurrence of sound with a human fidelity capability. The ossicles protect the inner ear from damage by dampening the tympanic membrane vibratory energy via a feedback loop from the endolymph. Second, the endolymph buffers the shearing potential of the vibrational force to protect the Corti cells. Third, bone conduction occurs even when the ossicles are removed, creating a resultant flaccid contact between the tympanic membrane and tympanic sulcus causing air conduction hearing loss. Fourth, bone is the ideal conductor for vibratory energy (the endochondral capsule is the only place in the human body where primitive bone which developed from fetal cartilage persists unchanged, without resorption, from before birth until after death). Bone conduction is the major route of sound conduction to the inner ear. Fifth, the cells of Corti are end organs rather than sensory cells. It is not the endolymph that vibrates the basilar membrane, but, rather, the endolymph vibration results from the resonating membrane. The hair cells play a role in cochlear mechanics. Sixth, the stapedius controls the stapes and regulates high-intensity and high-frequency audition; it is the only muscle of the human body to never rest (Tomatis, 1974b). It is constantly involved in sound perception regulation, from before birth till death (Howell, 1984).

Tomatis understands the ear to be neurologically involved with the optic (2nd), oculomotor (3rd), trochlear (4th), abducens (6th), and spinal-accessory (11th) cranial nerves by coming under the control of the acoustic nerve via what should correctly be called the audio-opto-oculo-cephalo-gyro cross-over. This is the major mechanism of reception and integration of perception (Tomatis, 1974a). He also makes a case for the skin to be viewed as differentiated organs of Corti, based on similarities in cellular structure of these two types of cells.

The vagus nerve connects with the tympanic membrane of the ear and then wanders to connect with and innervate the spino-accessory (11th cranial nerve) and the larynx area responsible for vocalization. The vagus subsequently connects the ear to every organ in the body and, through sound stimulation, can effect neurovegetative changes via this connection.

Tomatis and others (Hudspeth, 1989) acknowledge the importance of the ear due to the volume of the human nervous system devoted to the auditory and vestibular systems. In exploring the many functions of the human ear, Tomatis also describes what most view as two systems (cochlear and vestibular) as really being portions of one system. By understanding the functions, we can understand the ear's role in learning and define problems with listening which come from poor functioning.

Functions of the Ear

The human ear has at least the following functional capabilities, which can be altered at any age:

1. to transmit energy (cortical charge) to the brain
2. to integrate information from sound and motor movements to enable the development of verticality, laterality, and language
3. to establish a right lead ear for efficient audiovocal control
4. to establish balance/equilibrium and to stimulate neurovegetative balance
5. to perceive sound (hear)
6. to attend to and to discriminate between sounds we want to hear and to tune out those we do not want (listen)
7. to locate sounds spatially

Tomatis acknowledges all of these functions and developed techniques to restore to the ear its essential functional effectiveness when the cause is not sensorineural damage. Sometimes what appears to be an organic or sensorineural difficulty is at least partly due to poor functioning, delayed development, and/or to one's emotions. When poor functioning occurs, poor self-esteem, low motivation, and even depression may follow. It is worthwhile to take a more indepth look at each function to better identify symptoms of poor listening.

Cortical Charge from High-Frequency Sounds. We have some approximately 32,000 Corti cells (hair cells) in each ear. Hudspeth (1989) reviewed the anatomy of the ear and described these hair cells of the two cochlea as responding more than 100,000 times a second to the minute motions presented. Each hair cell (Corti cell) is tuned to a particular frequency of stimulation. Hudspeth infers that the responsiveness of hair cells to high frequencies of stimulation implies that transduction channels are very rapidly gated. Whatever the exact count, researchers agree on the presence of more densely packed Corti cells in the area of the basilar membrane reserved for high-frequency stimulation. In comparison, the area for low-frequency stimulation is much less dense. This leads Tomatis to theorize that high-frequency sounds are very energizing and stimulate and charge the brain so it has a greater possibility to learn to think. The effect of this fight against gravity, which is needed to observe a good vertical posture so one can better hear the high-frequency range, is a great gain of energy. For Tomatis, the ear is primarily a system to effect a cortical charge and increase the electrical potential of the brain.

Sound is transformed into nervous influx by the cells of the Organ of Corti in the inner ear, sent on to the cortex of the brain, and from there to the entire body to tone up the whole system and impart greater dynamism. Not all sounds give this charging effect. Lower-frequency sounds not only supply insufficient energy to the cortex, but may even tire the person by inducing motor responses which absorb more energy than the ear can provide.

Tomatis observes that those who lose high-frequency reception often have an accompanying loss of energy and motivation, fatigue, bad posture, and problems with attention, concentration, and memory. People who tend to be tired or depressed often have dull, toneless voices with very little high-frequency content. Changes in all of these factors, but particularly inreased concentration and memory, can help the person considerably to improve communication and learning.

The Ear as Integrator. Tomatis describes how the vestibular (balancing) and cochlear (decoding of sound) functions of the ear are joined in a single system. Phylogenetically, the vestibule analyzes larger movements, those within the body, and the cochlea evolved as an addition to analyze smaller acoustical type movements.

The influence of the ear is vast. In fact, its involvement can be found at every level of the nervous system.... Modern physiology is leaning towards a more unified view of the whole...the cochleo-vestibular apparatus, having reached a completely new dimension...is involved as an inductor, or organizer in the embryological sense of the word. I see it as the inductor which leads the nervous system to become what it is. (Tomatis, 1979, p. 5).

Anatomically, the vestibular nerve presents itself at every level of the medulla and is thereby directly connected with all the muscles of the body. Tomatis proposes the vestibular integrator role for the ear, noting that all muscles depend on the vestibule for their tone, equilibrium, and relative position with relation to the whole body (Tomatis, 1979).

Closely associated with this integrator is the optic or visual integrator. It is composed of the retina, optic nerve, thalamo-cortical tract, occipital area, and the tecto-spinal tract going down to the anterior roots of the medulla. The eye muscles are ordered by the vestibular integrator, as are all other muscles of the body.

Third and last is the cochlear or linguistic integrator, which gathers nerve tracts from the dorsal and ventral nuclei reaching the temporal area of the brain after passing through the pulvinar, back part of the thalamus. It then goes to the neocerebellum, where it connects with the vestibular analyzers through the surface network on the cerebellum, and then it returns to charge the brain through the frontal and parietal nerve tracts and some fronto-pontic and parieto-pontic fibers. This mass also connects with the vestibular tracts at the anterior roots after branching through the red nucleus. Tomatis thinks of the cochlear integrator as a linguistic dynamic that "step by step, guides the nervous system to its human fulfillment...[and] appears to be so much better adapted to language than what it was fashioned for" (Tomatis, 1979, p. 9). From this perspective, "learning appears as the result of a saturation, of a massive intake by the nervous system...[and] the whole body is involved in this process" (Tomatis, 1979, p. 9).

Tomatis (1971, 1978) observes that these integrators establish three humanizing characteristics, all of which are required for developing good audiovocal control: verticality, laterality, and language.

Vertical posture differentiates humans and animals and allows humans to construct a particular view of the world. Laterality provides a clear differentiation for controlling the body in its upright position. Use of language through voice emerges and, according to Tomatis (1978), "is harmonically related to this developing image of the body" (p. 137).

Laterality refers to the differentiation of function in the brain. A delay in lateralization probably means that the language function is not locked into one cerebral hemisphere. Laterality is a controversial issue, according to Sutaria (1985), and is based on the notion that, "in order for learning to occur normally, the central nervous system must be developed completely and sequentially" (p. 77). Orton (1928) and Delacato (1963) propose this need and describe problems, such as lack of internal awareness of the right and left sides of the body and consequent difficulties in reading and writing.

Listening becomes the foundation skill for learning when we understand this "learning anatomy" involving the ear at every level—physical, mental, and emotional (or as others describe them, body, mind, and spirit).

Right Lead Ear. Closely associated with laterality is an emphasis on which ear should be the lead ear. Tomatis (1953a, 1959, 1962, 1963, 1970a, 1971, 1974a, 1976, 1979) and others (Eisenberg, 1976; Kimura, 1967; Dwyer, Blumstein, & Ryalls, 1982) find that most people need to be right ear dominant to have the most efficient pathway from the auditory input to the brain's processing center in the left hemisphere. Control for speech and voice from the right ear allows the best timbre, speech flow, and melody and rhythm control to develop.

Balance. Most people know that the ear is involved in equilibrium, or vertical balance. Another kind of balance can occur through sound stimulation, that of the sympathetic and parasympathetic nervous systems. Tomatis (1974b) describes how the vagus nerve, the sensory auricular branch of the pneumogastric nerve, regulates through its branches the larynx, the pharynx, and the organs of the body. The auricular branch connects to the outer surface of the eardrum, thus forming a link between our inner, neurovegetative life, and the outside world.

Figure 7.1 shows this connection of how listening affects the entire body.

Hearing and Auditory Perception. Tomatis (1974a,b, 1989a) gives a good account of how hearing occurs, and Hudspeth (1989) describes hearing in the inner ear via the hair cells (Corti cells). Hearing occurs without effort or analysis, much like an open microphone that picks up sounds indiscriminantly. Hearing and listening are often confused, but, according to Tomatis (1974b, 1987), they are not the same.

> Hearing is a passive action falling within the realm of sensation, whereas listening is an active process that falls within the realm of perception. The two are totally different. Hearing is essentially passive; listening requires voluntary adaptation. When hearing gives way to listening, one's awareness increases, the will is aroused, and all aspects of our being are involved at the same time. Concentration and memory, our tremendous memory, are testimony to our listening ability. (Tomatis, 1987, p. 23)

Figure 7.1.   Pneumogastric nerve connects the ear to the entire body or the visceral organs

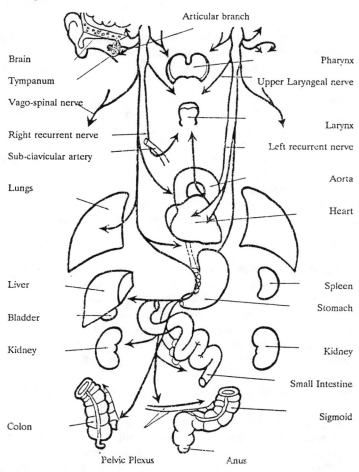

From *Vers l'ecoute humaine,* by Tomatis, 1974b, p. 68. Reprinted by permission.

Berry and Eisenson (1956) say that children with auditory perception problems can hear sounds but do not recognize their meaning. From Tomatis's view, they hear but do not listen. Myklebust (1954) defines *auditory perception* as the ability "to structure the auditory world and select those sounds which are immediately pertinent to adjustment" (p. 158). This definition of auditory perception is more similar to that of *listening,* because it adds selectivity. According to Lerner (1981), auditory perception has remained a relatively neglected research area.

Sutaria (1985) lists four types of auditory perception problems: (a) auditory discrimination of differences and similarities, (b) auditory foreground-background differentiation, (c) auditory blending, and (d) auditory sequencing.

If hearing and listening are different, then one can have good hearing and poor listening. On tests that do not differentiate between them, one can appear to have poor hearing when in fact poor listening accounts for part or all of the problem.

Increasing attention is being given to children who find it painful to listen to certain sounds they perceive to be overly loud. A number of autistic children are reported to have this difficulty. In fact, one, and only one, autistic girl was described as cured after receiving a treatment using sounds that allowed her oversensitivity to lessen, thus opening many more learning opportunities because she no longer had to protect herself by tuning out (Stehli, 1991). Stehli's book in particular has done much to focus public attention on the role of auditory processing and listening in many children with communication problems and to programs which may help.

Focusing on Sounds. Tomatis brings attention to a unique motor activity, that of the muscles in the middle ear that allow a person to focus on specific desired sounds and tune out those not wanted. Little is written about the two tiniest muscles of the body, even in medical literature. Tomatis wrote extensively about the role of the stapedius and tensor tympani muscles (1974ab). Simmons (1964), and more recently Borg and Counter (1989), examined this topic. Tomatis accords these two small muscles a fundamental role in the process of listening, which is a neurophysiological focusing process mediated by the muscles of the middle ear.

Listening is the active focusing of the middle ear to accommodate and enhance the sensory perception of those sounds of particular interest, those the individual wishes to analyze and interpret with maximum efficiency (Tomatis, 1954, 1963, 1971, 1974a,b, 1977; Tomatis & Moulonguet, 1960). It acts more like a directional microphone to highlight that part of the sound spectrum that needs analysis and diminishes the extraneous or background sound. This is accomplished by adjusting the tensions of the tympanum and the pressure of the endolymphatic fluid in the cochlea.

> One very important factor is the ability to analyze sound, to listen selectively, and to make subtle discriminations between sounds. When the selectivity is open, the ear is able to analyze sounds across the spectrum, which, you remember, goes from 16 Hz to 16,000 Hz. (Tomatis, 1987, p. 24)

In its fullest elaboration, listening is implicated, not only in aural comprehension, but also in voice, speech, body posture and body image, and the whole of our relational world.

Spatialization of Sound. Finding the spatial origin of a sound is a matter of timing. The two ears must work together well to locate the direction from which a sound comes. When this timing is off, difficulties with reading and writing are also reported. While some may minimize attention to this problem, Tomatis believes it is of major importance, because it reveals the surprising degree of confusion some people experience in auditory processing (1971, 1978).

Problems in any of these functions can trigger or cause listening disabilities at any age. They can begin prenatally.

Prenatal Listening and Human Development

The area that is the most enticing for Tomatis in his work is that related to fetal audition. He says his own premature birth caused him to search for what he had missed (1977, 1991). He was among the first to postulate that the fetus hears (1963)—common knowledge now (Eisenberg, 1976; Verny, 1981; Chamberlain, 1983; Spence & DeCasper, 1986), but not 30 years ago.

Listening actually begins in the womb. The ear and the neuronic tracks between the ears and the brain are already fully developed and operational in the fifth month of pregnancy (Tomatis, 1987). If human auditory development is similar to that of animals, then research by Abrams et al. (1987) with sheep lends support to Tomatis' contention that the ear plays a vital role in developing human potential. Abrams et al. found that, at least for fetal sheep, normal growth and maturation of the brain depends on an intact auditory system.

To what is the fetus listening anyway? Certainly to the sounds of the mother's body, and more importantly, to her voice. For decades preceding other researchers, Tomatis contended that the voice of the mother speaking and singing plays a key role in the child's language acquisition and development and in social communication skill development (Tomatis, 1963, 1981). His research showed that the fetus listens to the highly filtered mother's voice and that high-frequency sounds thereof are received and charge the brain of the fetus. Although his theory has changed over the years regarding the exact mechanism by which this is done, research by others now supports many of his contentions.

We know the following from research by DeCasper and Fifer (1980), Spence and DeCasper (1982, 1986), Eisenberg (1976), Querleu et al. (1988a, 1988b), and Querleu and Renard (1989):

1. The fetus hears by at least $4^1/_2$ months in utero.
2. Newborns prefer the voice of their mother over other voices. More specifically, they prefer her intonation pattern.
3. Newborns prefer familiar stories and poems read by their mothers to nonfamiliar ones.
4. At 2 months, French babies (the only ones researched) distinguish between individual syllables.
5. One-day-old babies synchronize their movements to an adult's speech articulation.
6. New amplification techniques have indicated that the attenuation of both music and speech sounds above 2,000 Hz have been overestimated and that high speech frequencies would be transmitted.

Gilmor (1989c) provides a summary of the genesis of listening and the Tomatis Method. Tomatis contends that during pregnancy, especially the last half, the intonation, richness, and emotional coloring of the mother's voice are important determinants of the desire to deploy one's listening for communication with the external world. The rhythm and structure of the native language spoken by the mother will also be imprinted on the nervous system of the developing fetus. Everything except the semantic meaning of the prenatal listening experience will be registered and stored for future reference. But what is most important is the kindling of the desire to communicate.

The inability to hear the natural mother's voice (the one familiar connection between fetal and birth worlds) may have a traumatic emotional impact on infants, whether it is because the child functionally cannot hear her voice due to a physiological difficulty or developmental delay or because the mother is not there with the child, due to some extended physical separation such as adoption, illness requiring hospitalization of either child or mother, or death of the mother. The constitution of the child is certainly a factor, too, for while some will succumb to trauma, others will not. If the infant decides to tune out some sounds that are too loud or traumatic in self-defense, he or she may not be able to tune in at will later because of nonuse. Parents may be unaware this is occurring and even be listening disabled themselves!

Early emotional and functional auditory problems can greatly influence the developing child's learning potential. De Villiers and de Villiers (1979) comment on language acquisition and individual differences therein:

> There may well be several alternative routes to the mastery of the full adult language.... The documentation of these individual differences and the range of normal variation in the rate and pattern of language development is

crucial for determining the nature and extent of many language disorders. But it is also important to our understanding of the process of first-language learning that we continue to seek the sources of these individual differences, be they in the child's intellectual or physical development, in his interaction with his parents, or in the particular language input that he gets. (p. 138).

A solution must access and turn on more of the child's inner natural ability and potential, so that he or she can learn and communicate more effectively in whatever situation is experienced. It may be that the biases and strategies for language acquisition arise from the parents' speech to the child, the parents' reaction to the child's speech, the parents' encouragement or lack thereof toward speech, and/or the child's memory and organization abilities. Listening is certainly involved in all of these. On top of the external influences and personal abilities, a critical period for learning a first language seems to exist and is described in relation to the wild children found in captivity who have difficulty picking up language if they do not get enough exposure to it during infancy (de Villiers & de Villiers, 1979, pp. 128–129). Regarding second-language learning, "the critical period applies more to the sounds of speech than to grammar or vocabulary" (p. 127). One of the leading researchers on language acquisition, Menyuk (1981), divides language development into three periods: infancy, age 2–11, and adolescent and postadolescent. The effect of any developmental difficulty will depend on both the nature of the difficulty (physiological, cognitive, or social) and the internal and external mechanisms employed to overcome the difficulty.

> Both neurological and cognitive factors have been suggested to account for the observed differences in second-language acquisition, pre- and postpuberty, and the effect of trauma. It may be that speech perception and production are set in the preadolescent period. This would account for the retention of the native language accent by adult second-language learners. (Menyuk, p. 156)

Hearing, Listening, and Learning

While hearing is a major function of the ear, problems with hearing must be distinguished from problems with listening. Berg (1987), in a study supported by the U.S. Department of Education ("Project Listening in Urban and Rural Noise (LURN)"), presents a summary of research relevant to listening and acoustics for normal and hard of hearing students.

According to Berg, hearing screening levels for identifying hard of hearing students under the All Handicapped Children's Law are now more likely to be set at 15 dB, rather than 25 to 30 dB. A hearing loss of 15dB is enough to cause learning problems. Physicians say a loss of 25 or 30 dB represents a loss as medically defined. Hearing loss is often accompanied by listening problems.

The term *listening disabilities* frequently is confused with *hearing disfunction*. The two are not the same. Confusions occur when poor listening is tied first to hearing loss. In defining listening problems related to hearing loss, Berg (1987) defines *listening* as "detection, discrimination, recognition, or comprehension of speech through audition, vision, or both in combination" (p. 65). Interestingly, his definition focuses on the relationship of the ear for language and meaning through speech, just as Tomatis does.

Many studies (Wrightstone, Aronow, & Moskowitz, 1962; Lennenberg, 1967; Quigley, 1969; Gentile, 1972) show hearing-impaired students perform less well academically than non-hearing-impaired students.

The impact of hearing loss is tied to language deficit as researched by Quigley and Thomure (1968) and Blair, Peterson, and Viehweg (1985). Using the Stanford Achievement Test in the former and the Iowa Test of Basic Concepts in the latter, these researchers found that as hearing deficits increased, academic deficits increased. Although differences in achievement are noted, differences in intellectual potential do not show up between these two groups (Moores, 1982).

If, on the other hand, hearing is normal and listening is poor, Tomatis explains why differences in IQ subscores, such as on the Weschler Intelligence Test, show up. In those subtest scores showing a high performance quotient but a low verbal quotient, lack of integration of incoming information causes the difference. The child may be very intelligent and have to struggle greatly because of verbal difficulties. Here is additional substantiation that good listening allows intelligence potential to develop, and research reported by Gilmor (1982) tends to support this.

Other data about hard-of-hearing students reviewed by Berg (1987) from Gengel (1971) show that those with bilateral loss have the worst time with listening, those with unilateral loss the next worst, and "even students with normal hearing cannot listen optimally in a typically noisy school classroom, even when the room has considerable acoustical treatment" (Berg, 1987, p. 98).

Noise and reverberation both affect listening scores. Bess and Tharpe (1988) concur that even students with unilateral hearing loss are 10 times more likely to experience academic failure than the normal population. And those with a loss in the right ear do worse than those with loss in the left ear (Oyler, Oyler, & Matkin, 1987).

The following from Berg (1987) are other important concepts that connect hearing loss, listening difficulties, and learning, as well as distinguish hearing loss from listening disabilities:

The degree of hearing loss need only be minimal to cause deficit. (p. 1)

The most frequent and most basic secondary consequence of hearing loss is listening deficit. (p. 1)

In addition to the hard of hearing, many other children have listening problems. (p. 3)

Listening is particularly important to children during their early language learning years. Often the hearing loss or auditory processing problem is not discovered until age five, and the child begins kindergarten with a language problem that makes listening even more difficult (p. 3).

Hearing, Listening, and Speaking

Literally from the beginning stages of fetal development, the voice and ear are connected. Tomatis reminds us that the muscles of the ear and the muscles of the jaw and the face have the same fetal development origin, the first and second branchial arches. A person's language and voice will be good if his or her listening function is good. Tomatis implicates the vestibular system, including breath and posture, when problems are observed in a person's speech and voice development (Tomatis, 1978, 1987).

Berg (1987) describes one speech need for those suffering from hearing loss: "Students must be able to detect speech sounds before they can learn to recognize them" (p. 75). This finding is identical to Tomatis's finding for all people (Tomatis, 1956) and was subsequently replicated at the Sorbonne in 1957. That "the voice can only produce what the ear can hear" is known as the Tomatis Effect (le Gall, 1961). Both the quality of voice and speech fluency are largely affected by the quality of the ear's listening.

Tomatis discovered this ear-voice link during his early work with professional singers (1974c, 1977, 1991). He applied engineering principles to train or retrain their listening in order to improve their speech and singing voices by focusing on the missing sounds (Tomatis, 1953a,b, 1956; Tomatis & Moulonguet, 1960). The ear-voice link became an ear-voice-learning link when those using the method discovered changes beyond those related to their voices.

While Berg's focus is on testing for hearing ability, he observes that audiologists work almost exclusively with identifying children with hearing loss, while speech language pathologists work primarily with students without hearing loss. To improve listening for those with hearing loss, Berg recommends identifying hearing loss, speech deficits, and listening problems. He also recommends changing classroom acoustics and student proximity to the teacher as well as managing hearing aids and amplification equipment. Tomatis suggests that even with a hearing loss, some speech problems may be due to poor listening.

WHAT EXACTLY ARE LISTENING DISABILITIES?

Learning Disabilities and Listening Disabilities

Are learning disabilities and listening disabilities the same? Are poor readers learning and/or listening disabled? Despite several decades of research, programs, legislation, and funding, we still have varying, and sometimes conflicting, definitions of learning disabilities, little research about auditory perception problems, and a multitude of different projects and programs to improve some aspect of learning.

Gerber and Bryen (1981) give an overview of the historical trends in the field of learning disabilities. They have been defined as the result of organic sources such as cerebral dysfunctions, perceptual motor dysfunctions, and neurological development maturation delays associated with cerebral dominance developmental delay.

In 1963, when the term *learning disabilities* was coined by Samuel Kirk, differing categories were created; these categories roughly fall into two groups: those with an organic origin in the brain (dysfunction, damage, injury, disease), and those whose symptoms were behaviorally displayed (dyslexia, disability, handicap, syndrome). They were also called brain dysfunction syndrome and minimal brain dysfunction syndrome. Either the part has a problem, the integration of the part with other parts has a problem, or the programming itself has a problem. Sensory problems with hearing, vision, motor control and balance were acknowledged, but no notice was given to the ear as integrator.

The Illinois Test of Psycholinguistic Abilities (ITPA), developed by Kirk, McCarthy, and Kirk (1968), significantly changed the context in which learning disabilities were held, from being visual processing dysfunctions to having auditory and language processing deficiencies. Lerner (1976) showed this trend in special education.

Johnson and Myklebust (1967) and Ayers (1974) connected certain types of learning disability to dysfunctions in the brain's integrative functions. Birch (1973) showed neurologically impaired children were significantly delayed in their ability to integrate information from the visual and auditory channels.

According to Kephart (1960), Barsch (1968, 1976), Frostig, Lefever, and Whittlesey (1964) and Ayers (1974), many learning disabilities can be attributed to deficits in perceptual and motor development.

Tallal (1975, 1976, 1978; Tallal & Piercy, 1973, 1974) concluded that delays in language acquisition are somehow related to deficits in the ability to process rapidly presented auditory information. Increasing the length of the acoustic stimulus helped improve sound discrimination. Rosenthal (1974) hypothesized that, underlying delayed or disordered language, is a generalized (not specific auditory) processing disorder in all perceptual modalities.

Much has been done in the field of reading, too. Lerner (in Kirk & McCarthy, 1975) shows a discrepancy in how reading specialists focus on developing skills for the *dyslexic child* (typically defined as one who has difficulty with reading or writing but with no observable cause) and how learning disabilities specialists focus on underlying deficits or disorders with broader ranging remediation. Early on, the underlying cause was thought to be visual perceptual problems. Jansky and de Hirsch (1973) show an important predictive relationship between oral language ability and reading achievement. They conclude that both receptive and expressive spoken language abilities are essential foundation skills for reading and that good reading training takes this into account.

Rudel and Denckla (1976) found that, regardless of sensory modality, reading age only correlates with temporal-spatial matching. Gibson and Levin (1975) conclude that some process similar to that required for initial reading success probably "involves extraction of structure of patterned information, the relations between subordinate units, both over time and space and within and across modalities. Both analyzing a pattern and perceiving the structure of a pattern are necessary for reading" (p. 250). Spatial and relationship analyses require good auditory functioning and integration. Listening disabilities are at the heart of many reading problems.

The ear's role in learning disabilities began to emerge from these earlier investigations, but it only becomes clear once the ear's role of integrator is acknowledged. Where, then, do we place listening disabilities in the realm of learning disabilities?

Perhaps it will help to keep this role of integrator in mind as we consider the confusion about the definition of learning disabilities from the law which attempts to deal with such disabilities. Public Law 94-142 gives the following operational definition of a learning disability:

> The child does not achieve commensurate with his or her age and ability levels in one or more of seven specific areas when provided with learning experiences appropriate for the child's age and ability levels. (Lerner, 1981, p. 13)

The U. S. Office of Education's definition of learning disability, as it appeared in the 1977 Federal Register, is presented by Donahue, Pearl, and Bryan (1982):

> Children with learning disabilities are defined as those with normal intelligence, intact sensory and emotional functioning, but who still exhibit a disorder in one or more of the basic psychological processes involved in understanding or using language, spoken or written. (p. 399)

In 1981, the National Joint Committee on Learning Disabilities (Hammill, Leigh, McNutt, & Larsen, 1981) defined learning disabilities such that other disfunctions (such as hearing loss) could occur simultaneously with them.

The inclusion of normal intelligence implies the person's potential is probably normal, but average school-based achievement is usually not attained. Instead, the result in actual circumstances is for schools to document greatly the disabilities, ignore the potential, and make both parent and child focus on past performance rather than on developing potential. It is a frequent lament in my consultations with parents and children.

Uncertainty reigns when there is lack of agreement over even the basic definition of a learning disability. This situation creates confusion among those professionals working with learning disabled persons. Still another review, by Wallach and Butler (1984), regarding historical trends identified two general categories of processing models that originally attempted to identify mental processes that cause learning disabilities: one related to auditory processing deficits, and the other to general cognitive processing deficits. Their perspective adds to our understanding of poor listening as an underlying disability.

The auditory/linguistic processing model arose primarily to extend the medical model and attempted to explain causes primarily within the category of developmental language dysphasia. It suggested that language disorders result from deficits specific to auditory/linguistic processing, including sequencing, memory, and discrimination processes. Deficiencies in these skills were thought to cause the language disorder, and the solution was to work on them directly in order to improve general language development.

But Wallach and Butler believed that the skills being called processing skills were actually just one particular use of language. Some attention was given to possible subtle neurological damage, but a way to identify such damage did not exist. They concluded that efforts turned away from attempting to specify anatomical or physiological deficits characteristic of medical model interpretations of language learning disabilities.

Cognitive processing models developed out of influences from information-processing theory, linguistics, and cognitive psychology (especially symbolic function). Treatment of learning disabilities by professionals using this model varies according to which of the following two views is held: (a) the processes underlie the use of language; or (b) the processes are one type of language use. If the first is held, then one would believe that remedial work on the processes would affect the social-interactive use of language in context. If the second is held, then work on metalinguistic skills would enhance only the metalinguistic uses of language. The models alert us to the possibility of multiple deficits and to the possibility that while some individuals may need to work on symbolic function, others may need to work on hierarchic organization.

Listening and Listening Disabilities: Definitions

The ear provides many functions, and listening does, in fact, involve the whole body. Our definition of *listening* and *listening disabilities* keeps this in mind. The definition of *listening* proposed here is that of Tomatis, that listening is the active, motivated whole-body tuning in to sounds one wants to hear and tuning out those one does not. *Listening disabilities* are the dysfunctions physically, emotionally, and mentally caused by the inability of the ear to focus on sounds (movements of the air) it wants to hear, to tune out those it does not want, and to naturally integrate and analyze those sounds and the internal movements of the body (motor) for our use. This definition acknowledges the singularity of the cochlear-vestibular system, desire as an important component of listening, and the ear's role of integrator.

From this context, a listening disability exists when we have (a) poor functioning of either cochlear or vestibular portions, or (b) poor control of and lack of harmony between both systems, and/or (c) we are emotionally not willing to tune in. Symptoms of listening disabilities are observable in many areas.

Symptoms of Listening Disabilities

The Listening Checklist shown in Figure 7.2 is for some people their first encounter with connecting problems of expressive and receptive language, motor control, attitude/behavior, and developmental difficulties to a single source, that of poor listening.

People of any age can show these symptoms. This checklist is a good screening device for parents, teachers, and other professionals interested

Figure 7.2. Listening Checklist.

The trouble with listening, you'd think, is that it's an invisible act. You can't see if a child's ears are shut, even though the consequences of not listening, in terms of self-esteem, happiness and achievement may be devastating.

To help parents and teachers identify children with a listening problem, we've devised the following checklist. There is no "score" on this checklist; it is only a guide to identification.

Receptive Listening/Language

This is the listening which focuses outside, on what another is saying, or what is going on in the home or school environment.

- ☐ has short attention span
- ☐ is easily distractible, especially by peripheral noises
- ☐ is oversensitive to certain sounds
- ☐ misinterprets questions or requests
- ☐ has difficulty with auditory discrimination (confuses similar sounding words or consonants), often asks for repetition
- ☐ is able to follow only one or at most two instructions in sequence

Expressive/Listening/Language

The listening which focuses inside, which monitors and reproduces correctly what one hears, especially one's own voice.

- ☐ voice quality (flat, monotonous)
- ☐ speech lacks fluency, rhythm, is hesitant
- ☐ vocabulary is weak
- ☐ sentence structure is poor or stereotyped
- ☐ singing is out of tune
- ☐ confuses or reverses letters
- ☐ has difficulty with reading (dyslexia), especially out loud
- ☐ poor spelling

Motor Skills

"Listening to the body." These skills are intimately related to the vestibular system of the ear, which controls balance, coordi- nation and body image.

- ☐ poor posture; slouching and slumping
- ☐ uncoordinated body movement, fidgeting, clumsiness
- ☐ poor sense of rhythm
- ☐ messy handwriting
- ☐ a hard time with organization, structure
- ☐ confusion of left and right, mixed dominance

Behavioral and Social Adjustment

A listening problem is often accompanied by the following:

- ☐ low tolerance of frustration
- ☐ poor self-image, self confidence
- ☐ difficulty in making friends, relating with peers
- ☐ withdrawal/avoidance
- ☐ irritability
- ☐ hyperactive tendencies
- ☐ is inordinately tired at the end of the school day
- ☐ low motivation, loss of interest in work
- ☐ immaturity (indicates lack of desire to grow)

Developmental History

Listening difficulties usually develop well before school age. If you've noted any of the signs above, you can trace the problem further by checking into the following:

- ☐ a stressful pregnancy
- ☐ difficult birth
- ☐ adoption
- ☐ early separation from the mother
- ☐ delay in motor development
- ☐ delay in language development
- ☐ recurring ear infections

From *Listen, Newsletter of the Listening Centre*, Gilmor & Madaule, 1988, p. 3. Reprinted by permission.

in identifying listening disabilities. It draws the attention of professional and nonprofessional alike, for it brings together symptoms of problems in different areas of research, all of which could lead us to the ear—if we know to follow. A description of some behaviors of children who have these symptoms is given by Thompson, Madaule, and Gilmor (1988–1989) and is found throughout the anthology by Gilmor, Madaule, and Thompson (1989). A review of research connects problems in several areas to listening if we keep in mind the definitions and list of symptoms given here.

Specific Areas of Disability

Speech/Language. Listening and speaking are intimately tied together in their anatomical development (Tomatis 1953b, 1954, 1956, 1963, 1967, 1972a, 1974b, 1979, 1987; Tomatis & Moulonguet, 1960). Might a listening disability cause a speech disability just because of this functional connection? Might we change speaking just by changing listening, as the Tomatis Effect implies?

Tomatis's clinical research, and that in schools and centers using his method (including ours in Phoenix), show that, when a child's listening improves, parents report many and varied changes: sentences become longer and more complex, participation in conversations increases, speech becomes clearer and possesses more modulation, relationships with friends and siblings improve, and the child begins to hum and sing more frequently. The coordination extends to the children's bodies as well, and they notice more, pay attention to more, and therefore have more to say. They can find language to describe feelings and desires. They begin to fit in, to know how they are related to others. Drawings take on dimension and colors change; names and other language are written on them with no prompting.

Belk (1989) describes use of the Tomatis Method from a speech pathology/audiology perspective and tells why improving listening first (so one can hear the sounds to be made) sometimes succeeds or accelerates improvement when traditional speech methods do not. Her training in both areas and in Special Education allows her to see connections others without this integrated background might miss. Used to establish good audio-vocal control and/or to prepare the client for additional traditional speech-language therapy, she concludes that the Tomatis Method is an appropriate treatment modality. It works even when major psychological or physiological causes have stopped communication.

Dyslexia. Serendipitously, Tomatis's work with professional singers led to the discovery that learning disabilities, especially reading and writing difficulties (dyslexia), are tied to listening. Some of the singers Tomatis helped reported additional beneficial changes in their reading and writing abilities, memory, concentration, sleeping and eating patterns, and energy levels. Later some of the singers brought him their children to see if the Method would help them overcome problems in school in these same areas (Tomatis, 1978, 1991).

Tomatis comments on dyslexia at length in his book *Education and Dyslexia* (in French, 1971; in English, 1978). "The dyslexic's real problem is an inability to interpret the world of human beings. Because he is unable to apprehend this world, he is also unable to see himself as an integral part of it" (Tomatis, 1978, pp. 133–134). Here is a description of what it is like to be dyslexic from psychologist Paul Madaule (1989), who has experienced dyslexia and the Tomatis Method first hand.

> The dyslexic, because of a dysfunctional auditory receiver, is a stranger to his own language. Any educational method used with dyslexic children must deal with the fact that the sound information they perceive, regardless of its original quality, is always distorted. (p. 55)

> The dyslexic is absorbed to such an extent in his problems that he often cuts himself off from the best parts of his own nature. His own image is reflected back to him in a deformed fashion, as if he were seeing himself through a trick mirror that makes everything look ugly. The therapist's role is to focus the patient's attention and interest on the healthy side of his being, to offset his distorted, dyslexified perception and to awaken him to the genuinely positive dimension within. (p. 59)

It appears to Tomatis, and others such as Levinson (1984), that reading and writing problems are just one symptom of dyslexia, not the definition of dyslexia itself. Tomatis says these problems affect one-third of French children (1971, 1978, 1988), and recommends a program, such as the Tomatis Method, to help them construct a normal perspective of the surrounding world.

Connecting the ability to listen with the ability to read becomes easy when we acknowledge that reading is a language-based skill, not a visual-based skill per se; that is, deficits in language more than in visual perception explain the problems. Orton (1925) explained the basis for developmental dyslexia in neurological terms as a lack of a well-established hemispheric dominance. Vellutino, Steger, and Kandel (1972; Vellutino, Smith, & Steger, 1975) showed that verbal labeling problems, rather than visual perceptual confusion, were the basis for reading reversal and orientation errors. Wallach and Butler (1984) concur that, though visual problems can cause reading problems, "in most cases alternative explanations, relating to linguistic rather than visual-processing deficits, appear to have more salience" (p. 272).

Liberman et al. (1980) also tie audition to reading:

the consonant segments of the phonemic message are typically folded, at the acoustic level, into the vowel. The result is that there is no acoustic criterion by which the phonemic segments are dependably marked. However, every syllable that is formed in this way contains a vocalic nucleus and, therefore, a peak of acoustic energy. These energy peaks provide audible cues that correspond to the syllable centers (Fletcher, 1929). Though such auditory cues could not in themselves help a listener to define exact syllable boundaries, they should make it easy for him to discover how many syllables there are and, in that sense, to do explicit syllabic segmentation. (p. 196)

Most recently, using REM brain scans to monitor reading, Montgomery (1989) made some surprising findings contrary to common theory. It has been commonly believed that, to neurologically understand a word that we read or repeat aloud, the brain must first translate the written symbol into an auditory form by sounding out the words in our head. But to the surprise of Marcus Raichle, head of the brain study group at St. Louis, REM images show that this translation is not necessary: "Somehow the visual form of a common word like screen can be directly shot forward to the motor areas controlling the mouth, or the semantic areas within the forehead, without being internally sounded out in the auditory cortex" (p. 60). But something different occurs on the images when a person reads verse and has to consider the way words sound. "Then we see an area near the auditory cortex become active.... This word sounding region in the auditory cortex appears to come into play, even though the sounds are 'only heard in our head'" (p. 60). Furthermore, what is true for adults reading simple, commonly used words may not be true of children learning to read. "'As I remember,' says Raichle, 'when learning to read in first grade, I had to learn to sound out the words on the page.' During this learning experience, he speculates, these phonological coding areas are active. But when one becomes a proficient reader they're no longer necessary," unless, he hypothesizes, a foreign or more complicated word appears, requiring components of this phonological system to come back into the process (p. 65).

This clearly supports the use of oral repetition of sounds and oral reading for poor and beginning readers. This active work is a necessary part of retraining the ear and simulating the most complex stages of language development in order to improve one's reading ability and develop one's learning potential.

The role of auditory processing in reading difficulties is gaining more attention from professionals and researchers such as Bryant and Bradley (1985). They conducted a comprehensive 10-year literature search in many countries and for many ages and grade levels with the following conclusion:

The most obvious and the most consistent of the difficulties which backward readers encounter is with sounds in words. They find it hard to isolate these sounds, to use them to build words, and to see that different words have sounds in common. This means that they are slow to learn about the relationship between letters and sounds, and between groups of letters ('chunks') and sounds. The result is dire. Any child who cannot grasp these relationships is bound to fall behind in learning to read, and even further behind in learning to spell. (Bryant & Bradley, 1985, p. 152)

Laterality/Modality. A *modality* is a channel through which a person interacts with his or her environment. Audition is considered to be a modality, as are vision, motor movement, and speech. Much has been written about laterality and modality separately, yet they may be more related than we at first thought, if only we see the ear as the link they share. If a person is to perceive and make sense of information from his or her environment, he or she must be internally organized first. Perceptual difficulties result in the person seeing, hearing, and experiencing the world differently from those who perceive well. Typical programs to improve modality integration use motor control and perceptual-motor activities. Research by Ayers (1978), Quiros (1976), and Quiros and Shrager (1975) link motor and posture functions to language and learning problems.

Any trauma, illness, or accident that interrupts the child's explorations and interactions adversely affects the development of the organized self. Over confinement to a playpen, restrictions to free movement, some even slight injury to the central nervous system, and an early separation from the natural mother may impede the development of the internal structure. And it is this internal structure upon which school learning depends for success.

When integration of two or more modalities is required, some people do poorly. In a well-functioning child, all the modalities operate well and in a balanced way. Research by Early (1973) shows a sharp difference between normal and learning-disabled children, the former being markedly superior in cross-modal function. In particular, the act of oral reading is a highly integrated skill. Motor and voice functions may organize and promote visual and auditory integration. Listening is the feedback loop for this integration to occur.

To help screen for integration difficulties, Heiniger (1990) offers a 20-minute test a classroom teacher can give to students. Tomatis' Listening Test battery includes a laterality test that does the same (Tomatis, 1953b, 1963, 1971, 1978).

Motor control also impacts the body's skeleton (Upledger & Vredevoogd, 1983). One Doctor of Osteopathy works with some clients from our center and explains to them how the skeleton of the body can be misaligned in specific areas, including craniosacral areas, causing difficulties with speech and language. He adjusts the physiology of the nervous system, musculature, and skeleton to enhance each of their functions. The result ranges from no improvement to improved capacity to use the neuromusculoskeletal system, improved response to other forms of therapy (physical, occupational, speech, and listening), and improved behavior.

Attention Deficit. Bloom and Lahey (1978) believe that auditory language processing problems may result from either an attentional deficit or the inability to integrate information from different sensory modalities. Attending and integrating both involve the ear. Being unable to attach meaning to sound may cause a child to "tune out" either complex input or particular types of input.

Medication, especially methylphenidate (commercially, Ritalin), has been used with hyperactivity (another descriptor often associated with attention deficit), and a review of studies describing its benefits for over 40 years has been made (Millichap, 1977). Its impact is to improve attention, visual perception, conceptualization, and eye-hand coordination, and to decrease hyperactivity. Auditory perception has not been observed to benefit as much as visual perception (Gerber & Bryen, 1981).

Children with attention disorder are theorized to be troubled by too many stimuli that are not task specific. Such children cannot tune out distractions. Studies by Swanson and Kinsbourne (1976) show no academic gains for children on drugs for hyperactivity. One conclusion is that they need to acquire motivation for learning in addition to improved processing. Farnham-Diggory (1978) recommends using special methods to teach complex learning tasks and to focus the attention of hyperactive children, rather than using drugs which have risky side-effects.

Richardson (1975) and Kinsbourne and Caplan (1979) support this view that neuropathology is not the cause of learning disabilities except for a small percentage of cases. Gerber and Bryen (1981) summarized this trend, showing a movement away from medical/etiological emphasis and toward either broadening the spectrum of possible causation or questioning the value or validity of organic diagnosis (p. 19).

Psychology. Whether a listening disability begins with a functional difficulty or an emotional need to tune out, many psychological implications exist for listening disabled youngsters and adults. In fact, it would be a disservice to motivate and enable someone to listen again if you leave him or her in the same disruptive or traumatic environment that caused the problem, either in fact or from his or her perspective. They would just have to "tune out" again for self-protection! Therefore, the use of counseling to assist both the listening disabled and those who interact with them is needed. Psychologist Tim Gilmor (1989a) summarizes psychological factors involved in poor listening that begin very early in life:

> A number of encounters in a person's life can detrimentally affect the desire to listen, and thus to communicate. A difficult prenatal life, traumatic birth, early separation from the mother, health problems in infancy and early childhood, all of these can be critical. Often the child's only possible response is to 'tune out' his environment by selectively dampening critical frequencies in the sounds around him. This is an unconscious process, which can quickly become a permanent filter through which the child's world is perceived darkly. (Gilmor, 1989a, pp. 9–10)

According to Tomatis (1963, 1967, 1970a, 1971, 1972a,b, 1977, 1978, 1991), a listening problem that is not the result of organic lesion generally has a psychological origin. In thousands of case studies he observed that many clients experienced or described times in their early lives when there were refusals or reluctance to accept certain stimuli from the environment, specifically those of spoken language. It manifests itself at the physiological level by a relaxation of the muscles of the middle ear, which considerably impedes the passage of sound. If the muscles of the middle ear are inactive for too long, they lose their tonicity. Sounds are imprecisely perceived, and as a result incorrectly analyzed.

Frostig (1976) attributes learning disabilities to the interplay among organic and environmental causes. Gerber and Bryen (1981) conclude explanations and assessment and treatment for learning disabilities "must include cognitive, psychosocial, and linguistic components" (p. 20). Tomatis (1963, 1967, 1971, 1977, 1978, 1991) developed the science of audio-psycho-phonology to acknowledge the relationship of ear, voice, and psyche.

Programs such as psychologist Lee Gibson's PEAKE Experience provide intensive process-oriented workshops that educate older teens and adults about ways to begin to perceive what they have been tuning out for years for self-defense. They learn techniques to improve relationships, to acknowledge others by listening, to become responsible for their communications and behavior, and to feel emotionally empowered and able to more fully develop their potential. They learn to listen to themselves and others—to the degree they have the functional ability to do so. Some of our clients have participated in both his workshop and the Tomatis Method, some starting with one, and some with the other. PEAKE is an acronym for the personal change process (Perceive, Experience, Acknowledge, Know, and Expand). The combination of methods as powerful as both of these is encouraging. The changes are lasting, as clients attest, and empower the participant to know that he or she is responsible for these changes, not the therapist facilitating the process. Tomatis concurs, the process of improvement must leave the client responsible for the change, not transfer responsibility to the facilitator.

Another therapist who concurs about nontransfer and brings a different dimension to the definition of listening is Ilana Rubenfeld. She developed Rubenfeld Synergy Method™, integrating Feldenkrais body movement, Alexander technique, Ericksonian hypnotherapy, and Gestalt therapy (Rubenfeld, 1988). Rubenfeld says she "listens with her hands." When a person who has been isolated by and from a previous emotionally and/or physically painful experience lies on a table, Rubenfeld invites and facilitates his or her listening to his or her own body, words, and feelings and then putting language to them. Meanwhile, she gently uses her hands to encourage the person's body to release old holding patterns affecting posture and movement.

Some of these traumas might be prevented by learning how to speak so others will listen and listen so others will speak, as suggested by Faber and Mazlish (1980) and Hamlin (1988). Taylor (1986) in *Positive Illusions* and Ornstein and Sobel (1989) in *Healthy Pleasures* recommend having optimistic perspectives over pessimistic ones for maintaining health and positive self listening.

Are we to be considered listening disabled if we have not the experience of listening these ways to ourselves—so that we can let go of the physical, emotional, and mental barriers that keep us from relating to self, others, and environment? From Tomatis' insights, the ear and listening ability are integral components of this lifelong process.

Music. Others besides Tomatis know of the importance of listening to and producing various tones. The famous violin teacher Suzuki (1983) observes that tone deafness often occurs in young children when they are trained by a tone deaf parent and learn to perfectly represent an imperfect tone.

Suzuki and Tomatis hold some ideas in common: the important function of listening *in utero*, listening as the basis for music ability, the need to focus on the child's potential, a love for Mozart's music, and the need to have the family support the child's listening development.

Musician, composer, writer, and teacher Don Campbell has done much to educate people about listening disabilities and the role of music. In *Rhythms of Learning* (1991), Brewer and Campbell place much emphasis, and rightly so, on rhythm's role in learning. At the heart of rhythm and movement is the ear, and once more, we are drawn to listening ability as the key for integration.

Besides the Tomatis Method, several other learning methods (such as Accelerated Learning and Orff-Schulwerk) use music and listening to enable the learner to accelerate the learning process. The music therapists use many forms of music to improve mental health, decrease pain, improve coronary care, assist childbirth and premature infant care, and reduce migraine headaches. A problem occurs when listening is poor from the beginning and cognitive approaches do not succeed in overcoming them. Campbell (1983, 1989, 1991) recommends chant activities to improve listening and open up one's awareness and classroom activities to integrate right and left brain functioning.

Through his original work with singers, Tomatis discovered that the ideal listening ear is a good musical ear and that Caruso had the perfect musical ear.

Are we listening disabled if we lack this kind of precision or call ourselves tone deaf? Is it important that matter is made up of rhythmic energy and that we relate to everything through our ear? Listening disabilities tie into an inability to experience or respond to music, the rhythmic sounds of voice and instruments that many take for granted.

Foreign Language. Learning a foreign language is considered to be a necessity in some countries, though not usually in the U.S. OptimaLearning (1988) recently published cassette tapes to teach very young children who are native English speakers how to speak French and Spanish and describes Tomatis's insistence that we must be able to hear the sounds of a language before we can learn it. "Before your children can speak a language, they must be able to *hear* the particular sounds and auditory frequencies of that language, according to Dr. Alfred Tomatis.... When children learn a second and third language, they are actually increasing their cognitive flexibility, a key to problem solving and creativity" (p. 1).

If early exposure is not possible, an older child or adult may use the Tomatis Method to develop an ear for a language, meaning he or she listens to sounds of a native speaker through the Electronic Ear's adjustments to that language in order to learn its intonation and frequency patterns. Tomatis discovered that every language has a particular frequency range within which most of the sounds therein are intensified, which he calls the *envelope curve* or *ethnogram* (Tomatis, 1960, 1963, 1970b, 1977, 1991; Tomatis & Moulonguet, 1960).

Are we listening disabled, in a sense, if we can hear only the sounds of our own language? For those who want to learn a foreign language, it is certainly a valid consideration.

Education. We can hardly pick up an educational journal or book without hearing about students at risk, learning disabilities, special education, drop-outs, illiteracy, poor teaching, and low funding. It is not uncommon to change standardized tests, textbooks, educational goals, curriculum, report cards, and teacher certification requirements, but maybe it is also time to change how we look at learning disabilities and perhaps see that something more basic than "the 3 Rs" is where we must start.

It is necessary to get to the problem source of many learning problems—listening disabilities—rather than to continue to merely address the symptoms (Thompson, 1989, 1990). Recommendations include perceiving the problem source to be poor listening, providing for early screening for listening problems, providing programs to improve both the functional and emotional aspects of poor listening, educating students (parents, too) about how to take care of their ears, preparing teachers to use techniques which develop and reward good listening, and addressing the need to prevent listening problems. Instead of just looking at the short-term costs of providing these measures, we must also count the long-term cost to the person and the entire society when we don't.

There is every indication that we need programs to improve listening and that some people need more than just cognitive-based methods. According to Friedlander (1973), 25% of kindergarten children from advantaged milieus fall into the category "learning disabled" because of poor listening. He connected poor listening with learning difficulties and saw the connection as the cause of poor scores on standardized tests; the students couldn't comprehend language well enough to complete questions correctly. According to de Hirsch (1981), "A child who does not comprehend fairly complex language in first grade will retreat into daydreaming, and the more he dreams the less he will listen. There are many youngsters who have learned *not* to listen before they are seven" (p. 64).

Can we keep our emphasis on standardized testing and continue to ignore the impact of poor listening on the scores? Content validity may give way to process validity, in a way of describing what must additionally be addressed.

Listening training programs are needed as early as possible in the child's life, yet we are often told, "Don't worry, he'll outgrow the problem." For many children, one year makes a difference in maturity and academic abilities, yet one should not sit back and do nothing for a year. "During transitional stages—and the age between 5 and 7 is such a stage—training stimulates maturation" (de Hirsch, 1981, p. 64). Exposure to information results in learning. A poor listener's perception alters the information so that it has to be unlearned and then relearned through an altered perception. (And also, a good listener learning distorted information has to unlearn the distortion before relearning the correction.) With the poorly functioning ear as integrator of information, what is the impact?

Learning disabled children do not see a relationship between what they do and what happens to them. It is suggested that this view of self and the world may hinder these children from actively seeking appropriate learning strategies such as verbal rehearsal (Hallahan, Gajar, Cohen, & Tarver, 1978). In other words, these children are disconnected. When students are disconnected, they resort to tuning out and to using whatever learning strategies they find to allow them at least some response. What can be done?

Learning Strategy Change. Simon (1985) and Lasky (1985), among others, describe a number of strategies to improve listening and speech. Insight that teachers must teach to the student's strength area is common knowledge. Developing the weak areas so they have a greater learning resource base is the challenge.

Proponents of Neuro-Linguistic Programming™ view every strategy one has as useful for something. When a strategy is applied in the wrong way or in an inappropriate situation, then one has problems. NLP is a controversial yet rapidly expanding communication technology based on the initial work of John Grinder and Richard Bandler. Some people object to its misuse by people who lack integrity in its applications, while others point to efficient techniques to improve gaining rapport and making desired communication and learning changes. The integrity of the user of any method is always a key to the acceptance of the method. The specific application of NLP techniques to education is provided by Cleveland (1987), Jacobson (1983), and Van Nagel, Siudzinski, Reese, and Reese (1985). Often only one step in a process separates success from failure. For example, while poor spellers compare a visually constructed image of how they think the word is spelled to an auditory image of how that visual image would sound, good spellers compare two visual images—the word as they construct it and as they remember seeing it. NLP, a fairly new and still evolving technology, has many techniques and insights that can help people use auditory and other sensory skills appropriately.

Are we listening disabled if we use auditory processing when some other strategy is more appropriate or, vice versa, do not use it when we should? Might we not use one strategy because of a functional disability therein and will that affect our learning ability?

HOW DO WE TEST FOR LISTENING DISABILITIES?

Test Requirements and Research Concerns

Public Law 94-142 has many formal test administration requirements but does not preclude using systematic behavioral observation and other nonstandardized clinician-constructed evaluation tools. Critical determinations cannot be made on the basis of only one test, so emphasis on testing comes through legal requirements to protect a child's civil rights. Descriptions of several auditory and language-based tests are given by Gerber and Bryen (1981) and Wallach and Butler (1984). They include standardized tests and subtests of auditory reception, discrimination, and closure, and those of sound blending, word recognition, oral directions, selective attention, and other language development and comprehension tests requiring reading/speech/auditory feedback. One such set of tests was developed by Flowers (1983). "The Flowers Auditory Test of Selective Attention is one of the first assessment instruments suggested for use with young children suspected of auditory perceptual deficits" (Gerber & Bryen, 1981, p. 13).

As Carver (1974) and Schery (1981) point out, the stability and reliability of standardized tests make them effective measures of group differences but reduce their ability to pick up important changes in the individual. For this reason, criterion referenced tests (CRTs) are often better for identifying specific changes. For both standardized tests and CRTs, problems in testing occur when a test assumes competence of lower-level skills or does not acknowledge that this lower-skill competence underlies abilities being tested.

Beyond the evaluation of listening abilities of individuals, the evaluation of programs must be considered. In a summary of the effect of language intervention programs for learning-disabled children, Wallach and Butler (1984) noted that no really comprehensive program evaluation research in speech and language intervention could be found. Research of any type is not an easy mistress to master.

Tomatis Listening Test

If one looks for a way to test the seven functions of the ear listed earlier, one test, the Tomatis Listening Test, is seen to address all of them and to incorporate the components in the proposed definition of listening and listening disabilities. A trained consultant using this composite test battery gathers information using electronic equipment to perform several types of test to identify both listening problems and listening strengths (Tomatis, 1967, 1971, 1978). A summary of the description given in *Education and Dyslexia* (Tomatis, 1978) follows for the test that is done in a sound quiet room and follows a specific protocol.

Threshold Evaluation. The person's ability to hear at a specific, predetermined intensity threshold the normal sound scale frequencies ranging from 125 to 8,000 Hz are tested for both air and bone conduction for both ears. A curve is derived for each of these. The good listener has parallel curves, while the disabled listener has distortions of varying types. The curves are examined in three ranges—bass (125-800 Hz), middle (800-2,000 Hz), and treble (2,000-8,000 Hz)—and as a whole. When a French person's self-monitoring is perfect, the curve rises at the rate of 6 db per frequency tested from 125 to 3,000 Hz and descends slightly thereafter. Disturbances in the curves indicate different problems.

Selectivity Evaluation. The person's ability to recognize pitch differences between frequencies is determined for each ear. The test is usually given using a sound input of about 45 db. This discrimination ability should be present by the time a child is 8 to 10 years old. People who have difficulty with this test are unable to discriminate tonal values of sound.

Spatialization Evaluation. The person's temporal spatial orientation ability is tested. Not everyone is able to orient himself or herself spatially. Confusion here indicates a fundamental difficulty in localizing oneself within one's environment.

Leading Ear Evaluation. The person is tested while speaking to determine his or her dominant ear. Sound is directed to each ear at the same intensity level at first and then changed to a different intensity toward the nondominant ear until there is a shift in facial expression, voice modulation, muscle tone around the mouth and jaw, general posture, and breathing depth. An audiolaterometer developed by Tomatis is used to do this test.

Additional Tests. Additional tests include the tree test, family test, and human figure test. Optional tests may be done or requested from other professionals.

WHO HAS LISTENING DISABILITIES AND WHAT IS THEIR IMPACT?

Listening disabilities occur at any age as a result of illness, accident, a major lifestyle disruption, or stress. Those children with listening disabilities are impacted in any of several ways, as described by Tomatis (1963, 1967, 1971, 1976, 1978, 1989a, 1991), and can be identified from their behavior as shown in the list of symptoms of poor listening in Figure 7.2.

In the classroom or elsewhere, students with poor listening develop problems using and expressing cognitive potential at three levels. They are (a) less focused, centered, and verbally articulate, (b) less curious and less interested in seeking information, and (c) less capable of solving communication-relational-social problems. According to Tomatis, when we can listen well, we have the possibility of thinking well.

Listening disabilities affecting adults account for problems with work, relationships, career achievement, and self-esteem loss. They are a huge problem. A 1988 2-year, joint project of the American Society for Training and Development and the United States Department of Labor, says that what businesses want most is workers who can listen, create, set goals, work in teams, and solve problems (Carnevale, Gainer, Meltzer, & Holland, 1988). Listening disabilities are as common in adults as in children. As an indicator, half the clients of Tomatis centers around the world are adults.

Both individual and cultural listening disabilities exist. The cultural ones, related to noise, negative and abusive verbal communication, too loud music, and abuse of television by cutting off dialogue, demand some mention because they provide an environment in which the individual disabilities exist (Jaret, 1990).

CAN LISTENING DISABILITIES BE ELIMINATED, OR MUST WE LEARN TO LIVE WITH THEM?

To overcome listening disabilities means preventing them whenever possible, using cognitive approaches when appropriate, and using programs that improve functioning when needed. The appropriateness of programs varies according to individual needs and the goals to be achieved for that person.

Traditional Approaches

Descriptions and summaries about listening disabilities programs that work are offered by Simon (1985), Sutaria (1985), Wallach and Butler (1984), and Gerber and Bryen (1981). In general, one-on-one instruction or therapy that has school-system support are effective. Beyond institutional support, support and belief in correction by the professional in charge, the person with the disability, and others in his or her support system are absolutely essential.

Studies in education, beginning with *Pygmalion in the Classroom* (Rosenthal, 1968), show that a teacher's expectations are responsible for some degree of a student's success. When expectations about a student's abilities do not change, it is almost impossible for the student to do well even though capabilities are improved. When teachers, and parents as well, lose sight of potential and stop directing attention down that path, the possibility of success is less.

Harmon (1988) suggests a fundamental change is happening in Western society to acknowledge that mind gives rise to matter. Ferguson's *(1980) Aquarian Conspiracy* guided many during the past decade to transform beliefs of inadequacy from the past and to choose some that are more empowering: "Our past is not our potential" (p. 417). Taylor (1986), Williams (1989), Pennybaker (1990), and Burns (1990) describe how to cognitively change listening and thinking to feel good and to be physically healthy. Beliefs tell us what to listen to, how to filter incoming information. They can work for or against our health.

A new program, the Reading Recovery Program (Pinnell, Fried, & Estice, 1990), requires one teacher to tutor a poor reader for 1/2 hour daily over several months as he or she reads aloud and writes about what was read. We should expect it to be successful, as is claimed, because the focus is on audiovocal control (self-listening), daily reading aloud, focus on the student's potential and competence (instead of problems), and development of a strategy to integrate information in the complex reading and writing process. And as Pinnell et al. (1990) raise the question for their program, others might relate their thoughts to their own program about the "real" costs of providing or not providing it. "Since we know we *can* provide this powerful instruction, are we *obligated* to provide it to those who need it despite the cost?" (p. 294).

Though some teachers help the poor listener compensate for listening weaknesses, their aim is not correction. Still, they should use all means possible to permit children to listen to themselves, to express themselves orally (sing, read, spell and study their homework aloud), and to sit at the front of the class with their right ear receiving the information from the teacher. For severe listening problems, placing the child in a small class and giving constant teacher support and positive reinforcement increases motivation and concentration.

Education is part of our very fabric. Language skills are the medium of instruction through which all other learning is fostered. The use of verbal instruction is a large part of teaching. So not only is listening the basis of learning, it is also a large basis for teaching. A listening disability could even be considered something a student has if the teacher is a poor speaker or user of language when teaching.

If we are to define what skills students must have in order to be effective learners, not disabled learners, we must begin with listening. It is more basic than the three R's.

The Tomatis Method

Tomatis's books are primarily in French, and his method has been difficult to learn about for those who speak English. Most research about it is based on clinical work in private centers, doctoral research, and special unpublished reports.

The Tomatis Method exists within our expanded definition of listening. It is a sound stimulation, counseling, and educational intervention to improve the ear's functioning, communication through language, desire for communication and learning, body image awareness, audiovocal control, and motor control. An initial assessment is given by a trained listening therapist and is interpreted during a consultation by a trained Tomatis consultant. It includes tests of listening and lateral dominance and figure drawings. Information from the test and consultation is supplemented by a detailed personal history.

In 1953, Tomatis developed an apparatus called the Electronic Ear, whose purpose is "to help the ear acquire its three functions: listening, monitoring of language, and laterality" (Tomatis, 1978, p. 141). The Electronic Ear uses four mechanisms: filters, electronic gate, balance control, and bone and air conduction reception.

The method simulates the five stages of listening development, depending on the program goal and the level attained by the person: (a) prenatal (filtered high frequency) listening, (b) sonic birth (integration of lower frequencies similar to what occurs when the fluid drains from the middle ear after birth), (c) prelanguage (humming), (d) language (repeating words and phrases), and (e) reading aloud. The length of each specific stage varies from person to person, depending on motivation and goals; breaks are interspersed to allow for integration of new listening patterns. Phases (a) and (b) are primarily passive, where the person simply listens for two hours each day, while he or she participates in some activity such as painting, playing games, doing puzzles, or even sleeping or talking with others. Phases (c), (d), and (e) include active work with one's own voice as well as continued passive listening. The Electronic Ear is used throughout the program phases. A typical program length is 30 days, broken into several intensive sessions.

During the auditory training the client listens to sounds of electronically filtered and unfiltered music (primarily Mozart and Gregorian chant) and voice to improve the focusing ability of the ear. If the client is a child, a tape of his or her mother's filtered voice is used. If the client is learning a foreign language, a tape of a native speaker of the language is used. By increasing the selective power of the ear, the person can perceive sound with less distortion and analyze it more precisely over the whole frequency range, from fundamental frequencies to the highest harmonics. For a nontrained ear, the fundamental frequency of a sound too often masks its harmonic spectrum, and the person has difficulty in controlling voice timbre (the mix of higher harmonics). Consequently the voice stays flat, with no modulation. By improving listening, the speaker has the opportunity to improve voice quality, fluency, modulation, and articulation, for the benefit of one's self as one's own first listener and of those others who listen. Implications for education and workplace are vast. When one's voice conveys energy and interest to others, the invitation to listen is more readily accepted.

Research reviews by Stutt (1983) and Gilmor (1984, 1989b) indicate that the experimental evidence is "growing and positive." A recent study by Kershner, Cummings, Clarke, Hadfield, and Kershner (1990) did not find significant changes favoring a group of learning disabled students who received the Tomatis Method in its group format (called the Listening Training Program or LTP). A number of methodological shortcomings and overdrawn conclusions limit the extent to which the results obtained in the study can be generalized (Tim Gilmor, personal communication, June 5, 1991). All the children in this study were attending a private school with low teacher–pupil ratio and individual remedial programs. It is probable that the LTP could not add significantly to such an intensive private school program which was so strongly supported by staff and parents.

On the positive side, a study by du Plessis and van Jaarsveld (1988) using two treatment groups (one counseling and one Tomatis) and one control group confirmed "significant positive changes following both [treatment] programs, but no change in the control group. On a number of variables the APP [Tomatis] group achieved significantly better results than the alternative therapy group, especially with regard to hearing and listening. A follow-up study confirmed the long-term effect of the intervention" (p. 144). This study followed another review (van Jaarsveld & du Plessis, 1988) that described eight empirical studies conducted in South Africa on topics such as laterality, stuttering, anxiety, and the use of the Tomatis Method with severely mentally retarded persons) and that showed positive gains within methodological deficiencies that limited the degree to which the gains could be attributed to the Tomatis Method alone.

The Method is still evolving and is used in a 150 centers worldwide and a few public and private schools by professionals from such varied backgrounds as education, psychology, speech pathology, audiology, medicine, music, and physical and neurodevelopmental therapies.

CONCLUSION

Just as with many programs that have been evaluated by specific criteria and found wanting, then reevaluated by other criteria and found effective, so it is with listening training programs. Do we want to test merely for specific auditory skills and ignore desire for communication, motivation to learn, integration of information, and other not easily testable concepts? Or do we want to view listening in a broad sense, to see its relationship to learning and development of intelligence, and to attack listening related problems from as many fronts as possible? The answer may well be that it is a political question. Luis Machado, former first Minister of Intelligence for Venezuela, insists "intelligence is a teachable and learnable faculty....This is now a fundamentally political problem. The teaching of intelligence is an affair of state" (1980, p. 27). We must want others to listen, then to think and to question. Only then, when we are willing to acknowledge the thoughts and perceptions of others, knowing acknowledgement is not the same as agreement, will we open up a truly safe place for all to speak. The power of one person over another is the power to speak but not listen. Individuals who are empowered use their voices, are no longer quiet victims; they question, listen, and search for answers everywhere.

What can we do? We can begin by acknowledging the existence of listening disabilities, having a goal to overcome them, and being excellent models of good listeners ourselves. We must seek out programs that work. We must make listening the focus of our foundation work in learning—for children and adults.

We're facing a new decade, and soon a new century, where listening on every level is required. We must listen to our own voice and body, the family and community voice, and the earth's voice. We can start by seeing the connection between listening and learning and by looking for solutions to related disabilities.

There is a price for success. Then again, there is a price for failure. Is it "Listening Disabilities, the Plight of Many" or "Listening Abilities, the Right of All"?

REFERENCES

Abrams, R.M., Hutchinson, A.A., & McTiernan, M.J. (1987). Effects of cochlear ablation on local cerebral glucose utilization in fetal sheep. *American Journal of Obstetrical Gynecology, 157*, 1438–42.

Ayers, A.J. (1978). Learning disabilities and the vestibular system. *Journal of Learning Disabilities, 11,* 30–41.

Ayers, J. (1974). *The development of sensory integration theory and practice.* Dubuque, IA: Kendall/Hunt.

Barsch, R.H. (1968). *Enriching perception and cognition* (Vol. 2). Seattle: Special Child Publications.

Barsch, R.H. (1976). *Ray H. Barsch.* In J.M. Kaufman & D.P. Hallahan (Eds.), *Teaching children with learning disabilities* (pp. 58–92). Columbus, OH: Charles E. Merrill.

Belk, J.B. (1989). The journey and its new roadmap: Clinical experience with the Tomatis Method. In T.M. Gilmor, P. Madaule, & B. Thompson (Eds.), *About the Tomatis Method* (pp. 129–143). Toronto: The Listening Centre Press.

Berg, F.S. (1987). *Facilitating classroom listening: A handbook for teachers of normal & hard of hearing students.* Boston: College-Hill Press.

Berry, M.F., & Eisenson, J. (1956). *Speech disorders: Principles and practices of therapy.* New York: Appleton-Century-Crofts.

Bess, F.H., & Tharpe, A.M. (1988). Performances and management of children with unilateral sensorineural hearing loss. *Scandinavian Audiological Supplement, 30,* 75–79.

Birch, H.G. (1973). Two strategies for studying perception in "brain-damaged" children. In S.G. Sapir & A.C. Nitzburg (Eds.), *Children with learning problems.* New York: Brunner/Mazel.

Blair, J., Peterson, M., & Viehweg, S. (1985). The effect of mild hearing loss on academic performance among young school-age children. *Volta Review, 87*(2), 87–94.

Bloom, L., & Lahey, M. (1978). *Language developmental and language disorders.* New York: John Wiley & Sons.

Borg, E.S., & Counter, A. (1989). The middle-ear muscles. *Scientific American, 261*(2), 74–80.

Brewer, C.B., & Campbell, D.G. (1991). *Rhythms of learning: creative tools for academic development.* Tucson: Zephyr Press.

Bryant, P., & Bradley, L. (1985). *Children's reading problems.* New York: Basil Blackwell.

Burns, D.D. (1990). *The feeling good handbook.* New York: Plume.

Campbell, D.G. (1983). *Introduction to the musical brain.* Saint Louis: Magnamusic-Baton, Inc.

Campbell, D.G. (1989). *The roar of silence.* Wheaton, IL: The Theosophical Publishing House.

Campbell, D.G. (Ed.) (1991). *Music physician for times to come.* Wheaton, IL: Quest Books.

Carnevale, A.P., Gainer, L.J., Meltzer, A.S., & Holland, S.L. (1988, October). Workplace basics: The skills employers want. *Training & Development Journal, 42*(10), 22–30.

Carver, R. (1974). Two dimensions of tests: Psychometric and edumetric. *American Psychology, 29,* 512–518.

Chamberlain, D.B. (1983). *Consciousness at birth: A review of the empirical evidence.* San Diego: Chamberlain Communications.

Cleveland, B.F. (1987). *Master teaching techniques.* Stone Mountain, GA: The Connecting Link Press.

DeCasper, A., & Fifer, W. (1980). Of human bonding: Newborns prefer their mother's voices. *Science, 208,* 1174–1176.

de Hirsch, K. (1981). Unready children. In A. Gerber & D.N. Bryen (Eds.), *Language and learning disabilities* (pp. 61–74). Baltimore, MD: University Park Press.

Delacato, C.H. (1963). *The diagnosis and treatment of speech and reading problems.* Springfield, IL: Thomas.

de Villiers, P.A., & de Villiers, J.G. (1979). *Early language.* Cambridge, MA: Harvard University Press.

Donahue, M., Pearl, R., & Bryan, T. (1982). Learning disabled children's syntactic proficiency on a communicative task. *Journal of Speech and Hearing Disorders, 47,* 397–403.

du Plessis, W.F., & van Jaarsveld, P.E. (1988). Audio-psycho-phonology: A comparative outcome study on anxious primary school pupils. *South African Tydskr. Sielk, 18*(4), 144–151.

Dwyer, J., Blumstein, S.E., & Ryalls, J. (1982). The role of duration and rapid temporal processing on the lateral perception of consonants and vowels. *Brain Language, 17,* 272–286.

Early, G.H. (1973, March). *Using motor functions to promote visual-auditory integration.* Paper presented at the Tenth Annual International Conference of the Association for Children with Learning Disabilities, Detroit.

Eisenberg, R. (1976). *Auditory competence in early life.* Baltimore: University Park Press.

Faber, A., & Mazlish, E. (1980). *How to talk so kids will listen and listen so kids will talk.* New York: Avon.

Farnham-Diggory, S. (1978). *Learning disabilities.* Cambridge, MA: Harvard University Press.

Ferguson, M. (1980). *The aquarian conspiracy: Personal and social transformation in the 1980's.* Los Angeles: J.P. Tarcher, Inc.

Fletcher, H. (1929). *Speech and hearing.* New York: Van Nostrand.

Flowers, A. (1983). *Auditory perception, speech, language and learning.* Dearborn, MI: Perceptual Learning Systems, Publishers.

Friedlander, B. (1973). Receptive language anomaly and language/reading dysfunctions in "normal" primary grade school children. *Psychol. Schools, 10,* 12–18.

Frostig, M., Lefever, D.W., & Whittlesey, J.R.B. (1964). *Marianne Frostig Developmental Test of Visual Perception.* Palo Alto, CA: Consulting Psychologists Press.

Frostig, M. (1976). Marianne Frostig. In J.M. Kaufman & D.P. Hallahan (Eds.), *Teaching children with learning disabilities* (pp. 164–190). Columbus, OH: Charles E. Merrill.

Gengel, R. (1971). Acceptable speech-to-noise ratios for aided speech discrimination of the hearing impaired. *Journal of Auditory Research, 11*, 219–221.

Gentile, A. (1972). *Academic achievement test results of a national testing program for hearing impaired students: 1971* (Series D, Number 9). Washington, DC: Office of Demographic Studies, Gallaudet College.

Gerber, A., & Bryen, D.N. (1981). *Language and learning disabilities.* Baltimore: University Park Press.

Gibson, E., & Levin, H. (1975). *The psychology of reading.* New York: Academic Press.

Gilmor, T.M. (1982). *A pre-test and post-test survey of children's and adolescent's performance before and after completing the Tomatis Program.* Unpublished manuscript, Tomatis Centre.

Gilmor, T.M. (1984). *Participant characteristics and follow-up evaluations of children and adolescents who have participated in the Listening Training Program (Tomatis Method), 1978–1983.* Unpublished manuscript, Tomatis Centre.

Gilmor, T.M. (1989a). Introduction to the Tomatis Method. In T.M. Gilmor, P. Madaule, & B. Thompson (Eds.), *About the Tomatis Method* (pp. 7–12). Toronto: The Listening Centre Press.

Gilmor, T.M. (1989b). Overview of the Tomatis Method. In T.M. Gilmor, P. Madaule, & B. Thompson (Eds.), *About the Tomatis Method* (pp. 15–42). Toronto: The Listening Centre Press.

Gilmor, T.M. (1989c). The Tomatis Method and the genesis of listening. *Pre- & Peri-natal Psychology, 4*, 9–26.

Gilmor, T.M., & Madaule, P. (Eds.). (1988). Listening checklist. *Listen, Newsletter of the Listening Centre* (600 Markham Street, Toronto, Ontario, *M6Q2L8 2*, p. 3.

Gilmor, T.M., Madaule, P., & Thompson, B. (Eds.). (1989). *About the Tomatis Method.* Toronto: The Listening Centre Press.

Hallahan, D.P., Gajar, A.H., Cohen, S.B., & Tarver, S.G. (1978). Selective attention and locus control in learning disabled and normal children. *Journal of Learning Disabilities, 11*, 231–236.

Hamlin, S. (1988). *How to talk so people listen.* New York: Harper & Row.

Hammill, D.D., Leigh, J.E., McNutt, G., & Larsen, G.C. (1981). A new definition of learning disabilities. *Learning Disabilities Quarterly, 4*, 336–342.

Harmon, W. (1988). *Global mind change: The promise of the last years of the twentieth century.* Indianapolis: Knowledge Systems, Inc.

Heiniger, M.C. (1990). *Integrated motor activities screening: Screening interpretation guide.* Tucson, AZ: Communication Skill Builders.

Howell, P. (1984). Are two muscles needed for the normal functioning of the mammalian ear? *Acta Otol* (Stockholm), *989*, 204–207.

Hudspeth, A.J. (1989). How the ear's works work. *Nature, 341*, 397–404.

Jacobson, S. (1983). *Meta-cation.* Cupertino, CA: Meta Publications.

Jansky, J., & de Hirsch, K. (1973). *Preventing reading failure.* New York: Harper & Row.

Jaret, P. (1990). From Elvis to the Stones to Def Leppard, the music has taken its toll on your hearing. But you don't have to lose what's left. *In Health, 4*(4), 50–58.

Jenny, H. (1974). *Cymatics* (Vol. II). Switzerland: Basilius Presse AG, Basel.

Johnson, D., & Myklebust, H. (1967). *Learning disabilities: Educational principles and practice.* New York: Grune & Stratton.

Kephart, N.C. (1960). *The slow learner in the classroom.* Columbus, OH: Charles E. Merrill.

Kershner, J.R., Cummings, R.L., Clarke, K.A., Hadfield, A.J., & Kershner, B.A. (1990). Two-year evaluation of the Tomatis listening training program with learning disabled children. *Learning Disabilities Quarterly, 13,* 43–53.

Kimura, D. (1967). Functional asymmetry of the brain in dichotic listening. *Cortex, 3,* 163–178.

Kinsbourne, M., & Caplan, P.J. (1979). *Children's learning and attention problems.* Boston: Little, Brown & Company.

Kirk, S.A., & McCarthy, J.M. (1975). *Learning disabilities: Selected ACLD papers.* Boston: Houghton-Mifflin.

Kirk, S., McCarthy, J., Kirk, W. (1968). *The Illinois test of psycholinguistic abilities.* Urbana, IL: University of Illinois.

Lasky, E.Z. (1985). Comprehending and processing of information in clinic and classroom. In C.S. Simon (Ed.), *Communication skills and classroom success: Therapy methodologies for language-learning disabled students* (pp. 113–132). San Diego: College Hill Press.

le Gall, A. (1961, March). *The correction of certain psychological and psycho-pedagogical deficiencies by the Electronic Ear using the Tomatis Effect.* Paris: Office of the Inspector General of Public Instruction.

Lenneberg, E.H. (1967). *Biological foundations of language.* New York: Wiley.

Lerner, J.W. (1976). *Children with learning disabilities* (2nd ed). Boston: Houghton-Mifflin.

Lerner, J. (1981). *Learning disabilities: Theories, diagnosis and teaching strategies* (3rd ed.). Boston: Houghton Mifflin.

Levinson, H.N. (1984). *Smart but feeling dumb.* New York: Warner Books.

Liberman, I.Y., Liberman, A.M., & Mattingly, I.G. (1980). Orthography and the beginning reader. In J. Kavanagh & R. Venezky (Eds.), *Orthography, reading, and dyslexia.* Baltimore: University Park Press.

Machado, L.A. (1980). *The right to be intelligent.* Elmsford, NY: Pergamon.

Madaule, P. (1989). The dyslexified world. In T.M. Gilmor, P. Madaule, & B. Thompson (Eds.), *About the Tomatis Method* (pp. 45–61). Toronto: The Listening Centre Press.

Menyuk, P. (1981). *Language and maturation.* Cambridge, MA: MIT Press.

Michaud, M.A. (1989). One who listens speaks: An interview with Dr. Alfred Tomatis [on Radio-Canada]. In T.M. Gilmor, P. Madaule, & B. Thompson (Eds.), *About the Tomatis Method* (pp. 201–207). Toronto: The Listening Centre Press.

Millichap, J.G. (1977). Medications as aids to education in children with minimal brain dysfunction. In J.G. Millichap (Ed.), *Learning disabilities and related disorders.* Chicago: Year Book Medical Publishers.

Montgomery, G. (1989). The mind in motion. *Discover, 10*(3), 58–68.

Moores, D.F. (1982). *Educating the deaf* (2nd ed.). Boston: Houghton-Mifflin.

Myklebust, H. (1954). *Auditory disorders in children* (2nd ed.). New York: Wiley & Sons.

OptimaLearning. (1988). *French for tots: For ages 2¹/₂ and up*. San Rafael, CA: OptimaLearning Language Company.

Ornstein, R., & Sobel, D. (1989). *Healthy pleasures*. Reading, MA: Addison-Wesley.

Orton, S.T. (1925). "Word-blindness" in school children. *Arch Neurol Psychiatry, 14*, 581–615.

Orton, S.T. (1928). Specific reading disability—Strephosymbolia. *Journal of the American Medical Association, 90*, 1095–1099.

Oyler, R.F., Oyler, R.F., & Matkin, N.D. (1987). Warning: A unilateral hearing loss may be detrimental to a child's academic career. *Hearing Journal, 40*, 18–22.

Pennybaker, J.W. (1990). *Opening up: The healing power of confiding in others*. New York: William Morrow and Company, Inc.

Pickles, J.O. (1988). *An introduction to the physiology of hearing* (2nd ed.). San Diego, CA: Academic.

Pinnell, G.S., Fried, M.D., & Estice, R.M. (1990, January). Reading recovery: Learning how to make a difference. *The Reading Teacher*, pp. 282–295.

Querleu, D., Renard, X., & Versyp, P. (1988a). Fetal hearing. *European Journal of Obstetrics & Gynecology and Reproductive Biology, 29*, 191–212.

Querleu, D., Renard, X., & Versyp, F. (1988b). La transmission intra-amniotique des voix humaines. *Rev Fr Gynecol Obstet, 83*, 43–50.

Querleu, D., & Renard, X., Boutteville, C., & Crepin, G. (1989). Hearing by the human fetus? *Seminars in Perinatology, 13*(5), 409–420.

Quigley, S.F. (1969). *The influence of fingerspelling on the development of language, communication and educational achievement in deaf children*. Urbana, IL: Institute for Research on Exceptional Children, University of Illinois.

Quigley, S., & Thomure, F. (1968). *Some effects of hearing impairment upon school performance*. Springfield, IL: Division of Special Education Services.

Quiros, J. de. (1976). Diagnosis of vestibular disorders in the learning disabled. *Journal of Learning Disabilities, 9*, 50–58.

Quiros, J. de, & Shrager, O.D. (1975). Postular system, corporal potentiality and language. In E. Lennenberg (Ed.), *Foundations of language development* (Vol. 2). New York: Academic Press.

Richardson, S.O. (1975). Learning disabilities—an introduction. In S.A. Kirk & J.M. McCarthy (Eds.), *Learning disabilities: Selected ACLD papers*. Boston: Houghton-Mifflin.

Roberts, C.V. (1988). The validation of listening tests: Cutting of the Gordian Knot. *Journal of the International Listening Association, 2*, 1–19.

Rosenthal, R. (1968). *Pygmalion in the classroom: Teacher expectation and pupils' intellectual development*. New York: Holt, Reinhart, and Winston.

Rosenthal, W.S. (1974). *The role of perception in child language disorders: A theory based on faulty signal detection strategies*. Paper presented at

American Speech and Hearing Association national convention, Las Vegas, NV.

Rubenfeld, I. (1988). Beginner's hands: Twenty-five years of simple; Rubenfeld Synergy—The birth of a therapy. *Somatics, 4*(4).

Rudel, R.G., & Denckla, M.B. (1976). Relationship of I.Q. and reading scores to visual, spatial and temporal matching tasks. *Journal of Learning Disabilities, 9*, 169–178.

Schery, T. (1981). Selecting assessment strategies for language disordered children. *Top Language Disorders, 1*(2), 59–73.

Simon, C.S. (1985). The language-learning disabled student: description and therapy implications. In C.S. Simon (Ed.), *Communication skills and classroom success: Therapy methodologies for language-learning disabled students* (pp. 1–56). San Diego: College-Hill Press.

Simmons, F.B. (1964). Perceptual theories of middle ear muscle function. *Annals of Otology, Rhinology and Laryngology, 73*, 724–739.

Spence, M., & DeCasper, A. (1982). *Human fetuses perceive maternal speech.* Paper presented at the SRCD Conference, Austin.

Spence, M., & DeCasper, A. (1986). Prenatal experience with low frequency maternal voice sounds influences the newborn's perception of maternal voice. *Infant Behavioral Development, 10*, 133–142.

Stehli, A. (1991). *Sound of a miracle.* New York: Doubleday.

Stutt, H. (1983). *The Tomatis Method: A review of current research.* Unpublished manuscript, McGill University.

Sutaria, S. (1985). *Specific learning disabilities: Nature and needs.* Springfield, IL: Charles C. Thomas.

Suzuki, S. (1983). *Nurtured by love* (W. Suzuki, Trans.). Athens, OH: A Senzay Publications.

Swanson, J.M., & Kinsbourne, M. (1976). Stimulant-related state dependent learning in hyperactive children. *Science, 192*, 1354.

Tallal, P., & Piercy, M. (1973). Developmental aphasia: Impaired rate of nonverbal processing as a function of sensory modality. *Neuropsychologia, 11*, 389.

Tallal, P., & Piercy, M. (1974). Developmental aphasia: Rate of auditory processing and selective impairment of consonant perception. *Neoropsychologia, 12*, 83.

Tallal, P. (1975). Perceptual and linguistic factors in the language impairment of developmental dysphasias: An experimental investigation with the token test. *Cortex, 11*, 196.

Tallal, P. (1976). Rapid auditory processing in normal and disordered language development. *Journal of Speech Hear. Res., 19*, 561.

Tallal, P. (1978). Implications of speech: Perceptual research for clinical populations. In J. Kavanaugh & W. Strange (Eds.), *Language research in the laboratory, clinic and classroom.* Cambridge, MA: MIT Press.

Taylor, S.E. (1986). *Positive illusions: Creative self-deception and the healthy mind.* New York: Basic Books, Inc.

Thompson, B., Madaule, P., & Gilmor, T. (1988–1989). Listening, learning & the Tomatis Method. *Human Intelligence Newsletter. 9*(4), 8–9.

Thompson, B.M. (1989). Listening, the basic basic we've been seeking. In T.M.

Gilmor, P. Madaule, & B. Thompson (Eds.), *About the Tomatis Method* (pp. 113–127). Toronto: The Listening Centre Press.

Thompson, B.M. (1990, January). *Tomatis technique: Application of sound listening and learning.* Paper presented at Region V Workshop, National Academy of Sciences Mathematical Sciences Education Board.

Tomatis, A.A. (1953a, Juillet). L'Oreille musicale. *Journal Français O.R.L.,* p. 1.

Tomatis, A.A. (1953b). Correction de la voix chantée. In *Cours International de Phonologie et de Phoniatrie* (pp. 335–353). Paris: Librairie Maloine.

Tomatis, A.A. (1954). La sélectivité auditive. *Bulletin du Centre d'Etudes et de Recherches médicales de la SFECMAS,* No. 10.

Tomatis, A.A. (1956). Relations entre l'auditon et la phonation. *Annales des Telecommunications, 2,* 7–8.

Tomatis, A.A. (1959). *Audiologie et phonologie expérimentales et appliquées* (Cours à l'Ecole des Psychologues Praticiens). Paris.

Tomatis, A.A. (1960). *L'electronique au service des langues vivantes.* Presented at the Conference with UNESCO and published in *Bulletin de l'Union des Associations des Anciens Elèves des Lycées et Collèges Francais,* No. 3.

Tomatis, A.A. (1962). La voix. *Revue Musicale,* édition spéciale consacrée a "Médecine et Musique." Paris.

Tomatis, A.A. (1963). *L'oreille et le langage.* Paris: Seuil.

Tomatis, A.A. (1967). *La dyslexie* (Course à l'Ecole d'Anthropologie). Paris: Editions Soditap.

Tomatis, A.A. (1970a). *Le langage-examen clinique-pathologie-traitement.* Société de médecine de Paris: Revue d'Enseignement Post-Universitaire.

Tomatis, A.A. (1970b). *L'intégraton des langues vivantes.* Paris: Editions Soditap.

Tomatis, A.A. (1971). *Educaton et dyslexie.* Paris: Les Editions E.S.F.

Tomatis, A.A. (1972a). *Nouvelles théories sur la physiologie auditive.* IIéme Congrés International d'Audio-Psycho-Phonologie, Paris.

Tomatis, A.A. (1972b). *La libération d'Oedipe.* Paris: Les Editions E.S.F.

Tomatis, A.A. (1974a). *Vers l'écoute humaine* (Vol. I). Paris: Les Edition E.S.F.

Tomatis, A.A. (1974b). *Vers l'écoute humaine* (Vol. II). Paris: Les Edition E.S.F.

Tomatis, A.A. (1974c). La rééducaton de la voix. *La Vie Médicale, 5*(20), 4.

Tomatis, A.A. (1976, January). *Detection of dyslexia among preschool children.* Paper presented at the National Congress of the South African Society for Education.

Tomatis, A.A. (1977). *L'Orielle et la vie.* Paris: Laffont.

Tomatis, A.A. (1978). *Education and dyslexia* (L. Guiney, Trans.). Fribourg, Switzerland: A.I.A.P.P.

Tomatis, A.A. (1979, March). *The ear and learning difficulties* (T. Brown, Trans.). Paper presented at the Quebec Association for Children with Learning Problems.

Tomatis, A.A. (1980, April). *Le défi de l'autio-psycho-phonologie.* Paper presented at the Symposium d'Audio-Psycho-Phonologie, Université de Potchefstroom.

Tomatis, A.A. (1981). *La nuit uterine.* Paris: Stock.

Tomatis, A.A. (1987). Ontogenesis of the faculty of listening. In T.R. Verny (Ed.),

Pre- and peri-natal psychology: An introduction (pp. 23–35). New York: Human Sciences Press.

Tomatis, A.A. (1988). *Les troubles scolaires.* Paris: Ergo.

Tomatis, A.A. (1989a). *Vertiges.* Paris: Ergo.

Tomatis, A.A. (1989b). *Neuf mois au paradis.* Paris: Ergo.

Tomatis, A.A. (1991). *The conscious ear.* Barrytown, NY: Station Hill Press.

Tomatis, A.A., & Moulonguet, M. (1960). Conditionnement audio-vocal. *Bulletin de l'Académie Nationale de Medecine, 144,* 11–12.

Upledger, J.E., & Vredevoogd, J.D. (1983). *Craniosacral therapy.* Chicago: Eastland Press.

van Jaarsveld, P.E., & du Plessis, W.F. (1988). Audio-psycho-phonology at Potchefstroom: A review. *South African Tydskr. Sielk, 18*(4), 136–142.

Van Nagel, C., Siudzinski, R., Reese, E.J., & Reese, M.A. (1985). *Megateaching and learning.* Indian Rock Beach, FL: Southern Institute Press.

Vellutino, F.R., Smith, H.I., & Steger, J.A. (1975). Reading disability: Age differences and the perceptual deficit hypothesis. *Child Development, 46,* 487–493.

Vellutino, R.R., Steger, J.A. & Kandel, G. (1972). Reading disability: An investigation of the perceptual deficit hypothesis. *Cortex, 8,* 106–118.

Verny, T. (1981). *The secret life of the unborn child.* New York: Dell Publishing Co.

Von Bekesy, G. (1960). *Experiments in hearing.* New York: McGraw Hill.

Wallach, G.P., & Butler, K.G. (Eds.). (1984). *Language learning disabilities in school-age children.* Baltimore: Williams and Williams.

Weeks, B.S. (1989). The therapeutic effect of high-frequency audition and its role in sacred music. In T.M. Gilmor, P. Madaule, & B. Thompson (Eds.), *About the Tomatis Method* (pp. 159–189). Toronto: The Listening Centre Press.

Weeks, B.S. (1991). The physician, the ear and sacred music. In D.G. Campbell (Ed.), *Music physician for times to come.* Wheaton: Theosophical Publishing House.

Williams, R. (1989). *The trusting heart: Great news about type A behavior.* New York: Times Books.

Wolvin, A.D., & Coakley, C.G. (1991). *Listening* (4th ed.). Dubuque, IA: William C. Brown Company.

Wrightstone, J.S., Aronow, M.S., & Moskowitz, S. (1962). *Development of reading test norms for deaf children* (P.N. 22–262). New York: Bureau of Educational Research, Board of Education.

Chapter 8

Functions and Processes of Inner Speech in Listening

Jack (John) Johnson
Department of Communication
University of Wisconsin-Milwaukee

The purpose of this chapter is to elaborate a theoretical perspective useful in explaining listening. This theoretical perspective outlines the role of inner speech, ostensive speech, decentering-egocentrism, and semantic and syntactic elaboration in the process of assigning or generating meaning. It is also suggested that the degree to which listeners need internally to elaborate or expand on the word meanings and word arrangements of a speaker's message depends on three factors: (a) level of the speaker's egocentrism, (b) level of immediacy of feedback present and/or available in the interaction, and (c) amount of shared meaning between the speakers and listeners.

Previous research has acknowledged the central role that the assignment of meaning has to the process of listening. Wolvin and Coakley (1988), for example, conceptualized listening as a three phase process involving: "receiving, attending to and assigning meaning to aural stimuli" (p. 91). Similarly, Goss (1982) proposed a tripartite information processing model of listening involving (a) signal processing—understand the phonetic, syntactic, and semantic characteristics of messages; (b) literal processing—initial assignment of meaning; and (c) reflective processing—inference making, evaluating and judging speaker and message.

The purpose of this chapter is to elaborate a theoretical perspective useful in explaining and predicting how we assign or generate meaning while listening. This theoretical perspective is grounded in the concept of "inner speech" and is based on the theory and empirical research of Dance (1979), Johnson (1982, 1984), Korba (1986, 1989), Luria (1966, 1981), Sokolov (1972), and Vygotsky (1986).

INNER SPEECH

The concept of *inner speech* has been used to label a variety of phenomena, some of which do not share the same attributes. I am using the concept of inner speech to refer to subvocalized or silent speech used to *facilitate* symbolic thought in the process of creating word meanings. Vygotsky (1986) was one of the first to argue that the meaning of words is based on generalizations, and that these generalizations are a consequence of symbolic thought's capacity to make association between or among words. It is important to remember that while inner speech and symbolic thought are related, they are not one and the same. Inner speech is not merely thinking silently to oneself. Vygotsky (1986), in commenting on the relationship between thought and word meaning, aptly points out, "Word meaning is a phenomenon of thought only insofar as thought is embodied in speech, and of speech only insofar as speech is connected to thought and illuminated by it" (p. 212). Inner speech and symbolic thought exist in a symbiotic relationship with each dependent on the other for the generation of word meaning. Symbolic thought functions to make associations between or among words/concepts and, thus, creates word meanings. Inner speech, like all speech forms, dramatically influences and shapes this associative process. Inner speech influences symbolic thought by making the associative process faster and more efficient.

Inner speech operates in many ways like taking notes. While using inner speech, we silently generate a few key words to remind ourselves of a much larger ideas or concepts. For example, when we prepare a grocery list we write *eggs, bread, butter, milk*. This abbreviated list is a quick and efficient way to jog our memory when we go shopping or when we recall messages. The grocery list, like inner speech, does not need to elaborate the quantity of *eggs* (1 dozen), or the types of *bread* (whole wheat or rye), or that *butter* to us really means margarine.

Inner speech, as a consequence of its unique method of processing information, shapes how we think. Inner speech is an extremely complex process. To help you better understand how it operates, let us examine the structural and functional characteristics of inner speech as outlined in the writings of Dance (1979), Johnson (1982, 1984), Korba (1986, 1989), Luria (1966, 1981), Sokolov (1972), and Vygotsky (1986).

Structure of Inner Speech

A.R. Luria, in *Higher Cortical Functions in Man*, reminds us that inner speech is "one of the most structurally complex processes of speech and the investigator must not forget for one minute the extent of its complexity" (1966, p. 402). With this warning in mind, let us examine its structural characteristics to determine how it is similar to, yet different from, other forms of spoken language. Structurally, inner speech has four independent characteristics.

Egocentric. The first and overarching structural characteristic of inner speech is that it is designed for oneself rather than others. Therefore, it is a form of *intrapersonal* spoken language (the producer and intended receiver of the spoken language is one and same person). More importantly, inner speech is highly egocentric. According to Piaget, *egocentrism* is:

> a lack of differentiation between one's own point of view and other possible ones. (Piaget, 1962, p. 4)

> difficulty in understanding differences in points of view between the speakers and therefore in decentration. (Piaget & Inhelder, 1969, p. 118)

The majority of discussions of communicative egocentrism (e.g., Chandler, Greenspan, & Barenboim, 1974; Flavell, 1968; Greenspan & Barenboim, 1975; Piaget, 1955, 1969, 1973) have treated it as an exclusively speaker or sender phenomenon. However, egocentric qualities manifest themselves in both the production (speaking and writing) and *reception* (listening and reading of spoken or written language) of communication (Johnson, 1982, 1984). Therefore, communicative egocentrism is present whenever an individual(s) fails to assume cognitively the perspective of a listener(s) or a speaker(s) when either encoding or decoding extrapersonal (between persons) messages. Egocentrism does *not* refer to selfish, self-indulgent, or egotistical behaviors, nor is it evident through the frequent use of personal pronouns of *I* and *me* (Johnson, 1982).

A major difference between Piaget's and Vygotsky's theories of human development is based on their positions regarding the development and evolution of egocentrism. Piaget claimed egocentrism disappears as the result of a child's cognitive development (Piaget, 1955, 1969, 1973);

Vygotsky (1986) asserted that, sometime between the ages of 3 and 7, egocentrism is transformed into or "goes under ground" and is transformed into inner speech. Vygotsky also claimed that this evolution was designed so that egocentrism could serve cognitive functioning (Vygotsky, 1986). Vygotsky's thesis, that the genesis of inner speech rests in egocentrism, provides the rationale as to why egocentrism is one of inner speech's structural characteristics. Inner speech's remaining structural characteristics, to a large degree, reinforce its egocentric nature.

Silent. The second structural characteristic of inner speech is that it is silent. All of us talk or even mumble to ourselves out loud. However, when we use inner speech, our vocalizations are inaudible to the human ear, and, therefore, inner speech is characterized as being silent. Although we are unaware of the speech movements of inner speech, previous research has shown the physiological and articulatory activities of the auditory–speech mechanisms are used to produce inner speech (Korba, 1986; McGuigan, 1978; Sokolov, 1972).

Compressed Syntax. Inner speech's third structural characteristic concerns its syntax, or how it arranges words. The peculiar syntax and grammar of inner speech has been referred to as predicated (Sokolov, 1972; Vygotsky, 1986), elliptical (Leontiev, 1969), crushed or condensed (Johnson, 1984). These various descriptions refer to the compressed form of inner speech's syntax and grammar. Inner speech uses extremely low levels of syntactic elaboration. The syntactic compression or synthesis allows for the omission of the subject of sentences. The syntax or arrangement of words in inner speech is, therefore, incomplete.

The spoken language we use to communicate with others (*extrapersonal*) often contains syntactic qualities similar to those found in inner speech. For example, compressed syntax occurs in extrapersonal situations when everyone in a conversation knows the answer to a question or the subject of a sentence. The answer to the question, "Would you like to go to the store with me?" is seldom answered with, "No, I don't want to go to the store with you; instead, it is followed with a simple "No" or "No, not really." The compressed syntax of the answer is possible only because the subject of the request is understood by all parties involved in the communicative interaction. Here's another example. Let's say your roommate and you are at the airport waiting for a mutual friend to arrive on an incoming flight from Lansing, Michigan. Upon seeing your friend's plane land, you would probably not say to either yourself or to your roommate, "The plane from Lansing, Michigan, on which our friend, Amanda, is traveling, has just landed." You would be more likely to say, "It's here," "All right, let's get going!" or some other abbreviated statement. The reason you can compress the syntax of your utterance is that both you and your roommate understand the subject of your statement based on the situation or context.

While extrapersonal spoken language often involves compressed syntax, it does not compare to the high levels of syntactical compression found in inner speech. The process of inner speech, as previously discussed, is analogous to preparing a grocery list. The grocery list, like inner speech, lists the main items (eggs, bread, butter) to be purchased but does so without the complicated syntactical structure normally used in extrapersonal conversations or writings.

Semantic Embeddness. The fourth structural characteristic of inner speech is referred to as *semantic embeddness*. With inner speech, it is possible for a single word to signify or refer to much more than it would if the same word were used at an extrapersonal level. The semantic embeddness of the words used in inner speech is very high, and, therefore, the number of words used can be very low. The grocery list example also applies to this fourth characteristic of inner speech. If you examine your grocery list, you will note that you probably did not specify the type of bread (whole wheat, rye, or white spongy); milk (whole, skim, 2%); or cheese (Swiss, cheddar, provolone). The reason for this absence of elaboration is that the terms you used have embedded and detailed meaning. Therefore, there was no need for you to elaborate on the type of goods.

In contrasting the semantic content of inner speech with that of extrapersonal communication, we note that the subject of inner speech is always known to the user of inner speech and therefore requires no semantic elaboration or detail. However, a public speaker's subject matter is seldom known to all listeners; therefore, the content of the public message must be elaborated in order to be understood.

It is impossible, owing to the fact that inner speech is silent, to provide a concrete sample of inner speech. However, let's assume for a minute that you are considering going out to get some pizza. After deciding to do so, you would *not* generally say to yourself, "I'm going to go out to Mama Dindia's to get some pizza"; rather, you might silently say to yourself "Mama Dindia's pizza" or just simply "pizza." Note that your inner speech statement does not identify why you are going out, or perhaps even where you are going to go to get the pizza. This semantic synthesis is possible because you know the purpose of your trip and the name and location of where you are going to buy the pizza. Also note that your statement is not syntactically complete. It is obvious that the subject is "I" and there is no need to identify yourself. This characteristic eliminates the need to identify or elaborate the subject of the action. There is also an absence of conjunctions and other parts of speech.

Inner speech, as a result of these four structural characteristics, is an extremely fast and efficient method for decoding, storing, and encoding information to make associations between or among concepts (Johnson, 1984; Korba, 1986). While inner speech and symbolic thought are not the same process, inner speech's unique structural characteristics shape symbolic thought and the generation of symbolic meaning. To more fully understand how this process operates, we need to examine the functions of inner speech and the role inner speech plays in symbolic thought and the word meaning process. Vygotsky, in referring to the centrality of inner speech to thought and word meaning, asserted, "The relation of thought and word cannot be understood in all its complexity without a clear understanding of the psychological nature of inner speech" (Vygotsky 1986, p. 224).

Functions of Inner Speech

Examining the function(s) of a phenomenon permits us to understand the natural and inevitable consequences of the phenomenon (Dance & Larson, 1972, 1976). When we ask "What are the functions of inner speech?", we are asking what are the natural (without intent) and inevitable consequences of inner speech.

Korba (1986) provides one of the most elaborate functional analyses of inner speech by using the tripartite functional schema of Dance (1967) and Dance and Larson (1972, 1976). Korba (1986), using the work of others (e.g., Dance, 1967, 1979; Feldman, 1976; Galperin, 1969; Johnson, 1982, 1984; Kuczaj, 1986; Kuczaj & Bean, 1982; Luria, 1966, 1981; Luria & Yudovich, 1959; Sokolov, 1972; Vygotsky, 1986), argues that the functions of inner speech parallel those of other forms of spoken language and therefore can be categorized as (a) linking or helping humans associate with and relate to their physical, psychological, and sociological environments; (b) regulating or controlling human behavior; and (c) developing and maintaining higher mental processes or symbolic thought. Inner speech, while serving each of these functions, is critical to the third function, developing and maintaining symbolic thought.

Inner speech, as previously noted, can be characterized as an intrapersonal process and is therefore designed to serve self rather than others. In serving the self, inner speech is used to encode, decode, and store symbolic meanings that are used to make associations between or among concepts. Inner speech is, therefore, the functional opposite of ostensive speech (Johnson, 1984). The function of ostensive speech is to facilitate extrapersonal communication by ostensifying or revealing intrapersonal symbolic meanings. This process involves elaborating or encoding the syntax and semantics of inner speech to a level sufficient to be understood by others. The structure and function of inner speech makes it a central process of human communication. Korba (1986), in referring to this centrality, stated:

> All verbal interaction (and a great deal of nonverbal interaction) requires the use of inner speech, either in the preparation (encoding) of spoken language for others, or in the understanding (decoding) of spoken language of others. (p. 33)

Inner speech is a process central to how humans process and act upon information. The next section will further elaborate the role of inner speech in listening.

INNER SPEECH AND LISTENING

The direct communication of symbolic meaning between the minds of humans is both physiologically and psychologically impossible (Vygotsky, 1986). Instead, symbolic communication occurs in a very indirect manner, and inner speech plays an important role in this process. In the process of symbolic communication our symbolic thoughts are transformed into word meanings, and these meanings, through the process of ostensive speech, are elaborated and converted into extrapersonal spoken language. When we listen to spoken language, the process is reversed, and extrapersonal spoken language is transformed or synthesized into word meanings through inner speech and finally into symbolic thoughts. In previous writing, I outlined a series of models that illustrate this process (Johnson, 1984). Figure 8.1 presents an overview of this process. Vygotsky (1986) notes that this process is highly dynamic and nonlinear, involving a continuous progression from symbolic thought to word and word to symbolic thought. Thus, symbolic thought "does not merely find expression in speech; it finds its reality and form" (Vygotsky, 1986, p. 219).

The four structural characteristics of inner speech make it an extremely fast and efficient means for encoding, decoding, and storing information. However, inner speech's structural characteristics also directly and irrevocably affect the process of listening.

The structure of inner speech affects the "generation of meaning" or the "literal and reflective information processing" stages of listening in several ways. For example, as we listen and decode messages through inner speech, we significantly reduce the syntax of these messages. This reduction in syntax accounts for the estimated difference between speaking and listening rates that is often referred to in the listening literature (e.g., Nichols, 1955, 1957; Wolvin & Coakley, 1988). Numerous studies

Figure 8.1. An inner and ostensive speech model of human communication.

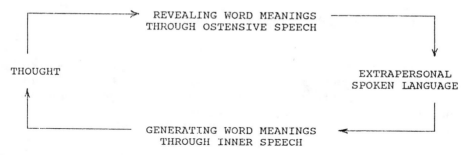

(e.g., Feldman, 1976; Foulke, 1971; Gough, 1972; Landauer, 1962) have examined word recognition and message comprehension rates during inner speech and estimated them to be somewhere between 275 and 400 words per minute. Korba (1986), in a study of the rate of inner speech, argued that, while these subvocalized rates may indicate a maximum number of words used in inner speech, they do not account for the semantic complexity of inner speech. Korba elaborated the logic of this argument by stating:

> It clearly stands to reason that if one word, conjured through inner speech, requires 100 words to adequately express its meaning in fully prepared, syntactical external speech, then each internal word carries a tremendous amount of idiosyncratic meaning for the individual. (1986, p. 84)

Korba (1986), to ascertain the number of words embedded in inner speech, asked subjects to list the key words they used while completing simple problem solving tasks and to expand these words into fully conversational speech. The self-report data were triangulated against the results of a spectral analysis of electromyography frequencies of the subjects' speech to verify that the subjects had subvocalized. The results indicate it takes over 4,000 words to semantically and syntactically expand 1 minute of inner speech into extrapersonal or conversational speech.

Regardless of how we determine the rate of inner speech, there is overwhelming agreement among researchers that inner speech operates at a significantly higher word-per-minute rate than extrapersonal spoken language. Inner speech's extremely high speed of processing and interpreting messages can be extremely beneficial but also hazardous. Nichols (1957) reminds us of this fact:

Not capitalizing on thought [inner speech] speed is our greatest single handicap. The difference between thought [inner speech] and speech speed breeds false feelings of security and mental tangents. Yet, through listening training, this same differential can be readily converted into our greatest asset. (p. 4)

We also know that the meanings of the words we use in inner speech have extremely complex and robust meanings. Quite simply, a single word used in inner speech has a multiplicity of meaning far beyond that found in extrapersonal spoken language. Furthermore, as a consequence of inner speech being inherently and structurally egocentric, the meanings we give to the words we speak and listen to are extremely idiosyncratic.

One of the major problems of listening is that understanding someone else requires us to decode the message based on the speaker's intended meaning. To overcome the natural egocentricity of inner speech, we must elaborate the word arrangements (syntactics) and word meanings (semantics) of our inner speech to a level sufficient to comprehend the intended meanings of a message. A large percentage of misunderstanding can be attributed to the inherent egocentrism of listeners' inner speech (Johnson, 1983). The cognitive behavior used to overcome this natural egocentricity is referred to as *decentering*.

Decentering

Decentering refers to the uniquely human ability to differentiate one's own point of view from the point of view of another. Decentering, like empathy, involves perspective taking. However, in decentering, one assumes the *cognitive* perspective of the other(s), whereas, in empathy one assumes the *emotional or physiological* perspective of the other(s) person (Johnson, Powell, & Reynolds, 1983).

Piaget (1955, 1962, 1973) was one of the earliest researchers to identify the process of decentering and asserted that decentering and egocentrism were opposites. That is, the lack of decentering implies the presence of egocentrism, and vice versa. Piaget and other researchers have labeled various forms or types of decentering, including physical, intellectual, spoken language (Piaget, 1955; Elkind, 1972; Flavell, 1963), perceptual (Bowd, 1974; Elkind, Larson, & Van Doorninck, 1965), and spatial (Rubin, 1974; Shantz & Watson, 1971). The vast majority of researchers treat the process of communicative decentering, like that of communicative egocentrism, as a speaker or sender phenomenon. This treatment, however, overlooks the major role decentering plays in listening.

Decentering occurs during listening when the listener assumes the cognitive perspective of the speaker in order to understand the speaker's intended meaning. To a degree, the process of decentering used in listening and in speaking is similar. Consequently, decentering in listening parallels the process described in Flavell's (1968) speaker model of decentering. In this process listening involves (a) perceiving an aural message; (b) covertly decoding, encoding, and storing the word meanings of the message using inner speech; and (c) making associations or generalizations (symbolic thought) based on the word meanings generated by inner speech. During this process the listener is confronted with suppressing the ever-present tendency to egocentrically interpret the words of the speaker. Decentering allows the listener to avoid the natural tendency to egocentrically interpret the messages of others.

Each of us produces and receives countless message, which, although intended to be understandable, are not. This problem is, to a large degree, the result of (a) inner speech being central to both speaking and listening, and (b) inner speech being highly egocentric. For example, it is possible for you to produce an egocentric message but have it make sense to your listeners because they decentered to your perspective and figured out your intended meaning. Similarly, it is possible for a speaker to produce a nonegocentric message but have it make no sense, because the listener(s) egocentrically interpreted the message. There is also the possibility that a message could make little or no sense because a speaker constructed a highly egocentric message and the listener(s) could not or did not decenter to interpret the speaker's intended meaning.

Listeners, therefore, are required to decenter to avoid their own levels of interpretive egocentrism and to counteract speakers' tendency to produce egocentric messages. Messages, of course, vary in their levels of egocentrism. Listed below are some moderately egocentric statements taken from insurance claim forms. While reading them, try to decenter and attempt to understand their intended meaning.

- I had been driving my car for 40 years when I fell asleep at the wheel and had the accident.
- Coming home, I drove into the wrong house and collided with a tree I don't have.
- The guy was all over the road. I had to swerve several times before I hit him.
- The accident happened when the right front door of a car came around the corner without giving a signal.

While these examples of egocentric spoken language are humerous, they are also representative of the levels of ambiguity often found in human communication. More often than we want to believe, our communication with others is filled with egocentric statements, and therefore it is necessary for listeners to decenter. Recently, I became interested in building a rock garden. One afternoon, while visiting a garden center, I spotted a pile of rocks and commented to my wife that they would be perfect for a rock garden. She smiled and said the rocks were too small for a garden, and that besides, we didn't really need a rock garden. Talk of the rock garden ceased, and after another 30 minutes of browsing, we left the center. While driving home, I spotted a truck loaded with rocks. Without referring to or pointing at the truck, I said to my wife, "That's what we need." Her response was, "So you're still thinking about building a rock garden." My wife, because she had seen the truck and decentered to my perspective, was able to understand my egocentric statement. However, on another occasion, my wife and I made arrangements to meet after work at the local art museum. She said to meet her at 6:00 p.m., in the front lobby. The museum, however, has two main entrances, one facing Lake Michigan and the other facing the parking lot. I assumed the front of the museum faced the lake, and she assumed the front entrance faced the parking lot. After 15 minutes of "patiently" waiting for her, I knew something was wrong and convinced myself to assume her perspective and tried to figure out what she had meant by her directions. I reminded myself that she had said, "Meet me at 6:00 p.m. in the front lobby." Within seconds, I remembered an earlier conversation in which we had disagreed on whether the side of a house facing a lake or river was the front or back. I immediately proceeded to the "back" entrance and found her "impatiently" waiting for me.

Estimating the Amount of Semantic and Syntactic Elaboration

The degree to which a listener needs to decenter and internally elaborate or expand on the word meanings (semantics) and word arrangements (syntactics) of a speaker's message depends on three factors: (a) level of the speaker's egocentric spoken language; (b) level of immediacy of feedback present and/or available in the communicative interaction; and (c) amount of shared meaning between or among the speakers and listeners (Johnson, 1984). Let's examine these three factors in detail.

Level of Speaker's Egocentrism. If a speaker decenters or assumes the perspective of the listener(s) and elaborates the semantics and syntactics of his or her messages to a level required by the listener(s), there is a corresponding decrease in the need for the listener to elaborate the semantic and syntactic structure of the speaker's statements. On the other hand, if a speaker fails to decenter, then it becomes necessary for the listener(s) to assume the speaker's perspective while elaborating the semantics and syntactics of the intended message. This form of message elaboration significantly increases the amount of time and effort it takes to listen.

Level of Immediacy of Feedback. Generally, as immediacy of feedback increases, there is a corresponding decrease in the need for the listener to elaborate internally the semantic and syntactic of a speaker's messages. For example, let's examine several communicative interactions. In the first interaction, you are listening to a public speaker deliver a formal speech to an audience of 500 people. Public communication allows almost no opportunity to verify the accuracy of our interpretations of the speaker's intended meaning. In situations where feedback is not available, there is a high probability of information overload because the listener(s) is not given the opportunity to ask questions or seek clarification. Therefore, in situations where feedback is not available, both speaker(s) and listeners need to be concerned with the egocentrism of their speaking and listening. On the other hand, let's say you are engaged in face-to-face communication in which all participants can equally feedforward and feedback information to one another. In this situation there is less need to internally elaborate the other speaker's word meanings and the word arrangements because you can stop the conversation and ask the speaker(s) for clarification. Public communication contexts, or situations in which feedforward and feedback are restricted, present a higher probability for listeners to interpret the messages of others egocentrically.

Level of Shared Meaning. The degree of decentering and semantic and syntactic elaboration required by the listener(s) is also influenced by the amount of shared meaning, or what George H. Mead called "significant symbolization," between or among speakers and listeners (Mead, 1922). Significant symbolization occurs when participants in a communicative interaction use words and gestures that have mutual or shared meanings. Generally, there is a greater chance for significant symbolization when individuals are familiar with each other's language systems. If both speakers and listeners share the same meanings for the words they use (significant symbolization), there is less of a need for either parties to elaborate the semantic and syntactics of messages. We all have undergone the difficulties of listening to a speaker who uses words we don't understand or for which we have different meanings. These communicative interactions tend to be highly tedious and time consuming. If I tell you that your fascia is sagging and needs replacing, will you know that I am talking about the board that covers your house's rafters, or will you make an appointment to see a plastic surgeon? The more significant symbolization, or shared meanings we have with speakers, the easier the process of listening.

SUMMARY AND CONCLUSION

This chapter has presented a theoretical perspective for understanding Wolvin and Coakley's (1988) third phase of listening (the assigning of meaning to aural stimuli) and Goss's (1982) second and third listening steps (literal and reflective information processing). Particular attention was given to describing and explaining the function of inner speech. It was suggested that inner speech, ostensive speech, decentering-egocentrism, and semantic and syntactic elaboration are key variables in assigning or generating meaning. Understanding how these variables influence the listening process provides a valuable tool for enhancing our listening effectiveness.

REFERENCES

Bowd, A. (1974). Factorial independence of perceptual egocentrism. *Perceptual Motor Skills, 38*, 453–454.

Chandler, M., Greenspan, S., & Barenboim, C. (1974). Assessment and training of role-taking and referential communication skills in institutionalized emotionally disturbed children. *Development Psychology, 10*, 546–553.

Dance, F.E.X. (1967). Towards a theory of human communication. In F. Dance (Ed.), *Human communication theory: Original essays* (pp. 288–309). New York: Holt, Rinehart and Winston.

Dance, F.E.X. (1979). Acoustic trigger to conceptualization. *Health Communication Informatics, 5*, 203–213.

Dance, F.E.X., & Larson, C. (1972). *Speech communication concepts and behaviors.* New York: Holt, Rinehart and Winston.

Dance, F.E.X., & Larson, C. (1976). *The functions of human communication.* New York: Holt, Rinehart and Winston.

Elkind, D. (1972, February). Egocentrism in young children. *Education Digest, 37*(6), 34–41.

Elkind, D., Larson, M., & Van Doorninck, W. (1965). Perceptual decentration learning and performance in slow and average readers. *Journal of Educational Psychology, 56*, 50–56.

Feldman, J. (1976). Why I move my lips when I read. *Claremont Reading Conference, 40*, 128–134.

Flavell, J. (1963). *The development psychology of Jean Piaget.* New York: D. Van Nostrand.

Flavell, J. (1968). *The development of role-taking and communication skills in children.* New York: Robert E. Krieger.

Foulke, E. (1971). Perceptions of time compressed speech. In D.L. Horton & J. Jenkins (Eds.), *The perception of language.* Columbus, OH: Charles Merrill.

Galperin, P. (1969). Stages in the development of mental acts. In M. Cole & I. Maltzman (Eds.), *A handbook of contemporary soviet psychology.* New York: Basic Books.

Goss, B. (1982). Listening as information processing. *Communication Quarterly, 30*, 304–307.

Gough, P. (1972). One second of reading. In J. Kavanagh & I. Mattingly (Eds.), *Language by ear and by eye: The relationship between speech and reading.* Cambridge, MA: MIT Press.

Greenspan, S., & Barenboim, C. (1975, June). *A matrix test of referential communication.* Paper presented at the Fifth Annual Symposium of the Jean Piaget Society, Philadelphia.

Johnson, J.R. (1982). Egocentric spoken language and reading achievement: An examination of relationship. *Communication Education, 31*, 115–123.

Johnson, J.R. (1983). Understanding misunderstanding: A key to effective communication. *Training and Development Journal, 37*(8), 62–68.

Johnson, J.R. (1984). The role of inner speech in human communication. *Communication Education, 31*, 211–222.

Johnson, J.R., Powell, R., & Reynolds, E. (1983, November). *Empathy: An analysis of the lack of intersubjectivity.* Paper presented at the Speech Communication Association Convention, Washington, DC.

Korba, R. (1986). *The rate of inner speech.* Unpublished doctoral dissertation, University of Denver.

Korba, R. (1989). The cognitive psychophysiology of inner speech. In C.V. Roberts & K. Watson (Eds.), *Intrapersonal communication processes: Original essays.* New Orleans, LA: Spectra.

Kuczaj, S. (1986). *Children's acquisition of word meaning.* Hillsdale, NJ: Erlbaum.

Kuczaj, S., & Bean, A. (1982). The development of noncommunicative speech systems. In S. Kuczaj (Ed.), *Language development, Volume 2: Language thought and culture.* Hillsdale, NJ: Erlbaum.

Landauer, T. (1962). Rate of implicit speech. *Perceptual and Motor Skills, 15*, 646.

Leontiev, A. (1969). Inner speech and the processes of grammatical generation of utterances. *Soviet Psychology, 7*(3), 11–16.

Luria, A. (1966). *Higher cortical functions in man.* New York: Basic Books.

Luria, A. (1981). *Language and cognition.* New York: John Wiley and Sons.

Luria, A., & Yudovich, F. (1959). *Speech and the development of mental processes in the child* (J. Simon, Trans.). London: Staples Press.

McGuigan, F. (1978). *Cognitive psychophysiological measurement of covert behavior.* Hillsdale, NJ: Erlbaum.

Mead, G. (1922). A behavioristic account of the significant symbol. *The Journal of Philosophy, 14*, 157–163.

Nichols, R. (1955). Ten components of effective listening. *Education, 75*, 292–302.

Nichols, R. (1957). Listening is a 10-part skill. *Nation's Business, 45*, 4.

Piaget, J. (1955). *The language and thought of a child.* New York: New American Library.

Piaget, J. (1962) Comments on Vygotsky's critical remarks. In L. Vygotsky, *Thought and language.* Cambridge, MA: MIT Press.

Piaget, J. (1973). *The psychology of intelligence,* Totowa, NJ: Littlefield, Adams and Company.

Piaget, J., & Inhelder, B. (1969). *The psychology of the child,* New York: Basic Books.

Rubin, K. (1974). The relationship between spatial and communicative egocentrism in children and young and old adults. *The Journal of Genetic Psychology, 125*, 295–301.

Shantz, C., & Watson, J. (1971). Spatial abilities and spatial egocentrism in the young child. *Child Development, 42*, 171–181.

Sokolov, A. (1972). *Inner speech and thought* (G.T. Onischenko, Trans.). New York: Plenum Press.

Vygotsky, L. (1986). *Thought and language* (A. Kozulin, Trans.). Cambridge, MA: MIT Press.

Wolvin, A., & Coakley, C. (1988). *Listening*. Dubuque, IA: Wm. C. Brown.

Chapter 9

Empathy and Listening*

Tom Bruneau

Department of Communication
Radford University
Radford, VA

Empathy in the practice of listening is central and complex. The concept and processes of empathy are explained, and a synthesis of important ideas is offered. The definitions and explanations are then applied to instructional considerations. Practical applications are implied throughout, and some specific strategies are outlined. The teaching of empathic listening is a relatively new area of listening pedagogy.

INTRODUCTION

This chapter concerns the elusive meanings of a complex concept and process of communication—being empathic toward others as listeners. The first section offers a definitional and conceptual focus, showing how complicated the concept is and its varied meanings. The second section involves kinds or ways of being empathic and processes of empathy. In this

---

* This chapter only briefly reviews the concept of empathy as necessary. For those interested in a fairly detailed review of the concept of empathy as well as a review of historical and current literature about empathy, the reader is referred to Bruneau (1988a, 1989a).

section, empathy will be discussed as it relates to biological, signalic (nonverbal), psychological, and social aspects of both speakers and listeners. In the last section, empathic processes will be discussed as they relate to practical listening attitudes, everyday philosophy, and instruction.

Empathy is a central communication variable. The practice of empathy implies individuality, otherness, as well as people in relationships. Empathy also implies feedback, caring for others, understanding others, etc. Empathy further implies communicating accurately and efficiently as well as the reduction of communication noise and uncertainty. The conceptual review to follow will provide further support for our claim as to the centrality of the concept of empathy in communication study, as well as the importance of empathic practice and the complexity of empathic concepts and processes.

THE CONCEPT OF EMPATHY

A Definitional Focus

Empathy literally means "feeling into" another, an animal, environment, or even an object, structure, or work of art. The concept has come to be understood commonly as "feeling with" another, while *sympathy* is commonly understood as "feeling for" another, at a distance or noninvolved. The empathy concept is related to other concepts such as *apathy* (no feeling) and *telepathy* (feeling across) in uncanny ways. The concept, however, is not just concerned with feeling or sensing another's emotions or subjective experiencing. It can also pertain to how we share behavior together, how we logically, strategically, or analytically infer the thoughts, attitudes, and assess the thinking styles of others. Thinking as another thinks is a complex listener variable.

Empathy is related to many other communication-based variables, compounding its conceptual complexity: intuition, caring, inference-making, role taking, concern, mind-reading, other directedness, involvement, compassion, introspection about others, loving and intimacy, mutuality, prediction and projection, perspective taking, and so on.[1] Defining empathy can be simple, e.g., "putting" yourself in someone's "shoes"; the definition can be complex, for example, vicariously experiencing another in mirrored reciprocity. The act of putting or "placing" ourselves elsewhere is quite obscure when we begin to analyze *how* we do this

---

[1] These variables are discussed further by Bruneau (1988a, 1989a).

feeling-wise, perceptually, and psychologically. In short, a complete or even adequate definition of empathy may never be possible, because there are so many complex and interacting levels of experiencing involved.

EMPATHY AS PROCESSUAL

Empathy can be understood as interconnected levels of information processing: object identification, imitation and replication, psychological operations, interactive sequencing, and as social role taking and role interplay.

Object Identification

Concepts of empathy first developed in relation to the study of the perception of objects (Lipps, 1907), whereby one imitates and attempts to become the structural attributes of what is perceived. At a crude level of human interaction, including certain modes of objective observation, a person attempts to go "over there," to another place, to perceptually shift his or her viewpoint toward the other (but not back to one's self). While the objectification of others as perceptual objects or spatial surfaces (figure/ground) is crude in terms of developing relations with others, it is necessary developmentally and it is important to the localization, identification, and recognition of others.

Developing out of a two-dimensional observation of others is a personal depth, a three-dimensionality; others become localized in a dynamic spatiality. We can then begin to sense others in their own personal spatiality. We begin to be able to see others looking *at us* from their viewpoints and we begin to understand that the object (person) of our observations concerns our own position relative to the one observed. Objectivity is initial to the relativity of others *to our own relativity.*

Imitation and Replication of Others

Much of early communication behavior learning is acquired by imitating and attempting to replicate the communication acts of others; for example, we attempt to replicate the speech and gestures of others in language learning. Once we have achieved a dynamic objectification of another (which goes beyond thingifying and localizing another as a position), a mirrored reference to ourselves as observers is possible. We are then capable of seeing ourselves as part of the observational field and the initial relativity in our perception, vis-á-vis the other, *in us.* We can then begin to go beyond earlier forms of imitation and replication of others and we can experience an active entrainment of the other *as part of our own sensory and perceptual processes.* Buber (1948, p. 97) referred to this phenomenon as one coming to understand the "motorality of the object with the perception of one's own muscles." Lipps (1926) described the process as "motor mimicry" whereby a perceiver develops internal cues similar to those experienced and reflected by the other. In this light, Cottrell (1942) described many aspects of empathy as resulting from and related to a "process of responding by reproducing the acts of the other(s)" (p. 384). Kenneth Burke's (1945, 1950) theory of identification also concerns the imitative basis of empathy in that, by striving to overcome generic differences between people, we transcend them when we adopt similar dress, behavior, language, attitudes, etc. Howell (1979) elegantly defined *empathy* as "the ability to replicate what one perceives" (p. 33). Restak (1984) developed the notion that empathy has, not only physiological and perceptual correlates, but also neurological ones such as mutual entrainment, information-processing similarities and differences based on biological and psychological rhythms, and kinesic synching processes. To be finely and intensely attuned to another, especially emotionally and nonverbally, is to lose one's own ego as objective. It is to act and perceive as the other does, to be mutually entrained. A kind of empathy called *umwelt* projection seems to occur (Bruneau, 1988a, 1989a). *Umwelt* means one's world, one's space-time reality. Von Uexkull (1921, 1957) developed the idea of a species-specific world of animals (and people) that is comprised of the signals and sensory data as reception and signal-giving or emitting capabilities. When one practices *umwelt* projection, he or she displaces his or her spatio-temporality and attempts to become vicariously the space-time world of another (or animal). Such an empathic presence in a listener may be considered to be, optimally, an "active listening." It seems reasonable to suggest that excellent listeners are so because they can attune or accommodate their biological and perceptual processes to those of a speaker in a variety of communication contexts. A more thorough review of empathic processes as related to biological rhythms and rhythmic interactions between communicators can be found in (Bruneau, 1988b), especially in terms of mutual entrainment and the synchronicity of personal tempos.

Empathic Psychological Processes

A number of mental processes are involved in empathizing. Arising out of the objective identification of another, as well as sensorial and perceptual accommodation, are a number of important psychological processes.

These processes involve the conception and understanding of the other as well as the symbolic and interpretive representation of the other *as one's own psychological mode*. Here we are concerned with guessing or inferring how another is thinking, including the contents, meanings, or significations of his or her thoughts. Also involved are processes of thinking reflectively or retrospectively about another *after* interaction has occurred. Psychological projections or projective anticipations and expectations concerning how another will act, what and how they will say, will think, and so on, are also highly involved. Of course, thinking as another is thinking *while they are thinking* concerns psychological forms of mutual empathy and the entrainment or attunement to the other(s) mentally, that is, forms of interactive empathy.

There are times when being objective and analytical about another, especially during emotional situations, is a form of psychological empathy. Selfish listening, especially from one's interests, experiences, and motivations, is not obverse to empathic listening, except when it is all-pervasive. It seems to be the case that, with some communicative expertise, being judgmental and critical about others can be construed as being empathic. However, for the most part, these forms of empathy are often projectively egocentric and not other-directed; they mostly concern one's own viewpoints, needs, values, beliefs, assumptions, opinions, attitudes, and so on, and often are not those of the other from his or her mental perspective. Certain kinds of thinking styles or thought modes appear to discourage or aggravate empathic understanding: quick assumptions, quick inferences about another, simplistic evaluations of another, stereotyping the other's appearance or thought or actions, thingifying or categorizing the other, naming the other, personality typing and so on. Mainly, these are problems of the need of observers or listeners for certainty, simplicity, or for the negating of the other as a complex person. They are problems of simplistic two-dimensional or dialectical thought. While such psychological processes pertain to empathy as perceptual object identification, they are initial and crude forms of empathy as psychological otherness and seem to restrict more authentic experiencing of otherness.

To attempt to identify the thought content or the style of thought, logical operations, and so on, is an act of inference; to value or evaluate or devaluate the thought or style of thought is an act of judgment. These can be empathic psychological forms, depending on the purpose, intent, or ego involvement of the would-be empathizer. They can be initial mental acts of empathy—if they are accurate projections and can be used as portals with which to enter the thoughts or thinking of another *as if one were the other*.

The literature concerning psychological modes of emphasizing is somewhat confusing. Acts of perception (mainly visual perception) are often considered psychological acts (signalic, nonverbal processes are given psychological or symbolic import). There is a great confusion in the literature concerning empathic feeling-with, experiencing another's emotions, and experiencing another's mental activity vicariously. The line (if such a line actually does exist or is credible) between thoughts and emotions in the conceptualizing of empathy has been obscure since the turn of the century. Several sample conceptualizations are in order.

Rogers (1966) defined *empathy* as "the ability of the therapist to perceive experiences and feelings accurately and sensitively" (p. 186). Koestler (1949) considered one aspect of empathy to be a projection or introjection into another in order to participate in his or her emotions. Danish and Kagen (1971) discussed empathy as "affective sensitivity," which is "the ability to detect and describe the immediate affective state of another (p. 51). Stotland (1969) described empathy to be "a state in which an observer reacts emotionally because he perceives experiencing or about to experience an emotion" (p. 12).

Other representative ideas concerning empathy as a psychological process include: losing consciousness of one's self in the other (Lipps, 1907); the experience of foreign consciousness in general (Stein, 1917/1970); the nowness of Youness (Buber, 1923/1970); trial identification (Fliess, 1942); "I-and-the-Other" (Sartre, 1943/1956); identification (Burke, 1945, 1950); a creative act (Schafer, 1959); inference making (Berlo, 1960); personal introspection about another in the here-and-now (Waedler, 1960); vicarious introspection (Katz, 1963); sudden intuition (Kohut, 1966); a mode of cognition (Kohut, 1971); an information-gathering activity (Kohut, 1982); predicting what another will feel, say, or do about you, himself, and others (Smith, 1966); accuracy in being sensitive to the current feelings of another (Truax & Carkhuff, 1967); projecting one's consciousness into another (Assagioli, 1973); resonating the other as a special unconscious ability (Karush, 1979); and creating an "interpersonal space" in the analytic situation (Schlesinger, 1984). This brief review not only shows how difficult it is to conceptualize empathizing as a psychological mode, it seems to indicate a wide range of kinds of thinking and feeling related to empathizing with another. Also, a great deal of semantic and conceptual confusion seems apparent. Nonetheless, there appear to be many kinds of conscious (or even unconscious) processes involved and any caring listener in any context seems to have to be inherently empathizing to be fully active and aware communicatively.

Empathy as a Step-Flow or Interactive Process

Empathy as a step-flow or interactive process can be described as a series of conscious acts or alterations of viewpoint in a linear sequence. It can also be conceptualized as a cyclic process that continues for a given period of time whereby an interaction event is articulated in distinct steps of an ongoing alternating process. In many models of empathic processes various biological, imitative, and psychological forms of empathizing (or combinations thereof) appear to be effected. The intention of such models is to describe an entire interactive process as more than a single act, inference, intuition, and so on, and to visualize people in an interactive, face-to-face situation or event. A few selected examples from the empathy literature should help to clarify this conceptualization.

Lipps (1907) described a process of inner imitation: one is stimulated by an object and imitates the object, the observer feels himself or herself into the object, loses consciousness of himself or herself, and then experiences the object as his or her identity, as if he or she had become the object (Katz, 1963, p. 85). The sociologist Moreno (1914) described empathy as "a meeting of two: eye to eye, face to face. And when you are near I will take your eyes out and place them instead of mine, and you will take my eyes out and will place them instead of yours, then I will look at you with your eyes and you will look at me with mine" (p. 63). Stein (1917/1970) described a three-step flow: the emergence of the experience (empathy), the fulfilling explication (sympathy), and the comprehensive objectification of the explained experience (oneness). In a psychoanalytical approach, Katz (1963, p. 41) described the process as (a) identifying with the other by becoming absorbed in the other, (b) taking the experience of the other into ourselves (incorporation), (c) the other's experience echoes within the empathizer (reverberation), and (d) the empathizer then distances himself or herself from the other by objective analysis (detachment). Rogers (1975) described empathy as a "way of being" where the empathizer first enters and becomes at home in the private world of another; secondly, is sensitive, moment by moment of felt changes or meanings in the other; and, lastly, communicates with the other to describe the empathizer's sensing of his or her world (p. 4). Bennett (1979) described an empathic process in intercultural communication situations: assuming difference, knowing self, suspending self, allowing guided imagination, allowing empathic experience, and reestablishing self (pp. 419–421). These as well as other examples mainly describe an observer either objectively or subjectively attempting to enter the interior world of another or others and in various ways attempting to create subject–object interplay between his or her own world view and that of the other. These descriptions are often specific to therapeutic strategies.

Empathizing in transactional and interpersonal contexts complicates considerations of empathic processes. In such contexts empathizing can occur as alternating viewpoint taking: alternating between one's own viewpoint (biologically, emotionally, or psychologically) and the as-if-I-were-the-other viewpoint. Also, being empathic can take the form of alternating between *what* another is saying (symbolic, meaningful interest) and *how* another is saying it (signalic, nonverbal processes). In a way, one alternates from symbolic to signalic information processing while also switching viewpoints, for example, myself emotionally, the other meaningfully, myself-as-other emotionally, myself meaningfully, myself-as-other meaningfully, and so on. A syntax of such alternations is possible as to intrapersonal–interpersonal sequencing. In terms of interactive empathic processes, dynamic transactions can further include being similarly conscious, feeling mutually, as well as being mutually synchronous biologically and nonverbally.

Empathy as Social Role Taking and Role Interplay

Mead (1934) viewed empathy as "the capacity to take the role of the other and to adopt alternative perspectives vis-a-vis oneself" (p. 27). Taking the role of significant others and seeing from their perspectives, according to Mead, concerns how we develop a self capable of deeper kinds of empathy with others. Berlo (1960) developed a theory of empathy whereby one attempts to recreate another's perspective by imaginatively taking his or her role as if it were one's own. Generally, role taking can be considered as a way of learning about others in terms of their life roles (mother, father, brother, etc.), their occupational roles, their leadership roles, as well as their roles situationally, for example, this speaker's role with this audience at this time, under these circumstances, etc. Excellent listeners, it is often assumed, practice role taking continuously in trying to understand messages and speaker intent, purpose, implications, etc.

While role taking implies mainly psychological perspective taking and thinking about another's role obligations, attitudes, assumptions, and so on, role taking also implies imitation. Simulating or enacting the role of another *in situ* or vicariously through imagined settings and situations are also aspects of role taking. The imitation of another's role through speech, gesture, motor behavior, and so on, however dramatistic, is a way of learning, a way of understanding. It is a way of securing information through trial and error (role discrepancy) in order that one can feel and understand the other better so that more accurate reflective and projective empathy (defined below) can occur. Such role taking through enactments, too, can provide the basis for greater awareness in interactive contexts. In listening actively, listeners can take the role of the speaker as to demographic characteristics (status, authority, age, etc.), speaker purpose, relationship to the audience, and so forth. Further, listeners can co-enact the speaker's intent mentally and also assume the speaker's voice and nonverbal mannerisms vicariously, both imaginatively at a distance as well as through active here-and-now imitation and replication—within necessary constraints.

Kinds of Empathy

In conceptualizing empathy, its processual complexity becomes more manageable if we differentiate kinds of empathy related to levels of mental and perceptual experiencing, kinds of behavior, and communication contexts. First of all, it is convenient to categorize empathy in terms of time perspectives that can help to answer questions as to "when" and, implicitly, "how" empathy is processual. Recently, Bruneau (1988a, 1989b) attempted to describe empathic processes as an interplay of perception (present), memory (past), and anticipation/expectation (future). A brief outline of these theoretical formulations is offered below.

Interactive empathy (or *momentary empathy*) concerns communicative processes during act-ual or event-ual transactions, becoming the other in the moment, in the here-and-now, as an immediate apprehension of the other perceptually (signalically) and as *momentary otherness*. The imitative and biological bases of empathy are highly involved.

Interactive empathy whereby two (or more) are attempting to share messages can become a kind of *mirrored reciprocity*. People attempt to replicate and reflect the other in the transactional moment. When more than one interactant is empathically engaged momentarily in a positive synchronous or rhythmic manner, we can refer to a *mutual empathy*. Mirrored reciprocity seems to exemplify, in part, Howell's (1979, p. 33) definition of empathy: "the ability to replicate what one perceives." In social and group situations, interactive and mutual empathy become more complex and notions of group identity, solidarity, and cohesion appear to be related to developing empathic processes in groups large and small.

Reflective empathy refers to re-sensing, remembering, forgetting, perceiving again, and mnemonic processes *after* the occurrence of communicative acts, events, occasions, etc. Reflective empathy refers to "re-seeing" (after images of self and others visually) and "re-hearing" or "re-listening" (auditory images). In some ways, "re-spect" (to see again, literally), or "re-inspection," or introspection about others, all concern reflective empathy. Out of necessity, concern, interest, and so on, the act of reflecting upon past communication acts can be symbolically analytical or without conscious volition. Re-feeling, or re-sensing, or re-experiencing moods, past communication climates, and other elusive aspects of communication encounters often happen, but how and why these reflections occur is often elusive. The idea of residual messages has received very little serious attention by communication theorists and pragmatists alike.

However this may be, it seems reasonable to assume that, for ongoing relationships, for the re-occurrence of like acts and events, and for the continuation of communication activities, empathic reflection provides for the contents with which to make empathic projections.

Projective empathy concerns futurity, thinking ahead, planning ahead, anticipation, expectation, feelings toward events, occasions, acts, and so on, *to come*. Stotland's term *predictive empathy* (1969, p. 275) is involved when measured accuracy of one's own forward guessing is tested against future outcomes. Projective empathy concerns the ability to plan for, to forecast, and to imagine communication acts, events, and occasions of one's self and others in interaction. The essence of audience analysis by speakers concerns projective empathy. Listeners, too, can obviously prepare to listen, to anticipate, and not just merely reflect upon what has been said. Thinking ahead is an art form that is slighted or often ignored. Rehearsal for the future concerns practice and preparation, caring about future messages, the response to those messages, and the potential after-effects of these messages.

Interactive, reflective, and projective empathy are highly interrelated processes. It seems reasonable to believe that the more one is interactively aware and attentively entrained with others, the more one can be adequately and accurately engaged mnemonically later. Further, it seems reasonable to posit that the more one can and does engage in reflective empathy, the more one has information of many kinds which can serve as the basis for projective empathic processes. These are all critical and interrelated hypotheses in dire need of creative and imaginative research. The implications of these hypotheses for communication training and instruction are many.

TO LISTEN EMPATHICALLY

Empathic Listening: Philosophy and Attitudes

To listen empathically, as suggested above, has many meanings. Empathic listening concerns many levels of human experiencing; it is a way of being, a way of learning effectively, a style of being fully human. It concerns the dynamic processing of both verbal and nonverbal information.

Empathic listening can even be considered to be a philosophy of communicating, of responding, in that such listening implies a fuller personhood, a healthy view of otherness and self, as well as a guide to living and loving more fully. Empathic listening is to be respectful of the dignity of others. Empathic listening is a caring, a love of the wisdom to be found in others whoever they may be. Empathic listening is to be open to the world and others as unique and separate realities. Listening empathically is to be continually discovering our own special uniqueness in others, seeing ourselves from other perspectives, and it helps us to unfold our own individuality. Empathic listening is an active philosophy, a way of growth in authentic selfhood.

To be an empathic listener obviously requires an active and pervasive attitude about the worth of empathic listening. While the obvious advantages briefly outlined above are incentives, being empathic is a commitment to another or others and, sometimes, an obligation to be involved in their problems and livelihoods. It is difficult to be empathic with one's enemies (though often beneficial), with those who are ignorant and crass, or with those who may do us harm in some manner. Being empathic does imply a cost–benefit ratio in that being empathic with some people may cost us dearly in terms of time, effort, and a lack of positive results. This should not be a deterrent to empathizing in selected ways in order to understand the negative or even psychological or sociological pathologies of others. Indeed, empathizing will help us gain an understanding of the commonly misunderstood and what we often avoid.

Empathic listening not only necessitates an awareness of advantages, it requires an inherent interest in empathic processes as well as a motivated interest in people. To be an empathic listener is to be a lover of "people watching." Those who are consumed in their own ego involvements, consumed in difficult emotional problems or psychological pathologies of many sorts, are not likely to be empathically involved with others or to be motivated toward listening empathically. Such pathologies are often characterized by alienation from interaction.

Listening empathically requires attentive vigilance and endurance; it demands both physical health and mental alertness, perseverance, as well as fortitude. To be actively empathic implies that one is fully involved biologically, physiologically, perceptually, psychologically, and socially. Being empathic as a listener or speaker requires that one process a great deal of information and be capable of integrating and synthesizing this information. To be fully empathic is to experience an overloading or taxing of one's own neurological systems. Empathic listening can be exhausting; to be negentropic (reducing uncertainty) in the uniqueness of others requires an intensity of focus and the willingness to shift focus. It requires an ability to process many different kinds of information (both left and right brained) in a dynamic manner. Being an empathic listener requires a willingness to alter one's own habits and regularities in receiving and interpreting information; it requires a love of strangeness, novelty, and change. Being empathic seems to require a courage to lose one's own ego and self-as-central to one's own identity, to decenter and recenter again and again.

Being empathic as a listener implies a healthy self-concept and an adequate level of self-esteem. To venture forth in the minds and feelings of others is to be able to lose or displace one's own identity. Those with fragile or fractured identities seem to fear further confusion in the joy of otherness. Also, those who hold to their own identities as permanent, perfect, or too stable may have difficulty in experiencing otherness authentically and as dynamically variable. To change one's identity, at least temporarily, is required in empathizing fully.

The ability to feel one's own biological systems to feel one's own emotions fully, and to feel a wide variety of affective motion, moods, *phoria*, and so on, may be essential to listening empathically. Those who have learned to inhibit or restrict their own feelings (for a variety of reasons) may have difficulty as empathic listeners. To be highly dogmatic and closed-minded, too, appears to be the obverse of empathic listening, especially in terms of speech content or topic. To be overly objective and analytical can sometimes prevent empathizing.

Empathic Listening: Applied Perspectives

Focus on clarifying the concept and articulating the process of empathy in communication studies has been sorely lacking (Redmond, 1983; Stewart, 1983; Gordon, 1985; Bruneau, 1989a; Thomlison, 1991). It should not be surprising, then, to find empathic communication instruction and training to be "embryonic" (Coonfield et al., 1975, p. 12) and that we have "so loose a grasp...on ways of increasing the empathic tendencies of human communicators" (Gordon, 1985, p. 1). The reasons why such a central communication concept and process should be neglected in applied communication literature appear to be several: (a) the concept and process of empathizing are extremely complex and highly variable, (b) differing communication contexts concern differing ways of empathizing, (c) the valid measure of empathic abilities is froth with great difficulties (and sorrowful results), and (d) in the case of empathic listening, no valid measures exist, and how we can effectively teach it to others is pedagogically infantile.

A number of attitudinal and motivational prerequisites about understanding empathy and becoming better empathic listeners have been suggested in the previous section and throughout this chapter. Also, a number of directions for empathy instruction have been implied throughout. While it is not in the scope of this chapter to detail training exercises or instructional techniques, some suggestions for teaching empathic listening are in order.

Increasing the amount and kinds of listener feedback responses (active listening) and developing an "attentive style" (Norton, 1982) are essential to empathic listening. Active attentiveness seems to be necessary to one's biological arousal as well as activating the imitative bases of empathic projection. Active attentiveness appears to be essential to being capable of feeling as a speaker (regardless of context) feels. This arousal concerns the ability to be involved and committed, not only to the expression of others, but to one's own abilities in affective decentering. The study and analysis of listeners responding on videotape or in the here and now can sensitize people to their own response styles and affective involvement in the expression of others. Those reluctant to feel or those pervasively objective in perspective taking need to affectively engage and, then, affectively decenter, again and again.

Having listeners recognize and discriminate between emotional connotations (paralinguistics and nonverbal communication) and the logical and lexical content of spoken discourse can help them to recognize their own abilities to decenter affectively or to decenter cognitively—and to switch between modes of decentering. Asking listeners to report how a speaker felt or feels while expressing can be a testing of these decentering abilities as well as to provide motivation in listening to both the content and treatment of spoken messages. Exercises can be designed to have learners alternately assess the feelings and thoughts of speakers, that is, empathic code switching. Listeners who are usually highly involved affectively may need to be involved in activities that help them become aware of speech content, main ideas, how a speaker is thinking, a speaker's values, beliefs, motives, intentions, purpose, etc. Listeners can be asked to assess such cognitive structures at intervals during live or videotaped expressions in formal or informal contexts.

Having trainees or students practice, "you just said—you were feeling when you said" exercises can be important to empathic listening instruction. Listeners are forced into an attentive style, expanding attentive vigilance and exercising reflective empathy. These kinds of carefully given feedback exercises seem to not only help in the active practice of listening comprehension, they seem to test other-directedness abilities. Many listeners are unable to assess the feelings of others talking objectively. Many listeners seem unable to assess the feelings of others who are talking about various personal or emotionally arousing topics, past experiences, and so on. Having listeners feedback to speakers what they said and how they felt can be followed up with requiring listeners to state "why" they said it. This latter variation requires accuracy in inference making and other modes of psychological empathizing.

In terms of the imitative bases of empathic listening, trainees or students can be asked to "replay" short spoken expressions just heard from a dyad partner, attempting to say the same words *exactly*, in the same order, and in the same voice with the same vocal variety. Additionally, trainees can be asked to mirror-image the nonverbal expressions of speakers (or simply mirror-image nonverbal scripts without spoken discourse). Paralinguistic (sounds without words) exercises can also be conducted similarly. These kinds of exercises and variations of them are practice in interactive empathizing. Once the trainees become spontaneous and begin to enjoy such exercises, the "monkey-see-monkey-do" novelty can be used to discuss the powerful bonding processes which seem to occur.

Enacting the roles of others is a common communication training technique and, when coupled with assessing role discrepancy, can create empathic understanding and feeling. Role playing one's own future can also create empathy for one's own self. For people who are well beyond the acquaintance stage, role-reversal techniques are helpful. "I'll talk like you, then you talk like me" exercises can lead into exercises where "I will talk like you talking to me while you talk like me talking to you" exercises. By adding the role playing of other focal participants in the web of triads or networks of interactants much empathic understanding and the perception of the feelings of others can be discovered, assessed, and accommodated.

Asking people to report their message residues, their delayed recall, can help to develop reflective empathy. The raising of consciousness about after-images, hearing again, re-experiencing feeling tones, and so on, is an important empathy listening exercise. Such training exercises can be conducted immediately after a message is heard or even long after.

Asking listeners to report what a speaker actually sees out of his or her eyes (in visual snap shots or sequences) in terms of perceptual viewpoint taking seems to develop otherness in listeners. Asking listeners to scan the audience (of one or many) through the eyes of a speaker is an important exercise. Having listeners attempt to imagine hearing the speaker as he or she may be hearing his or herself is important.

While it may be impossible to teach some people to care for and commit themselves to helping others for many reasons, the above instructional suggestions are good starting points for empathic listening training and instruction. Many other approaches to teaching empathic communication in general and empathic listening in particular are deserving of more focus than permits here. The need to develop and collect together empathy training and teaching devices is certainly necessary in the years to come. Empathic listening instruction is new—in a world where the cry to "have empathy" for others is old.

REFERENCES

Assagioli, R. (1973). *The act of will.* New York: Viking Press.

Bennett, M.J. (1979). Overcoming the golden rule: Sympathy and empathy. In D. Nimmo (Ed.), *Communication yearbook 3* (pp. 407–422). New Brunswick, NJ: Transaction Books.

Berlo, D.K. (1960). *The process of communication.* New York: Holt, Rinehart and Winston.

Bruneau, T. (1988a). Conceptualizing empathy in intercultural contexts. *Human Communication Studies* (Japan), *16*, 37–70.

Bruneau, T. (1988b). Personal time and self-identity. In P. Reale (Ed.), *Time and identity* (pp. 102–115). Milan: Franco Angeli.

Bruneau, T. (1989a). Empathy and listening: A conceptual review and theoretical directions. *Journal of the International Listening Association, 3,* 1–20.

Bruneau, T. (1989b). The deep structure of intrapersonal communication processes. In C. Roberts & K. Watson (Eds.), *Intrapersonal communication processes: Original essays* (pp. 63–81). Scottsdale, AZ: Gorsuch Scarisbrick.

Buber, M. (1948). *Between man and man.* New York: Macmillan.

Buber, M. (1970). *I and thou* (W. Kaufmann, Trans.). New York: Charles Schribner's Sons. (Original work published 1923)

Burke, K. (1945). *A grammar of motives.* New York: Prentice-Hall.

Burke, K. (1950). *A rhetoric of motives.* Berkeley, CA: University of California Press.

Coonfield, T. (1975, May). *Listening skills training.* Paper presented at the International Communication Association conference, Chicago. (ERIC research document 122337).

Cottrell, L.S. (1942). The analysis of situational fields in social psychology. *American Sociological Review, 7,* 370–382.

Danish, S.J., & Kagan, N. (1971). Measurement of affective sensitivity: Toward a valid measure of interpersonal perception. *Journal of Counseling Psychology, 18,* 51–54.

Fliess, R. (1942). The metapsychology of the analyst. *Psychoanalytical Quarterly, 10,* 211–227.

Gordon, R.D. (1985, August). *Empathy: The state of the art and science.* Paper presented at the World Communication Conference, Baguio, Republic of the Philippines. (ERIC research document 260470).

Howell, W.S. (1979). Theoretical directions for intercultural communication. In M. Asante (Ed.), *Handbook of intercultural communication.* Beverly Hills, CA: Sage Publications.

Karush, A. (1979). Introductory remarks on the role of empathy in the psychoanalytic process. *Bulletin of the Association of Psychoanalytical Medicine, 18,* 75–80.

Katz, R.L. (1963). *Empathy: Its nature and uses.* Glencoe, NY: Free Press.

Koestler, A. (1949). The novelist deals with character. *Saturday Review, 32,* 7–8.

Kohut, H. (1966). Forms and transformation of narcissism. *Journal of the American Psychoanalytical Association, 14*, 243–272.

Kohut, H. (1971). *The analysis of the self*. New York: International Universities Press.

Kohut, H. (1982). Introspection, empathy, and the semicircle of mental health. *International Journal of Psycho-Analysis, 63*, 395–408.

Lipps, T. (1907). Das wissen von fremden ichen. *Psychologischen untersuchungen, 1*, 694–722.

Lipps, T. (1926). *Psychological studies*. Baltimore: Williams and Wilkins.

Mead, G.H. (1934). *Mind, self, and society*. Chicago: University of Chicago Press.

Moreno, J.L. (Ed.). (1914). *Progress in psychotherapy*. New York: Grune and Stratton.

Norton, R. (1983). *Communicator style*. Beverly Hills, CA: Sage Publications.

Redmond, M.V. (1983, November). *Toward resolution of the confusion among the concepts "empathy," "role-taking," "perspective-taking," and "decentering."* Paper presented at the Speech Communication Association Conference, Washington, DC. (ERIC research document 236748).

Restak, R.M. (1984). Possible neurophysiological correlates of empathy. In J. Lichtenberg et al. (Eds.), *Empathy I* (pp. 63–75). Hillsdale, NJ: Analytic Press.

Rogers, C.R. (1966). Client-centered therapy. In S. Arieti (Ed.), *Handbook of psychiatry* (Vol. 3, pp. 183–200). New York: Basic Books.

Sartre, Jean-Paul. (1956). *Being and nothingness* (H.E. Barnes, Trans.). New York: Philosophical Library. (Original work published 1943)

Schafer, R. (1959). Generative empathy in the treatment situation. *Psychoanalytic Quarterly, 28*, pp. 342–373.

Smith, H.C. (1966). *Sensitivity to people*. New York: McGraw-Hill.

Stein, E. (1970). *On the problem of empathy* (W. Stein, Trans.). The Hague: Martinus Nijhoff. (Original work published 1917)

Stewart, J. (1983). Interpretive listening: An alternative to empathy. *Communication education, 32*(4), 379–391.

Stotland, E. (1969). Exploratory investigations of empathy. In L. Berkowitz (Ed.), *Advances in experimental social psychology* (Vol. 4, pp. 271–313). New York: Academic Press.

Thomlison, D. (1991, March). *Approaches for teaching empathic listening*. Paper presented at the International Listening Association Conference, Jacksonville, FL.

Truax, C.B., & Carkhuff, R.R. (1967). *Toward effective counseling and psychotherapy*. Chicago: Aldine.

Uexkull, Jacob von. (1921). *Umwelt and innerwelt de tiere*. Berlin: Springer.

Uexkull, Jacob von. (1957). A stroll through the worlds of animals and men: A picture book of invisible worlds. In C.H. Schiller (Ed. and Trans.), *Instinctive behavior* (pp. 5–80). New York: International Universities Press.

Waelder, R. (1960). Psychoanalysis, scientific method, and philosophy. *Journal of the American Psychoanalytic Association, 10*, 617–637.

Chapter 10

Listening For Narrative

Paul G. Friedman

Department of Communication Studies
University of Kansas

This chapter deals with listening to narratives, arguing first that stories comprise a major and distinct form of discourse, and therefore warrant unique listening strategies. Stories give coherence to peoples' experiences in particular contexts, involve intentions and feelings, and operate as integrated, holistic units. Narratives reflect a discrete mode of thought, evidenced by how we impose a narrative structure upon human experiences and how stories capture our attention. For these reasons, stories are used to persuade. Some persuasive uses of narrative are benevolent; others are manipulative. Five elements are identified as essential to critical analysis of any narration—its fidelity, coherence, inclusion, sequence, and meaning—and specific questions and examples are provided to illustrate how to conduct such an analysis. This framework provides teachers with a valuable tool for helping students listen more perceptively to narratives.

The 20th century has seen invalidated the assumption that scientific research will yield a single, undeniable description of each event and process in human affairs. Concurrently, the narrative—an ancient form of discourse that provides dramatized "versions" of phenomena—is receiving increased attention. Most extant literature on listening, however, does not address narratives independently of other forms of discourse.

Scholars and practitioners concerned with listening in contemporary society should distinguish and analyze messages expressed in narrative form. The narrative is a distinct kind of discourse, a powerful one, and one being used to manipulate listeners in our society. Learning to identify narratives embedded in everyday discourse, to interpret their implications, and to critique them are vital skills for contemporary auditors. Elaborating on these points is the purpose of this chapter.

CHARACTERISTICS OF NARRATIVES

Most current listening theory applies primarily to expository prose, the kind used in lectures, instructions, and simple information exchanges among people. But narrative prose is different. By *narrative* I refer to a story that explains or gives meaning to a series of human events. A story draws together human actions, highlights their sequence, and attributes to them a role in achieving an ending. In other words, a narrator imposes a *plot* on what would otherwise be independent, disconnected events. Sometimes, these events actually have occurred. *True* stories range from anecdotes about episodes that transpired in only a few minutes, to biographies of individuals' lives, to histories of entire epochs. Composed or *fictional* stories include jokes, ballads, short stories, plays, films, and novels.

No matter what form narratives take, all have certain characteristics that distinguish them from expository prose. To illustrate, imagine as prototypes these two forms of oral discourse: (a) a factual account of the Holocaust during World War II, such as a historian's lecture related in expository prose; and (b) a narrative account of just one victim's experience, as it might have been told perhaps by Anne Frank. Consider how these two accounts of the same phenomenon would likely differ. (Of course, each account would contain some elements of the contrasting form of discourse, but presume each emphasizes one over the other.)

The expository speaker would provide verifiable, objective pieces of information and express them in quantitative terms if possible; the narrator would provide personal experiences described in his or her own subjective language or that of another character. The expository version would collapse large amounts of information into parsimonious statistics and statements; the narrative account would describe particular events in rich, vivid detail. The expository description would refer minimally, if at all, to details of the particular contexts in which the events took place; the narrative description would be anchored in a specific times and places. The expository message would be dispassionate and use the language and logical reasoning of science; the narrative message would include references to feelings, to inferences about participants' intentions, and to comparisons between what was intended and what occurred.

Moreover, the expository explanation would provide many bits of information, each comprehensible and meaningful on its own. If the lecture happened to be terminated at the half-way point, listeners still would feel that they had received some useful information. The narrative explanation, in contrast—if told as a single story—would only be coherent if heard in its entirety. It would have a beginning, middle, and end, and the meaning of each part would depend upon its relationship to the rest of the story. Listeners would have to hear how the whole story "turned out" before the implications of any event, even one that occurred at the beginning, would be fully apparent. Aborting the telling half-way through would render the story pointless and leave listeners feeling frustrated.

Narrative accounts, in short, are distinct from expository prose, because they give coherence to peoples' experiences in particular contexts; they include description of intentions and feelings; and they are integrated, holistic units of discourse.

Acknowledging that narratives are distinctive, however, merely warrants them a *discrete* position in the listening literature. It doesn't indicate how *important* that place should be. Narratives deserve, I believe, a *central* role because they (a) reflect listening patterns *essential* and *inherent* in human cognition, and (b) they have great *power* to elicit desired responses.

NARRATIVES AND COGNITION

What indicates that narratives reflect an essential mode of cognition and are not merely a trivial artifact of our entertainment-hungry society? First, narratives are universal. Stories are told in every society on earth, primitive and sophisticated. Barthes (1974, p. 1) wrote, "The narrative is present at all times, in all places, in all societies; the history of the narrative begins with the history of mankind; there does not exist, and never has existed, a people without narratives."

Second, children's earliest listening desires include hearing stories from their parents and other caregivers. Some of their earliest self-initiated play involves making up stories about the phenomena that surround them. Studies indicate that children at a remarkably young age possess an internalized *story grammar* (Olson & Gee, 1988). That is, they expect stories to have a basic internal structure and readily recognize when this structure is violated.

Third, people appear to impose narrative structures instinctively on phenomena they don't understand. Michotte (1963) demonstrated this some time ago when he showed observers two or more colored rectangles moving randomly and asked them to describe what they saw. Most imposed elaborate cause and effect stories on the rectangles' actions and used plots to assign meaning to their random motions. Likewise, in thematic apperception tests, subjects are presented with still pictures and asked to invent stories about them, and they do so readily.

Fourth, the content of stories is stored in cognitive memory and retrieved more easily than is expository prose. A number of studies (e.g., Tun, 1989) indicate that, when comparable information is embedded in both an expository and a narrative passage, and recall of that material is tested, the material in the narrative passage is recalled better.

Fifth, when given a choice of material, people tend to prefer the narrative. Drama programs on television (narratives) consistently achieve higher ratings than documentaries (expository messages). This point was illustrated in a letter (August 19, 1989) sent to columnist Ann Landers from a woman who was so mad she "could spit tacks." Why? She and her husband "love to watch the soaps." They have come to know the characters so well they are "like members of our own family." Recently, at a critical moment, the network cut in with a news bulletin reporting that the Chinese government was executing students, causing the couple "to miss out on the crisis involving Scorpio, Sean and Frisco in 'General Hospital.'" The writer reminded Ann, "They don't rerun soaps, Ann. If you miss something, it's gone." And she implored her to let the networks "know that these interruptions are disruptive and they make viewers angry."

Of course, this outraged viewer's viewpoint might not be broadly representative, nor attributable to the preference for narrative over expository prose. But it is indicative of how captivating the narrative mode can be. Clearly, we naturally use the story form in our thinking and listen for it in the messages we hear.

Finally, narratives are used by researchers to diagnose the deep structure of peoples' thinking about topics they are investigating. One certainly can learn respondents' views (or schema for conceptualizing an area of behavior) by asking about them directly in an expository exchange. Such an interview, however, elicits responses that actually tell only a fraction of what respondents really think about the domain of life under question. Recently, investigators have learned that deeper, unconsciously held views can be inferred from narratives told about that domain.

For example, by studying narratives about mothers in reports of forensic psychiatrists, Smit (1988) extrapolated ten commandments of "appropriate" mothering or expectations the psychiatrists held about the mothers' behavior. By asking teachers to tell stories of their encounters with academically "at-risk" students, Winfield (1986) identified the factors to which teachers attribute these students' difficulties in school. And by comparing narratives told by students who experience low and high performance anxiety when reading literature aloud, Pelias and Pelias (1988) learned how the two groups of students' perceptions of their performance experiences differed. These insights would not have appeared in a more straightforward expository interview. Embedded within our narratives are clues to what we really think and can not, or will not, articulate in an expository way. Discerning belief systems that drive narrative accounts is a listening skill vital to social researchers.

Other researchers examine narratives in mass media to learn how they reflect (or influence) their audience's concepts about social relations. For example, Herschman (1988) investigated the "ideology of consumption" encoded within episodes of the popular television series *Dallas* and *Dynasty*. Furnham and Schofield (1986) studied how men and women were portrayed in narratives incorporated into radio advertisements to detect instances of sex-role stereotyping. In short, the narratives we tell and hear contain clues to our deepest operating principles, because we construe much of our lives in the narrative mode.

IMPACT OF NARRATIVES

For all of the above-mentioned reasons, narratives also can be used to *manipulate* the thinking and behavior of listeners. Many of these manipulations are benevolent in intent. For example, psychotherapy may be viewed as a process in which an incoherent or demoralizing conceptualization of one's own *life story* is heard empathically and then gradually replaced, through dialogue, with a reconstructed, more self-enhancing story (Keim, Lentine, Keim, & Madanes, 1987).

Suppose a patient, Joe, is despondent over failing to fulfill his culture's life script, perhaps because he isn't married and settled into a career by age 35. He views himself as "ill" because he is out of step with the life story he should be leading and believes he is a protagonist in a "tragedy." A therapeutic intervention might include probing for and identifying factors in his early life that hampered his progress and relabeling what he has done thus far as "remarkable" considering the obstacles he has had to overcome. Thus, a benevolently manipulated version of his story renders him a "hero" and makes a "happy" ending more probable.

Listeners must be wary, however, of accepting *non*therapeutic attempts to manipulate their self-perceived life story. For example, the *Wall Street*

Journal (WSJ) recently sought subscriptions by contrasting the life stories of two individuals who started out under the same circumstances. One read the *WSJ*, achieved fame and fortune, and rose to the top of his organization. The other didn't and had a much less successful career. Implicit in his story are two assumptions: (a) success is measured by how much one earns and how high in the hierarchy one rises, and (b) reading the *WSJ* increases both. We are bombarded by manipulative life story narratives like this one that purport to be helpful. Listeners must be wary of them.

Other narratives are developed to give *purpose and direction to a group's efforts* to improve social conditions. For example, in 1985 the *Christian Science Monitor* sponsored the "Peace 2010" contest. They asked their readers to write a story from a vantagepoint 25 years in the future and to assume that the world had achieved lasting peace. If we only have countless "war stories" to look back upon and no clear "peace story" to guide our actions in the years ahead, they reasoned, we might simply repeat the past, this time at even greater cost. The *Monitor* received 1300 entries and published selections from the best in the book *How Peace Came to the World* (Foell & Nenneman, 1986). These stories provide vivid scenarios of how a desired state of affairs, world peace, might come to pass. In the same vein, many studies or organizational communication indicate that effective leaders create visions, scenarios, or stories about the future that inspire employees to committed performance.

On the other hand, narratives also may be employed to *legitimize exploitive or unethical behavior.* Geis (1987), for example, points out that many political speakers spin narratives that sustain oversimplified myths about players and plots on the local or international scene. He provides as examples three basic mythic themes: (a) The Conspiratorial Enemy—an outgroup (usually portrayed as hostile, different from us, homogenous, and highly potent) that is plotting to commit harmful acts; (b) The Valiant Leader—our current political leader (usually portrayed as benevolent, courageous, aggressive, and capable) who is acting to save us from danger; and (c) United We Stand—our group can achieve victory over our enemies if only we work hard, sacrifice, and obey our leaders.

Such myths are not necessarily fictional. The term *myth* merely signifies a widely accepted, readily evoked story. Myths help give coherence to a morass of confusing information. But they present several dangers. First, they presuppose simple causal theories of events. Most stories told orally tend to be pared down to basics, more than stories conveyed in written form. Also, few social processes actually have one easily identified cause, so myths provide the illusion of understanding what's going on and often preclude openness to additional relevant data. Moreover, when myths are widely accepted, they render unnecessary the presentation of any evidence supporting their validity. They need only be invoked, not proven.

Second, myths can be used to "justify" questionable courses of action. Bennett and Edelman (1985) count "among the most common narrative plots in U.S. mass media the saga of the government and its agents confronting formidable 'facts of life,' such as the deceitfulness of Communists, the immorality of criminals, or the aversion to honest work that swells the ranks of welfare recipients and the hard-core unemployed" (p. 156). They maintain that these characterizations *perpetuate* rather than accurately portray and help relieve the problems of international belligerance, crime, and poverty. For example, they describe in detail how myths were used to justify U.S. involvement in El Salvador's 1984 election. Our government depicted Jose Napoleon Duarte's success as a victory for democracy, while a closer analysis supports retelling the story as a prearranged outcome intended to legitimize the maintenance of power by the established right-wing aristocracy of that country. Regardless of which story is more valid, Bennett and Edelman's analysis describes how narratives can be used to justify policies that favor the current ruling elite in any organization or political system.

Narratives also play an important role in small groups by sustaining members' identity and interactions with each other and outsiders. Bormann (1985) developed "symbolic convergence theory" to describe how group members create a common consciousness through shared narratives (jokes, stories, reminiscences, anecdotes, and, rituals). He reports that, frequently during ostensibly task-oriented discussions, a participant will use imagery or tell a story in which characters enact a dramatic scenario occurring in some other place or time. Other members get caught up in the narrative and participate in telling it or commenting on it. Embedded in the story are important themes that relate to what the group is doing. Part of becoming a cohesive group is sharing such common stories. The process of inferring the themes in these stories he calls "fantasy theme analysis." These shared fantasies help the group develop what Bormann calls a *rhetorical vision,* a broader view of who and what they are in relation to each other and the outside world. Often the rhetorical vision can be summed up by a master analogy or slogan, such as "We're one big, happy family" or "We are fighters for justice in a selfish world." Stories told in this context set the group off from others and instruct members in appropriate behavior.

Other storytelling in interpersonal communication is less well-intentioned. Moine (1982) compared highly effective salespeople in various organizations with average producers to identify techniques the top performers use to persuade. He found that story telling is one method that distinguished the two groups. In fact, Moine says, "some sales agents I have studied do almost nothing but tell stories" (p. 153). He gives this example of how a top life insurance agent closed a deal for a policy with a young man who was considering signing with a smaller company: "It's like taking your family on a long ocean voyage across the Atlantic Ocean, and you want to get from here to England, and you have the choice of either going on this tugboat or the Queen Mary. Which one would you *feel safe* on?"

A recent book on sales techniques (Torquato, 1988) refers to "The Parable Tactic." Salespeople are advised to "deal with a sticky situation by describing a similar situation that happened to somebody else. Therefore, you are not confronting the buyer with a set of unpleasant facts, related to him. You are merely telling him a story" (p. 238). Torquato suggests that safety and fear are motivators to which the Parable Tactic especially applies.

He describes one "top-of-the-line" insurance salesman who used parables effectively. He would always insist on speaking with both husband and wife, with the overt objective of consolidating the family's insurance in order to reduce the premiums. His real goal was to sell them more. The salesman would allow the husband to explain that he was insurance poor and would commiserate by saying, "I understand. Sometimes, I think I have too much insurance myself." Then he would launch into a horror story about someone named Joe who died in a car accident and add, "Isn't it a shame about his wife, Mary Ann?" The customer's wife would invariably ask, "What about her?" Then the salesman would reluctantly paint a picture of her and her children's fallen lifestyle and deprivation. He would add other accounts of similar disasters caused by insufficient insurance.

This storytelling salesman bragged that he never sold anybody anything. He said, "All I had to do was choose my stories wisely and tell them properly." Torquato points out that we are conditioned to listen to stories and to be taught lessons by them (by hearing as children, for example, Aesop's fables and Biblical parables). A salesman's lecture on buying more insurance would be rejected, but a story can induce a mind change without triggering a defensive reaction. Investment and franchise salespeople are armed with a number of success stories.

Some companies even make up stories to aid their marketing campaigns. A trend in marketing food products, for example, is to provide a "founder" or a "founding story" on the package to personalize the product, that is, to identify the product with a single individual rather than a large corporation. Betty Crocker, Aunt Jemima, Uncle Ben, and many other food personalities never existed. They were invented as marketing tools. Several new health foods, as well as chocolate chip cookie and brownie products, now include lengthy stories on their packages about how the founders started making the products in their home kitchens. Their culinary achievements were so tasty and wholesome, friends insisted they quit their regular jobs and make their food discoveries available to the wider society. These stories convey the false impression that the product still is homemade by the founder and not produced in large vats at a factory staffed by low-paid employees, although that's usually the case. The manufacturers use stories to convey an inaccurate product image, one that appeals to consumers' desires, rather than the facts.

LISTENING CRITICALLY TO NARRATIVES

How does one listen to narratives critically? Few guidelines exist. Most extant narrative criticism refers primarily to aesthetic or literary qualities. Other criteria are more relevant from a listening standpoint. Fisher (1987) maintains that stories should be judged by the standards of "probability" and "fidelity." Narrative probability refers to coherence or internal consistency. Narrative fidelity requires that the story "ring true" or be consistent with what listeners experience in their lives. (These standards are comparable to measures of "reliability" and "validity" with which conclusions drawn from experimental research are evaluated.) These two criteria provide a good starting point for listening critically to narratives. However, to do so comprehensively, other important criteria need to be added. I believe cautious listeners should keep in mind five standards for judging narratives:

Fidelity

Whether a story has narrative *fidelity* is a first and self-evident criterion for evaluation. Thus, listeners should ask:

• *Did the narrated events actually take place as described:*

In a criminal trial, both the prosecutor and the defendant argue for the fidelity of their narration. The jury listens to determine what actually took place. Of course, the fidelity criterion applies to all statements, both expository and narrative. However, veridicality is *sufficient* for evaluating expository statements but not for narratives. An expository statement may be true or false. A "true" narrative can be only one version among several that can claim authenticity. In other words, among stories that pass the test of fidelity, one may be *better* than another rather than being simply "right" or "wrong."

For example, consider these two stories:

1. The husband didn't help with the kids, so the wife took over their care.
2. The wife took care of the kids, so the husband didn't help with them.

Both stories contain accurate statements, but one story probably is better than the other. In a criminal trial, every witness testifying under oath may be telling the truth, yet the real story can still remain in doubt. Therefore, additional criteria must be considered.

Coherence

A story ties events together into an integrated whole and, thereby, gives coherence and meaning to them. Polkinghorne (1988) maintains that we give raw perceptions "meaning" in several ways, two of which are inherent in narrative. Narrative meaning includes defining one phenomenon as *part* of another or one as the *cause* of the other. In other words, "narrative meaning is created by noting that something is a *part* of some whole and that something is the *cause* of something else" (p. 6). So listeners should pose these questions next:

*   *Do the events described belong within the same story?*

For example, major political changes that pleased the current U.S. administration have taken place over the past few years in Panama, Nicaragua, South Africa, and several countries in Eastern Europe. If a reelection candidate in a campaign speech were to claim responsibility for specific changes, each narration of events would have a different level of coherence because the U.S. government's degree of influence differed in each case. In the first case (Panama), American actions obviously are a critical part of the story; in the last (Eastern Europe), we played a much smaller role, and listeners may question the candidate's place in that story.

*   *Are the events related to each other as the story implies?*

In narrating her marital dissatisfaction, a wife might ascribe cause to her husband's reticence and might view her own efforts "to bring him out of his shell" as an appropriate solution. The husband's narration might label as a cause his wife's aggressive nagging and as a solution his own withdrawal for some "peace and quiet." Each gives different coherence to their relationship. Anyone listening to just one side would do well to question how aptly each party relates the story's events.

William Bennett, former czar of the federal "war on drugs," in his narration of how drug abuse in America should be reduced, advocated giving drug users stiffer jail sentences. Others, who view drug use as a symptom of other social problems, such as poor housing, education, and job opportunities, disagree. Bennett believes these social problems are a result of drug abuse; his opponents see them as its cause. Their disagreement is a matter of narrative coherence.

- *Is a social critique substantive or based on a coherence judgment—that people, dialogue, or a context are out of place in a story?*

Some social critiques are based on narrative coherence and should be heard as such. The critic has a preference for how a particular story should be enacted and challenges the status quo, not because a substantive error was made, but because it violates how the critic believes the story should be cast, what the characters should say, or where it should take place.

Sometimes the critic objects to an individual's *role* in a story. When Rev. Jesse Jackson helped arranged the release of several Americans from Iraq after its invasion of Kuwait, for example, U.S. State Department officials objected to his playing the part of international negotiator. Listeners should note that this objective is a matter of narrative coherence. The officials didn't criticize what Jackson did; they felt it inappropriate for him to perform this diplomatic role.

Likewise, some people objected to David Souter's nomination to the Supreme Court—not because of a particular opinion (he had expressed few), but because they believed he was an inappropriate candidate for this position. Because Souter is a reclusive bachelor, they worried that he wouldn't understand the feelings of a woman facing an unwanted pregnancy. Their concern was based on assumptions about the kind of person who should be in that role, not on anything Souter had done or said that disqualified him.

Objections also are raised to what people in various roles in a story *ought to say*. The objection is one of coherence if the complaint is not about the content of comments, but about the legitimacy of making a certain *kind* of comment. U.S.A.F. General Michael Dugan, at the time Air Force Chief of Staff, for instance, was abruptly dismissed after speaking to the press about plans for waging war against Iraq, including specific targets for American air strikes. Higher-ups in the administration didn't dispute the content of his comments. They felt that by speaking publicly on this topic Dugan had violated the parameters of his role in the Persian Gulf military operation.

More aesthetically based appropriateness judgments were voiced when Kitty Dukakis, wife of the former presidential candidate and governor of Massachusetts, published a book in which she related without inhibition the course of her addictions to drugs and alcohol. Some questioned the appropriateness of such forthright disclosures. Others applauded her for them. No one disputed the veracity of her revelations. The debate was over whether someone in her position should have revealed as much as she did.

In a similar vein, questions are raised about the *setting* for particular narratives. When the Persian Gulf crisis started, for example, President Bush was on vacation at his home in Kennebunkport, Maine. He refused to allow the Iraqi invasion of Kuwait to keep him "hostage" in the White House, so he kept his vacation plans and supervised the American mobilization from there. His political advisors were concerned about the Maine coast serving as a backdrop for interviews about dispatching troops to the deserts of Saudi Arabia. No one questioned Bush's management of the operation, just the appropriateness of the setting in which he chose to conduct it.

To summarize, listeners to critiques on peoples' roles, comments, and context should distinguish when these critiques are substantive and when they are based on judgments of narrative coherence.

Inclusion

A third criterion is whether the story structure incorporates all salient events and their component parts. A critical listener asks: "Is anything omitted or not accounted for?"

A narrated event includes *actions* performed through some *means* by *characters* in particular *settings*. An oversimplified story telescopes these elements into a truncated myth about the event which provides the illusion of understanding. Consideration of what might be omitted, therefore, raises several other questions:

* *Are relevant actions or events left out of the story?*

In the Iran-Contra trials of both Oliver North and John Poindexter, for example, a key issue was how important a part of the whole story were messages they received from and sent to then President Reagan.

* *Are important characters omitted?*

In the debate over abortion, for instance, Pro-Life advocates insist the fetus is being ignored as a character in the narrative of what occurs when a woman becomes pregnant unwillingly. In contrast, Pro-Choice advocates believe the mother is overlooked by those who would outlaw abortion. Listeners to narratives biased toward either side of this controversy must be attuned to whether the concerns of all key characters are being considered.

In traditional organizational theory, a company's owners are depicted as the appropriate source of the company's decisions. Recently, attention has been given to the concerns of all the "stakeholders" affected by the organization (such as its employees, suppliers, customers, community members, and so on). They are seen as essential characters in narratives about the organization's activities.

- *Do important actions take place in any other locale?*

City and state officials are being blamed for decreases in social services available in local communities and for recent tax hikes. They retort that their behavior is influenced by policies initiated in Washington, DC. We often must look beyond the setting where a narrative takes place for important story elements.

Vaclav Havel, former president of Czechoslovakia, insisted that changes in Soviet policy be given major credit in the narration of his own country's peaceful revolution. Nelson Mandela maintains that U.S. sanctions are necessary in his scenario of what will make South Africa continue dismantling apartheid. Both believe actions in distant locales are inherent parts of the stories in their own context.

- *Are events, characters, or settings included inappropriately?*

A jury decided Imelda Marcos was not a responsible party in her husband's monetary transactions in the Philippines. Likewise, Captain Joseph Hazelwood was deemed not culpable for the Exxon Valdez oil spill. In both cases, it appears they were given inappropriate roles in highly publicized narrations of events.

Sequence

Stories organize events in time. A narrative account has a beginning, a middle, and end. This event sequence must be examined critically, as well, by asking these questions:

- *Did the events occur in the order presented? Are simultaneous or overlapping events presented as sequential?*

Recently, several major corporate acquisitions, mergers, and bankruptcies have made headlines. Each was followed by journalists' accounts purporting to describe the sequence of events that led to them. For example, when the firm of Drexel, Lambert, and Burnham went bankrupt, narratives poured out describing a sequence of events (and implying cause) that included that firm's involvement in junk bond trading, its guilty plea to insider trading charges, the large bonuses paid to executives, and Michael Milken's resignation, among others. What events actually contributed to the bankruptcy? Which were irrelevant? Which were coincidental but not causal? A discerning listener needs to question narrative sequence.

- *Did the story really "start" at the beginning of this account? Are there different versions of what action began the chain of events that constitute the story?*

When children tell the story of a schoolyard fight, they often disagree about who "started it." The same issue arises in marital and organizational disputes, as well as international affairs. In narratives about German reunification, for example, some accounts refer back to earlier periods in the 20th century. These narrators believe reunification is a step in a process that began with the start of World War II. Others believe the situation today is unlike any that existed before and should be viewed without reference to the past. When the story started is a key issue.

- *Is the story over yet? Are other outcomes still to come?*

Some people prefer to wrap up a story and declare it over before others are willing to do so. Is an argument over when the disputants have worked out an agreement? Or should they continue talking until they have examined how the argument got started in the first place and make plans for preventing future disputes? (An arbitrator might prefer the former closure point, but a counselor the latter.)

Recently, civil rights leaders reenacted the march led by Martin Luther King from Selma, Alabama on its 25th anniversary. Their intention was to communicate that much more needs to be done before the civil rights movement can be narrated with a "happily ever after" ending. Others believe it is time to dismantle affirmative action legislation because its basic goals have been met; they claim the equal opportunity story is over. Listeners also must be alert to story endings.

Meaning

Stories are organized around a point, or theme. The meaning ascribed to a story may be questioned:

- *Are the inferences made obviously supported by the events? Or can other interpretations be imposed?*

When the story of homeless people in America is told, some conservatives relate it as the failure of individuals to be industriousness enough to afford housing. Liberals blame the government's failure to provide sufficient social protections and services.

A story is told of a woman who came before a judge for the crime of stealing food. The judge levied a $10 fine, because stealing food is illegal, but then added to everyone else in the court, "I also fine each of you one dollar for the crime of tolerating a society in which this woman had to steal in order to eat." This story points up the varied interpretations that can be ascribed to an event.

- *Is the intent of relating the story to liberate or manipulate the listener?*

This criterion questions the impact of the story on its listeners. Implied is the moral imperative of increasing awareness and thereby enhancing the freedom of people to choose intelligently for themselves. Some stories are told to manipulate or suppress thought rather than to free listeners. For instance, stories told by unscrupulous salespeople have a manipulative intent. Stories told by "cult" leaders that unjustly accuse or promote fear of "outsiders" also stifle free choice. On the other hand, most stories told by therapists and theologians are meant to give listeners another viewpoint with which to view familiar events they had construed in a dissatisfying way.

To summarize, since stories unify events into a meaningful structure, listeners must consider whether the events related occurred as described, are parts of a coherent whole, are connected in cause–effect patterns, are complete (or whether anything important has been omitted or added), are aptly sequenced, and are interpreted appropriately.

CONCLUSION

Narratives provide a distinct and powerful mode of organizing information, a mode that corresponds to how perceptions are construed. Listening scholars and teachers should address this mode as one independent of expository discourse. Listeners must be able to recognize when narratives are present in the discourse they hear and to question their adequacy. This chapter provides teachers with a framework and examples for preparing students to develop their ability to listen critically to narratives.

REFERENCES

Barthes, R. (1974). *S/Z*. New York: Hill & Wang.

Bennett, W.L., & Edelman, M. (1985). Toward a new political narrative. *Journal of Communication, 35*(4), 156–171.

Bormann, E. (1985). *The force of fantasy: Restoring the American dream.* Carbondale, IL: Southern Illinois University Press.

Fisher, W.R. (1987). *Human communication as narration.* Columbia, SC: University of South Carolina Press.

Foell, E.W., & Nenneman, R.A. (1986). *How peace came to the world.* Cambridge, MA: The MIT Press.

Furnham A., & Schofield, S. (1986). Sex-role stereotyping in British advertisements. *British Journal of Social Psychology, 25*(2), 165–171.

Geis, M.L. (1987). *The language of politics.* New York: Springer-Verlag.

Herschman, E.C. (1988). The ideology of consumption: A structural-syntactical analysis of "Dallas" and "Dynasty." *Journal of Consumer Research, 15*(3), 344–359.

Keim, I., Lentine, G., Keim, J., & Madanes, C. (1987). Strategies for changing the past. *Journal of Strategic and Systemic Therapies, 6*(3), 2–17.

Michotte, A.E. (1963). *The perception of causality.* London: Metheun.

Moine, D.J. (1982). To trust, perchance to buy. *Psychology Today, 8*, 51–54.

Olson, M.W., & Gee, T.C. (1988). Understanding narratives: A review of story grammar research. *Childhood Education, 64*(5), 302–306.

Pelias, M.H., & Pelias, R.J. (1988). Communication apprehension in the basic course in performance of literature. *Communication Education, 37*(2), 118–126.

Polkinghorne, D.E. (1988). *Narrative knowing and the human sciences.* Albany, NY: Stane University of New York Press.

Smit, J. (1988). Mothers and their boys: A never-ending fantasy: An exploration of mothers' discourse in forensic psychiatry. *International Journal of Law and Psychiatry, 11*(3), 279–287.

Torquato, J. (1988). *Why winners win!: Techniques of advocate selling.* New York: AMACOM.

Tun, P.A. (1989). Age differences in processing expository and narrative text. *Journal of Gerontology, 44*(1), 9–15.

Winfield, L.F. (1986). Teacher beliefs toward academically at-risk students in inner urban schools. *Urban Review, 18*(4), 253–268.

Chapter 11

Listening: A Relational Process

Steven C. Rhodes

Department of Communication
Western Michigan University

This chapter describes listening from a relational perspective. From a relational perspective *listening* is defined as a continual process that occurs within the context of relationships. Systems theory is used as the guiding theoretical perspective. As such, the dyad is described as a system, communication is described as a transactional process occurring within that system, and listening is described as an inseparable part of the transactional processes that occur continuously and simultaneously within a system. Practical applications of the perspective presented in this chapter are described for both research and instruction. In terms of research, the predictability of communication patterns is presented as a way to operationally define effective listening. For instruction, response styles are offered as an area of instruction applicable to improving effective listening.

Over the years, there have been numerous attempts to define *listening* from a variety of perspectives. Some scholars have focused on the components of listening: hearing, attending, understanding, and remembering (e.g., Lundsteen, 1979; Bostrom & Waldhart, 1980; Steil, Watson, & Barker, 1983; Brownell, 1986). Some have focused on the types of listening: serious and social, empathic and informational, discriminative and judgmental (e.g., Howell, 1982; Wolff, Marsnik, Tacey, & Nichols, 1983; Wolvin & Coakley, 1988). Others have been concerned with certain skills related to listening: identifying main ideas, distinguishing between fact and inference, paraphrasing, and asking questions (e.g., Nichols & Stevens, 1957; Weaver, 1972; Floyd, 1985). Still others have concentrated on the covert nature of listening: perception, concentration, interpretation, understanding, remembering (e.g., Barker, 1971; Weaver, 1972; Hirsch, 1979; Goss, 1982), while others have suggested that the overt process of responding appropriately is an important part of effective listening (e.g., Steil, 1981; Steil, Watson, & Barker, 1983; Brownell, 1986; Rhodes, 1987).

As the title implies, the perspective of listening discussed in this chapter will be relational. Listening will be described as a relational process—a continual process that occurs within the context of relationships. In order to focus on listening as a relational process, systems theory will be used as the guiding theoretical perspective. As such, the dyad will be described as a system, communication will be described as a transactional process occurring within that system, and listening will be described as an inseparable part of the transactional processes that occur continuously and simultaneously within a system. Practical applications of the perspective presented in this chapter will be described for both research and instruction. In terms of research, the predictability of communication patterns will be presented as a way to define operationally effective listening. For instruction, response styles will be offered as an area of instruction applicable to improving effective listening. However, before applying systems theory to develop a relational perspective of listening, some background regarding other attempts to define listening is necessary.

BACKGROUND

Regardless of their focus, most definitions of listening can be classified according to certain similarities and differences. Wolvin and Coakley (1988) surveyed 20 definitions and found them to be similar or different in the following areas: processes mentioned (e.g., analyzing, concentrating, understanding); symbols to which the listener attends (e.g., verbal and/or nonverbal stimuli); and purpose (e.g., appreciate, comprehend, evaluate). Extending Wolvin and Coakley's survey, Glenn (1989) conducted a content analysis of 50 definitions of listening. Her analysis revealed that similarities and differences among definitions of listening depend on the presence or absence of seven concepts: perception, attention, interpretation, memory, response, spoken sounds, and visual cues. Glenn concluded that "a universal conceptual definition of listening from which operational guidelines may be established will not be easy to formulate" (p. 29). Also addressing the difficulty of formulating a universal definition of listening, Fitch-Hauser and Hughes (1988) questioned whether attempts to define the cognitive aspects of listening are a dream or a reality. They concluded that, "although much remains to be done, we can now say that we have begun to define listening and have begun the process of developing a theory of listening" (p. 88). However, they also point out that "to continue progressing toward the goal of developing a valid theory of listening, using sound definitions of the concepts involved, we must establish some commonalities in our *operationalizations* of the construct" (p. 87; emphasis added).

Tests as Operational Definitions of Listening

To date, most attempts to define listening *operationally* have been limited to the development of listening tests (Villaume & Cegala, 1986; Rhodes, 1987, 1989a). In fact, in the last 10 years, there has been a greater concentration of articles about listening tests and/or the nature of listening assessment published in communication journals than articles related to other aspects of listening (Rhodes, 1984, 1985; Roberts, 1988; Rhodes, Watson, & Barker, 1990). For example, of the 37 articles published in *The Journal of the International Listening Association* in its first 4 years of publication, a little over 25% of the articles addressed questions related to assessment. Almost half of the articles about listening that have appeared in *Communication Education* since 1980 have been concerned with assessment. During that same time period, over half of the listening articles that have appeared in *Communication Monographs, Central States Speech Journal, The Western States Speech Journal, Communication Quarterly,* and *The Southern States Speech Journal* have been concerned with assessment.

In spite of these efforts, some listening scholars feel that attempts to define listening operationally as scores on a listening test are too limited—they fail to capture the conceptual and theoretical essence of listening (Erway, 1972; Roberts, 1988; Fitch-Hauser & Hughes, 1988; Emmert, 1989; Rhodes, 1989a). As Roberts (1988) suggested, "a valid and reliable test [has] not been agreed upon by a majority of the listening researchers [because they] continue to focus on measurement to the detriment of theory building" (p. 3). He went on to say that it would seem "prudent to first discover what it is that we should be studying before deciding how we should measure it" (p. 3). Erway suggested this earlier when she tried to explain why more listening research has not been published. As part of her explanation, Erway indicated that it "has been difficult to measure valid changes in behavior because we have not yet decided what listening is" (p. 22). Rather than lack of understanding about what listening is, Fitch-Hauser and Hughes (1988) suggest that "one possible explanation for the paucity of research about the receiving component [listening] may be found in the abstract nature of that component" (p. 75).

In sum, attempts to define listening operationally have been limited to the development of listening tests or have suffered because of a discrepancy between the operational definition and its conceptual counterpart. Such a discrepancy usually stems from the listening researcher's inability to define operationally the abstract, *intra*personal components found in conceptual definitions of listening (Fitch-Hauser & Hughes, 1988; Rhodes, 1989b).

The Intrapersonal Nature of Listening

As the Wolvin/Coakley and Glenn surveys suggested above, every definition of listening contains some aspect of intrapersonal communication. In fact, many definitions of listening are entirely intrapersonal. This places an emphasis on the abstract dimensions of listening. An examination of three definitions illustrates this point.

Hirsch (1979) contends that "listening is something that takes place between people" (p. 1), and that his focus is on how listening "relates to the total communication process among people" (p. 1). He even goes so far as to indicate that his focus will be on interpersonal listening rather than intrapersonal listening. And yet, he defines interpersonal listening as "the process whereby the human ear receives sound stimuli from other people and through a series of steps *interprets the sound stimuli in the brain and remembers it*" (p. 1; emphasis added). Other than indicating that the stimuli for listening come from other people, Hirsch's definition does little to advance an interpersonal view of listening. Receiving, interpreting, and remembering sound stimuli are all intrapersonal processes. Even when Hirsch expands his definition to include nine distinct, but interdependent stages, each stage is still an intrapersonal process.

Goss (1982) also stressed the intrapersonal nature of listening. He defined *listening* as a three-phase intrapersonal process that involves signal processing (related to hearing), literal processing (determining meaning), and reflective processing (critical analysis and appreciation). In developing his definition, Goss argued that the conceptual confusion about listening resulted from the lack of a theoretical perspective that permitted integration of the essential components of listening. He offered human information processing as an appropriate theoretical perspective, and thus described listening as intrapersonal communication in action.

Wolvin and Coakley (1988) defined *listening* as "the process of receiving, attending to, and assigning meaning to aural stimuli" (p. 91). In presenting their definition, they point out that the three processes within their definition—receiving, attending to, and assigning meaning—are intrapersonal processes. They indicate that these three processes can be found in most definitions of listening, and that a fourth process—overt responding—that is found in some definitions should not be considered a part of the listening process.

Building Operational Definitions of Listening

Obviously, a relationship exists between listening and intrapersonal communication. Rhodes (1989) emphasized the importance of this relationship when he said that, "although the terms 'listening' and 'intrapersonal communication' do not always appear together in the literature, the two processes are conceptually related....understanding intrapersonal communication is a necessary, but not sufficient, condition for understanding listening" (p. 564). Wolvin (1989) took an opposite, but similar position, when he said "to a considerable degree, the process of listening is a major component of intrapersonal communication....The study of listening can, thus, assist one's understanding of intrapersonal communication" (p. 508).

Recognizing and emphasizing the nature of the relationship between listening and intrapersonal communication does not solve the problem of the gap that typically exists between conceptual and operational definitions of listening. If anything, recognizing and emphasizing the relationship simply highlights the difficulty listening scholars face when they try to define operationally the abstract, intrapersonal components of listening.

Fitch-Hauser and Hughes (1988) recognize that "the process of defining listening is essentially the process of construct validation" (p. 82). According to Bowers and Courtright (1984), "a researcher concerned with construct validity seeks to understand what underlying constructs account for patterns of relationship between *the measure in question* and other variables" (p. 120). In other words, to what extent does a test measure what it says it measures?

According to Fitch-Hauser and Hughes, three elements are involved in the process of construct validation: the trait measured (e.g., listening), the measuring instrument (typically a listening test), and the interpretation of the measuring instrument (i.e., what the test is purported to measure).

These three elements necessitate asking two questions. To what extent does a test measure a trait that actually exists? And, how well does the proposed interpretation correspond to what is measured by the test? To find answers to these questions, Cronbach and Meehl (1955) indicate that a network must be created that connects (a) observable properties or quantities to each other, (b) theoretical constructs to observables, or (c) different theoretical constructs to one another.

Fitch-Hauser and Hughes contend that listening researchers are well on the road to creating such a network. They suggest that attempts to compare listening tests to one another and to components of listening common to most definitions are attempts to establish this first link (relating observable properties to each other). They provide connecting listening to comprehension and connecting listening to various types of memory as two examples of linking theoretical constructs to observables. They offer Goss's reliance on information processing theory as the basis for defining listening as a cognitive process and Bostrom and Waldhart's (1980) use of models of memory as evidence of attempts to establish the third link (connecting different theoretical constructs together).

Cronbach and Meehl (1955) indicate that a fourth criterion—at least some of the laws must involve observables—must be met if valid constructs are to be developed. Rhodes (1989b) and Roberts, Edwards, and Barker (1987), along with Fitch-Hauser and Hughes, suggest that this fourth criterion may be the easiest one for listening researchers to meet. They posit that, although intrapersonal processes such as the physiological, electrochemical chain of events that take place during listening cannot be directly observed, the external manifestations of such internal processes can be observed. "We can see evidence supporting the notion that someone has received information auditorily, and we can see that person respond to that stimulus. We can also observe that same person either use or recall the information given in the stimulus at a later time" (Fitch-Hauser & Hughes, 1988, p. 86). They go on to conclude that "to continue progressing toward the goal of developing a valid theory of listening, using sound definitions of the concepts involved, we must establish some commonalities in our operationalizations of the construct" (p. 87). In other words, listening researchers must establish commonalities among the listening tests they use in order to operationalize the listening process. Having made this plea, Fitch-Hauser and Hughes point out that there is very little overlap among the assortment of tests that are currently used to measure listening, and they call on listening researchers "to begin the process of establishing convergent validity of our instruments" (p. 87).

I concur with this call for the establishment of convergent validity of already established listening tests. *However, I question whether scores on listening tests are the only observable manifestations of the* intrapersonal *aspects of listening.* As I have suggested elsewhere,

Although the terms 'listening' and 'intrapersonal communication' do not always appear together in the literature, the two processes are conceptually related. This can be seen from an examination of typical definitions of both processes. To understand listening as a process, one must understand its intrapersonal dimensions. *However, not all of listening is intrapersonal. To understand listening totally, one must also understand its relational dimensions.* (Rhodes, 1989b, p. 564; all emphases added)

Adding the Response Stage to Our Definitions

Earlier in this chapter, I mentioned that Wolvin and Coakley (1988) purposely exclude overt responding from their definition of listening. They indicate that "When listeners respond overtly, they are no longer listeners; instead they become senders—that is, the encoders of new messages—in the communication process" (p. 90). In making this argument they cite the following example from Weaver (1972):

> Let us assume that the single word "come" is a command. Whether you obey it or not does not concern the process of listening. You have "heard" it, which means you have received and attended to the data. The listening process concerns only the selecting of such stimulus data in order to "receive" it and the cognitive structuring of it. (p. 6)

There are two problems inherent in the positions taken by Wolvin/Coakley and Weaver. One is that by not recognizing the response stage as a part of listening they make it difficult to identify when listening takes place. Although most of what happens when people listen involves internal processing, a listener must respond for others to know how a message has been processed. Steil et al. (1983) argue that "the response stage of listening is especially crucial for judging the success of the listening act as a whole" (p. 22). And while they indicate that listening consists of at least four connected activities—sensing, interpreting, evaluating, and responding—it is the last activity—responding—that is particularly important. They recognize that listening cannot take place without the first three activities. But they point out that these are internal processes, and until a person makes a concrete response, it is difficult to determine whether listening has taken place.

Brownell (1986) also stresses the importance of responding. To her, "the proof of good listening is an appropriate response" (p. 206). Rhodes et al. (1990) concur when they say that, "to the degree that a listener responds overtly, competence can be assessed.... Thus, how a listener responds is an important part of assessing listening effectiveness" (p. 64). Other theorists agree and stress that competence in listening cannot be recognized as only a cognitive process—effective, or competent listening is a behavioral act (e.g., Mead, 1980; Wiemann & Backlund, 1980; Spitzberg, 1981; Mc-Croskey, 1982; Ridge, 1983; Villaume & Cegala, 1986). A competent, or effective listener then, must be able to respond appropriately. We can only know if a listener has responded appropriately if we can look at a response in relation to its stimulus.

The second problem with the Wolvin/Coakley and Weaver position is that it highlights a distinction between *senders* and *receivers* that many communication theorists have tried to put to rest. Contemporary communication theory describes communication as a transactional process (e.g., Littlejohn, 1987; Williams, 1988; Trenholm, 1991). From a transactional perspective, the use of terminology such as *senders* and *receivers,* or *speakers* and *listeners,* creates an artificial distinction. In any communication transaction each participant is simultaneously sending and receiving messages. To look at listening, then, from a transactional perspective, it is necessary to look at a "listener" in relation to a "speaker"—to look at both parties simultaneously—to look at both parties together as a whole.

CONCEPTUALIZING LISTENING AS A RELATIONAL PROCESS

For a long time, communication theorists have worked very hard to describe communication as a process, and researchers have worked equally hard to bring a process focus to their research (e.g., Berlo, 1960, 1977; Scheidel & Crowell, 1966; Brooks & Scheidel, 1968; Smith, 1972; Hawes, 1973; Cahn & Hanford, 1984). As a result, we have come to describe communication as a transactional process.

When communication is transactional, all persons in the process are actively involved and are interdependent. Each person is at any moment continuously and simultaneously sending messages and receiving messages. The way a person sits, his or her tone of voice, or other nonverbal factors makes each person a source even when the other person is talking. Obviously, people are also receiving communication messages from others even when they are talking. As I listen, I simultaneously "speak" to you with my nonverbal responses, and periodically provide you with verbal responses. As you speak, you simultaneously "listen" to the nonverbal messages, periodically tune in to the verbal messages, and continuously adapt your communication behaviors according to your assessment of the extent to which you feel you have been understood. I do the same. In addition, we both continuously and simultaneously "listen" to ourselves.

Some people do not view communication as transactional, but rather they see it as interactive. An interactive view holds that one person says something, the other reacts, and the first person alters his or her next statement. From this point of view, communication is a series of actions and reactions. Such a view fails to capture the essence of the communication process. From a transactional perspective we cannot actually say whether a communication participant is a speaker or a listener. He or she may be a source of the messages to which you are reacting, but at the same time he or she is receiving the messages you are sending. Who is the source, who is the receiver?

To capture the essence of communication, and thus the essence of listening, we must try to visualize it as a process in which we are a source and at the same time a receiver—in which we are speaking and listening at the same time. We encode and send messages while we are decoding and receiving other messages. We are not sources, then receivers, then sources, then receivers. We are both participants involved in a communication event—affecting and affected by one another, functioning continuously and simultaneously.

Listening, then, is a complex process that includes both covert (intrapersonal) and overt (relational) activities. During a communication event I take in and process "messages" from you (interpersonal); I use these "messages" to create meaning (intrapersonal); and I provide you with a response that lets you know the meaning I have created (relational). You do the same. By continuously and simultaneously listening carefully, we use one another's responses to monitor our progress toward understanding and to modify subsequent communicative choices, if necessary.

Systems Theory as a Theoretical Base

Any description of communication—and thus listening—as a transactional process uses systems theory as its theoretical base (Monge, 1977; Fisher, 1978; Wilmot, 1979; Littlejohn, 1987; Cushman & Cahn, 1985; Trenholm & Jensen, 1988). A *system* can be defined as any interrelated group of elements (components) that work together as a whole to achieve certain outcomes. The idea of a systemic process implies interdependence among the components involved in the process (von Bertalanffy, 1968; Churchman, 1968; Ackoff & Emery, 1972; Cherry, 1978).

As noted above, any conceptually complete attempt to study listening must presuppose the inherent systemic nature of that process, and thus take into account both intrapersonal and relational dimensions of the process. Fisher and Hawes's (1971) human system model (HSM) and interact system model (ISM) offer places to begin. Essentially, the difference between their models rests in what each one considers a system's prevailing systemic components to be. For the HSM, the prevailing components are the people in the system and their characteristics. For the ISM, the prevailing components are the communication patterns created in the system.

In the HSM, even though people are the components, a system is seen as characterized by the interrelationships and organization of its components, and not by the components themselves. This is not to say that the people are not important, but merely points out that the HSM is most concerned with how the relationships among people affect a system's operations. These relationships can be characterized by "cognitive and affective constructs such as cohesiveness and commitment, power and influence, leadership and authority" (p. 448). Constructs like these are characteristics of the people who make up the system. According to Fisher and Hawes, these characteristics do two things: (a) they characterize the relationship among components, and (b) they affect a system's operations.

The intrapersonal (cognitive—information processing) dimensions of listening are characteristics of people that could be added to Fisher and Hawes's list of cognitive and affective constructs. Since the intrapersonal dimensions of listening are characteristics of the human components of a system, and since the HSM considers humans as systemic components, the HSM is an appropriate model for studying the effects of the intrapersonal dimensions of listening. Villaume and Cegala (1986) provide an example of such listening research with their study of subjects' orientation to conversational text (intrapersonal variable) and subjects' interaction mode as predictors of conversational recall. They found that a person's type of orientation to text and type of interpersonal stance affected how he or she participated in a conversation. Work by Beatty and Payne (1981) and Rhodes (1989a) that looked at the effects of receiver apprehension and cognitive complexity (intrapersonal dimensions) on listening effectiveness also serve as examples. But, the intrapersonal aspects of listening are only part of the overall listening process; the other part involves the relational dimensions (responses). Since these relational dimensions are not direct characteristics of the human components of a system, Fisher and Hawes would argue that their ISM is also needed.

Individuals are not the direct concern of the ISM—communication patterns are. As Fisher and Hawes see them, these patterns "are components of a system which are codable units of verbal and nonverbal communication" (p. 448). The relationships among these components are "defined by the formal consistency of recurring patterns of communication units" (p. 448).

Examining these communicative units as indications of the communication patterns that develop during listening as a relational process requires a measure consistent with a conception of listening that includes a

Figure 11.1   Sample conversation showing interacts and communication patterns.

C1 Interviewer: What kind of position would you like?

D1 Applicant: I think I'd like to work in marketing or sales. Something where there is contact with people. I enjoy working with people.

C2 Interviewer: Have you ever considered personnel work?

D2 Applicant: No, I don't think I would want to get into personnel. At least not into benefits or labor relations. Maybe your kind of job, you know, recruiting.

C3 Interviewer: Do you think recruiting is something you'd enjoy?

D3 Applicant: Yes. It seems challenging and like a sales position in some ways. Do you think I would qualify?

C4 Interviewer: You might. We could check on that after we get the test results back.

D4 Applicant: I hadn't thought about personnel work in a recruiting sense.

C5 Interviewer: Well, let's put it down as a possibility.

D5 Applicant: Good. What do we do next?

response stage. It has already been noted that effective listening is a process that involves an initial behavior, a reaction, and the subsequent use of that reaction. Thus, any unit used to measure effective listening must take into account these three factors. Fisher and Hawes define the *interact* as such a unit.

Given a stream of ongoing communication between you and me, an *interact* is any pair of communication behaviors that connect us. For example, $C_1-D_1-C_2-D_2-\ldots C_n-D_n$ is a stream of ongoing communication (see Figure 11.1). I *initiate* communication C_1, which is received, processed, and *reacted* to by you in the form of communication D_1 and produces C_2. The first interact is C_1-D_1, the second is D_1-C_2, the third is C_2-D_2, and so on. In this example we see that the logical requirements for an accurate conception of the response stage of listening—initial, reactive, subsequent behaviors—have been met. Thus, the interact can be an index of the response stage of listening. Depending on how participants in a dyad listen, the interacts take on certain characteristics. In other words, over time, interacts depict communication patterns.

THEORETICAL IMPLICATIONS

Listening and Communication Patterns

The dyad is the system level that provides a maximum opportunity to observe listening as a relational process by observing communication patterns. Listening is easy to observe at this system level because of the large degree of interdependence characteristic of the dyadic situation. Since listening processes at an *intra*personal level are almost always internal, they are not easily observed. On the other hand, in an *inter*personal (dyadic) system some listening processes serve to connect the two conversants, and these signals are *external* and *observable*.

Let us again look at you and me as a dyadic system. Assume that you and I share a common goal X (understanding) that we must obtain if the system (you and I together) is to reach some relational goal Y (resolution of our conflict). Selecting myself as an arbitrary starting point, I encode communication content C in relation to X. Given X, I have expectations concerning my transmission of C, so using listening processes on the intrapersonal level, I decode C—comparing it with certain standards. Making subsequent adjustments based on the information obtained from the decoding comparison, I adjust C, formulating C_1. I now transmit C_1 to you. During this time you may or may not have been encoding your own communication content. In either case, given X and C_1, I have expectations concerning any response from you. Thus, if an observer knows X and C_1, your response will be somewhat predictable.

You decode C_1, encode communication content C_2, and respond to me by returning or reflecting back what you decoded as C_1—this response being C_2. Perceived and utilized, your response (C_2) serves to correct any expectations I previously had. These corrections on my part result in C_3. I transmit C_3 to you. Given X and expectations concerning my response to C_2, you respond by reflecting C_4, and so on until we are satisfied we have obtained X which will lead to Y, or until the system dissolves (cannot accomplish X, Y, or both), or until time runs out.

When your responses match my expectations and my responses match your expectations, subsequent action is likely to continue along lines we both anticipate, given X and Y. Conversely, where there is a mutually perceived gap between expected and actual responses, between expected responses and X, between actual responses and X, or between expected, actual responses and X, we each adjust our subsequent actions, bringing them more into line with one another's orientations and the system's assigned goal. If either of us is not listening effectively, it becomes difficult to send messages that communicate understanding or misunderstanding, or agreement or disagreement, because any single message reflects a previous message. If effective listening is taking place, the response is predictable, because it is logically connected to an earlier message. If effective listening is not taking place, then it becomes difficult to predict my response based on your previous message—and vice versa. Therefore, the communication patterns that form in a dyad where

Figure 11.2. Communication Contents Forming Interactive Loops Between Two Conversants.

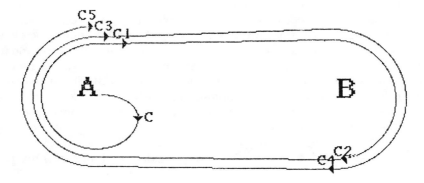

effective listening is taking place will be more predictable than the communication patterns where this is not true.

Figure 11.2 provides a diagram of the communication content initiated in the example above. In a crude and static manner, this diagram illustrates that you and I are completing communication loops commonly referred to as interaction. Remembering what has already been said about listening and sources and receivers in a dyadic system, the diagram illustrates that, on one level, listening can be identified in the following manner. For me (A), it is the decoding, encoding, and reflection of C_1 by you (B) in the form of C_2, which resulted in C_3. For you (B), it is the decoding, encoding, and reflection of C_2 by me (A) in the form of C_3, which resulted in C_4. If we overlook the arbitrary starting point for observation and assume that the process of communication has no beginning or end (Berlo, 1960), then all of the communication contents make up the set of all possible occurrences of listening. Therefore, observing the communication patterns formed by a dyadic system is the equivalent of observing listening as a relational process.

PRACTICAL IMPLICATIONS

The theoretical perspective described in this chapter has practical implications for both research and instruction. The implications for research have to do with a means to define listening effectiveness in operational terms that are very different from the typical listening test presented in a one-to-many setting. The instructional implications rely on thinking about traditional material in a different light.

A Research Application

From initial contact to separation, listening as a relational process involves a continuous set of encounters during which one person continues the contact without separation only as long as the other offers communications that facilitate the relationship and thus create movement toward understanding by providing necessary information. One person can obstruct or facilitate progress toward understanding almost at will. Behaviors that will prevent understanding from taking place include ceasing communication, responding irrelevantly, responding in a confused manner, or doing just the opposite of what is required—in other words, not listening effectively. One of the things that will help the dyad move toward understanding is to listen effectively, which includes responding appropriately.

Not every signal in a communication situation will be perceived as providing an equal amount of information. According to a basic concept of phenomenological psychology, all human behavior, without exception, is determined by the perceptual field of the behaving individual. Each individual's perceptual field is made up of the entire universe. It includes the self and the individual's personal and unique field of awareness about others and the environment. In short, the individual's perceptual field is the foundation of his or her experiences and his or her behavior is a function of this perception (Combs & Snygg, 1959). Therefore, the more I perceive a signal as informative, the more I will behave as though ambiguity or uncertainty have been removed from the situation. If I *perceive* your response as an attempt to "conceal" rather than "disclose" information, the extent to which that signal can be utilized to determine understanding will be reduced rather than enhanced. If I *perceive* your response as confusing, the extent to which those signals can contribute to understanding will be minimized.

For example, when your response is composed of irrelevant information with reference to understanding, I may perceive such a signal as an indication that you are not listening effectively, or listening but generating confusing information about the task that binds us together. On the whole then, for effective listening to take place, we must perceive one another's responses as "disclosing" rather than "concealing" potential information. If a majority of the responses are perceived to be "concealing," then the communication patterns that develop will not be predictable.

As the term is used with reference to communication patterns, *predictability* can be defined as an index of the amount of information a source conveys to a destination. When there is a lack of information or when the amount of available information is small, the degree of predictability will be low. When information is in abundance or readily available, predictability will be high. More exactly, predictability can be described as a consequence of an increase in information. Therefore, as information decreases, predictability may be presumed to have decreased (Garner, 1962, pp. 1–7, 19–28).

Effective listening, then, can be operationalized by measuring the certainty with which one person's communication can be predicted from another person's communication. Using acts and interacts, given an interact's antecedent "act," with what degree of certainty can its subsequent "act" be predicted? For example, I have argued that a listener must respond before we can say whether listening has taken place. The restrictions that listening involves responding and effective listening involves appropriate responding, constrain what happens next in a communication event. In other words, when two people are listening effectively some communications are more likely to follow certain communications than others. As Hawes (1970) put it, we predict that "given any behavior, some behaviors are more likely to precede and follow it than others" (p. 208). Thus, the more effective the listening, the more constrained communication becomes. As a result, if we know generally what two people are talking about and we know what one of them has just said, we should be able to predict how the other person will respond—if the other person is listening effectively.

In this light we would seek to estimate degrees of effective listening by the measure of predictability in the communication patterns—the more certain we are in our predictions about a dyad's communication patterns, the more we can say that effective listening has taken place; the more uncertain, the less effective the listening has been. The theoretic range for predictability is from "absolute certainty—the antecedent state is always followed by the same subsequent state to...maximum uncertainty of prediction the antecedent state is equally likely to be followed by any subsequent state" (Hawes, 1973, p. 211).

More recently, the predictability of communication patterns has been studied by scholars interested in identifying and studying the structural and functional complexities of conversation (e.g., Craig & Tracey, 1983; Flood, 1984; McLaughlin, 1984). The focus of much of this research has been concerned with understanding the processes related to establishing coherence in a conversation. The arguments presented above regarding the predictability of communication patterns suggest that predictable communication patterns are indications of coherence in a conversation. Thus, recent studies in discourse analysis provide researchers interested in studying listening as a relational process with a background and framework for a new line of listening research.

An Instructional Application

Focusing on how a person responds also has practical implications for instruction. By defining an effective listener as a listener who *responds appropriately,* the teacher or trainer can help students examine their response styles and provide them with instruction about various response options. For example, Rogers and Farson (1981) suggest that most people naturally tend to evaluate when they respond to someone they have been listening to, and yet most people prefer not to be evaluated. When this happens, the person listening has responded *inappropriately,* and according to the model presented in this chapter, listened ineffectively. Listeners have five response options: evaluative, supportive, interpretive, probing, and understanding.

1. An *understanding* remark reflects back what the person has said, indicating that the respondent understands and accepts the information without attempting to go beyond it, investigate it, or evaluate it.
2. A *probing* response indicates the receiver's intent is to seek further information, provoke further discussion along a certain line, or question the sender. The receiver has in some way implied that the sender ought to or might profitably develop or discuss a point further.
3. A *supportive* remark indicates the receiver's intent is to reassure, to pacify, to reduce the sender's intensity of feeling. The receiver has in some way implied that the sender does not need to feel as he or she does.
4. An *interpretive* response indicates the receiver's intent is to teach, to tell the sender what his or her problem means, or how the sender really feels about the situation. The receiver has either obviously and subtly implied what the person with the problem might or ought to think.
5. An *evaluative* response indicates the receiver has made a judgment of relative worth, appropriateness, effectiveness, or rightness of the sender's problem. The receiver has in some way implied what the sender might or ought to do.

As the needs of a situation change, a listener has all five options available to him or her, but the responsibility for establishing understanding must be met first. In other words, these response styles are hierarchically related moving from the first (understanding) to the fifth (evaluative).

Gibb's (1961) classifications of communication into defensive and supportive categories can also be thought of in terms of inappropriate and appropriate response styles. Gibb identified six distinct communication behaviors that promote a defensive attitude. He also described six positive counterparts that promote a positive communication climate.

1. *Evaluation vs. description:* No one enjoys being evaluated, criticized, and judged. Evaluation is "you" language. Description is "I" language. It describes the speaker's thoughts and feelings.
2. *Control vs. problem orientation:* Implicit in attempts to control lies the assumption that the controller is more knowledgeable or knows better what is good for the "controllee." Rather than trying to get others to do what you want them to do, strive to find an alternative that is equally beneficial.
3. *Strategy vs. spontaneity:* If others detect that you are following a preplanned script rather than being open and honest with them, they become defensive. It is better to respond immediately and honestly without hidden agendas or motives.
4. *Neutrality vs. empathy:* Neutrality is the lack of emotional involvement and commitment. It conveys the message, "You're simply not worth getting excited about."
5. *Superiority vs. equality:* Interpersonal relationships must be based on mutual respect.
6. *Certainty vs. provisionalism:* To act with certainty is to act as if we have all the answers. If we appear to be more flexible—to be genuinely committed to solving problems rather than simply taking sides on an issue—then people will be less defensive towards us.

The arousal of defensiveness is the antithesis of effective listening. If a listener responds with communicative behaviors that force the other person to defend himself or herself, then the listener has responded ineffectively. On the other hand, an effective listener in a relational setting responds in ways that show the other person that the listener is being supportive.

A similar logic applies to using Sieburg and Larson's (1971) confirming and disconfirming behaviors as a model for looking at a listener's appropriate or inappropriate responses. They define confirming behaviors as those responses that make the other person feel good about himself or herself—messages a listener sends that tell the other person that the listener values him or her as a person. Disconfirming behaviors are the opposite. These are responses a listener uses to tell the other person that the listener does not value him or her as a person.

Disconfirming Responses.

1. *Impervious response:* When one speaker fails to acknowledge, even minimally, the other speaker's communicative attempt, or when one

ignores or disregards the other by not giving any ostensible acknowledgment of the other's communication, his or her response may be
called impervious.

2. *Interrupting response:* When one speaker cuts the other speaker short
    or begins while the other is still speaking, his or her response may be
    called interrupting.
3. *Irrelevant response:* When one speaker responds in a way that seems
    unrelated to what the other has been saying, or when one speaker
    introduces a new topic without warning or returns to his or her earlier
    topic, apparently disregarding the intervening conversation, her or his
    response may be called irrelevant.
4. *Tangential response:* When one speaker acknowledges the other
    person's communication but immediately takes the conversation in
    another direction, his or her response may be called tangential.
    Occasionally, individuals exhibit what may appear to be direct
    responses to the other, such as "Yes, but..." or "Well, you may be
    right, but..." and then may proceed to respond with communicative
    content very different from or unrelated to that which preceded. Such
    responses may still be called tangential.
5. *Impersonal response:* When a speaker conducts a monologue, when
    his or her speech communication behavior appears intellectualized
    and impersonal, contains few first-person statements and many
    generalized "you" or "one" statements, and is heavily loaded with
    euphemisms or cliches, the response may be called impersonal.
6. *Incoherent response:* When the speaker responds with sentences that
    are incomplete, or with rambling statements difficult to follow, or
    with sentences containing much retracing or rephrasing, or interjec-
    tions such as "you know" or "I mean," his or her response may be
    called incoherent.
7. *Incongruous response:* When the speaker engages in nonvocal be-
    havior that seems consistent with the vocal content, his or her
    response may be called incongruous. For example, "Who's angry? I'm
    not angry" (said in a tone and volume that strongly suggests anger). Or,
    "I'm really concerned about you" (said in a tone that suggests lack of
    interest or disdain).

Confirming Responses.

1. *Direct acknowledgment:* One speaker acknowledges the other's com-
    munication and reacts to it directly and verbally.
2. *Agreement about content:* One speaker reinforces or supports infor-
    mation or opinions expressed by the other.

3. *Supportive response:* One speaker expresses understanding of the other, reassures him or her, or tries to make him or her feel better.
4. *Clarifying response:* One speaker tries to clarify the content of the other's message or attempts to clarify the other's present or past feelings. The usual form of a clarifying response is to elicit more information, to encourage the other to say more, or to repeat in an inquiring way what was understood.
5. *Expression of positive feeling:* One speaker describes his or her own positive feelings related to prior utterances of the other. For example, "Okay, now I understand what you are saying."

All three of the examples above indicate that a practical implication for instruction of conceptualizing listening as a relational process is that it allows the teacher or trainer to provide direct instruction in specific, observable communication behaviors. By focusing on the responding stage of the listening process, those individuals interested in how to teach effective listening can turn to the wealth of material available in the interpersonal literature concerning feedback and response styles.

CONCLUSION

Over the years, the number of conceptual definitions of listening has grown considerably. Recently, listening scholars have made some progress in identifying commonalities among the conceptual definitions, but we have continued to have difficulty bridging the gap between our conceptual definitions and our measures. In spite of this gap, progress has been made in establishing some valid and reliable operational definitions. However, most of those operational definitions have been related to the construction of listening tests. Although listening tests are an important part of the process of studying listening, they stem from a limited way to conceptualize listening and are only one way to operationalize listening.

Although the terms *listening* and *intrapersonal communication* do not always appear together in the literature, the two processes are conceptually related. Most conceptual definitions of listening contain references to *intra*personal processes. However, as I have indicated in this chapter, not all of listening is *intra*personal. To understand the complete process of listening, we must also understand its relational dimensions.

For this author, understanding the relational dimensions of listening involves turning to systems theory and approaching the listener/speaker relationship from a holistic perspective. As participants, we strive to communicate, and our success or failure depend upon a number of factors.

Some of these factors include the understanding we have of one another and the situation (*intra*personal); the clarity of our own goals and our perceptions of and sensitivity to one another's needs (*intra*personal); the strategic, communicative choices we make (*intra*personal); and our ability to put those choices into action—to respond appropriately (relational).

This chapter has also argued that focusing on the response stage of listening is central to any attempt to conceptualize listening as a relational process. From a research perspective, operationalizing listening effectiveness as the predictability of communication patterns within a dyadic system was presented as one practical implication. It should be noted, however, that measuring the predictability of communication patterns within a dyadic relationship will require a coding system that can be used during interaction analysis. The coding system should be related to conceptual definitions of listening. At this stage in my thinking, I have not found or developed such a system. I did examine the communication patterns of effective and ineffective listeners in dyads in an earlier research project (Rhodes, 1987). At that time, however, I was simply testing the line of thinking I have presented in this chapter. Although that category system worked for my preliminary test, it was not grounded in listening theory. I suggested at that time, as I am again, that a coding system designed to examine listening behaviors should be developed.

It should also be noted that presenting traditional response style categories as a means of offering direct instruction in listening effectiveness is also only one possibility. All of the work that has gone on for years in the areas of empathy and humanistic psychology provide other avenues for pursuing listening as a relational process. Work in the area of referential communication provides still another avenue, as does any of the work done in interpersonal areas such as conversational involvement or coorientation. As listening scholars we should not be afraid to look elsewhere for ideas that might help us find more creative ways to study and teach about listening.

As we pointed out in the beginning of the chapter, listening research has typically focused on the one-to-many situation, followed a lecture retention model, and operationalized listening effectiveness as a score on a test. The relational perspective described in this chapter allows for a more valid and heuristic investigation of how listening operates in the interpersonal setting. Some of the advantages of the relational perspective described in this chapter would include the following:

1. Listening would occur in an interactive setting where the participants would have goals guiding their behavior.
2. Participants would have the opportunity to respond immediately to what they have heard. Each response would operate as evidence of

how effective one participant has been in listening to prior portions of the conversation (predictability of communication patterns).
3. Listening would be investigated in more realistic, everyday situations with varied constraints.
4. The function of making appropriate response choices during the process of listening could be more easily investigated as participants utilized situational information to process what is being said during a conversation (combination of *intra*personal and relational components).
5. Listening would be closely aligned with speaking in actual interaction.
6. Response strategies in relational listening could be identified along with the effect such strategies have on speaking and vice versa.
7. Instruction in how to respond appropriately in different situations could play an important role in listening instruction.

Because of advantages such as these, a relational perspective toward research in listening offers a fresh way to investigate listening. Many of the disadvantages of operationalizing listening through standardized tests are avoided. Furthermore, the conclusions coming from a relational research model will be more valid for studying listening in one-to-one rather than one-to-many settings.

REFERENCES

Ackoff, R.L., & Emery, F. (1972). *On purposeful systems,* Chicago: Aldine.

Barker, L.L. (1971). *Listening behavior.* Englewood Cliffs, NJ: Prentice-Hall.

Beatty, M.J., & Payne, S.K. (1981). Receiver apprehension and cognitive complexity. *The Western States Speech Journal, 45,* 263–269.

Berlo, D.K. (1960). *The process of communication.* New York: Holt, Rinehart and Winston.

Berlo, D.K. (1977). Communication as process: Review and commentary. In B.D. Ruben (Ed.), *Communication yearbook I* (pp. 11–27). New Brunswick, NJ: International Communication Association.

Bostrom, R., & Waldhart, E. (1980). Components in listening behavior: The role of short-term memory. *Human Communication Research, 6,* 221–227.

Bowers, J.W., & Courtright, J.A. (1984). *Communication research methods.* Glenview, IL: Scott, Foresman and Company.

Brooks, R.D., & Scheidel, T.M. (1968). Speech as a process: A case study. *Speech Monographs, 35,* 1–7.

Brownell, J. (1986). *Building active listening skills.* Englewood Cliffs, NJ: Prentice-Hall.

Cahn, D.D., & Hanford, J.T. (1984). Perspectives on human communication research: Behaviorism, phenomenology, and an integrated view. *Western Journal of Speech Communication, 48,* 277–292.

Cherry, C. (1978). *On human communication*. New York: Science Editions.

Churchman, C.W. (1968). *The systems approach*. New York: Dell Publishing Co.

Combs, A., & Snygg, D. (Eds.). (1959). *Individual behavior, a perceptual approach to behavior*. New York: Harper.

Craig, R.T., & Tracy, K. (Eds.). (1983). *Conversational coherence: Form, structure, and strategy*. Beverly Hills, CA: Sage Publications.

Cronbach, L.J., & Meehl, P.E. (1955). Construct validity in psychological tests. *Psychological Bulletin, 42*, 281–302.

Cushman, D.P., & Cahn, D.D. (1985). *Communication in interpersonal relationships*. Albany, NY: SUNY Press.

Emmert, P. (1989, March). *The reification of listening*. Paper presented at the annual meeting of the International Listening Association, Atlanta.

Erway, E. (1972). Listening: The second speaker. *Speech Journal, 10*, 22.

Farra, H.E. (1983, Fall). Relational listening. *Listening Post Supplement*, pp. 21–40.

Fisher, A. (1978). *Perspectives on human communication*. New York: Macmillan.

Fisher, A., & Hawes, L.C. (1971). An interact system model: Generating a grounded theory of small groups. *Quarterly Journal of Speech, 57*, 444–453.

Fitch-Hauser, M., & Hughes, M.A. (1988). Defining the cognitive process of listening: A dream or reality? *Journal of the International Listening Association, 2*, 75–88.

Flood, J. (Ed.). (1984). *Understanding reading comprehension: Cognition, language, and the structure of prose*. Newark, DE: International Reading Association.

Floyd, J.I. (1985). *Listening: A practical approach*. Glenview, IL: Scott, Foresman and Company.

Garner, W.R. (1962). *Uncertainty and structure as psychological concepts*. New York: John Wiley and Sons.

Gibb, J.R. (1961). Defensive communication. *Journal of Communication, 11*(3), 141–148.

Glenn, E.C. (1989). A content analysis of fifty definitions of listening. *Journal of the International Listening Association, 3*, 21–31.

Goss, B. (1982). *Processing communication*. Belmont, CA: Wadsworth.

Hawes, L.C. (1970). *An empirical definition and analysis of physician-patient communication systems*. Dissertation Abstracts International, 71–78, 741, 576A.

Hawes, L.C. (1973). Elements of a model for communication processes. *Quarterly Journal of Speech, 59*, 11–21.

Hirsch, R.O. (1979). *Listening: A way to process information aurally*. Dubuque, IA: Gorsuch-Scarisbrick.

Howell, W.S. (1982). *The empathic communicator*. Belmont, CA: Wadsworth Publishing Co.

Littlejohn, S.W. (1987). *Theories of human communication*. Belmont, CA: Wadsworth Publishing Co.

Lundsteen, S.W. (1979). *Listening: Its impact at all levels on reading and other language arts*. Urbana, IL: National Council of Teachers of English.

McCroskey, J. (1982). Communication competence and performance. *Communication Education, 31,* 2–4.

McLaughlin, M.L. (1984). *Conversation: How talk is organized.* Beverly Hills, CA: Sage Publications.

Mead, N. (1980). *Developing oral communication skills: Implications of theory and research for instruction and training.* Paper presented at the National Basic Skills Orientation Conference, Arlington, VA.

Monge, P. (1977). The systems perspective as a theoretical basis for the study of human communication. *Communication Quarterly, 25,* 19–29.

Nichols, R., & Stevens, L. (1957). *Are you listening?* New York: McGraw-Hill.

Rhodes, S.C. (1984). *What communication journals tell us about listening.* Paper presented at the annual meeting of the Central States Speech Association, Chicago.

Rhodes, S.C. (1985). What the communication journals tell us about teaching listening. *Central States Speech Journal, 36,* 24–32.

Rhodes, S.C. (1987). A study of effective and ineffective listening dyads using the systems theory principle of entropy. *Journal of the International Listening Association, 1,* 32–53.

Rhodes, S.C. (1989a). *Receiver apprehension, cognitive complexity, and conversational involvement as indices of perceived listening effectiveness.* Paper presented at the annual meeting of the International Communication Association, San Francisco.

Rhodes, S.C. (1989b). Listening and intrapersonal communication. In C.V. Roberts & K.W. Watson (Eds.), *Intrapersonal communication processes: Original essays,* (pp. 547–569) New Orleans, LA: SPECTRA.

Rhodes, S.C., Watson, K.W., & Barker, L.L. (1990)l. Listening assessment: Trends and influencing factors in the 1980s. *Journal of the International Listening Association, 4,* 62–81.

Ridge, A. (1983). *Methods of listening assessment.* Paper presented at the annual meeting of the Central States Speech Association, Schaumberg, IL.

Roberts, C., Edwards, R., & Barker, L. (1987). *Intrapersonal communication processes.* Scottsdale, AZ: Gorsuch Scarisbrick.

Roberts, C.V. (1988). The validation of listening tests: Cutting of the Gordian knot. *Journal of the International Listening Association, 2,* 1–19.

Rogers, C.R., & Farson, R.E. (1981). In J.A. DeVito (Ed.), *Communication: Concepts and processes,* Englewood Cliffs, NJ: Prentice-Hall.

Scheidel, T.M., & Crowell, L. (1966). Feedback in small group communication. *Quarterly Journal of Speech, 52,* 273–278.

Sieburg, E., & Larson, C. (1971). *Dimensions of interpersonal response.* Paper presented at the annual meeting of the International Communication Association, Phoenix.

Smith, D.K. (1972). Communication research and the idea of process. *Speech Monographs, 39,* 174–182.

Spitzberg, B. (1981). *Competence in communicating.* Paper presented at the annual meeting of the Speech Communication Association, Anahiem, CA.

Steil, L. (1981). On listening…and not listening. *Executive Health, 18,* 3.

Steil, L., Watson, K., & Barker, L.L. (1983). *Effective listening: Key to your success*. Reading, MA: Addison-Wesley.

Trenholm, S. (1991). *Human communication theory* (2nd ed.). Englewood Cliffs, NJ: Prentice-Hall.

Trenholm, S., & Jensen, A. (1988). *Interpersonal communication*. Belmont, CA: Wadsworth Publishing Co.

Villaume, W. A., & Cegala, D.J. (1986). *Implications of discourse strategy for listening*. Paper presented at the annual meeting of the International Listening Association, San Diego.

von Bertalanffy, L. (1968). *General system theory*. New York: George Braziller.

Weaver, C.H. (1972). *Human listening: Processes and behavior*. Indianapolis, IN: Bobbs-Merrill.

Wiemann, J.M., & Backlund, P.M. (1980). Current theory and research in communicative competence. *Review of Educational Research, 15,* 187.

Williams, F.W. (1988). *The new communications*. New York: Wadsworth.

Wilmot, W.W. (1979). *Dyadic communication*. Reading, MA: Addison-Wesley.

Wolff, F.I., Marsnik, N.C., Tacey, W.S., & Nichols, R.G. (1983). *Perceptive listening*. New York: Holt, Rinehart and Winston.

Wolvin, A.D. (1989). Models of the listening process. In C.V. Roberts & K.W. Watson (Eds.), *Intrapersonal communication processes: Original essays* (pp. 508–527). New Orleans, LA: SPECTRA.

Wolvin, A.D., & Coakley, C. (1988). *Listening* (3rd ed.). Dubuque, IA: Wm. C. Brown Publishers.

Chapter 12

Listening Environment: A Perspective

Judi Brownell

Department of Managerial Communication
School of Hotel Administration
Cornell University

This chapter focuses on how organizational leaders create and maintain strong listening environments. Such environments are characterized by effective listening behaviors, and facilitate both task accomplishment and relationship development within organizations.

Listening environment is defined as a set of enduring organizational characteristics that contribute to the development of common perceptions and expectancies among organizational members with regard to listening practices. Strong listening environments emerge, then, when members of a work group perceive specific managerial behaviors and interpret them as positive, supportive, and helpful. In particular, managers must understand what employees say, communicate empathy, and respond appropriately to worker needs.

In addition to demonstrating specific listening skills, managers can strengthen listening environments by attending to three other elements. They must ensure that the organization's physical setting encourages frequent employee encounters as well as provide listening training for all workers. Effective managers also assume the role of symbolic leader, communicating both directly and indirectly that listening is valued.

Organizational leaders who create strong listening environments are preparing their employees to deal effectively with a constantly changing, complex workplace. Few skills contribute more directly to employees' life-long learning and organizational development than effective listening. In addition, strong listening environments may well alter employees' perceptions of the organization and of work. The perception of colleagues as supportive and trusting has implications for the ways in which individuals view traditional boundaries between their personal and professional lives. Clearly, the concept of listening environment can be extended into a variety of other contexts. This perspective may provide insights that will enable us to bridge gulfs that have existed not only between individuals and workgroups but between organizations, communities, and nations.

Wherever individuals depend on accurate and complete information—whether in homes, schools, or work organizations—the environment in which these exchanges occur has a significant impact on the quality and nature of the interaction. Supportive communication climates are characterized by strong listening environments; such environments facilitate the development of healthy and open interpersonal relationships. Educators, parents, doctors, managers, counselors, and numerous other professionals increase their effectiveness when they make it clear that listening is practiced and valued.

This chapter focuses specifically on listening in work organizations and on how organizational leaders create and maintain an environment that encourages information sharing and trust. The role managers play in creating strong listening environments is discussed and four esential elements of such environments are reviewed. Finally, the theoretical and practical implications of this perspective are presented.

DEVELOPING LISTENING ENVIRONMENTS IN ORGANIZATIONS

Organizational leaders have become increasingly proactive as they analyze their unique work settings and plan for positive change. Today's effective managers focus on the individual and his or her beliefs, needs, and goals (LaFollette, 1975; Schermerhorn, 1977). There are few better ways to demonstrate the importance placed on the organization's human resources than to encourage employee trust, participation, and information sharing through effective listening. Developing a supportive communication environment where listening is practiced and valued is essential to an employee-centered workplace (Ashworth & Meglino, 1982; Diffie-Couch, 1984; Loftu Nave, 1986; Nicholas, 1982). As Peters (1988) explains, strong listening environments are characterized by the following:

> Managers listening to their people...teammates listening to each other...people paying attention to those in other functions, battering down the time-honored, action-slowing functional boundaries. (p. 367)

The term *listening environment* is relatively new (Bruschi, 1986; Peters, 1988) and has not yet been well defined or firmly established in the literature. For our purposes, a listening environment refers to a set of relatively enduring organizational characteristics that contribute to the development of common perceptions and expectancies among organizational members with regard to listening practices. These perceptions, once established, influence employees' attitudes and subsequent communication behavior (Ashworth & Meglino, 1983; Schlesinger & Balzer, 1985). The specific listening environment, then, emerges out of the interactions that members of a work group have and employees' subsequent interpretation of the meaning of these actions. An aspect of organizational culture, a listening environment refers to how listening is perceived, interpreted, and experienced by members of a work group. Strong listening environments are created when listening is valued and when norms have developed that support effective listening practices. In work organizations, it becomes a management responsibility to ensure that such conditions are fostered and supported.

Pearson (1989) writes that "whatever the environment a manager inherits from the past, shaping—or reshaping—it is a critically important job" (p. 94). His implication is clear: Managers have the responsibility for creating the environments in which their employees work. Through setting standards, modeling desirable behaviors, rewarding high performance, and building trust, managers define what it is like to work in their companies.

In 1985, Daniel reported a study designed to prove whether or not managerial style alone correlated with subordinate perceptions of organizational climate. He defined organizational climate as "characteristics of the work environment, perceived directly or indirectly by the people who work in the environment" (p. 416). His findings are particularly interesting for our purposes; he discovered that management style did, indeed, show a definite and consistent relationship to climate measures. We can assume, then, that managers who demonstrate effective listening skills contribute to the development of a strong listening environment—their behaviors do make a difference (Kaiser, 1982; King, 1978).

Managers also realize that to build healthy relationships and accomplish tasks, they must pay close attention to employees' behaviors, attitudes, and feelings; they must create environments that encourage all employees to become effective listeners (Sypher, Bostrom, & Seibert, 1989).

CREATING A STRONG LISTENING ENVIRONMENT: MANAGEMENT RESPONSIBILITIES

If managers of the 1990s are to achieve their goals, they must focus on the listening environment as an important organizational variable (Redding, 1984; Stegman, 1988; Blank, 1985; Peters, 1989). There is little doubt that excellent companies work to foster strong listening environments (Peters & Austin, 1985; Peters & Waterman, 1982). Although far too little research exists to support the link between effective listening practices and improved individual and organizational performance, there are specific actions managers can take to facilitate effective listening throughout their organizations.

First, the listening process is briefly discussed and the skills that contribute most directly to strong listening environments are described. Later, three additional elements of strong listening environments are explained.

THE SKILLS OF LISTENING

Perhaps one of the reasons why listening has only recently been emphasized as a key factor in organizational development is because it is relatively difficult to conceptualize (Glenn, 1989). Wolvin and Coakley (1988) have been widely cited for their vivid presentation of the problems involved in defining the listening process. Listing a representative sample of various definitions from 1925 to 1985, they write:

> A quick glance at these definitions shows us that listening scholars do not agree on what listening is. A more careful study, however, reveals to us that they raise many questions crucial to the construction of a definition. (p. 57)

Since listening is largely a covert process, scholars have long debated whether it can be taught in the same manner as other, more overt, communication skills. In addition, it may be that individuals who are *perceived* to be effective listeners do not perform significantly better than do their colleagues when given standardized listening tests. A number of other factors, such as motivation, the individual's background, attitudes, and gender, also influence one's listening ability. Nevertheless, behavioral approaches to understanding and assessing listening effectiveness are essential if managers are to deliberately create strong listening environments.

A study by Brownell (1988) is particularly relevant to our purposes. In an effort to answer the question, What do employees mean when they say their manager listens?, she discovered that perceptions of listening effectiveness were most closely associated with the projection of empathy. Two other dimensions that employees used in forming judgments of their managers' listening ability were accurate understanding of the message and the appropriateness and timeliness of the response. Although other dimensions of the listening process also contribute to perceptions of listening behavior (Husband, Cooper, & Monsour, 1988; Gilbert, 1989), accurate comprehension, empathy, and an appropriate response appear to be key in managers' ability to accomplish the tasks involved in creating strong listening environments. Thus, managers themselves must first demonstrate desirable listening skills.

Insure Accurate Comprehension

In order to clearly and accurately understand someone, the listener must perform several related tasks. First, he or she must direct attention to and concentrate on the specific message; the person must accurately hear what was said. Concentration alone, however, is not enough. The listener must also share the speaker's vocabulary and meanings as well as distinguish between important main points and less significant details. Finally, in order to demonstrate understanding, the listener must use information appropriately. To do this, he or she must have remembered what was said.

Concentrate. In their text, Wolvin and Coakley (1988) address some of the primary reasons for lack of concentration. These include ego-centricity, lack of self-discipline, and lack of self-motivation. Concentration is affected by the extent to which the listener sincerely cares about both the topic and the person speaking (O'Neil & O'Neil, 1974). To a marketing specialist, a description of a new product line is much more attention getting than gossip about an upcoming fashion show; the problems of family members or good friends are inherently more interesting than those experienced by casual acquaintances.

One of the most common obstacles to concentration that listeners face, however, is noise in the environment. Regardless of the setting, listeners confront numerous other stimuli in addition to the speaker and message. These distractions may be environmental (external) or self-generated (internal), or they may come from the speaker (Floyd, 1985). Some types of noise, such as the appearance or presentation habits of the speaker, are difficult to control; others, like the physical environment, can be changed or adapted to reduce as much noise as possible. Designing physical environments conducive to effective listening is the topic of a later section.

One reason why it's so difficult to concentrate is that there is a significant differential between speaking speed and thinking speed. While individuals speak at approximately 125 to 150 words per minute, most listeners can comprehend at three times that rate—up to 500 words per minute. This is of particular importance to teachers and trainers who are concerned with sustaining participants' attention over long periods of time. Effective listeners use spare listening time efficiently; they consider the ideas presented in terms of their personal interests and needs, apply the information to concrete situations, formulate relevant questions, and otherwise participate in the communication event (Wolff, Marsnik, Tacey, & Nichols, 1983; Wolvin & Coakley, 1988; Floyd, 1985).

Clearly, the listening process is blocked if the individual never receives the entire message in the first place. Whether the specific problem is fatigue, stress, lack of interest in the topic, or some external distraction, managers must do whatever is necessary to avoid or reduce factors that interfere with concentration. If strong listening environments are to be established, participants must be able to concentrate fully on the exchange. Managing chaos (Peters, 1989), in the final analysis, requires managing each individual encounter—the small but significant moments of human interaction.

Share Perceptions and Consider Contexts. When employees from different cultures and with different world views interact, it becomes readily apparent that words can be exchanged—and heard—without meanings being shared (Bormann, 1983; Goodall, 1983). Under such circumstances, those who are responsible for ensuring that effective communication takes place must work hard to accurately understand the speaker's intent. Even within one organization or one community, subcultures develop different meanings for various words and events. Common understandings develop as meanings are negotiated within the context of specific interactions.

In their role as boundary spanners, managers must link the perceptions of different divisions and departments. Specialized vocabularies and unique role relationships often distance individuals who work in the same building or on the same floor. Creating a strong listening environment requires managers to recognize differences as well as similarities among employees and to ask appropriate questions so that each individual's unique world view is taken into account. Heightened awareness and increased sensitivity to these and similar factors improve listening ability.

Another sensitivity effective listeners develop is an awareness of nonverbal cues. Ideally, verbal and nonverbal messages reinforce one another. In some instances, however, messages received from the two channels appear discrepent. An employee may say he or she doesn't mind coming in to work early, but his or her facial expression and voice convey a different message. In such cases, managers must determine the communicator's true intent by considering both verbal and nonverbal indicators. An understanding of nonverbal behavior is particularly important to those who manage a diverse work force, since the meaning of specific nonverbal behaviors is often culturally determined. You can imagine the misunderstandings that result when two communicators not only use different verbal codes but assign different meanings to nonverbal behaviors as well.

As the workplace becomes more complex and as information sources multiply, all employees must quickly distinguish between important and superficial information, between main ideas and supporting details. Effective listeners learn to determine the most relevant aspects of the message conveyed. They are able to see relationships among ideas and events, distinguish fact from opinion, and seek additional information when messages are unclear or incomplete (Brownell, 1986, 1990).

Remember Messages. Although memory is a cognitive activity separate from listening, managers discover that, unless they are able to remember what is said, it is impossible to demonstrate their understanding by taking appropriate action. In one study of hospitality managers, individuals gave themselves the highest ratings on the question, "When I say I will take care of something, I do it" (Brownell, 1988). Demonstrating to employees that their concerns are taken seriously requires that what they say also be remembered beyond the specific communication encounter. Perception checking, note taking, and other deliberate techniques increase the chances that ideas will be recalled accurately. When strong listening environments are operative, individuals feel that their ideas and opinions are heard and considered. Although paying undivided attention to a message is prerequisite to remembering it, long-term memory techniques based on deliberate association are tools well worth learning.

In their efforts to facilitate information sharing, managers must also present themselves in a manner that communicates warmth and openness. Unless employees feel free to speak up about their concerns, managers will not have access to important information. Another key element of effective listening, then, is the communication of empathy.

Demonstrate Empathy

Although most of us have a general understanding of what is meant by empathy, it is important to clearly distinguish it from such related concepts as "sympathy" or "understanding." If an individual genuinely empathizes, he or she identifies with another's thoughts and emotions by entering the other person's frame of reference, by sharing the other person's world view (Kennedy, 1977) in an open and nonjudgmental manner. It is particularly difficult to empathize when colleagues have few common experiences. As Wolvin and Coakley (1988) write:

> separate worlds create separate perceptions, experiences, feelings, and thoughts, and prevent two people from ever sharing complete empathy. (p. 254)

Know the Speaker. One of the first steps in developing empathy is to find out as much as possible about the person speaking. Wolff and her colleagues (1983) explain that the purpose of empathic listening—as opposed to other forms—is to facilitate the speaker's personal learning and growth. Empathic listeners build trust by communicating a sincere concern for the person speaking.

There is little question that empathy is an essential ingredient in any communication encounter. The multicultural work environment and the increasing specialization of the workforce place even greater demands on managers' ability to project their sincere interest in each employee and to make every effort to take each speaker's perspective into account.

Develop Skills and Sensitivity. What are the skills of empathic listening? Perhaps Gerald Egan (1985) said it best:

> One does not listen with just his ears; he listens with his eyes...he listens by becoming aware of the feelings and emotions that arise within himself....He listens to the words of others but he also listens to the messages that are buried in the words....He listens to the voice, the demeanor, the vocabulary, and the gestures. (p. 228)

Empathic listeners attend both to the verbal and the nonverbal aspects of a speaker's message (Wolff et al., 1983). Managers who seek complete and accurate communication look beyond the obvious verbal statements to more subtle nonverbal and paralinguistic cues. Further, they show their interest and concern through their own nonverbal behavior. Unless employees perceive that their manager is listening in an open and accepting manner, they may hesitate to take risks or to share their true feelings (Shea, 1984).

The effective empathic listener not only listens openly but also communicates his or her understanding to the speaker (Kelly, 1977). Nothing else is as important to the development of strong listening environments as the rapport created through skilled empathic listening. Regardless of the context, however, listeners must be willing to spend time in the encounter; the speaker must feel free to explore his or her feelings in a nonevaluative setting. Silence becomes an important part of the process as listeners limit the amount of advice, questions, and opinions they provide, and instead rely on supportive verbal and nonverbal behaviors. Eye contact, head nods, and supportive verbal cues become important indicators to employees that their manager is listening. One of the strongest indicators of effective listening, then, is the nature and quality of the listener's response. Appropriate and timely verbal and nonverbal behaviors contribute to strong listening environments.

Provide an Appropriate Response

Although researchers are in disagreement about whether or not the element of response is legitimately part of the listening process, those who study perceptions of listening in organizational contexts are convinced that employees' interpretations of managers' listening behavior are directly related to what managers do with the information they acquire. Consequently, feedback and subsequent action have become important management concerns as individuals look to ways in which they can facilitate strong listening environments.

Demonstrate Supportive Behaviors. Gibb's (1960) guidelines for supportive communication climates are particularly relevant. Supportive responses are nonevaluative and encourage employees to speak out. Among Gibb's recommendations are:

1. describe rather than judge
2. qualify statements rather than presenting ideas as if there were only one "right way"
3. project an attitude of equality, not superiority, through language and tone
4. invite problem solving by all parties involved rather than dictating practices or solutions

Whereas the supportive behaviors mentioned above contribute to information sharing and risk taking, other behaviors—such as interruptions, changing the subject, or ignoring employees' feelings—discourage employee contributions and participation. Unfortunately, as Wolvin and

Coakley (1988) note, "the listener's good intentions do not always result in a helpful response" (p. 258). When the goal is to facilitate information sharing and problem solving, it is essential to keep in mind that too much advice, evaluative statements, or an emotional response may inhibit further discussion. Since sensitive communication situations arise repeatedly in the workplace, managers who are able to identify and select appropriate types of feedback facilitate the strongest listening environments.

Respond to Employee needs. Managers must also take every opportunity to demonstrate their responsiveness to employee concerns. As Peters (1988) advises,

> Fix small things on the spot.... Listening is abetted by notetaking... but the clearest indicator is that something happens—either on the spot or soon after. (p. 518)

Employees' judgments of their managers' listening effectiveness, without doubt, directly correspond to the appropriateness of the actions managers take upon hearing employee concerns. When managers delay action or respond in unanticipated or inappropriate ways, employees judge that their managers have not heard them.

Although accurate comprehension, the communication of empathy, and an appropriate response are key to creating strong listening environments, other elements are also important.

ELEMENTS OF STRONG LISTENING ENVIRONMENTS

Peters (1988) lists three "essentials" of a listening environment: a physical setting that encourages frequent, nonthreatening encounters; listening training for all employees; and, symbolic actions that communicate "listening is valued in this organization" (pp. 369-370). Each of these elements is examined below.

Create a Setting and Opportunities to Listen

The physical environment itself has a significant impact on both the quantity and quality of listening that takes place. Peters (1988) emphasizes the need to provide a convenient physical location where groups or teams can meet and know that they won't be interrupted. Open doors, comfortable chairs, and the availability of chalkboards, flip charts, and bulletin boards all send messages to employees about whether or not communication is encouraged. The distance between communicators, often influenced by where chairs are located, also affects interaction by sending messages regarding the formality of the situation or the status of various group members.

Other factors, such as temperature, lighting, and furnishings, also influence individuals' comfort level and their subsequent listening behavior. Rooms that are too hot or not well lit may make participants drowsy. Chairs that are uncomfortable cause discomfort and fatigue, making it more difficult for individuals to concentrate. By carefully designing an environment that facilitates active, two-way communication, managers send a clear signal to their employees that listening is valued.

Physical environments affect listening behavior in offices, boardrooms, and seminar rooms alike. Davis and Hagaman (1976) pose some questions that direct attention to the factors that affect listening environments:

1. Can the physical environment be designed to reduce fatigue?
2. Are there any environmental features that might distract communicators?
3. What physical factors contribute to the ease of the interaction?
4. How does the size and shape of the room affect communication behavior?

Bruschi (1986) reminds us that creating a strong listening environment is particularly important in training seminars, where the emphasis has traditionally been placed on the participant-as-listener rather than on what can be done to encourage two-way listening between participant and trainer. As Finkel (1980) writes, effective listening is most likely to take place when participants are removed from "the noise, excitement, bustle, and stress of everyday work life" and when the trainer makes every effort to meet the "physical, emotional, and psychic needs of the whole person" (p. 56).

If listening is valued, then opportunities to share ideas must also be built into the daily work schedule just like lunches and client appointments. If offices are physically separated, it is even more important that regular opportunities be created for employees to meet and to interact. Managers who really want to hear what employees are saying make it a habit to walk around, to drop in unexpectedly, to be visible.

Listening is not always a planned activity. Some of the most important listening situations are informal; they arise in the halls, by the water cooler, and in the cafeteria. These informal discussions are potentially valuable management tools; they provide opportunities to connect with the grapevine, to hear about fears and rumors first-hand, and to assess how employees feel about their jobs. Peters (1988) describes one Dayton Power & Light executive who literally had his office dismantled so that he would not be hindered in his efforts to become more intimately involved in the company's daily operations. The manager realized that unless he made himself available—physically—he could talk about listening all he wanted, but it wouldn't make a difference in employees' daily experiences. Productive change can only take place when individuals make a commitment to "do things differently." One way to reinforce a commitment to improve listening is through comprehensive, ongoing employee training.

Train All Employees to Listen

Training is one effective means of rewarding high performance, enriching jobs, and motivating individuals. Managers who view every employee as an important resource ask themselves, What is being done on a regular basis to increase this person's knowledge and skill? Training is often the best answer. Training has been defined (Noe, 1986) as a "planned learning experience designed to bring about permanent change in an individual's knowledge, attitudes or skills" (p. 736). Notice that attitudes are included in this definition; clearly, years of research confirm that attitudes are often as important in achieving high performance as knowledge or skill. *In Search of Excellence* (Peters & Waterman, 1982) was not the first management book to note that, when it comes right down to it, "excellence is a matter of attitude."

The long-term positive effects of listening training also increase as a result of the environmental factors discussed earlier. In order for employees to effectively transfer their newly acquired behaviors from the classroom to the workplace, their work setting must be supportive and provide the necessary resources. Goals must be set and employee progress recognized. All members of the organization, from the CEO to line workers, must be involved in the training effort. If training is perceived as something "they" think "we" need, employees' resistance will undermine any potential positive outcomes. Listening training that is organization-wide and viewed as vital to professional development as well as to gaining a competitive edge will be embraced by employees at all levels (Wexley & Latham, 1981).

Ideally, effective listening becomes recognized and valued as an organizational norm; by creating strong listening environments within their departments and divisions and by training new employees as they enter the organization, managers perpetuate a culture that facilitates and rewards effective listening practices. In addition to formal training, however, listening can also be encouraged through informal management strategies.

Peters and Austin (1985) have written that "coaching is the essence of leading" (p. 447). If we carefully examine how learning occurs in an organization, we see that only a small portion of an employee's time is spent in a structured classroom setting. Almost everything that happens to an employee after entering an organization (Strauss & Sayles, 1980) can be seen as a potential learning situation. Managers who view themselves as coaches seize these informal opportunities to enhance their employees' listening abilities. They engage in an ongoing, face-to-face process of influencing employees' performance. This collaborative effort in itself contributes to the supportive atmosphere and positive attitudes essential to strong listening environments.

Managers as coaches observe employees' listening behavior, help each individual to set realistic goals, provide opportunities to practice the appropriate behaviors, and then provide timely and constructive feedback. Allenbaugh (1983) provides useful insights on how the coaching relationship facilitates both the task and the relationship dimensions discussed earlier. He suggests that the degree to which managers make themselves available for coaching directly affects an employee's accurate understanding of his or her job. He also believes that the interpersonal interactions inherent in the coaching process itself contribute to greater risk taking and stronger employee commitment. Listening training, then, contributes to the development of strong listening environments.

Demonstrate That Listening Is Valued

While the organization encourages effective listening through formal and informal training, managers demonstrate their commitment by modeling these behaviors and attitudes during their daily interactions. In addition, they recognize and reward individuals who practice effective listening behaviors at work.

Effective leaders teach and facilitate—but first and foremost, they provide a role model. Peters (1988) writes, "In the end, the manager's minute-to-minute actions provide a living model of his or her strategic vision" (p. 508). Managers who are committed to fostering strong listening environments visibly and consistently demonstrate their own willingness to listen. Frank and Brownell (1989) explain, "In demonstrating appropriate actions, leaders set standards of acceptable performance. They contribute to raising the level of expectations throughout the organization by setting an example" (p. 221).

Management behavior is, today more than ever, symbolic action

(Schein, 1985). Recognizing that employees are motivated and inspired as much by images, symbols, and stories as by statistical reports, effective managers intentionally use emotional as well as rational devices to facilitate important outcomes (Deal & Kennedy, 1982). As Peters and Austin (1985) put it, "All management is show business" (p. 311); effective leaders shape values and encourage desired attitudes and behavior through their own actions. Managers who value strong listening environments demonstrate, on a daily basis, their vision of what it means to listen well. Setting standards for effective listening behavior is a key management task.

In addition to serving as role models, managers encourage strong listening environments by recognizing and rewarding employees' listening behavior. Managers demonstrate that listening is valued by paying attention to it; as Peters (1988) explains, managers encourage others to improve their performance by taking the behavior seriously. Directly and indirectly, managers are in a position to reinforce and reward employees' performance, thereby fostering some behaviors and extinguishing others. Employees who look to their manager for guidance regarding the organization's values and norms must discover that effective listening is among the key competencies for which members are rewarded.

IMPLICATIONS: THEORETICAL AND PRAGMATIC

An impressive and growing collection of studies has documented the need for effective listeners in organizational settings (Wolvin & Coakley, 1988). Listening has drawn increasing attention as communication and management scholars have begun to treat it as a separate variable in the multifaceted work environment. Here, we look at what our understanding of listening environments may mean for the future of listening research and practice in organizational settings as well as in other communication contexts.

Theoretical Implications

The often-repeated story of the wise men and the elephant may apply to the study of listening as well. As scholars strive to define and conceptualize the listening process, their perspectives, methods, and purposes guide them to see quite different aspects of this complex activity. Perhaps, then, the goal is not so much to reach agreement on what listening does or does not include but rather to accurately and thoroughly understand selected aspects of the process. Those who focus on listening environments follow in the footsteps of others who have explored similar concepts. Early studies of organizational and communication climate, however, focused largely on the influence of organizational rather than individual variables. Typical of these was Lawler, Hall, and Oldham's (1974) "Organizational Climate: Relationship to Organizational Structure, Process, and Performance." Researchers were interested in how such factors as information flow and group size affected employees' behavior. Although these studies provided much valuable information, they did not generally provide insight into the human relations aspects of everyday life.

Egan (1985) provides some insight into the ambiguities involved in operationalizing concepts related to organizational—and for our purposes, listening—environments. He has developed three systems into which organizational variables are classified:

1. The Performance System encompasses the organization's mission, specific goals, and material resources.
2. The People System includes communication flow and other observable variables that relate to human interaction.
3. The third system is composed of less tangible variables that "rinse through" the organization. These include quality of worklife concerns, the organization's climate, culture, and—its listening environment.

It is here, in the third system, that researchers must focus their attention in the coming decades as they examine an individual manager's influence on larger dimensions such as the corporation's climate and culture as well as its change and development. Such study requires new approaches and new methods of conceptualizing human factors in organizational contexts.

Quantitative research is likely to be supplemented by a growing number of qualitative studies. Ethnographic methods and cases may well provide important glimpses into the symbolic interactions of organizational members. Since many of our definitions of "good" and "poor" listening rely either on self-reports or on the perceptions of others, scholars need to further operationalize these concepts so that studies can be duplicated and conclusions drawn.

Perhaps most importantly, longitudinal studies must be conducted to assess the long-term impact of listening environments on individual and organizational performance. How does the quality of work life affect other organizational dimensions over time? Although we know intuitively that strong listening environments are desirable, there is sparse evidence to support our notion that companies become successful and maintain their competitive edge because their employees listen. Researchers must look carefully at the assumptions upon which their studies are based and ask themselves whether it would be wise to take one step back and question the foundations upon which new theories are rapidly being built.

Finally, studies of listening environment must be conducted within a broad framework and interpreted in view of other important organizational dimensions. In order to put knowledge into practice, researchers must share findings and develop conceptual models that integrate listening environments with such dimensions as management style, the nature of the workforce, or organizational culture. Scholars must also relate their studies to research conducted in other disciplines and with other methodologies. Listening environments are of interest not only to organizational psychologists, human resources professionals, and organizational development specialists, but also to educators, doctors, lawyers, and therapists, to name a few. Only when scholars and researchers have made sense of the larger picture and applied their models to a variety of contexts can educators and practitioners put to use the information gained about the nature, outcomes, and development of listening environments.

Pragmatic Implications

As constant change becomes a taken-for-granted aspect of organizational life, employees must constantly reassess their personal competencies and professional goals. They must collaborate with their colleagues and adjust to sophisticated information technologies. If one skill contributes to employees' lifelong learning and facilitates organizational development, there is a great likelihood that it is listening. Not only are the skills of listening ever more vital in rapidly changing, complex organizations, but also the accompanying "listening attitudes," fostered by strong listening environments, now appear necessary for survival.

If listening is established as a vital communication skill, able to affect the dynamics of the workplace, the next question becomes, Can individuals be "taught" to listen? Researchers must come to terms with the fact that, as yet, we do not know if listening instruction makes any predictable and long-term difference in the way people behave on the job. Even if listening ability can be developed in classroom settings, the question of transfer—particularly into certain kinds of environments—looms large. If colleagues do not support or reinforce employees' listening behavior, the possibility of extinguishing newly learned skills increases. It may be particularly difficult to create strong listening environments in already established organizational cultures with norms that encourage independence and competition. Although Peters (1988) and others (Steil, Barker, & Watson, 1983) continually reinforce the notion that training dollars are well spent, the "listening attitude" so essential to high performance may not be something that can be acquired through laboratory practice alone.

Clearly, individuals must be high self-monitors to be effective listeners, able to judge the speaker's response accurately and adapt to his or her rational and ideosyncratic behavior. Other important dimensions of listening, such as empathy, may also be as much a personal characteristic as an acquired skill. If so, then psychological testing and personal inventories may find a more significant place in recruitment and selection processes as individuals are selected for their listening aptitude.

Strong listening environments may significantly alter employees' perceptions of the organization and of work. The concepts of colleagues as extended family and of jobs as satisfying a wide variety of individual needs have implications for the ways in which we view traditional boundaries between our personal and professional lives. The skills and attitudes required to build strong listening environments in organizational settings can be applied to numerous other contexts as well. As a research laboratory, work organizations provide an ideal setting for testing assumptions and hypotheses. The principles generated by such research, however, must be transferred to other contexts to improve the quality of listening in our homes, schools, and larger communities.

We must begin to ask questions that recognize our need for effective listening in all contexts; such questions include the following: What does the concept of listening environment mean on a global level? Might the insights and practices that work so well within organizational structures—work organizations, schools, and families—also apply more generally? What value are our research findings to such tasks as dealing with individuals with special needs or improving international relations? Is there a problem of human relations anywhere that could not benefit from sensitive and skilled listening?

CONCLUSION

Building a strong listening environment is one of management's most significant challenges. As Lewis and Reinsch (1988) conclude, "listening in work environments is a complex activity" (p. 63); the process nature of communication makes identifying and reinforcing effective listening behaviors a difficult task.

In their efforts to promote healthy work relationships, employee commitment, and organizational effectiveness, managers have begun to look more closely at the nature of their listening environment for clues to the best means of achieving these outcomes. As organizational leaders, their task is to create and maintain a climate that facilitates open communication and trust—an environment that encourages all employees to come forward to express ideas and share information.

Listening environments, however, are not unique to work organizations. Wherever individuals come together to share ideas, and whenever individuals look to others for understanding and support, the listening environment becomes an important concept as it influences the nature and outcomes of communication encounters. Every individual, functioning either as a group member or partner in a communication transaction, has the ability to influence the listening environment. By practicing effective listening behaviors, controlling the physical setting, and demonstrating that listening is valued, each participant plays a role in enhancing the quality of his or her relationships. In times of transition and in moments of uncertainty, it is unlikely that one individual can make a greater contribution to improving the quality of human communication.

REFERENCES

Allenbaugh, G.E. (1983). Coaching: A management tool for a more effective work performance. *Management Review, 72*(5), 21–26.

Ashworth, D.M., & Meglino, B.M. (1982). Organizational climate and employee performance. *Mid Atlantic Journal of Business, 21*(1), 1–8.

Blank, M.D. (1985). Managing the employee on the other side of the screen. *Personnel, 62*(7), 64–68.

Bormann, E.G. (1983). Symbolic convergence: Organizational communication and culture. In L.L. Putnam & M.E. Paconowsky (Eds.), *Communication and organizations: An interpretative approach,* Beverly Hills, CA: Sage.

Brownell, J. (1986). *Building active listening skills.* Englewood Cliffs, NJ: Prentice-Hall, Inc.

Brownell, J. (1988). *Perceptions of listening: A management study.* Unpublished working paper. Ithaca: Cornell University.

Brownell, J. (1990). Perceptions of effective listeners: A management study. *The Journal of Business Communication, 27*(4), 401–416.

Bruschi, P. (1986). Getting it by ear: Listening in the training process. *Data Training, 5*(5), 1–3.

Daniel, T.L. (1985). Managerial behaviors: Their relationship to perceived organizational climate in a high-technology company. *Group & Organization Studies, 10*(4), 413–428.

Davis, J., & Hagaman, J. (1976). What's right—and wrong—with your training room environment. *Training, 13,* 72–75.

Deal, T., & Kennedy, A. (1982). *Corporate cultures: The rites and rituals of corporate life.* Reading, MA: Addison-Wesley Publishing.

Diffie-Couch, P. (1984). Building a feeling of trust in the company. *Supervisory Management, 29*(4), 31–36.

Egan, G. (1985). Managing the rationale in organizations and institutions. *The 1985 Annual: Developing human resources, pp. 259–274.*

Finkel, C. (1980). The total immersion meeting environment. *Training and Development Journal, 34,* 52–56.

Floyd, J.J. (1985). *Listening: A practical approach.* Glenview, IL: Scott, Foresman and Company.

Frank, A.D., & Brownell, J. (1989). *Organizational communication and behavior: Communicating to improve performance (2 + 2 = 5).* New York: Holt, Rinehart, and Winston.

Gibb, J.R. (1960). Defensive communication. *Journal of Communication, 11,* 142.

Gilbert, M. (1989, March). *Perceptions of listening behaviors of school principals.* Paper presented at the ILA Convention, Atlanta, Georgia.

Glenn, E.C. (1989). A content analysis of fifty definitions of listening. *Journal of the International Listening Association, 3,* 21–31.

Goodall, H.L. (1983). *Human communication: Creating reality.* Dubuque, IA: Wm C. Brown.

Husband, R.L., Cooper, L.O., & Monsour, W.M. (1988). Factors underlying supervisor's perceptions of their own listening behavior. *Journal of the International Listening Association, 2,* 97–112.

Kaiser, L.R. (1982). Sensitive managers can improve the working environment. *Hospital Financial Management, 36(3),* 12–17.

Kelly, C.M. (1977). Empathic listening. In J. Steward (Ed.), *Bridges not walls.* Reading, MA: Addison-Wesley Publishing Company.

Kennedy, E. (1977). *On becoming a counselor: A basic guide for nonprofessional counselors.* New York: Seabury.

King, C.P. (1978). Keep your communication climate healthy. *Personnel Journal, 57(4),* 204–206.

LaFollette, W.R. (1975). How is the climate in your organization? *Personnel Journal, 54(7),* 376–379.

Lawler, E.E., III, & Hall, D.T., & Oldham (1974). Organizational climate—relationship to organizational structure, process and performance. *Organizational Behavior and Human Performance, 11(1),* 139–155.

Lewis, M.H., & Reinsch, N.L., Jr. (1988). Listening in organizational environments. *The Journal of Business Communication, 25(3),* 49–67.

Loftu Nave, J.L. (1986). Gauging organizational climate. *Management Solutions, 31(6),* 14–18.

Nicholas, I.J. (1982). Organizational climate and strategic decision-making. *Journal of General Management, 7(3),* 57–71.

Noe, R. (1986). Trainees' attributes and attitudes: Neglected influences on training effectiveness. *Academy of Management Review, 7(4),* 736–749.

O'Neil, N., & O'Neil, G. (1974). *Shifting gears: Finding security in a changing world.* New York: M. Evans.

Pearson, A.E. (1989). Six basics for general managers. *Harvard Business Review, 7(4),* 94–101.

Peters, T. (1988). *Thriving on chaos.* New York: Alfred A Knopf.

Peters, T. (1989). Operating principles #1: Listen, understand, and respond to customers. In R. Zemke & R. Schaef (Eds.), *The service edge: 101* companies that profit from customer care (pp. 29–35). New York: NAL Books.

Peters, T., & Austin, N. (1985). *A passion for excellence*. New York: Warner Books.

Peters, T.J., & Waterman, R.H., Jr. (1982). *In search of excellence: Lessons from America's best run companies*. New York: Warner Books.

Redding, W.C. (1984). *The corporate manager's guide to better communication*. Glenview, IL: Scott, Foresman, & Company.

Schein, E.H. (1985). *Organizational culture and leadership*. San Francisco: Jossey-Bass, Inc.

Schermerhorn, J.R. (1977). Information sharing as an interorganizational activity. *Academy of Management Journal, 20*(1), 148–153.

Schlesinger, L., & Balzer, R. (1985). An alternative to buzzword management: The culture performance link. *Personnel, 62*(9), 45–51.

Shea, G. (1984). *Building trust in the workplace*. New York: American Management Association.

Stegman, J.D. (1988). The importance of managerial communication: An annotated bibliography. *The ABC Bulletin, 51*(3), 25–26.

Steil, L.K., Barker, L.L., & Watson, K.W. (1983). *Effective listening: Key to your success*. Reading, MA: Random House.

Strauss, G., & Sayles, L. (1980). *Personnel: The human problems of management*. Englewood Cliffs, NJ: Prentice-Hall.

Sypher, B.D., Bostrom, R.N., & Seibert, J.H. (1989). Listening, communication abilities, and success at work. *Journal of Business Communication, 26*(4), 293–303.

Wexley, K.N., & Latham, G.P. (1981). *Developing and training human resources in organizations*. Glenview, IL: Scott, Foresman, and Company.

Wolff, F.I., Marsnik, N.C., Tacey, W.S., & Nichols, R.G. (1983). *Perceptive listening*. New York: Holt, Rinehart, & Winston.

Wolvin, A.D., & Coakley, C.G. (1988). *Listening*. Dubuque, IA: William C. Brown.

Chapter 13

Listenability = Oral-based Discourse + Considerateness

Donald L. Rubin

Department of Speech Communication
The University of Georgia

Listening researchers and scholars recognize the need for a paradigm that casts listening as a unique modality. Too often listening theory and research depicts listening as quantitatively different than reading (e.g., more severe memory demands), but not qualitatively different. The listenability of a spoken message is too often equated with the readability of its transcription. Yet readability measures are seriously flawed, even as predictors of reading comprehension. Recent advances in orality/literacy theory, however, do provide a distinctive perspective on listening. Listeners are constrained by the same psycholinguistic and contextual factors that constrain oral production. Therefore, *oral-based* language—marked by redundancy, simple conjunction, first-person reference and second-person address, etc.—is inherently more listenable than literate-based language. Oral-based language, however, is not especially listenable when interactants do not share prior knowledge and expectations. In such cases—when listeners are sociopsychologically remote from speakers—listenable messages must also be *considerate*. Considerate language is marked by certain audience-adapted features of metadiscourse, information flow, cohesion, and the like. Messages produced in writing, as well as messages produced in speech, can be evaluated for listenability based on the degree to which they are (a) oral-based and (b) considerate.

REFOCUSING ON THE MESSAGE
IN LISTENING THEORY

A person's life turns on your response to what you will hear in the next few minutes. For the better part of a week, a complex drama has been enacted, all for your benefit. To be sure, sometimes the narration has been tedious: This investigator has so many years of training, that social worker has such and such a case load. But even then you try hard to attend, impelled by the handkerchief wringing of the defendant's kinfolk in the first row of the gallery, or by the fiercely fixed gaze of the victim's son seated two rows behind. More often, though, the riveting narrative transports you into another time and place: a weed-infested back yard hidden within a bank of overgrown shrubs, a musty parlor strewn with the pitiful contents of an impoverished senior citizen's purse.

Now arrives the time for your own starring role in these proceedings. But the certainty you'd prayed would grace you has yet to descend. You hang on the judge's words, searching for any small guidance they might offer. You're determined that no potential key the judge might utter will escape you.

And this is the nature of the message with which you must contend:

> In order for a hope of benefit or a fear of injury, if any, to render a confession, if any, inadmissable, such hope or fear must be induced by another. If you find there was hope or fear, yet, if you find that the hope or fear originated in the party's own mind, from seeds of his own planting and under the influence of a hope or a fear so originated the Defendant made a confession, this will not exclude the confession, if any. All the evidence of the hope or fear that excludes is that and that only which some other person kindles or excites.

No guidance, no key, no certainty emerges from hearing this message. No wonder that judges' instructions have minimal effects on jurors' deliberations; they can barely be understood even by the most committed listener (Buchanan, Pryor, Taylor, & Strawn, 1978; Charrow & Charrow, 1979; Fortson, 1970). The problem is not in the cognitive processes of the listener, not in the listening context, not even in the quality of the physical signal uttered by the speaker. Rather, the problem is that the text is simply not adapted to the demands of aural processing. It is not a listenable text.

Models and definitions of *listening* (e.g., Goss, 1982; Lundsteen, 1979; Watson & Barker, 1984; Wolff, Marsnik, Tacey, & Nichols, 1983; Wolvin & Coakley, 1982) tend to focus on the cognitive processes and skills of the listener. Thus, we know the effects on listening outcomes of individual "inside the head" factors such as short- and long-term memory capacity (Bostrom & Waldhart, 1988), cognitive complexity (Beatty & Payne,

1984), information "chunking" (Townsend, Carrithers, & Bever, 1987), and amount of prior knowledge (Larsen, 1983).

Interference in listening is most often attributed to dysfunctional listener traits like prejudices toward topics or speakers (Wolff et al., 1983) and low motivation (Petrie & Carrel, 1976). Or ineffective listening may be due to listener background variables that can result in listener expectations that don't match those of the speaker. These expectations, in turn, can lead the listener to distort meanings (Kintsch & Greene, 1978) or to otherwise draw faulty inferences (Weaver, 1972).

Clearly, though, the *input* to these listening processes must also exert important effects on listening outcomes. To be sure, many listening models do make passing mention of listening materials or stimuli, but they devote relatively little analysis to the nature of message variables. In receiver-centered accounts, qualities of the message text are too often taken for granted.

Neglecting the nature of the message text is surely a conceptual error, even for accounts of listening that are deliberately focused upon individual-difference cognitive and affective variables. Text qualities cannot be taken for granted, for they no doubt *interact* with listener characteristics, as well as exert their own independent effects on listening outcomes. For example, the judge's instructions to the jury reproduced above are in general poorly adapted to the conditions of aural uptake. A version of these instructions cast in less complex syntax would aid virtually every listener. Listener motivation is probably not a variable in affecting comprehension in the case of courtroom listening. On the other hand, it is likely that individual listener differences in syntactic processing capacity probably do interact with their ability to listen to this sort of message. Those with greater syntactic "fluency" can better handle conditional language and densely embedded clauses (Straw & Schreiner, 1982).

Early Approaches to Listenability: Relying Upon Readability Formulae

Although most work in listening relegates text variables to a subordinate role, a small literature does explore the listenability of messages as a variable of interest. Much of this research derives from a concern for measuring listeners' comprehension of broadcast communications. For the most part, this literature equates listenability with readability. And for the most part, empirical validations of the listenability/readability equation have been less than convincing.

Young (1950), for example, presented radio news stories that had been rewritten at four graded levels of reading ease, based on a standard readibility formula. No significant differences in listening comprehension were found, nor were research participants able to even rank order the passages in terms of difficulty. Harwood (1955a), in contrast, reported significant rank order correlations between readability levels of listening passages (he constructed seven graded versions of each radio news passage) and comprehension scores.

Some research designs are readability formulae to vary passages in studies that compared listening comprehension with reading comprehension. Denbow (1975) reviewed several such studies. While their results have hardly been unanimous, it appears that differences between reading and listening comprehension are most likely to emerge for texts of difficult readability. These passages are better comprehended by readers than by listeners (Harwood, 1955b). Denbow's (1975) own results, however, showed no reliable difference between reading and listening at any level of readability. But for listening and reading alike, readability level was associated with comprehension.

(Note that these relationships between reading and listening comprehension pertain to experienced readers, and not necessarily to children. Generalizing across varying levels of difficulty in reading or listening materials, reading comprehension tends to trail listening comprehension through most of the school years—Sticht & James, 1984. One study did manipulate readability levels of reading and listening passages presented to children—Horowitz & Samuels, 1985. Unlike the adult patterns of comprehension, sixth-graders' comprehension of difficult passages was better in the aural mode. Easier passages revealed no difference between reading and listening comprehension.)

Readability formulae, therefore, apparently can serve as rough indicators of listenability. Indeed, Fang (1966–1967) developed an "Easy Listening Formula" that operates by the same principles that govern readability formulae. All such formulae ascribe text difficulty according to some combination of sentence length and lexical complexity. The Fang listenability index simply counts the number of syllables less the number of words per sentence. Like several commonly used readability formulae, it presumes an inverse relationship between word length and familiarity. The most commonly used words, and hence the most readily recognizable words, tend to be short. At the same time, shorter sentences tend to be less taxing to process than longer ones.

Critiques of Traditional Readability/Listenability Formulae

The proposition that it is easier for people to comprehend simple language rather than complicated language is a truism that hardly explains a thing. Glasser (1975) questioned both readability and listenability approaches that blindly dictate brevity in sentences and in words, because these approaches obscure what should be the underlying semantic concerns for clarity and informativeness. Most editors know this to be the case. Sometimes a clearer sentence is a longer one (Campbell & Holland, 1982). Consider the following versions of a typical sentence found in a scholarly article about comprehending narrative texts:

1. It was suggested that a culture-specific schema aids both in comprehending and reconstructing stories.
2. This article suggested that a culture-specific schema aids listeners as they comprehend stories, and also as they reconstruct stories.

The second version is less terse and would receive lower readability scores, but is more readily comprehensible.

Indeed, a host of research studies shows that traditional readability formulae may do an adequate job of rank ordering the difficulty of texts, but they do not do an adequate job of predicting comprehension test scores (see reviews in Campbell & Holland, 1982; Duffy, 1985). For example, rewriting jury instructions merely to improve readability scores did not improve actual comprehension of those instructions (Charrow & Charrow, 1979). Dissatisfaction with readability formulae arises because they ignore qualitative differences even in syntax and vocabulary, the two factors upon which readability formulae are based. For example, syntactic patterns which place additional information at the ends of sentences rather than in the beginning or middles are relatively easy to understand (Felker, Redish & Peterson, 1985). Words that are long but represent concrete referents may be easier to comprehend than short but abstract words (Campbell & Holland, 1982; Glasser, 1975).

Furthermore, readability formulae are not at all equipped to consider text features beyond syntax and lexicon that may have even more profound effects on comprehensibility. These include (a) pragmatic factors like the ways in which a piece of discourse addresses an audience and motivates their attention, (b) use of metadiscourse cues to "sign post" important structures and direct readers through the text (see, for example, Crismore & Hill, 1988), (c) techniques for introducing information so as to build upon readers' prior knowledge, (d) organizational factors like highlighting superordinate information, and (e) use of rhetorical schema like analogy or narration for elaboration.

Because of these kinds of limitations, some researchers assert that traditional approaches to readability are wholly outmoded (Schumm, Konopak, Readance, & Baldwin, 1989). The factors that render readability formulae of dubious utility may exert an even greater effect on listenability. We do not yet know for certain. At very least, however, it would be a travesty to simply apply readability formulae to listening texts and label the result "listenability." Instead, a more productive project would seek to define listenability in terms of what is unique or distinctive about texts that are readily processed by ear rather than by eye.

WHAT IS DISTINCTIVE ABOUT LISTENING?

This chapter proposes that understanding how discourse structures affect listenability is critical to revivifying the study of listening. Although they may not agree on any mutually acceptable definition of listening, many scholars do concur that listening research languishes for a lack of a unique, theory-driven identity (Bostrom & Waldhart, 1988; Goss, 1982; Rubin & Roberts, 1987). Paradoxically, studies of listening frequently fail to characterize or even acknowledge the distinctiveness of listening processes. In listening research, listeners are treated essentially as people who are reading with their ears.

Standardized listening tests, for example, have long been subject to criticism as tests of reading comprehension that just happen to be administered by tape recorder (Kelly, 1965). Guidelines for improving the validity of such tests suggest moving away from standard reading test paradigms by incorporating elements of interactivity like question asking, or using shorter listening passages that don't tax memory so stringently (Rubin & Mead, 1984).

By the same token, research on listening has often relied upon listening passages that are merely reading passages presented orally. One study of listening comprehension (Ernest, 1968) is noteworthy just because it is so brazen in this regard. Research participants "listened" to selections taken from a book entitled, *Reading Improvement for Men and Women in Industry.* Even Goelman (1982), who at least professed concern about employing listening passages that reflect oral language patterns, found it most convenient to merely read aloud folktales found in print. (Conversely, Pearson & Fielding, 1982, observe that a great deal of contemporary research that has been appropriated as seminal to the field of reading has actually been conducted in aural channels. Research in listening is actually more advanced than it is given credit for.)

The presumption of many models of listening—a misleading one—is that listening differs from reading only in the addition of some more stringent constraints on short-term memory in the case of listening, and of some more difficult decoding processes in the case of reading. Thus accounts of listening (e.g., Wolff et al., 1983) often bear remarkable resemblance to theories of reading (e.g., Just & Carpenter, 1980). Where some contemporary models of listening do differ qualitatively from most reading models is in emphasizing listeners' interactive feedback to speakers (i.e., overt response) as a component of listening (e.g., Wolvin & Coakley, 1982). Readers, of course, interact with authors remotely and indirectly, if at all. (And yet contemporary reader response theory posits a sort of transaction between reader and text that parallels in some ways the interaction between speaker and listener; Rosenblatt, 1985.)

In short—with perhaps the single exception of the principle of interactive feedback—inquiry about listening lacks a principled paradigm for capturing the distinctive traits of listening. When a paradigm that ascribes a unique identity to listening processes is articulated, it is likely that scholarship in this area will begin to flourish well beyond its current state.

Orality and Literacy

Recent advances in scholarship on literacy/orality provide just such a framework for characterizing listening (see, for example, Horowitz & Samuels, 1987; Rubin & Rafoth, 1986). This body of scholarship contrasts speaking and writing (and hence listening and reading) from historical evidence (e.g., Goody & Watt, 1963/1968), from the perspective of discourse (Tannen, 1982) and linguistic (Chafe, 1982) analysis, through ethnographic methods (Scollon & Scollon, 1981), psycholinguistic methods (Olson, 1986), and educational research (Michaels, 1986).

Orality/Literacy theory observes that writing and speaking can obviously be regarded as distinct channels of communication. Readers take in linguistic information by eye, listeners by ear. But that distinction is hardly informative and may actually occlude important similarities between certain written and oral communication events (e.g., notes exchanged between lovers and whispered "sweet nothings"; see Rubin & Kantor, 1984)

Oral-based style. More fundamental than simply pointing to channel differences, orality and literacy can be regarded from a functional perspective as distinct ways of meaning (Halliday, 1987). Prototypical (i.e., conversational) oral discourse is grounded in proximity to a tangible audience and situation, issues from a tangible ego, can be flexibly modified, and is rapidly produced with little self-consciousness. Oral-based discourse (whether in the written or spoken channel) thus conveys involvement, spontaneity, tentativeness, solidarity.

Consider, as an example of talk that conforms to most norms for oral-based discourse, this exchange in a high school science class:

TEACHER: Okay, the other one now—the article in the second one, uhm, the first one I asked you to read—"Air from Dinosaur Age Trapped in Rock." What is that basically about?

STUDENTS: [multiple responses/unintelligible]

TEACHER: Kind of, kind of you know one at a time so I can get better....Go ahead, Kristy.

KRISTY: The resin off the tree and whatever trickled down the bark. The air had gotten caught into that. And it just hardened. And now we're just finding out that that's got a lot more oxygen in that particular air than in ours.

TEACHER: Okay. What is that—we just read an article earlier, or some of you read that one about Baby Jessica that talked about, about the oxygen...increasing oxygen pressure. What does it do?

MARK: It makes you breathe better.

DWAYNE: That's why dinosaurs are so big.

TEACHER: Growth possibly. That may be a reason why dinosaurs are so big. Good, Dwayne. Uh, we look now back at...

JOSH: That's why cavemen were so hairy.

TEACHER: We look—that could be—we look back at time now and we find that, uh, the amount of, of vegetation or biomass as they call it, just the amount of things growing was tremendous. Because what are we now using all this biomass or all these plants or animals for? Anybody know?

Literate-based style. Conversely, prototypical (i.e., edited essayist) written discourse presumes a universal, inchoate audience and situation, alienates the speaker from the utterance, fixes meaning in time, and is produced deliberately and free from the tyranny of real-time fragmentation. Literate-based discourse (whether in the written or spoken channel) thus conveys detachment, planfulness, conclusiveness, and authority. As an example of literate-based talk, consider the following remarks taken from a criminal trial transcript. Although it is taken as a slice of interactive discourse, it hardly sounds like oral language.

THE COURT: Mr. Nebel, I will have to tell you, you may not leave the courthouse, in fact, you may not leave the floor without special permission of the Court.

MR. NEBEL: My office is across the street.

THE COURT: Well, please tell me or ask for permission to go there.

MR. NEBEL: I left word with the Sheriff.

THE COURT: I understand that you did.

MR. NEBEL: May I go to my office?

THE COURT:	Yes, sir.
	[The jury was returned to open court.]
THE COURT:	Ladies and Gentlemen, your question is, do you have to present a check to be cashed before forgery can take place? If so, does the State have to prove that he tried to cash the check?
	I will charge you again, as I did before, a person commits the act of forgery in the first degree when, with intent to defraud, he knowingly makes, alters, or possesses any writing in a fictitious name or in any such manner that the writing as made or altered purports to have been made by another party, at another time, with different provisions, or by authority of one who did not give such authority and utter or deliver such writing.
	I have already given you instructions on uttering and delivering.
	Does that satisfy your minds?
MRS. JORDAN:	Yes, your honor.
THE COURT:	You may go back to the jury room.

Oral-Based Language and Listenability

With respect to discourse processing, oral-based language is typically easier to comprehend by ear; we're better at listening to talk than at listening to writing declaimed aloud. Thomas (1956), by way of illustration, compared students' comprehension when listening to a lecture marked by "oral style" (operationalized, admittedly, in a somewhat atheoretic manner) compared to an otherwise identical lecture composed in a "nonoral" style. The oral style message resulted in significantly higher comprehension scores, and also in higher quality ratings. The explanation lies in the reciprocal nature of oral composing and aural comprehending. Psycholinguistic and contextual factors cause speakers (in prototypical oral situations) to repeat themselves, to generate relatively larger verb clusters than noun clusters, to avoid complex subordinate constructions. Listeners, operating under the influence of many of those same real-time and real-space factors, are happily able to exploit the redundancy, the reduced nominalization, and the coordinate constructions that appear in prototypical oral texts.

For these very reasons, listenability is first of all a function of the degree to which texts convey meaning in oral-based modes (Rubin & Rafoth, 1986). In contrast to relying upon unsatisfactory readability formulae, listenability can be evaluated in terms of three dimensions of oral-based expression:

1. A message cast in the syntax of oral language is listenable.
2. A message cast in the rhetorical structures of oral language is listenable.
3. A message that evokes an oral communication situation, for example through the use of direct address in personal pronouns, is listenable.

Most observers agree that Ronald Reagan (the corporate being, including speech writers and teleprompter technicians) produced highly listenable prose. As an illustration of how oral-based language contributes to listenability, consider the following excerpt of a speech delivered in September 1982 (quoted in Carter, 1985, pp. 228–234):

> Today has been a day that should make us all proud. It marked the end of the successful evacuation of the P.L.O. from Beirut, Lebanon. This peaceful step could never have been taken without the good offices of the United States and, especially, the truly heroic work of a great American diplomat, Ambassador Philip Habib. Thanks to his efforts, I am happy to announce that the U.S. Marine contingent helping to supervise the evacuation has accomplished its mission. Our young men should be out of Lebanon within two weeks. They, too, have served the cause of peace with distinction and we can all be very proud of them....It seemed to me that, with the agreement in Lebanon, we had an opportunity for a more far-reaching peace effort in the region and I was determined to seize that moment. In the words of the scripture, the time had come to "follow after the things which make for peace." Tonight I want to report to you on the steps we have taken, and the prospects they can open up for a just and lasting peace in the Middle East.

In terms of oral-based syntax, some of Reagan's sentences are indeed short and pithy (e.g., the tragically mistaken line, "Our young men should be out of Lebanon within two weeks"). More often, though, sentences are expanded by coordination (e.g., "They served *and* we can be proud," "We had an opportunity *and* I was determined). Or else the sentences are expanded by right-branching modifiers, modifiers that follow base clauses (e.g., "I want to report on steps (base clause) [that] we have taken and prospects [that those steps] can open up for a just and...). Only one "periodic" sentence (see, for example, Brooks & Warren, 1972) interrupts the progressive, cumulative flow of information by intruding (i.e., "It seemed to me that, with the agreement in Lebanon, we had..."). Note also that Reagan uses but one passive construction ("this step could never have been taken"). In those instances in which Reagan does use nominal constructions (e.g., "a more far-reaching peace effort"), he at least avoids more complex nominalized forms of verbs that characterize hyperliterate language (e.g., "the intensification of the allocation of militarized resources").

Turning to analyses of oral-based rhetorical structures, concern focuses upon textual features that allow listeners to discern the organizational macrostructure of a passage (see, for example, Kintsch & Van Dijk, 1978). Rhetorical structures like problem–solution, listing, analogizing, and exemplifying build that macrostructure. Listing—as in oral recitations of genealogies (Ong, 1982), and narration—as in the use of folk tales and parables (Scollon & Scollon, 1981) have been identified as charac- teristcally oral rhetorical structures. Still, Meyer and Freedle (1984) found that adult listeners recalled more from texts organized by means of compare–contrast or cause–effect, relative to more listlike topical organi- zation. Their design did not include a narrative condition. In studies of listening to stories (as opposed to reading them), it appears that listeners more readily recall the gist—the essential macrostructure—of a narra- tion. Listeners, however, are at a disadvantage in recalling the incidental details of stories (Hildyard & Olson, 1978).

Reagan, in the speech above, adopts a clear narrative flavor. Elsewhere in the speech, to be sure, he introduces certain adversative structures (e.g., "But our policy is motivated by more than strategic interests. We also have an irreversible commitment to the survival...of friendly states.") He also uses listlike structures (e.g., "There were two basic issues we had to address. First...."). But the overall macrostructure in which these other elements are embedded is narrative. Narrativity is especially apparent in the frequent occurrence of temporal markers ("today," "the end," "within two weeks," "that moment," "time had come," "tonight"). And indeed, toward the conclusion of the speech Reagan explicitly invokes the narrative frame: "It has often been said...that *the story* of the search for peace and justice in the Middle East is a tragedy of oppor- tunities missed." Transforming his account of American Middle East policy into a story in this fashion increases the listenability of Reagan's speech.

The third element of oral-based discourse—evoking an oral communi- cation context—is readily apparent in Reagan's speech. Most obvious is his use of direct first and second person address (e.g., "*I* want to report to *you*"). Other discourse elements evoke orality by dint of convention. Oral formulae are phrases and expressions that are associated with communica- tion events by use and tradition. In this speech Reagan invokes the scriptural passage ("follow after the things which make for peace") much in the tradition of a preacher speaking to his congregation. Later in the speech, Reagan uses another oral formula common to a preaching context: "So tonight I am calling for a fresh start...I call on Israel to...I call on the Palestinian people to...And I call on the Arab states to..." This formula also capitalizes on the characteristically oral syntax of redundancy and further evokes an oral context.

Much of the audience for this speech heard it over broadcast media. Indeed, probably the largest segment of the audience actually read it in print. Still, these sorts of text features allow audience members to construe the face-to-face situation which the speech presupposes. In short, the speech is listenable because it is rife with oral-based discourse features.

CONSIDERATE TEXT

Rubin and Rafoth's (1986) proposal linking listenability to oral-based language may have been right-headed, but like many unidimensional theories, it was too simplistic. It does not account for the fact that some oral-based discourse is highly fragmented or presumes a high degree of shared context. Such speech is listenable only for very limited audiences, if any. Consider a sample of conversational language—very much oral-based, but not very listenable:

Interviewer: Can we go chronologically in terms of grade school, high school, college?

Respondent: I would...sure. Grade school, in my memory, grade school is dim as years stretch out gets dimmer. But I think I probably learned in grade school that the real basics, probably grade school and early junior high, the real basics of, of grammar and the English language. And, the later years that I really took it to, to, use it and, an..., and practice the basic and learn more I guess. I think probably it was a little bit m...I had more of an influence on me...than would ordinarily be the case because...my situation. I was in a small city school and I was one of the few black students at the white school that I went to, not in elementary school, but in junior high. I think I started in maybe sixth grade or something, the first year that we were able to go to the other schools.....

This conversational narrative was produced by a successful attorney who no doubt has the capacity to manage listenable monologue in other situations. Here, however, even the chronological organization invited by the interviewer breaks down. Even the speaker realizes the structure needs mending ("not in elementary school, but in junior high"). The contextual information that is missing here—but which is necessary for comprehension—concerns the history of racial desegregation of public schools in the South. Not every listener will be able to make the inference that the speaker attended a racially segregated school prior to the sixth grade. At any rate, a highly listenable text should not demand that listeners expend too much cognitive capacity creating coherence by engaging in such inferencing.

Recently, discourse analysts have introduced the concept of "thought-ful" (Pearson & Tierney, 1984), "friendly" (Singer, 1986) or "considerate" (Arbruster, 1984) text. A considerate text eases the readers' (or listeners') burden of information processing, reduces the inferential load. Redundancy, explicit transitions and organizational cues, and predictable flow from "given" to "new" information are all features of considerate text.

Based on the criteria developed by Singer (1986) and refined by Schumm et al. (1989), the following dimensions of considerateness can be identified:

1. *Text organization*—including appropriate introductory material, logical arrangement, clear signalling of superordinate/subordinate relations, internal summaries
2. *Cohesiveness*—including lexical, pronominal, and conjunctive ties across local and global stretches of discourse
3. *Discourse Consistency*—consistent style, including parallel uses of rhetorical devices (e.g., questions as advanced organizers throughout a text)
4. *Flow of Information*—including a macrostructure that reflects underlying conceptual structure, logical introduction of new information, judicious associations with presumed prior knowledge
5. *Elaboration of Information*—avoiding undue conceptual density, including appropriate use of developmental devices like example, analogy, and explanation
6. *Metadiscourse*—cues within a text wherein a speaker/writer directly addresses a listener/reader as to purpose, message structure, and processing strategies.

Some texts that are literate-based in most respects may be highly considerate: such is the intention of the "Plain English" movement in document design, for example. The "Plain English Will" (Kellogg, 1983, p. 1) humorously illustrates the notion of considerate text in document writing.

> I am John Doe. This is my will. See my signature on this will. See my witnesses' signatures. I revoke all my other wills and codicils. See Sam Brown. I want him to be my executor. Please Court, make him my executor. Sam is honest, I hope, and fair, I hope. Sam won't serve? See Bob Baker. Bob will be executor ...

Considerateness and Orality

The dimension of considerateness of text cuts across the dimension of orality/literacy. Considerateness is not isomorphic to orality nor to listenability. As the "Plain English Will" above demonstrates, some literate-based texts may be highly considerate. Some considerate documents, however, are hardly oral-based. This is especially true of well-designed forms and documents, like many computer manuals. Their use of bullets, heads and subheads, tables, side-bars, and white space render them highly considerate. But these very features concomitantly render them nonoral.

Conversely, some texts that are oral-based in most respects may be essentially inconsiderate. Such is the case of much formulaic and ritualistic discourse like prayers and declarations and even nursery rhymes. For some of these genres, the saying of the formula has social meaning quite apart from the formula's literal or even figurative meaning. A clear example of this phenomenon is the recitation of the Pledge of Allegiance to the American flag. The prosody with which youngsters are trained to recite this 31-word formula helps segment it into a viable oral chant. But it is hardly a considerate text; to comprehend it requires a great deal of inference making. We are well aware of what it means to recite "The Pledge" (indeed, George Bush exploited this meaning in his 1988 presidential campaign against Michael Dukakis). Many citizens, however, would be far less confident that they comprehend what the text of the pledge means, even after uncountable listenings.

Oral-based discourse, of itself, does not require considerateness because it can presume a high-context situation, one in which much information is shared extratextually because of understood exophoric reference. Indeed, entire cultures can be characterized as high-context cultures (Hall, 1976). In such cultures, a taciturn style may be valued more than a voluble style, and an indirect style may be more appropriate than a direct one (see, for example, Hymes, 1974).

These traits are characteristic of oral-based cultures as well. Scollon and Scollon (1981), for example, describe Athabaskan communication norms, in which it is thought to be rude to explicitly state the conclusion you wish your listeners to draw. For Athapaskans, even those who have learned to read and write, it is enough to just present a set of facts. Listeners are free to draw whatever conclusions they wish. In literate-based cultures, in contrast, stating explicit conclusions is not rude, it is considerate.

Thus, norms for considerateness are culture-specific. Oral-based cultures may therefore construe listenability in different terms than those presented in this chapter. The listener, and not the speaker, in an oral-based culture bears the burden of reproducing meaning (Rubin, 1989).

Language styles are, of course, continuous dimensions and not dichotomies (Tannen, 1982). For purposes of discussion, however, it is useful

Table 13.1. Listenability and Style

	CONSIDERATENESS	
	considerate text	inconsiderate text
oral-based	+ listenable in Western cultures	+ listenable in oral-based cultures
DISCOURSE STYLE		
literate-based	+ / – listenable; target of public speaking instruction	– listenable; prevailing in professional contexts

to visualize a matrix which crosses dimensions of considerateness with discourse style (oral/literate language) (see Table 13.1):

Considerateness and Listenability

In literate-based cultures, at least, listening comprehension is sometimes optimal for highly organized, explicit text—that is, considerate texts. These highly listenable messages can manifest many elements of oral-based discourse like redundancy and loose or cumulative sentence patterns. But as considerate texts, they diverge from a prototypically diffuse, nonintegrated conversational style. Here, for example, is a high school teacher who delivers minilectures to her students in a nonconversational but nonetheless listenable style. Notice in particular her use of organizational cues to guide the listener.

TEACHER: Okay, what we are going to do is take some more notes on the characteristics of the romantic hero. You need to take your notes out. The first thing that you need to know about the romantic hero is that he is not exactly superhuman, but he may have extraordinary powers. You also need to know that his vision of the world is larger and more perfect than the one that we inhabit. You should already have that down. Does everyone understand what I mean by a greater vision?

STUDENTS: [several in unison[] Yes.

TEACHER: Luke does, but Rhoda doesn't. What I mean is that he sees the world as being more perfect than the one we inhabit. He has greater vision of the world and sees things in a wider perspective. Okay.

This minilecture has the kind of cohesion, unity, and authority one usually associates with literate-based language—though it certainly contains other markers of oral-based style, as well (e.g., direct first- and second-person address). Literate flavored though it may be, this text is a more effective vehicle for its information than would be an inconsiderate, loosely structured conversation.

CONCLUSIONS AND RECOMMENDATIONS

Assessing Listenability

The thesis of this chapter can be summarized in a succinct equation:

LISTENABILITY = ORAL-BASED DISCOURSE + CONSIDERATENESS

Unfortunately, this equation cannot be evaluated algorithmically, like earlier readability approaches to listenability. Indeed, the great advantage of relying on sentence length and lexical complexity formulae was their objectivity and simplicity (Fang, 1966–1967). The overpowering disadvantages of such formulae, however, are that they are of limited empirical adequacy and of no conceptual validity. I have contended in this chapter that to advance scholarship in listening, it is critical that central constructs reflect what is unique and distinctive about listening. Any metric for listenability, therefore, must eschew outmoded (albeit highly practical) readability formulae.

Recent approaches to evaluating comprehensibility of text utilize rating systems instead of word counts (Duffy, 1985; Schumm et al., 1989). It is easy to envision the kinds of criteria that such a rating system will incorporate. Several scales will measure elements of oral-based discourse such as those summarized by Chafe (1982), Rubin (1987), Rubin and Rafoth (1986), and elsewhere. These scales will reflect discourse features such as sentence length, first- and second-person address, and transparency of macrostructure. Other scales will measure elements of considerateness, such as those summarized by Singer (1986). These scales will reflect discourse features such as explicitness, use of appropriate developmental devices, and metadiscursive signalling to listeners about effective listening processes.

Of course this listenability scale will need to be constructed in conjunction with empirical validation trials. In doing so, however, listening researchers need to move beyond standard formats devised for testing reading comprehension and recall. We cannot continue to test listening performance exclusively by means of lecture passages that presume literate-based processing of referential content. It's no surprise that reading comprehension of such "difficult" materials typically exceeds listening comprehension.

To balance the picture, researchers need to conduct reading/listening comparisons that involve nondiscursive, nonreferential, oral-based texts (e.g., preaching, or a session with a family planning counselor) and more diverse listening outcomes (e.g., enrapture, or even plain old persuasion) besides "comprehension." One does not test a listener's comprehension of a prayer or a greeting or an exhortation. It simply makes no sense. By the same token, it may make more sense to assess how different versions of jury instructions ultimately affect juror deliberations and decision making, rather than to test their recall on multiple choice tests. To validate listenability ratings, therefore, we will need to consider a fuller range of the ways listeners *respond to* and *use* oral messages, not merely what details listeners can remember.

Listening Skills

The listenability perspective has practical implications for guiding the practice of speakers. Effective speakers, barring those who achieve effect through obfuscation, will wish to develop facility in producing listenable messages. Since the theory proposes that good speakers minimize the demands on listeners, implications are less pronounced for guiding the practice of listeners. Under ideal conditions, all listeners will effectively process information simply by doing what comes naturally.

Under nonideal conditions, that is, reality, listeners must actively strive after meaning that may come packaged in more or less unlistenable messages. Much as a competent reader learns to "read like a writer" (Pearson & Tierney, 1984), so should listeners become accustomed to "listening like a speaker." To listen like a speaker means to represent to oneself the speaker's intended encoding strategies.

Often those speaker intentions go awry during the process of encoding. But knowing about the generic qualities of listenable text will aid listeners in making inferences about how a speaker ought to have crafted the message. When listening like a speaker, a listener might internally remark, "Oh, that must have been the second major point, coordinate with the first point he made. It sounded like it was going to be just an example to illustrate that first point. But now I see that he meant to give it equal emphasis and to set it apart from the first idea." In short, competent listeners use their knowledge of listenability to mentally repair or reconstruct nonideal messages. It is in this way that one's internalized sense of listenability aids not only in encoding listenable messages, but also in understanding messages received.

REFERENCES

Armbruster, B. (1984). The problem of "inconsiderate text." In G.G. Duffy, L.R. Roehler, & J. Mason (Eds.), *Comprehension instruction* (pp. 202–217). New York: Longman.

Beatty, M.J., & Payne, S. (1984). Receiver apprehension and cognitive complexity. *Western Journal of Speech Communication, 45,* 363–369.

Bostrom, R., & Waldhart, E.S. (1988). Memory models and the measurement of listening. *Communication Education, 37,* 1–13.

Brooks, C., & Warren, R.P. (1972). *Modern rhetoric* (3rd ed.). New York: Harcourt Brace Javonovich.

Buchanan, R.W., Pryor, B., Taylor, K.P., & Strawn, D.U. (1978). Legal communication: An investigation of juror comprehension of pattern instructions. *Communication Quarterly, 26*(4), 31–35.

Campbell, L.J., & Holland, V.M. (1982). Understanding the language of public documents because readability formulas don't. In R.J. DiPietro (Ed.), *Linguistics and the professions* (pp. 157–171). Norwood, NJ: Ablex Publishing Corp.

Carter, J. (1985). *The blood of Abraham.* Boston: Houghton–Mifflin.

Chafe, W. (1982). Integration and involvement in speaking, writing, and oral literature. In D. Tannen (Ed.), *Spoken and written language.* Norwood, NJ: Albex Publishing Corp.

Charrow, R., & Charrow, V. (1979). Making legal language understandable: Psycholinguistic study of jury instructions. *Columbia Law Review, 79,* 1306–1374.

Crismore, A., & Hill, K.T. (1988). The interaction of metadiscourse and anxiety in determining children's learning of social studies textbook materials. *Journal of Reading Behavior, 30,* 249–260.

Denbow, C.J. (1975). Listenability and readability: An experimental investigation. *Journalism Quarterly, 52,* 285–290.

Duffy, T. (1985). Readability Formulas: What's the Use? In T. Duffy & R. Waller (Eds.), *Designing usable texts* (pp. 113–144). Orlando: Academic Press.

Ernest, C.H. (1968). Listening comprehension as a function of type of material and rate of presentation. *Speech Monographs, 35,* 154–158.

Fang, I.E. (1966–1967). The "Easy Listening Formula." *Journal of Broadcasting, 11,* 63–69.

Felker, D.B., Redish, J.C., & Peterson, J. (1985). Training authors of informative documents. In T. Duffy & R. Waller (Eds.), *Designing usable texts* (pp. 43–62). Orlando: Academic Press.

Fortson, R.F. (1970). Judges' instructions: A quantitative analysis of jurors' listening comprehension. *Today's Speech, 18*(4), 34–38.

Glasser, T.L. (1975). On readability and listenability. *ETC, 32,* 138–142.

Goelman, H. (1982). Selective attention in language comprehension: Children's processing of expository and narrative discourse. *Discourse Processes, 5,* 53–72.

Goody, J., & Watt, I. (1968). The consequences of literacy. In J. Goody (Ed.), *Literacy in traditional societies.* London: Cambridge University Press. (Original work published 1963)

Goss, B. (1982). Listening as information processing. *Communication Quarterly, 30*, 304–307.

Hall, E.T. (1976). *Beyond culture*. New York: Anchor Press.

Halliday, M.A.K. (1987). Spoken and written modes of meaning. In R. Horowitz & S.J. Samuels (Eds.), *Comprehending oral and written language* (pp. 55–82). San Diego: Academic Press.

Harwood, K.A. (1955a). Listenability and rate of presentation. *Speech Monographs, 22*, 57–59.

Harwood, K.A. (1955b). Listenability and readability. *Speech Monographs, 22*, 49–53.

Hildyard, A., & Olson, D.R. (1978). Memory and inference in the comprehension of oral and written discourse. *Discourse Processes, 1*, 91–117.

Horowitz, R., & Samuels, S.J. (1985). Reading and listening to expository prose. *Journal of Reading Behavior, 17*, 185–198.

Horowitz, R., & Samuels, S.J. (1987). Comprehending oral and written language: Critical contrasts for literacy and schooling. In R. Horowitz & S.J. Samuels (Eds.), *Comprehending oral and written language* (pp. 1–53). San Diego: Academic Press.

Hymes, D. (1974). *Foundations in sociolinguistics: An ethnographic approach*. Philadelphia: University of Pennsylvania Press.

Just, M.A., & Carpenter, P.A. (1980). A theory of reading: From eye fixations to comprehension. *Psychological Review, 87*, 329–354.

Kellogg, I. (1983). The plain English will. *Simply Stated, 35*, 1, 3.

Kelly, C.M. (1965). An investigation into the construct validity of two commercially published listening tests. *Speech Monographs, 32*, 139–143.

Kintsch, W., & Greene, E. (1978). The role of culture-specific schemata in the comprehension and recall of stories. *Discourse Processes, 1*, 1–13.

Kintsch, W., & Van Dijk, T. (1978). Toward a model of text comprehension and production. *Psychological Review, 85*, 363–394.

Larsen, S.F. (1983). Text processing and knowledge updating in memory for radio news. *Discourse Processes, 6*, 21–38.

Lundsteen, S.W. (1979). *Listening: Its impact at all levels on reading and the other language arts* (rev. ed.). Urbana, IL: National Council of Teachers of English and ERIC/RCS.

Meyer, B.J.F., & Freedle, R. (1984). Effects of discourse type on recall. *American Educational Research Journal, 21*, 121–143.

Michaels, S. (1986). Narrative presentations: An oral preparation for literacy. In J. Cook-Gumperz (Ed.), *The social construction of literacy* (pp. 94–116). Cambridge, UK: Cambridge University Press.

Olson, D. (1986). The cognitive consequences of literacy. *Canadian Psychology, 27*, 109–121.

Ong, W.S.J. (1982). *Orality and literacy*. London: Methuen.

Pearson, P.D., & Tierney, R. (1984). On becoming a thoughtful reader: Learning to read like a writer. In A. Purves & O. Niles (Eds.), *Becoming readers in a complex society*. Chicago: National Society for the Study of Education.

Petrie, C.R., & Carrel, S.D. (1976). The relationship of motivation, listening capability, initial information and verbal organizational ability to lecture comprehension and retention. *Communication Monographs, 43*, 187–194.

Rosenblatt, L. (1985). The transactional theory of the literary work: Implications for research. In C. Cooper (Ed.), *Researching response to literature and the teaching of literature: Points of departure.* Norwood, NJ: Ablex Publishing Corp.

Rubin, D.L. (1989, February). *Orality, considerateness of text, and the social construction of listening.* Paper presented to the Annual Convention of the International Listening Association, Atlanta.

Rubin, D.L. (1987). Divergence and convergence between speaking and writing. *Topics in Language Disorders, 7*(4), 1–18.

Rubin, D.L., & Kantor, K.J. (1984). Talking and writing: Building communication competence. In C. Thaiss & C. Suhor (Eds.), *Speaking and writing* (pp. 29–74). Urbana, IL: National Council of Teachers of English.

Rubin, D.L., & Mead, N.A. (1984). *Large-Scale assessment of oral communication skills: K–12.* Annandale, VA: Speech communication Association and ERIC/RCS.

Rubin, D.L., & Rafoth, B. (1986). Oral language criteria for selecting listenable materials: An update for reading teachers and specialists. *Reading Psychology, 7,* 137–151.

Rubin, R., & Roberts, C.V. (1987). A comparative examination and analysis of three listening tests. *Communication Education, 36,* 142–153.

Schumm, J.S., Konopak, J.P., Readance, J.E., & Baldwin, R.S. (1989). Considerate text: Do we practice what we preach? In S. McCormick & J. Zutell (Eds.), *Cognitive and social perspectives for literacy research and instruction* (Thirty-eighth Yearbook of the National Reading Conference, pp. 381–390). Chicago: National Reading Conference.

Scollon, R., & Scollon, S. (1981). *Narrative, literacy and face in interethnic communication.* Norwood, NJ: Ablex Publishing Corp.

Singer, H. (1986). Friendly texts: Description and criteria. In E.K. Dishner, T.W. Bean, J.C. Readance, & D.W. Moore (Eds.), *Reading in the content areas: Improving classroom instruction* (pp. 112–128). Dubuque, IA: Kendall/Hunt.

Sticht, T.G., & James, J.H. (1984). Listening and reading. In P.D. Pearson (Ed.), *Handbook of reading research* (pp. 293–317). New York: Longman.

Straw, S., & Schreiner, R. (1982). The effects of sentence manipulation on subsequent measures of reading and listening comprehension. *Reading Research Quarterly, 17,* 339–352.

Tannen, D. (1979). Oral and literate strategies in spoken and written language. *Language, 58,* 1–21.

Tannen, D. (1982). The oral/literate continuum of discourse. In D. Tannen (Ed.), *Spoken and written language* (1–16). Norwood, NJ: Ablex Publishing Corp.

Thomas, G.L. (1956). Effect of oral style on intelligibility in speech. *Speech Monographs, 23,* 46–54.

Townsend, D.J., Carrithers, C., & Bever, T. (1987). Listening and reading processes in college- and middle school-age readers. In R. Horowitz & S. J. Samuels (Eds.), *Comprehending oral and written language* (pp. 217–242). San Diego: Academic Press.

Watson, K.W., & Barker, L.L. (1984). Listening behavior: Definition and measurement. In R. Bostrom (Ed.), *Communication yearbook 8* (pp. 178–197). Beverly Hills, CA: Sage.

Weaver, C.H. (1972). *Human listening: Processes and behavior.* Indianapolis: Bobbs-Merrill.

Wolff, F.I., Marsnik, N.C., Tacey, W.S., & Nichols, R. (1983). *Perceptive listening.* New York: Holt.

Wolvin, A., & Coakley, C.G. (1982). *Listening.* Dubuque: W.C. Brown.

Young, J.R. (1950). Understanding radio news: The effect of style. *Journalism Quarterly, 27,* 19–23.

AUTHOR INDEX

Subject Index